Understanding the imaginary war

Manchester University Press

Cultural History of Modern War

Series editors
Ana Carden-Coyne, Peter Gatrell, Max Jones, Penny Summerfield and
Bertrand Taithe

Already published

Carol Acton and Jane Potter   *Working in a world of hurt: trauma and resilience in the narratives of medical personnel in warzones*
Julie Anderson   *War, disability and rehabilitation in Britain: soul of a nation*
Lindsey Dodd   *French children under the Allied bombs, 1940–45: an oral history*
Rachel Duffett   *The stomach for fighting: food and the soldiers of the First World War*
Christine E. Hallett   *Containing trauma: nursing work in the First World War*
Jo Laycock   *Imagining Armenia: Orientalism, ambiguity and intervention*
Chris Millington   *From victory to Vichy: veterans in inter-war France*
Juliette Pattinson   *Behind enemy lines: gender, passing and the Special Operations Executive in the Second World War*
Chris Pearson   *Mobilizing nature: The environmental history of war and militarization in Modern France*
Jeffrey S. Reznick   *Healing the nation: soldiers and the culture of caregiving in Britain during the Great War*
Jeffrey S. Reznick   *John Galsworthy and disabled soldiers of the Great War: with an illustrated selection of his writings*
Michael Roper   *The secret battle: emotional survival in the Great War*
Penny Summerfield and Corinna Peniston-Bird   *Contesting home defence: men, women and the Home Guard in the Second World War*
Trudi Tate and Kate Kennedy (eds)   *The silent morning: culture and memory after the Armistice*
Spiros Tsoutsoumpis   *The People's Armies: A history of the Greek resistance*
Wendy Ugolini   *Experiencing war as the 'enemy other': Italian Scottish experience in World War II*
Laura Ugolini   *Civvies: middle-class men on the English Home Front, 1914–18*
Colette Wilson   *Paris and the Commune, 1871–78: the politics of forgetting*

Centre for the Cultural History of War

http://www.arts.manchester.ac.uk/subjectareas/history/research/cchw/

Understanding the imaginary war

Culture, thought and nuclear conflict, 1945–90

∼

Edited by
MATTHEW GRANT AND BENJAMIN ZIEMANN

Manchester University Press

Copyright © Manchester University Press 2016

While copyright in the volume as a whole is vested in Manchester University Press, copyright in individual chapters belongs to their respective authors, and no chapter may be reproduced wholly or in part without the express permission in writing of both author and publisher.

Published by Manchester University Press
Altrincham Street, Manchester M1 7JA, UK
www.manchesteruniversitypress.co.uk

British Library Cataloguing-in-Publication Data is available

ISBN 978 1 5261 3190 4 paperback

ISBN 978 1 7849 9440 2 hardback

First published by Manchester University Press in hardback 2016

This edition first published 2018

The publisher has no responsibility for the persistence or accuracy of URLs for any external or third-party internet websites referred to in this book, and does not guarantee that any content on such websites is, or will remain, accurate or appropriate.

Typeset by Out of House Publishing
Printed in Great Britain
Published with the support of the Gerda Henkel Foundation, Duesseldorf

GERDA HENKEL **STIFTUNG**

Contents

List of figures		*page* vii
Notes on contributors		viii
Acknowledgements		xi
1	Introduction: the Cold War as an imaginary war *Matthew Grant and Benjamin Ziemann*	1
2	The apocalyptic fiction: shaping the future in the Cold War *Eva Horn*	30
3	Building peace, fearing the apocalypse? Nuclear danger in Soviet Cold War culture *Miriam Dobson*	51
4	Sixty years and counting: nuclear themes in American culture, 1945 to the present *Paul Boyer*	75
5	The imaginative landscape of nuclear war in Britain, 1945–65 *Matthew Grant*	92
6	German angst? Debating Cold War anxieties in West Germany, 1945–90 *Benjamin Ziemann*	116
7	After Hiroshima: Günther Anders and the history of anti-nuclear critique *Jason Dawsey*	140

Contents

 8 Hiroshima/Nagasaki, civil rights and anti-war protest in
    Japan's Cold War   165
    Ann Sherif

 9 Catholic anti-communism, the bomb and perceptions of
    apocalypse in West Germany and the USA, 1945–90   189
    Daniel Gerster

10 'The nuclear arms race is psychological at its roots':
    physicians and their therapies for the Cold War   213
    Claudia Kemper

11 Imagining the apocalypse: nuclear winter in science and
    the world   238
    Paul Rubinson

12 Images of nuclear war in US government films from
    the early Cold War   260
    Lars Nowak

Index   287

Figures

1	*Medical Aspects of Nuclear Radiation* (1950). 'Cold War Hysteria', DVD Mill Creek Entertainment, 2008.	page 263
2	*You Can Beat the A-Bomb* (1950). 'Cold War Hysteria', DVD Mill Creek Entertainment, 2008.	268
3	*Military Participation on Tumbler/Snapper* (1952). 'Ultimate Nuclear Test Films', DVD Walthour Productions, 2007.	276
4	*Operation Ivy* (1952). Courtesy of US National Archives, photo 374-G-67-5.	279
5	*Operation Cue* (1955). https://archive.org/details/Operatio1955 (Creative Commons licence: public domain).	280

Notes on contributors

Paul Boyer (†) was Merle Curti Professor of History Emeritus at the University of Wisconsin-Madison (USA). His many book publications include *Urban Masses and Moral Order in America, 1820–1920* (Cambridge, Mass., 1978); *By the Bomb's Early Light: American Thought and Culture at the Dawn of the Atomic Age* (New York, 1985); *When Time Shall Be No More. Prophecy Belief in Modern American Culture* (Cambridge, Mass., 1992); *Fallout: A Historian Reflects on America's Half-Century Encounter with Nuclear Weapons* (Columbus, 1998).

Jason Dawsey is Lecturer in Modern European history at the University of Tennessee-Knoxville (USA). Dawsey is the author of 'Where Hitler's name is never spoken: Günther Anders in 1950s Vienna', in *Contemporary Austrian Studies*, Vol. XXI: *Austrian Lives*, edited by Günter Bischof, Fritz Plasser and Eva Maltschnig (Innsbruck and New Orleans, 2012). He is also the co-editor (along with Günter Bischof and Bernhard Fetz) of *The Life and Work of Günther Anders: Émigré, Iconoclast, Philosopher, Man of Letters* (Innsbruck, 2014). He is currently completing a monograph on Günther Anders' critique of modern technology.

Miriam Dobson is Senior Lecturer in Modern History at the University of Sheffield (UK). Her main publications are *Khrushchev's Cold Summer: Gulag Returnees, Crime, and the Fate of Reform After Stalin* (Ithaca and London, 2009), winner of the 2010 Wayne S. Vucinich Book Prize, and, as co-editor, *Reading Primary Sources. The Interpretation of Texts from Nineteenth- and Twentieth-century History* (London, 2008). In her current book project, she is exploring the history of Baptist and Pentecostal communities in the Soviet Union.

Notes on contributors

Daniel Gerster is Researcher (Wissenschaftlicher Mitarbeiter) at the Center for Religion and Modernity of the Westfälische Wilhelms-Universität Münster (Germany). He is author of *Friedensdialoge im Kalten Krieg. Eine Geschichte der Katholiken in der Bundesrepublik Deutschland, 1957–1983* (Frankfurt am Main and New York, 2012). He is currently working on a project analysing the impact of boarding schools on German elite formation during the nineteenth and twentiethth centuries.

Matthew Grant is Senior Lecturer in History at the University of Essex (UK). He is the author of *After the Bomb: Civil Defence and Nuclear War in Britain, 1945–68* (Basingstoke, 2010), and the editor of *The British Way in Cold Warfare* (London, 2009). He is currently working on a project charting the impact of the Cold War on British cultural and social life.

Eva Horn is Professor of Modern German Literature and Cultural Theory at the German Department of the University of Vienna (Austria). She is the author of *The Secret War: Treason, Espionage, and Modern Fiction* (Evanston, 2013) and *Zukunft als Katastrophe* (Frankfurt am Main, 2014), and co-editor, with Anson Rabinbach, of 'Dark powers: conspiracies in history and fiction', *New German Critique* 103 (2008). Her current research project is a literary history of climate.

Claudia Kemper is Research Fellow at the Institute for Social Research in Hamburg (HIS) (Germany). Her main research interests focus on intellectual and expert groups and organisations, as, for example, in her first book *Das Gewissen. Kommunikation und Vernetzung der Jungkonservativen 1919–1925* (Munich, 2010). She is currently preparing for the publication of her second book about the International Physicians for the Prevention of Nuclear War (IPPNW).

Lars Nowak is Assistant Professor of Media Studies at the University of Erlangen-Nuremberg (Germany). His main publications are *Deformation und Transdifferenz: Freak Show, frühes Kino, Tod Browning* (Berlin, 2011) and, as co-editor, *KartenWissen: Territoriale Räume zwischen Bild und Diagramm* (Wiesbaden, 2012). In his current research project, he is examining the use of photography and film as visualising techniques in ballistics and detonics.

Paul Rubinson is Assistant Professor of History at Bridgewater State University (USA). He has published articles in *Cold War History* and

Notes on contributors

Diplomatic History, as well as essays in *The Routledge Handbook of the Cold War* (New York, 2014) and *The Human Rights Revolution: An International History* (New York, 2012). His current book project is *Rethinking the Antinuclear Movement*, forthcoming from Routledge.

Ann Sherif is Professor of East Asian Studies at Oberlin College, Ohio (USA). Her publications include *Japan's Cold War: Media, Literature, and the Law* (New York, 2009) and *Mirror: The Essays and Fiction of Kôda Aya* (Honolulu, 1999). Her current research focuses on independent and regional publishers and literature in Cold War Japan.

Benjamin Ziemann is Professor of Modern German History at the University of Sheffield (UK). His many book publications include *War Experiences in Rural Germany, 1914–1923* (Oxford and New York, 2007); *Contested Commemorations. War Remembrances and Republican Politics in Weimar Germany* (Cambridge, 2013); *Encounters with Modernity. The Catholic Church in West Germany 1945–1975* (New York, 2014) and, as editor, *Peace Movements in Western Europe, Japan and the USA during the Cold War* (Essen, 2007).

Acknowledgements

How can the Cold War be called a 'war'? This question got us thinking about the role of the threat of nuclear destruction that the arms race since 1945 entailed. We first discussed this issue during a workshop that took place at the German Historical Institute in London and that was co-organised with the German Historical Institute at Rome and the Arbeitskreis für Historische Friedensforschung. For their generous financial support of this workshop we would like to thank the Gerda Henkel Stiftung, the German Historical Institute London and its director, Andreas Gestrich, the Deutsche Stiftung Friedensforschung and the Arbeitskreis für Historische Friedensforschung. During the workshop, we benefited from the intellectual input provided by those colleagues who have subsequently contributed chapters to this volume, and by Patrick Bernhard (who also co-organised the workshop), Jost Dülffer, Andreas Gestrich, Michael Geyer, Helge Pharo, Umberto Rossi, Thomas F. Schneider, Vera Wolff and particularly by the late Paul Boyer, who also gave the keynote lecture.

During the long gestation of this volume, we were supported by numerous colleagues. We are indebted to Martin Sherwin, Nadine Rossol, Andrew Priest, Tracey Loughran and Christine Brocks for their interest in our project and for practical help at various stages. We should like to acknowledge the help of Holger Nehring, who co-organised the workshop in London and helped to edit some of the chapters in this volume. We are grateful to the team at Manchester University Press for the constructive collaboration, and to the two anonymous reviewers for their incisive and extremely helpful questions and suggestions.

Note on translation: unless otherwise indicated, all translations are by the authors of individual chapters.

Matthew Grant and Benjamin Ziemann, August 2015

1

Introduction: the Cold War as an imaginary war

Matthew Grant and Benjamin Ziemann

The Cold War began as a metaphor.[1] It was an analogy that used temperature to indicate a state of conflict just short of an actual 'hot' war. When George Orwell coined the term 'cold war' in his article in *Tribune* on 19 October 1945, he situated the genealogy of this new type of conflict in the connections between democratisation, empire building and weapons technology. Military weapons, Orwell knew, are an instrument of power well beyond their actual use on the battlefield. And as only a limited number of countries might be able to harness the new technology of the atomic bomb (Orwell reckoned it might be only three or four, which was a fairly accurate prediction, at least for the fifteen years from 1945 onwards) it might lead them to 'a tacit agreement never to use the atomic bomb against one another'. The socialist writer and critic asked how the new empires would operate, being based on the possession of atomic bombs; that is, a state that was 'was at once UNCONQUERABLE and in a permanent state of "cold war" with its neighbours'. What was the 'world-view, the kind of beliefs, and the social structure' that might be fostered by such an empire? At least one thing seemed to be certain to Orwell: the real danger of the atomic bomb might be that of 'prolonging indefinitely a "peace that is no peace"'.[2]

Seventy years after its publication, Orwell's short article is still a powerful outline of the conceptual questions raised by this new type of conflict. Orwell was the first to understand that the atomic bomb not only ushered in the new state of ideology, politics and society in the emerging conflict that he tried to conceptualise in his article, but that it also stood as a powerful symbol of that new state. 'The bomb' quickly became a shorthand term for the dangerousness of the 'Cold War' – of the horror that would await if it turned 'hot' – and so itself became a signifier for a world in which the metaphorical play with the temperature of armed conflict was no longer confined to the realm of the military, but emanated from a single weapons' technology and pervaded all aspects of culture, society and politics. 'Cold War' quickly moved from being a simple metaphor of military tension to becoming an indicator of an entire complex system of global ideologies, politics and societies. As such, it became an entrenched, though disputed, concept. It went, as it were, from being the 'cold war' to the Cold War. Yet it never lost its metaphorical nature. It stood simultaneously for a 'sustained international conflict short of "hot" war', as its very opposite ('a form of peace'), and for the techniques and actions need to 'fight' it. In short, 'Cold War' could stand as a metaphor for both war and peace.

Nuclear weapons were crucial for these multiple meanings of the Cold War: and the 'bomb' itself became the central metaphor of the Cold War. It was the harbinger of destruction, the symbol of what became a vast arsenal of power that seemed to threaten the very existence of humanity. But it was also, by its very destructiveness, the guarantor of peace: the way both blocs could 'deter' aggression, providing peace through strength. Living 'under the shadow' of the bomb signified anxiety and dread, and the image of the mushroom cloud became the central icon of the entire Cold War, evoking not only the threat of nuclear war but the entire time-frame of the Cold War. On a more mundane level, the bomb was also called into metaphorical action to stand for any event, new, shocking, or powerful, such as when one physician in late 1945 called the new practice of artificial insemination by donor a development as 'startling' as the atomic bomb.[3]

In this volume, we propose to take the metaphorical character of the Cold War seriously and to place how the bomb was used as a symbol for nuclear war at the very heart of this conflict. Understanding the Cold War, and the bomb's place in it, requires an analysis of the complex linguistic inversions and paradoxical rhetorical interventions that allowed it to be envisaged in such contrasting ways. Thus, we consider the historical relevance of the political, cultural and artistic ramifications of nuclear weapons as signifiers for a new type of conflict in greater detail and in a more coherent fashion. We try to encapsulate this understanding of the metaphorical qualities of the Cold War in the notion of an imaginary war, or, more precisely, a war against the imagination. As an attack against the imagination, the nuclear threat forced politicians and ordinary people to accept the notion that preparations for nuclear annihilation would contribute towards peace, and that the existence of these weapons, and the anticipation of large-scale destruction that came with them, were an inescapable corollary of security, freedom and future prosperity on both sides of the Cold War divide.

Introduction: the Cold War as an imaginary war

In a short but important piece that he published shortly after the end of the bloc confrontation, historian Michael Geyer highlighted three aspects of the system of nuclear deterrence that allowed him to qualify the Cold War as a sustained attack against the imagination.[4] The first was the simulation of war games that calculated the potential impact of nuclear weapons on different theatres of war and under different strategic and operational parameters. As the actual use of nuclear weapons was of course avoided at all cost, the only way governments could seek to understand the consequences of nuclear war – both on the enemy and themselves – was to simulate nuclear war. Such simulations meant that the anticipation and imagining of how nuclear weapons might be used became itself a key battlefield of the Cold War. Proponents of different schools of nuclear strategy may have held different opinions on how to conduct nuclear war, but their plans and strategies relied on the assumptions of what a nuclear war would be like – on how it was simulated and imagined. Pacifist critics and peace researchers likewise tried to understand the consequences of any such strategy on the peoples and societies that would be affected. Implicitly, everyone involved in fighting the Cold War, nuclear strategists and peace campaigners alike, agreed that the key battlefield of the Cold War was how nuclear war was simulated and imagined. It is wrong to assume, as some analysts have done, that the imagination of nuclear war benefited only those who sought to foster peace. Such forecasts were, to the contrary, also used by those military planners who wanted to make a nuclear stand-off both knowable and manageable.[5] Vast sums were expended in attempting to understand the 'reality' of nuclear war, and the results of such attempts at modelling nuclear war greatly influenced Cold War Strategy. For example, exercise *Abel Archer-83* not only modelled NATO's potential use of its first-strike strategy in the early 1980s, but also raised alarms in Moscow that the war game was in fact a cover for a genuine strike.[6] Imagining war in this sense not only furthered knowledge of the nuclear 'reality', but was in fact inseparable from it.

This agreement over the imagination of the battlefield was closely related to the second aspect: the credibility of nuclear devastation as the capstone of deterrence. In its attempt to create such credibility, the blueprints for nuclear destruction had to pervade society and culture and to win the battle over the hearts and minds of populations in Cold War societies and convince them that nuclear deterrence worked and was the only way to keep the Cold War 'cold'. As Geyer clearly recognised, this making and unmaking of the credibility of nuclear destruction was in itself a rhetorical strategy, and as such it was part and parcel of the use of the bomb to stand as metaphor for a new type of warfare: the peace-ensuring weapon of total destruction.[7] Ultimately, this led to the third aspect of the imaginary war that Geyer identified: the destruction of the autonomy of the enemy and of their willpower. The Cold War as a metaphorical play on the possibility of nuclear destruction was destructive, as it forced people to give in to the underpinning logic of deterrence. Only through relying on the logic of deterrence could security be obtained. This led to the anguished attempts to ensure the credibility of the deterrent that typified the politics of both weapons technology and alliance strategy in the Cold War. It is reasonable to assume that it was precisely this loss of intellectual autonomy that Orwell meant when he described the core effect of the Cold War as 'the reimposition of slavery'.[8]

Taking the metaphorical quality of the Cold War seriously and emphasising the centrality of 'the bomb' as a symbol of its unprecedented destructive potential enables us to highlight both the discursive nature of this particular conflict and the centrality of that nature to how the conflict was understood and fought. The nuclear bombs that were used to destroy the Japanese cities of Hiroshima and Nagasaki in 1945 formed part of a conventional war effort. Yet, in the decades after August 1945, the understood 'reality' of nuclear devastation was created through the discursive practices that regulated the linguistic and pictorial references to a potential nuclear catastrophe – in short, it was imagined.[9] While nuclear war was a fiction, the rhetorical usages of this fiction created the very reality of the Cold War as the age of the atomic bomb. Different groups of actors made and unmade this reality by using media that allowed them to construct the discursive elements of nuclear deterrence and its purported consequences. The metaphorical nature of the Cold War, then, and the centrality of the bomb within that metaphorical landscape, structured the entire framework of the Cold War.

In arguing that we need to understand the metaphorical nature of the nuclear conflict within the Cold War, we are not suggesting that the Cold War has no concrete meaning. Metaphors do not mean anything we want them to mean. Rather, they provide a framework – a limited and, at times, tightly bound one – of acceptable political and social realities. A key aim of the book is to explore the ways nuclear weapons could be imagined during the Cold War, by analysing the historical range and implications of key metaphors for nuclear conflict in detail. As such, the emphasis of the volume is placed on the consequences of how the 'imaginary war' structured the way in which the Cold War was envisaged and fought, and not just to provide examples of how nuclear weapons were imagined within popular culture. This distinction, between the structural implications of imagining nuclear weapons on the one hand, and the hermeneutic study of a selection of potentially endless cultural productions on the other, is central to the volume. We move beyond a mere description of the ways in which popular media represented the bomb and the nuclear age more generally.[10] Such a cataloguing of the different ways in which the media portrayed the bomb is a first step towards a more complex analysis of the nuclear threat. Yet it has to be accompanied by two additional perspectives that highlight the profound significance of the bomb for the Cold War. On the one hand, representations of the nuclear threat have to be situated in discourses about national and international security and about the role of nuclear deterrence in the post-war world. On the other hand, the imaginary war has to be understood as a threshold of expectations, as a fundamental shift in the ever-changing interplay between the 'space of experience' and the 'horizon of expectations' as the two main temporal markers in modern society.[11]

In much the same way, we do not view the Cold War as an imaginary war in the sense that this confrontation was just the result of an elaborate propaganda machinery that was employed by governments in the West and the East in order to deceive the people in their respective countries.[12] The notion of propaganda is too simplistic to understand the continuing presence of, and the emotional investment in, the bomb as a signifier of total annihilation. To be sure, both governments and the military as well as anti-nuclear protest movements had their own vested interests in circulating their respective views on nuclear armaments, and used any means at their disposal to do so. But even while the political aims of key actors differed, they all shared a common terrain: the assumption that the prospect of nuclear war was best elaborated in the form of a simulation based on key signifiers. Any 'propaganda' effort could use these signifiers, but could not create them.

It would also be mistaken to assume that the Cold War was an imaginary war as it had no material reality. Hundreds of Minuteman missile silos were tucked away across the Great Plains, thus turning the American Midwest into another frontline of the Cold War and demonstrating the intersections between grand nuclear strategy and US domestic politics. While the silos were by and large invisible to the US public at large, they had a continuing presence for the local population that actually mostly supported nuclear deterrence.[13] The material reality of the imaginary war is also visible in the toxic legacy of the many former sites for the production of nuclear weapons that nowadays, after they have been decommissioned, need long-term solutions for the clean-up of nuclear waste and the preservation of key hardware structures.[14] The Cold War was not an imaginary war in the sense that the nuclear threat was immaterial. It was imaginary in the sense that formats that are usually described as fictitious – from dreams and nightmares, films and novels to forecasts and scenarios – had an important bearing on the reality of the Cold War as a nuclear confrontation. For example, the acute fears of nuclear destruction caused by the escalation of the Cuban Missile Crisis in 1962 were very real, an intense emotional response to the fear of global destruction. Yet these fears were by necessity 'imagined', and how they were imagined was the result of a complex process of cultural construction. When the US Defence Secretary Robert McNamara wondered whether he had seen his last sunset during the crisis, he was articulating his understanding of nuclear war that was based on both technological awareness of the power of nuclear weapons and on the 'scientific' modelling of the results of a nuclear attack on US cities conducted by the US Government.[15]

The TV documentary *The War Game*, produced by the British film director Peter Watkins in 1965, can help us to understand how the imaginary war operated on different levels. The film was commissioned by the BBC and shot on location in various towns in the county of Kent. In the form of a mock documentary, it portrayed the effects of a 1-megaton bomb dropped on the town of Rochester, from the initial blast and shockwave and the ensuing firestorm to the subsequent breakdown of societal order, while police and fire services try to dispose of the many corpses and crack down with brutal force on rioting people, who scour the debris of the destroyed town for bits of food and other usable items. Shortly before the scheduled screening, the BBC refrained from broadcasting the film, following intensive behind-the-scene debates with government officials from the Home Office and the Ministry of Defence that were followed by intensive scrutiny of the decision in parliament and in the print media. The film was subsequently released for screening in cinemas, attracting an estimated audience of six million people in the UK alone until it was finally broadcast on BBC television in 1985. At the political level, the story of the *The War Game* is one of self-censorship of the BBC for fear of endangering its position vis-à-vis the government, with the interesting point that the decision to pull the programme was not taken owing to the vivid nature in which the film portrayed the effects of a nuclear bomb on the bodies and souls of the surviving victims. As historian

Introduction: the Cold War as an imaginary war

Tony Shaw has convincingly argued, 'the central issue' in the debates between the government and the BBC was not 'that of the immediate psychological impact of the film's horror; rather, it was that of *The War Game*'s impact on the public's attitudes to the nuclear deterrent'.[16]

At this level, the story of *The War Game* is one of the liberal Cold War consensus that supported the policy of nuclear deterrence in the UK as in other Western countries, and of the limited political potential for a public critique of that consensus as for instance through the Campaign for Nuclear Disarmament (CND), which used the film in its appeal to the public. To understand the more complex ways in which *The War Game* was part and parcel of the nuclear war as an imaginary war, a closer look at the mediated reality that the film presented and at its use of the medium TV is needed.[17] As the title of the film already suggests, *The War Game* is firmly situated in the Cold War as a war of simulations and scenarios of nuclear warfare. It opens with a map of the UK that pinpoints all those places that are potential targets of Soviet nuclear missiles, comparable to the maps that were used by military planners at the time. Nuclear war games are also introduced through short fictitious interview statements by a nuclear strategist with a heavy American accent, clearly modelled along the lines of RAND-strategist Herman Kahn, who is also represented through an intertitle with the question 'Would the survivors envy the dead?', from his 1960 book *On Thermonuclear War*.

Yet *The War Game* is not only situated in the simulation of nuclear war as the actual battlefield of the Cold War. Within these parameters, the film tackles the credibility of nuclear deterrence head-on as it inverts some of the narrative tropes that civil defence films produced by the British government tended to use. Quoting extensively from civil defence manuals and from meetings with civil defence planners, and showing how civil defence measures unfold and dramatically fail in the wake of the atomic blast, the films shows that civil defence will not underpin the national or local community amidst an exceptional challenge, but rather lead to an anomic situation in which the rule of law collapses, and thus ultimately create a police state that would destroy the very liberties that the Cold War consensus claimed to defend. Ironically, the depiction of state brutality in post-attack Britain in *The War Game* was based on government policies that were every bit as imaginary as the rest of the film, as the state's ability to maintain any control, however murderous, was deeply doubted within Whitehall.[18]

In addition, Watkins' film also operates at a third level of discursive intervention – that of the medium television itself and its capacity to represent and shape reality. At first glance, *The War Game* is presented in the typical style of BBC news coverage of current affairs, with a hand-held camera that brings the viewer close to the location of the events, and short interviews with members of the public that ironically reveal their lack of knowledge about the actual effects of nuclear weapons. Yet as the effects of the atomic blast intensify, the film makes it clear that its impact cannot be captured through the medium of television. Rather than trying to show killing and dying, Watkins relied on lay actors who talk directly to the camera about their loss and devastation. Their confused 'stammering' can be read as an eyewitness testimony that replaces any attempt at a 'realistic' portrayal of the consequences of nuclear war. Indicative of the refusal of Watkins to conform with established ways of framing and representing nuclear war is also his portrayal of the nuclear explosion itself. Rather than normalising or even aestheticising this moment by showing a mushroom cloud, the film itself is 'blinded' for a few seconds through overexposure, thus showing the insufficiency of the medium for depicting nuclear catastrophe. Seen in a wider frame, *The War Game* is thus a critical reflection on television as the archetypical medium of the Cold War, a medium that stabilised an omnipresent political reality through a verisimilitude of events it could never actually produce.[19]

The War Game was not simply propaganda, although that was indeed the perception of many commentators in the British press, mostly the defence correspondents in fact, who took the view that the film was an inversion of their own political preferences and thus labelled it 'crude CND propaganda'.[20] It was a genuine attempt to understand the 'reality' of nuclear war on Britain, to cut through the mist of government lies and propaganda which Watkins thought clouded people's ability to understand the issue. It imagined the breakdown of deterrence as emerging from the internal logic of the bloc confrontation, and Watkins chose to contrast images of the havoc caused by the bomb in Rochester with statements from Roman Catholic and Anglican bishops about the legitimacy of nuclear deterrence, thus highlighting how the potential reality of nuclear war inverted the unspoken assumptions of deterrence. *The War Game* was successful in puncturing some of the intense secrecy with which the UK Government surrounded nuclear issues, but it was no less a simulation of the imaginary war than the bland reassurances promoted by the pro-deterrent governments of NATO: all shared the assumption that the politics of nuclear war rested on how it was imagined and simulated. As mentioned, the film used the language of deterrence and civil defence to critique those ideas, to highlight their inherent flaws and the

Introduction: the Cold War as an imaginary war

hypocrisy of government. Yet it relied on the logic of civil defence even as that logic was being critiqued, illustrating the fact that Watkins could not escape the bounded nature of how nuclear war was understood. He could, however, push those boundaries. *The War Game* constituted such a fundamental shift in the horizon of expectations, in fact it represented a revolution in British Cold War culture as it established the idea of a horrific post-nuclear society in which survival might be worse than death.[21] This opened up a new way of imagining nuclear war, and throughout the 1970s and 1980s, depictions of a future conflict gained much of the rhetorical force from imagining the horrors of the post-nuclear world.[22]

The imaginary nature of the Cold War was not static. The vast numbers of attempts to simulate or imagine nuclear conflict expanded the horizons of the imaginary war greatly. Nor did it just magically spring into being in 1945. While the bomb as a harbinger of potentially global devastation inaugurated a new quality of warfare, important aspects of what we call the imaginary war had already emerged during previous stages of twentieth-century warfare. The underlying theme can be perhaps described as the trend towards a virtualisation of warfare that had emerged since 1914. In a rather loose fashion, the French critic Paul Virilio has raised attention to the often parallel developments between weapons' technologies and the technology of cinematography during the twentieth century. The key point that can be borrowed from this analysis is the way in which the conduct of war increasingly depended on means of making the process of targeting and destruction visible, as the distance between the soldiers and their actual targets was rapidly increasing.[23] This process had moral consequences, not least visible in the behaviour of the military aircraft crews that dropped the bombs on Hiroshima and Nagasaki, and has been characterised as a 'Promethean slope' by the philosopher Günther Anders.[24] Yet the other crucial side-effect of this process, addressed by Virilio, is the increasing need for mediated representations of the battlefield in order to gauge the results of the employments of weapons. In that sense, he quite rightly called the First World War the 'first mediated conflict in history', as a supply of images through air reconnaissance was almost as vital as the supply of ammunition. The 'logistics of perception' thus became the second important battlefield of industrial warfare.[25]

This trend was compounded by another trend that was equally much exacerbated during the imaginary nuclear war since 1945: the 'crisis of representation' of the modern battlefield. As the distance between soldiers and their enemies widened and the battlefield was largely emptied of actual soldiers, as in the no-man's-land between the trench systems, it was increasingly difficult, if not impossible to visually represent the battlefield using a conventional vanishing point perspective. Photographers during the Great War and cinematographers in its aftermath tried to respond to this problem. One answer was the decision by the Australian war photographer Frank Hurley to recreate a battlefield in Flanders by putting together a montage of twelve different photos in the darkroom.[26] In the decades from 1945 to 1990, military planners, artists and protesters struggled to envisage the likely effects and consequences of an all-out nuclear war. In these endeavours, they still grappled with the consequences of the crisis of representations that had commenced in 1914.

The impact of the imaginary war was enormous. It fundamentally changed the 'present future' of those societies involved in fighting it during the Cold War period – the possible worlds that were envisaged during the present of the 1960s – as it threw into doubt the very availability of such a future.[27] From the very start of the atomic age, strategists, intellectuals and artists grappled with the idea that the Cold War could lead to the end of humanity. The way this idea was imagined took a variety of forms: activists dramatised the choice been peace and prosperity and war and death; strategists elevated the bomb in to the preserver of peace. A writer like Tove Jansson, in her children's book *Comet in Moominland* (1946), could depict an earth-ending scenario about which the central characters, standing for humanity, could do nothing about.[28] Decades later, in the 1980s, ways of imagining nuclear war – of fighting the imaginary war – had expanded dramatically. Models of nuclear war existed that allowed strategists to posit a limited, indeed winnable, nuclear war. Likewise, simulations of nuclear war abounded in popular culture depicting the gruesome horrors of radiation sickness and the breakdown of society. The depictions changed, but their centrality to the Cold War had not. They continued to form the bedrock of how the Cold War was fought, and how it was, and could be, conceptualised. The bomb, and the Cold War, continued to be metaphors of enormous power even though their content changed. How that content changed, and how it underpinned how the Cold War was understood and fought, is the topic of this volume.

Recent historiography on the nuclear age

There has been an enormous upsurge in scholarly interest in the Cold War over the last decade. Perhaps the best example of this is the recent three-volume synthesis, *The Cambridge History of the Cold War*, which comprises a collection of essays seeking to move beyond the traditional diplomatic confines of the subject in order to view it in the context of global political and social change.[29] Although still firmly focused on the Cold War as an ideological battle between the East and the West, there was a keen emphasis on both the role of ideas and concepts such as human rights and Eurocommunism, and on structural economic developments throughout the second half of the twentieth century, culminating in the demand for consumer goods. The *Cambridge History* gave due attention to the issue of nuclear weapons. Indeed, in his chapter on the contribution of nuclear weapons to the escalation of the Cold War up until 1962, David Holloway writes that 'nuclear weapons are so central to the history of the Cold War that it can be difficult to disentangle the two'.[30]

Holloway's essay, and the others in the *Cambridge History* are good examples of what we can usually categorise as the first of two historiographical approaches to the nuclear age. This discusses the political and diplomatic consequences of nuclear weapons, and there is a vast literature on this aspect of the nuclear confrontation. We have detailed histories of national nuclear strategies and the weapons-building programmes in the belligerent nations, on nuclear crisis management, and the thorny issue of the bomb's role in starting, escalating, easing or ending the Cold War.[31] The best of this research seeks not only to chart what happened, but to understand what protagonists thought was happening. Campbell Craig and Sergey Radchenko's recent book, for example, places the assumptions of the United States and Soviet Union about both the nature of atomic bomb, and the other's intentions towards it, centre stage in their account of the start of the Cold War period.[32] Jacques Hymans' sustained engagement on the history and politics of nuclear proliferation has sought to uncover the psychological and emotional dimensions of political choices to 'go nuclear', recognising that the decision to build nuclear weapons programmes was as much about the psychological need for such programmes within political systems, as it was 'rational' choice.[33] Similarly, Baylis and Stoddart's new book argues that the political desire within the United Kingdom for building, and maintaining, the nation's nuclear deterrent was firmly rooted in ideas of British national identity in an era of decline.[34]

In this sense, the historiography of nuclear politics and diplomacy is moving in the same direction of work on ideology or Cold War politics more generally, which has seen an attempt to pinpoint contemporary understandings in order to better analyse policy responses to the developing Cold War.[35] There has also been sustained work on how nuclear knowledge was formed in US military circles, particularly in terms of modelling the consequences of nuclear war on American cities. This highlights the intense efforts to 'understand' and 'imagine' nuclear war on the part of the American authorities in order to better develop nuclear and civil defence strategies.[36] In general, the histories of nuclear weapons have highlighted the processes by which they were produced and deployed. As yet, however, there has been relatively little attention paid to the nature of nuclear knowledge itself, or to the fact that even when mapping (both figuratively and physically) the power of these weapons and their political meaning, politicians, scientists and military planners were engaging in an active process of imagination that relied not only on scientific and political know-how, but also rested on assumptions about the nature of warfare, human society and emotions, which have yet to be analysed thoroughly.

The second broad historiographical approach to the nuclear age confronts the social and cultural implications of nuclear weapons.[37] The social history of nuclear weapons has been understandably dominated by research on peace movements around the globe. Excellent research has charted the formation and activities of a range of peace groups,[38] none more so than Lawrence Wittner's astounding three volumes on global disarmament movements.[39] In the same way as other pioneering work on the bomb's impact on American society,[40] this work takes the bomb's existence as a starting point and analyses how different groups attempting to influence what seemed to them a graspable, concrete political situation. Jeremi Suri's work goes further, arguing that a changed understanding of the nuclear confrontation from the mid-1960s directly influenced the explosion of political and social dissent that followed.[41] This is an immensely fruitful way of examining the nuclear politics of the 1960s, and following Suri other scholars have sought to embed the 'nuclear' aspect of Cold War dissent more firmly into the context of social and political ideas.[42] Although such work has provided major new insights into the social and political importance of nuclear weapons, it does not investigate fully how those dissenters understood or imagined nuclear weapons.

Cultural history approaches have differed from social history approaches, in investigating how knowledge about nuclear weapons is created and dispersed throughout national cultures. Often this work has been marked by their concentration on cultural production – histories of Cold War culture rather than cultural histories of the Cold War – and research on the depiction of nuclear weapons in films, books and magazines have greatly enhanced our understanding of how nuclear weapons have been represented within these types of popular culture.[43] At its very

Introduction: the Cold War as an imaginary war

best, the cultural history of nuclear weapons has sought to understand how the forms in which nuclear technology have been discussed have influenced the nature of nuclear knowledge. This is particularly true of the trailblazing work of scholars such as Paul S. Boyer and Spencer Weart.[44] To take one example, Boyer's analysis of apparently ephemeral material culture, such as the free toys given away with breakfast cereals, highlighted the centrality of the atomic bomb to domestic culture in the United States and showed how it was a source of national pride and technical wonder as well as destruction. The apparently mundane examples of 'nuclear culture' in the years immediately following 1945 showed a society which felt a brief confidence that they had controlled this new technology.[45] To take another example, Weart's nuanced look at how 'in the imagination, nuclear war often meant no future but an empty one' demonstrated the importance of how the bomb was imagined for any attempt to chart its history.[46]

The work of Boyer and Weart has been foundational to the study of Cold War culture, setting the conceptual terrain a later generation of scholars have since explored. They also highlighted the importance of nuclear technology, broadly conceived, in determining how nuclear weapons were understood. Narratives of civil nuclear energy helped allay fears about nuclear weapons from the very beginning of the 'atomic age'. Landmark works on the cultural ramifications of nuclear energy have been produced recently,[47] particularly Gabrielle Hecht's *The Radiance of France*, which ties the French civil nuclear programme, which generates more than three quarters of the nation's electric energy, to French national identity in the post-war period.[48] Jeff Hughes has criticised Weart's book, and Kirk Willis' work on early British nuclear culture,[49] for taking a fixed understanding of what nuclear culture was, and then seeking to chart how this vision of nuclear culture was discussed within popular culture. This, Hughes argues, is 'essentialising' nuclear culture, seeing it as an 'autonomous, homogeneous and transcendent entity'.[50] Although this criticism has some validity, Weart's book is still important for its sweeping ability to unpick the images of nuclear war that circulated within American culture.

More recent work has sought to detail the cultural specificity of the nature and formation of nuclear knowledge in a wide variety of cultures other than that of the United States.[51] A recent special issue on 'British Nuclear Culture' looks at the issue from a number of perspectives, attesting to the heterodox ways nuclear weapons were depicted.[52] An excellent essay on reactions to the atomic bomb in China highlights the central way in which the specific context of civil war and the building of state socialism influenced how the new weapon was understood.[53] National cultural and historical context is central to understanding the limits and influence of the imaginary war. Of particular importance is the growth of what we can call the really existing history of nuclear weapons, the physical consequences of the arms race as well as the cultural ones. Joseph Masco's pioneering work on *Nuclear Borderlands* is of central importance in understanding how the nuclear weapons programme transformed parts of the South-western United States.[54] Kate Brown's *Plutopia* examines the impact of civil nuclear disasters in the United States and the Soviet Union.[55] A recent special issue of *Urban History* has explored the impact of the nuclear stalemate on the urban environment.[56] We also have the beginnings of a historiography of the impact of nuclear knowledge on individual subjectivities, such as Frank Biess' pioneering work on the emotional consequences of nuclear armaments on the population of West Germany.[57]

Our volume builds on these approaches, in particular through its central focus on the fundamental instability of forms of knowledge about nuclear weapons. In putting the thinking of the unthinkable centre stage, the present collection emphasises both the bomb as the core element of the Cold War, and the key role that attempts really to imagine the unthinkable potentials of nuclear destruction had on the political, social and cultural realities of the Cold War. We are not suggesting that studies that concentrate on political decision-making are misguided or wrong. Far from it. We are arguing that such studies could be enhanced by paying greater attention to the way in which nuclear war was, and could be, imagined, and the consequences of that for the wider Cold War. Likewise, we are aware of some of the problems with a cultural history approach, and have sought to avoid a relativist approach that suggests that all ways of imagining nuclear war were equal. We have resisted the urge to detail a cavalcade of cultural production, but rather focus on how the imaginary war was formulated and fought in popular culture. Above all, we believe that the cultural history of the Cold War is vital to understanding every part of the conflict, that the ideas and images associated with the nuclear confrontation structured what the Cold War was or could possibly be.

The scope of this volume

By its very nature, the presence of the atomic bomb and its challenge to intellectual understanding transcended national borders as well as the

Introduction: the Cold War as an imaginary war

Iron Curtain. Ways of imagining the bomb, and the destruction it caused, were limited by scientific and technological understandings which were widely circulated. The boundaries of how the bomb could imagined were challenged and expanded by artists, intellectuals, defence planners and activists in remarkable ways. Our introduction has highlighted the conceptual and symbolic nature of the bomb during the Cold War period. The following chapter, by Eva Horn, extends this by highlighting the 'fictionality' of nuclear weapons. Combined, these chapters demonstrate the framework within which the bomb could be imagined: the attempt to grapple with an apocalypse that seemed urgent and real, a tangible threat to the whole concept of the future, but which also seemed ungraspable and unknowable, a 'blind spot' which obscured both the future and the 'reality' of the bomb. All those who sought to understand the imaginary war had to grapple with this.

Yet, despite the capacity of nuclear weapons to inflict global devastation, distinctive national cultures shaped the ways in which nuclear war was modelled and imagined. The imaginative framework of nuclear war was structured differently in very different national contexts, owing not least to the potential limits of information exchange. Chapters 3 to 6 of this volume contextualise these national trajectories in a long-term perspective for four countries: the Soviet Union, the United States, West Germany and the United Kingdom. These nations have been selected to provide analyses of how the imaginary war was understood in key Cold War belligerent nations. In our four main belligerent nations it is clear that the imagination of nuclear war was diverse and deeply embedded in national culture, and focusing on these nations in the first instance allows us to see this diversity and richness of responses to nuclear weapons, but also to understand the real differences and constraints within each national culture.

This is not to suggest that other national contexts are unimportant, and indeed it is obvious that much more research is needed to understand how the imaginary war structured the experiences of the Cold War in nations across the globe. Existing research suggests that Chinese reactions towards the atomic bomb were muted in the context of the civil war and early Communist period.[58] In France, the issue of nuclear war was more closely linked to civil technology than in any other society.[59] Even neutral countries were implied and affected, as, for instance, the imaginary war decisively shaped Sweden's position of neutrality.[60] The Swiss example is particularly striking and informative. Despite being a neutral country, Switzerland had some of the highest per capita spending on civil defence during the Cold War and the highest ratio between soldiers relative to the population in Europe. Between 1956 and 1971, the Swiss army conducted five 'national defence exercises'. These were large-scale simulations of a nuclear attack on the country. They involved an increasingly larger circle of participants – including civil authorities – and made substantial efforts to make the scenarios of these rehearsals ever more complex and realistic. Since the mid-1960s, the threat scenarios that underpinned the simulations changed. As the progress of détente made a direct attack by the Soviet Union increasingly unlikely, the scenarios also involved domestic threats such as leftist terrorism or communist subversion. That the imaginary war was also simulated and anticipated in neutral countries suggests that the Cold War was more than just a bloc confrontation between the two superpowers and their respective allies.[61] The Cold War has a much wider geography than it is usually assumed with a focus on US foreign and military policy, not least because Japan, the only country that had been targeted and devastated by nuclear weapons, played a crucial role in the scenarios and imaginations of total nuclear destruction.

In the Soviet Union, the progressive historical optimism of the Bolshevik project curtailed the extent in which anxieties about a nuclear apocalypse could be articulated. Nevertheless, an atomic culture gradually developed also in the Soviet Union, as Miriam Dobson argues in her chapter. From the 1950s to the 1980s, the Soviet press released an increasing amount of information about the nature and potential consequences of nuclear weapons. But in line with the emotional regime that the Bolsheviks tried to instil in the population, any outright expressions of nuclear fear remained a taboo. At the margins of Soviet society, however, it seems religious language allowed some groups and individuals to articulate an emotional response to the prospect of nuclear war and to express it by using the Biblical rhetoric of the apocalypse.

While atomic culture had only a limited presence in the Soviet Union, US society since 1945 has to be understood in the light of the pervasive nature of the bomb in media, politics and mass culture, as Paul Boyer argues in his chapter. In the decades from 1945 to the early twenty-first century, the challenge to think the presence of the bomb went through three distinctive cycles, each of them prompted by a specific cause: the bombs dropped on Hiroshima and Nagasaki in the first wave up to the mid-1950s, then the heightening of the bloc confrontation in the late 1950s and early 1960s, and finally the problem of nuclear proliferation in the third cycle that started in the late 1970s. One characteristic feature of US atomic culture that has often been noted was that the widespread

Introduction: the Cold War as an imaginary war

anxieties about nuclear weapons in these three cycles of engagement never translated into sustained political action or into a fundamental change in nuclear policy.[62] One crucial factor that shaped this trajectory seems to have been the early and substantial presence of the bomb in US popular mass culture which played on the claviature of nuclear anxieties, while at the same time rendering nuclear weapons as a playful and ultimately perhaps even harmless technical gizmo with a destructive capacity that evoked fear and fascination in equal measure. Thus, the ground was prepared for the kind of nostalgia in the cultural articulation of nuclear weapons that has characterised US mass media in the years since the dissolution of the Soviet Union, as the immediate threat of a nuclear confrontation between the East and the West had apparently disappeared.

In the representations of US popular culture, destruction through nuclear weapons often appeared to take place at sites that were far away from the American homeland, whether in Japanese cities or in remote atolls in the South Pacific. In a stark contrast, the immediacy of nuclear destruction was one of the central features of imagining nuclear war in West Germany, as Benjamin Ziemann argues in his chapter. German angst was not a strange romantic malady, but was nurtured by a clear sense of the geography of the bloc confrontation in Europe. From the 1950s to the 1980s, both politicians, top-brass officers in the Bundeswehr and peace protesters shared the perception that one certain outcome of any nuclear confrontation would be the devastation of large swathes of West German territory. Already during the 1950s, when West German rearmament triggered a controversy over the possibility to equip the Bundeswehr with nuclear weapons, the situation was aggravated by the fact that retaliation would require NATO troops to halt an alleged Soviet offensive by targeting German cities with their own nuclear warheads. During the 1980s, the Fulda gap – named after the most likely place for a conventional Soviet attack into West German territory – emerged as a symbol for nuclear destruction that might occur right at the doorstep of ordinary German citizens. At the same time, the Fulda gap linked the concerns of local citizens and peace activists with the modelling of nuclear war at US Army training facilities that were thousands of miles away. Despite specific national trajectories and concerns, the imaginary war linked distant communities via the mass media coverage of nuclear strategy.

Another peculiarity of West German perceptions of the atomic bomb were the ways in which images of nuclear destruction were saturated with recollections of the Allied bombing campaign from 1939 to 1945, thus making the new scale of devastation comprehensible and tapping into notions of victimhood. This peculiarity, however, was not exclusive to the Germans, as British discourses on the bomb also tapped into images of the Second World War bombing campaign. As Matthew Grant argues in his chapter, the physical and imaginative landscape of the Second World War helped shape reactions to the atomic bomb. Like West Germany, Britain differed from the United States in considering itself immediately and directly in the firing line of potential Soviet aggression. The gilded memory of nation's survival of the Blitz of 1940–41 helped to create a confidence, or rather sanguinity, concerning the capacity of Britain to resist and survive an atomic attack which tended to undercut the apocalyptic nuclear culture which emerged elsewhere. The advent of the hydrogen bomb, however, destroyed that confidence. From 1954 onwards, British culture was resolutely pessimistic about the chances of the population – and indeed of humanity itself – having any chance of survival in a nuclear war. This apocalyptic culture was promoted by both nuclear disarmers and pro-deterrent cold warriors who were keen to emphasise the power of Britain's own bomb, leading to a cultural inability to imagine, or conceptualise what life after a nuclear war would be like.

Following these chapters a series of pieces investigate aspects of the imaginary war in greater detail, providing rich examples of the complex, innovative and contradictory ways in which a variety of individuals and groups sought to understand the imaginary war for political, social and cultural ends. In virtually all discussions of nuclear weapons in European and US intellectual culture during the Cold War, there was a widespread but mostly implicit agreement that 8 August 1945, the day when the bomb was dropped on Hiroshima, was a deep caesura. Yet, as Jason Dawsey argues in his chapter, the German-Jewish philosopher Günther Anders acted as a trailblazer for a more complex understanding of 8 August 1945 as a 'zero hour' that required a fundamental rethinking of the basic categories of the anthropological premises of human existence: time, future and the implications of man-made mass death for human civilisation. Steeped in the German tradition of dialectical thinking, Anders had a keen interest in the inversion of traditional concepts of understanding that the bomb had brought about. Most notably, he contemplated the implosion of the means–end relationship through an instrument that was capable of obliterating the very notion of human purpose at all. Anders' thinking speaks to the core of the Cold War as an imaginary war, as he emphasised the challenge of imagining the unimaginable in order to arrive at a proper understanding of how the bomb had altered human civilisation.

Introduction: the Cold War as an imaginary war

Thinking nuclear war required understanding the perspectives of, and consequences for, both perpetrators and victims respectively. Anders addressed the complex moral issues emanating from the question of human responsibility in a highly mechanised type of warfare in his published correspondence with Claude Eatherly, the US Air Force pilot of the B-29 that had given the 'go-ahead' to the Enola Gay on 8 August 1945. The fundamentally altered nature of warfare in the wake of the bomb was also one of the starting points of a series of encounters between Japanese intellectuals and representatives of the hibakusha and US civil rights' activists from the Student Nonviolent Coordinating Committee (SNCC) that took place in Japan in 1966. The participants in these encounters were shaped by highly diverse experiences: the deliberately belated attempts to explore and address the medical and psychological knock-on effects of the Hiroshima bomb in a Japanese society that lived under direct US occupation until 1952 and subsequently under the nuclear umbrella of the Western superpower on the one hand; and the legacy of racial segregation and the presence of violent white supremacism in the Deep South on the other hand. Yet, despite these divergent backgrounds, hibakusha and SNCC activists such as Ralph Featherstone discovered a common ground for their critical intervention into Cold War politics, as Ann Sherif argues in her chapter. They tapped into a language of universal human rights that allowed them to connect their experiences of violent exclusion as effects of a shared history of colonialism and imperialism, in the Deep South as well as in the Japanese conduct of war until 1945. As the hibakusha joined forces with SNCC in their condemnation of the US war in Vietnam, they could use their own experiences for a powerful statement against the present state of the Cold War in East Asia. During these encounters in 1966, the atomic war was not a future possibility that could be contemplated in dialectical categories, but had a corporeal presence in that particular Cold War moment.

Thinking about nuclear war posed a fundamental challenge also for traditional Catholic discourses on war and peace, as Daniel Gerster argues in his comparative chapter on responses in the United States and West Germany. On both sides of the Atlantic, the early Cold War pointed to the strength of a liberal and anti-communist Cold War consensus in both churches and to the reaffirmation of 'just war' theology in the age of nuclear war by Pope Pius XII. Yet by the end of the Cold War, consensus had shifted in favour of a nuclear pacifism among both US and German Catholics. Yet papal letters and theological reflections were only one way in which the Catholic religion's complex patchwork of symbolic languages and ritual performances allowed to address the pressing issue of nuclear war. During the immediate post-war years from 1949 to 1953, a wave of Marian apparitions occurred at various places both in the United States and in West Germany. As Gerster argues, Marian apparitions as a traditional form of popular belief thus allowed to express lingering fears of an imminent nuclear war among the Catholic laity at the height of Cold War tensions during the early 1950s. Such traditional symbolic languages could be adapted and utilised to make the unimaginable comprehensible. Charged with stark moral dichotomies, they reflected – at least in the case of the Catholics – not only the Cold War confrontation, but also manifest anxieties about the sweeping secularisation of Western societies in the post-war period.

Although Catholics could rely on their traditional symbolism, more complex ways of imagining and forecasting nuclear war emerged since the 1960s. They were underpinned by a development that can be termed the 'scientisation of the social'. This somewhat bulky term denotes the increasing significance of expertise from the social sciences – in the widest sense, including empirical survey techniques such as opinion polling, forms of therapy as well as scientific approaches to remedy social ills – to identify and tackle a variety of societal problems.[63] Making their expertise heard in the public arena, scientists claimed that they could provide more accurate predictions of the immediate and long-term consequences of a nuclear war.

Chapters by Kemper and Rubinson detail two particular cases of the use of scientific expertise in modelling nuclear war. The case of physicians who criticised the nuclear arms race could be seen as a natural extension of their obligation to prepare themselves for medical knowledge in cases of major emergencies. Yet as Claudia Kemper argues in her chapter on the organisation International Physicians for the Prevention of Nuclear War (IPPNW), the public interventions of this group of physicians – initiated by the Harvard Medical School cardiologist Bernard Lown – were embedded in a broader conceptualisation of the nuclear arms race as a social 'disease'. By employing this metaphor, IPPNW could use their medical expertise as the springboard for a more substantial critique of the social pathology of societies in the East and the West that potentially endangered the lives of millions of people. Based on this line of reasoning, IPPNW was also able to frame the causes of the arms race in psychological categories and thus to offer an allegedly rational explanation for the repressed emotions that were driving the apparent irrationality of nuclear armaments.

Introduction: the Cold War as an imaginary war

In their public statements during the 1980s, IPPNW also drew on the phenomenon of the 'nuclear winter', another prediction about the effects of nuclear war that was based on scientific expertise. In the late 1970s, the astronomer-cum-media celebrity Carl Sagan developed the argument that nuclear explosions would release such vast amounts of soot and smoke into the atmosphere that the sunlight could be blocked and the global atmosphere turned into a state of hibernation that would substantially impede or even block farming altogether. This notion of the 'nuclear winter' quickly attracted intensive coverage and public debate both in the United States and in the Soviet Union, again demonstrating that scientific imaginations of nuclear war could particularly easily transcend the Iron Curtain. Yet, as Paul Rubinson argues in his chapter, there was an inherent tension between the academic credentials of the 'nuclear winter' hypothesis (which were, despite Sagan's efforts to simulate a peer-review process, somewhat dubious at any rate) and his intensive attempts to use his theory for a political intervention into the ongoing conflict over nuclear arms control. In a sense, the conflicts over the political use of his argument, which involved major nuclear physicists as well as leading US politicians, demonstrate that the politicisation of science is a corollary of the scientisation of the social.[64] Although Sagan's claims for scientific credibility repeatedly fell on deaf ears, the popularity of his modelling of the effects of nuclear war even continued after the collapse of the Soviet Union had allayed fears of an imminent nuclear stand-off between the superpowers. Like the talk of a nuclear 'disease' by IPPNW, 'nuclear winter' was proof that scientific models of understanding the potential effects of a nuclear war relied on metaphors as crucial linguistic devices to construct a societal reality.[65]

The final chapter in the volume demonstrates how film was widely employed to depict the destructive consequences of nuclear weapons. As Lars Nowak argues, US films engaged differing levels of realism in their portrayal of nuclear war and used different rhetorical strategies. Fictional feature films during the early 1950s often relied on metonymic connections and on the use of monsters as metaphors for the bomb. Many other films offered a detachment from catastrophic visions by portraying all-out nuclear war as a re-booting of human civilisation that would allow a group of survivors to start to rebuild their lives in a rural environment. Stanley Kramer's film version of Nevil Shute's *On the Beach*, released in 1959, kick started a turn to more critical readings of the causes and effects of nuclear war. Films that were produced by US civil defence agencies, on the other hand, tried to sanitise nuclear war by depicting not the bomb itself, but the emotional, panic-fuelled responses of the public as the real danger in the event of nuclear war. This rhetorical strategy was shared by many of the nuclear test films, documentary footage shot by a US Air Force unit from 1946 to 1962. In these films, the realism of the depiction of actual nuclear explosions was further enhanced by the use of real artefacts such as conventional weapons and props such as test houses or samples of various materials, whose destruction in the blast could be documented. In these films, the US military gave nuclear war a corporeal existence, and at the same was putting its conviction on the public record that fighting and surviving nuclear war was perfectly feasible.

Some general conclusions

In this volume, we argue that fantasies, dreams and nightmares, fictitious narratives and war games, religious prophecies and apocalyptic scenarios, and many other forms of depicting nuclear war were a pivotal part of the Cold War as an imaginary war. The Cold War was not only a conflict over the possession and potential use of nuclear weapons. We would assert that some key elements of the Cold War as a new, and in fact unprecedented, type of conflict can only be fully understood by putting the projection of potential outcomes of nuclear war centre stage. Different forms of knowing and depicting nuclear war were a crucial battlefield of the Cold War. They were used both by top-brass military and by peace activists, by outspoken supporters of nuclear deterrence as well as by their sharpest critics. The different uses of these forms of knowledge influenced their form. But ultimately, they were all elements of the same terrain, the war over the hegemony in making legitimate assumptions about the effects of an all-out nuclear war. Moreover, such assumptions transformed people's understanding of themselves, the Cold War, and their potential futures. In an essay on the social history of death written at the height of the renewed nuclear tensions of the early 1980s, British historian David Cannadine argued that 'for the first time ever in recorded history, global, total death has become, since 1945, a very real possibility. As in the medieval world, death once more not only reigns but rules. But this time it is the bomb, not the bacillus, which is his emissary.' For Cannadine, 'the threat of mass, accidental death' created an understandable link between his current present's limited future and the closed horizon of the medieval past.[66] A historian writing about death in early twenty-first-century Western Europe would be less likely to make such a link, whereas it was normal in a time when the imaginary war was compressing the very idea of a liveable future.

Introduction: the Cold War as an imaginary war

Based on the evidence and the arguments that are presented in the chapters of this volume, we can draw a few more general conclusions about the nature and historical dynamic of the Cold War. First of all, one of the peculiarities of the Cold War was the way in which fiction had become reality, and reality fictitious.[67] All modern wars had been accompanied by textual and visual representations of the bloodshed on the battlefields. These were essentially forms of mimesis, attempts to re-present an already existing external reality by means of artistic licence. Yet, in the case of an all-out nuclear war, this external reality did not yet exist, and hence everyone who tried to fight the Cold War had to invoke different narratives and tropes of fiction in order to make the reality of nuclear war plausible. In the visual arts, for example, art historian Annegret Jürgens-Kirchhoff has argued, the Hiroshima and Nagasaki bombings marked a decisive end to all attempts of portraying the destructive effects of war through mimesis, through images that claimed to be a somewhat realistic copy of the original impression.[68] For artists, one possible strategy was to depict the moment of catastrophe indirectly, through a portrayal of the horror on the faces of those who were to watch the bomb explode. The German artist Karl Hofer used this approach in his 1947 painting 'Atomic Serenade', in which only flashes of lightning represented the beam of light produced by a nuclear explosion. The Dutch artist Constant Nieuwenhuys referred to pictorial elements of primitive art in his 1951 painting 'Scorched Earth I', which has often been interpreted as an artistic examination of the meaning of Hiroshima.[69] In the 1960s, British artist William Crozier instead attempted to depict catastrophe through 'a series of desolate landscapes of Essex',[70] creating a series of empty, yet violent paintings to convey his anxiety about the nuclear future.

In many ways, the cross-over between fiction and reality that is so characteristic of the Cold War is part of a broader trend towards the virtualisation of warfare that had emerged since 1914, basically as a result of the First World War's destruction of the unity of place as one of the key frames of enacting traditional wars on a battlefield. What the Cold War added to this trend, however, was a fundamental disruption of the unity of time in the setting of war. Nuclear war was a calculation of the future responses to hypothetical potential future actions. As such, it was played out as a form of somehow knowledgeable anticipation of the future, an anticipation that incorporated elements of science fiction even when this was not the designated genre of reflecting potential outcomes of the use of nuclear weapons. Nowhere was the close interplay between science fiction and the reality of nuclear war planning more obvious than in the US strategic defence initiative (SDI), launched in 1983, with its core metaphor of space as the new 'frontier', as SDI provoked intensive commentary from the science fiction community and seemed for more than one observer to be itself conjured up by a science fiction writer.[71] Yet futuristic metaphors drawn from science fiction had been an important element of Cold War discourse from the beginning.

Second, to consider the interconnections between fiction and 'reality' as a key element of the imaginary war forces us to rethink issues of periodisation. In recent historiography there is a trend to downplay the coherence of the Cold War as a historical period, and to emphasise the discrepancies between the early Cold War, the phase of détente from the early 1960s to the mid-1970s, and the return of international tensions from 1977 during the 'second Cold War'.[72] This shift in emphasis also reflects a welcome reluctance to attribute literally all phenomena in society and politics from 1945 to 1990 to the Cold War. Against the backdrop of these historiographical developments, the focus on the imaginary war can help to emphasise the fact that the Cold War has primarily to be understood as a war, if only one that played out in the metaphorical sphere of nuclear scenarios and fantasies.[73] The specifics of the fear caused by the bloc confrontation occurred within a much wider periodisation relating to the cultural history of nuclear technology. Nuclear war has had an imaginary presence from the very onset of scientific discoveries in the field of nuclear physics at the end of the nineteenth century,[74] and it continued to have one after the end of the Cold War. The end of the bloc confrontation and the subsequent 'war on terror' have certainly led to fundamental changes in the commemoration of the Hiroshima bombing in the Western world, most notably in the United States. Indicative of this shift towards a robust defence of US military action in 1945 is not only the controversy over the planned exhibition of the Enola Gay at the Smithsonian Institute in 1995. Changes in nomenclature are also revealing, as the shift from 'ground zero' denoting the epicentre of the bomb in downtown Hiroshima to implying – post 9/11 – the site of the former Twin Towers in Manhattan.[75] Yet while the conditions for the use of nuclear weapons in high-level strategy and international politics have certainly changed since 1990, their lingering presence in the collective imagination and in popular culture has shifted emphasis but also remained. As George Orwell pointed out, the real significance of possessing nuclear weapons was not their actual use in a conflict, but the inversion of political languages that they incurred and the discursive power that the bomb wielded over nations that possessed and those that did not possess these arms. And in that sense, the era of the Cold War has yet to end.

Introduction: the Cold War as an imaginary war

Third, drawing on the themes of this volume there are good reasons to be very sceptical about portraying the Cold War as 'the long peace', as John Lewis Gaddis did in a seminal article first published in 1986.[76] From the vantage point of that year, with Gorbachev's reforms in the USSR having led to substantial negotiations between the superpowers and to a dramatic reduction in the stockpiles of nuclear weapons on the horizon, it was sensible to point out the undoubted element of outward stability that the bloc confrontation had brought to post-war international politics. With a bipolar international system in which two superpowers competed with each other, but also defined the rules of engagement, nuclear deterrence was successful in restraining any major independent escalation of military conflict, at least before the advent of militant Islamic currents in Iran and Afghanistan in the late 1970s. Yet such an interpretation from the perspective of international relations is bound to miss the extent to which the realistic fiction of an impending nuclear war consistently permeated society and culture on both sides of the Iron Curtain over the decades. In many ways, it is a fundamentally flawed use of political terminology to describe the 'peace that is no peace' – to quote Orwell again – with one of the key concepts that have been used to describe a stable political order in European thinking since Greek antiquity. To rephrase this argument from a different angle: even if the presence of total war during the decades since 1945 – as opposed to the global violent turmoil from 1939 to 1945 – was limited to a metaphorical state, it was still 'real' in the sense that the metaphors of nuclear annihilation shaped the social and political reality in all belligerent nations.

Notes

1 For important conclusions of a literary scholar from this core assertion, see D. Seed, *American Science Fiction and the Cold War: Literature and Film* (Edinburgh, 1999), pp.1–13; also D. Seed, *Under the Shadow: The Atomic Bomb and Cold War Narratives* (Kent, 2013); for a stimulating discussion on the concept of the Cold War, see A. Stephanson, 'Fourteen notes on the very concept of the Cold War', in G. Ó Tuathail and S. Dalby (eds), *Rethinking Geopolitics* (London, 1998), pp. 62–84.
2 G. Orwell, 'You and the atomic bomb', *Tribune*, 19 October 1945, online at: http://gutenberg.net.au/ebooks03/0300011h.html#part33 (accessed 15 February 2016).
3 G. Corea, *The Mother Machine* (London, 1985), p. 34.

4 M. Geyer, 'Der kriegerische Blick. Rückblick auf einen noch zu beendenden Krieg', *Sozialwissenschaftliche Informationen* 19 (1990), pp. 111-17, pp. 112-15.
5 U. Horstmann, *Abschreckungskunst. Zur Ehrenrettung der apokalyptischen Phantasie* (Munich, 2012), p 100.
6 L. Scott, 'Intelligence and the risk of nuclear war: Abel Archer-83 revisited', *Intelligence and National Security* 26:6 (2011), 759-77.
7 Horstmann, *Abschreckungskunst*, p. 114.
8 Orwell, 'You and the atomic bomb'.
9 T. Nanz and J. Pause, 'Das Undenkbare filmen. Einleitung', in T. Nanz and J. Pause (eds), *Das Undenkbare filmen. Atomkrieg im Kino* (Bielefeld, 2013), pp. 7-24, p. 8.
10 For essays which discuss representations of nuclear weapons in individual media outlets in depth, see the essays in D. Lente (ed.), *The Nuclear Age in Popular Media: Aa Transnational History, 1945-1965* (New York, 2012).
11 On these categories, see the seminal article by R. Koselleck, 'Space of experience and horizon of expectation: two historical categories', in R. Koselleck, *Futures Past: On the Semantics of Historical Time* (New York, 2004), pp. 255-75.
12 For such an interpretation, see M. Kaldor, *The Imaginary War: Understanding the East-West Conflict* (Oxford, 1990).
13 See G. Heefner, *The Missile Next Door. The Minuteman in the American Heartland* (Cambridge, Mass., 2012).
14 See, for instance, J. Krupar, 'The challenges of preserving America's nuclear weapons complex', in R. B. Mariner and G. K. Pahle (eds), *The Atomic Bomb and American Society. New Perspectives* (Knoxville, 2009), pp. 381-405; P.C. van Wyck, *Signs of Danger: Waste, Trauma, and Nuclear Threat* (Minneapolis, 2004).
15 J. G. Blight and D. A. Welch, *On the Brink: Americans and Soviets Re-examine the Cuban Missile Crisis* (New York, 1989).
16 T. Shaw, 'The BBC, the state and Cold War culture: the case of television's *The War Game* (1965)', *English Historical Review* 121:494 (2006), pp. 1351-84, quote p. 1366. For a wider perspective, see M. Grant, 'Images of survival, stories of destruction: nuclear war on British screens from 1945 to the early 1960s', *Journal of British Cinema and Television* 10 (2013), pp. 7-26.
17 For the key points that follow, see the incisive analysis by J. Pause, 'Will the survivors watch TV? Peter Watkins' *The War Game* (1965)', in Nanz and Pause (eds), *Das Undenkbare filmen*, pp. 53-84.
18 M. Grant, *After the Bomb: Civil Defence and Nuclear War* (Basingstoke, 2010).
19 Pause, 'Will the survivors watch TV?', pp. 69, 75.
20 Shaw, 'BBC, the state and Cold War culture', p. 1373.
21 Grant, 'Images of survival', p. 23.
22 D. Cordle, 'Protect/protest: British nuclear fiction of the 1980s', *British Journal for the History of Science* 45:4 (2012), pp. 653-69.

Introduction: the Cold War as an imaginary war

23 P. Virilio, *War and Cinema: The Logistics of Perception* (London, 1989).
24 See the chapter by Jason Dawsey in this volume.
25 Virilio, *War and Cinema*, p. 69.
26 B. Hüppauf, 'Experiences of modern warfare and the crisis of representation', *New German Critique* 59 (1993), pp. 41–76.
27 N. Luhmann, 'The future cannot begin: temporal structures in modern society', *Social Research* 43 (1976), pp. 130–52, p. 140.
28 T. Jansson, *Comet in Moominland* (London, 1951). Originally published as *Kometjakten* (Vasa, 1946).
29 M. P. Leffler and O. A. Westad (eds), *The Cambridge History of the Cold War. (3 vols)* (Cambridge, 2010).
30 D. Holloway, 'Nuclear weapons and the escalation of the Cold War, 1945-62', in Leffler and Westad (eds), *Cambridge History of the Cold War*, vol. 1, p. 376.
31 For example, R. Rhodes, *The Making of the Atomic Bomb* (New York, 1987); J. L. Gaddis, P. Gordon, E. May and J. Rosenberg (eds), *Cold War Statesmen Confront the Bomb: Nuclear Diplomacy since 1945* (Oxford, 1999); D. Holloway, *Stalin and the Bomb: The Soviet Union and Atmic Energy, 1939-1956* (New Haven, 1995); L. Freedman, *The Evolution of Nuclear Strategy* (London, 1982).
32 C. Craig and S. Radchenko, *The Atomic Bomb and the Origins of the Cold War* (New Haven, 2008).
33 J. E. C. Hymans, *The Psychology of Nuclear Proliferation: Identity, Emotions and Foreign Policy* (Cambridge, 2006).
34 J. Baylis and K. Stoddart, *The British Nuclear Experience: The Roles of Beliefs, Culture and Identity* (Oxford, 2015).
35 M. J. Selverstone, *Constructing the Monolith: The United States, Great Britain, and International Communism* (Cambridge, Mass., 2009).
36 D. L. Snead, *The Gaither Committee, Eisenhower and the Cold War* (Columbus, 1999).
37 See J. Hughes, 'Deconstructing the bomb: recent perspectives on nuclear history', *British Journal for the History of Science* 37 (2004), pp. 455–64.
38 B. Ziemann (ed.), *Peace Movements in Western Europe, Japan and the USA during the Cold War* (Essen, 2007).
39 L. S. Wittner, *The Struggle Against the Bomb. 3 vols* (Stanford, 1995–2003).
40 H. Laville, *Cold War Women: The International Activities of American Women's Organisations* (Manchester, 2002); L. McEnaney, *Civil Defense Begins at Home* (Princeton, 2000).
41 J. Suri, *Power and Protest: Global Revolution and the Rise of Détente* (Cambridge, Mass., 2003).
42 J. Burkett, *Constructing Post-Imperial Britain: Britishness, 'Race' and the Radical Left in the 1960s* (Basingstoke, 2012); H. Nehring, *The Politics of Security: British and West German Protest Movements and the Early Cold War, 1945-1970* (Oxford, 2013).

43 See, for instance, Seed, *Under the Shadow*; Lente (ed.), *The Nuclear Age in Popular Media*; A. Nadel, *Containment Culture: American Narratives, Postmodernism and the Atomic Age* (Durham, N.C., 1995); S. C. Zeman and M. A. Amundson (eds), *Atomic Culture: How We Learned to Stop Worrying and Love the Bomb* (Boulder, 2004); D. Cordle, *States of Suspense: The Nuclear Age, Postmodernism and United States Fiction and Prose* (Manchester, 2008).
44 P. S. Boyer, *By the Bomb's Early Light: American Thought and Culture at the Dawn of the Atomic Age* (Chapel Hill, 1985); S. R. Weart, *Nuclear Fear: A History of Images* (Cambridge, Mass., 1988).
45 Boyer, *By the Bomb's Early Light*.
46 Weart, *Nuclear Fear*, p. 217.
47 I. Welsh, *Mobilising Modernity: The Nuclear Moment* (London, 2000).
48 G. Hecht, *The Radiance of France: Nuclear Power and National Identity after World War II* (Cambridge, Mass, 2009).
49 K. Willis, 'The origins of British nuclear culture', *Journal of British Studies* 34 (1995), pp. 59–89.
50 J. Hughes, 'What is British nuclear culture? Understanding *Uranium 235*', *British Journal of the History of Science* 45:4 (2012), p. 498.
51 See, for example, P. D. Smith, '"Gentlemen, you are mad!" Mutual assured destruction and Cold War culture', in D. Stone (ed.), *The Oxford Handbook of Postwar European History* (Oxford, 2012), pp. 445–61.
52 See the articles in the special issue of *The British Journal of the History of Science* 45:2 (2012).
53 H. Harrison, 'Popular responses to the atomic bomb in China, 1945–55', *Past and Present* 218 supplement 8 (2013), pp. 98–116.
54 J. Masco, *Nuclear Borderlands: The Manhattan Project in Post-Cold War New Mexico* (Princeton, 2006).
55 K. Brown, *Nuclear Families, Atomic Cities, and the Great Soviet and American Plutonium Disasters* (Oxford, 2013).
56 See M. Farish and D. Monteyne, 'Introduction: histories of Cold War cities', *Urban History* 42:4 (2015), 543–46.
57 F. Biess, '"Everybody Has a Chance": civil defense, nuclear angst, and the history of emotions in postwar Germany', *German History* 27 (2009), pp. 215–43.
58 Harrison, 'Popular responses to the atomic bomb in China'.
59 Hecht, *The Radiance of France*.
60 R. Dalsjö, 'The hidden rationality of Sweden's policy of neutrality during the Cold War', *Cold War History* 14:2 (2014), pp. 175–94.
61 S. Marti, 'Den modernen Krieg simulieren. Imaginationen und Praxis totaler Landesverteidigung in der Schweiz', in D. Eugster and S. Marti (eds), *Das Imaginäre des Kalten Krieges. Beiträge zu einer Kulturgeschichte des Ost-West Konfliktes in Europa* (Essen, 2015), pp. 243–68.
62 A. M. Winkler, *Life under a Cloud. American Anxiety about the Atom* (New York. Oxford, 1993), p. 4.

Introduction: the Cold War as an imaginary war

63 K. Brückweh, D. Schumann, R. Wetzell and B. Ziemann (eds), *Engineering Society: The Role of the Human and Social Sciences in Modern Societies, 1880-1980* (Basingstoke, 2012).
64 B. Ziemann, K. Brückweh, D. Schumann and R. Wetzell, 'Introduction', in Ziemann *et al.* (eds), *Engineering Society*, pp. 1–40, here pp. 8f, 30f.
65 See P. Sarasin, *Anthrax: Bioterror as Fact and Fantasy* (Cambridge, Mass., 2006).
66 D. Cannadine, 'War and death, grief and morning in Modern Britain', in J. Whaley (ed.), *Mirrors of Mortality: Studies in the Social History of Death* (London, 1981), pp. 235–36.
67 See the chapter by Eva Horn in this volume.
68 A. Jürgens-Kirchhoff, *Schreckensbilder. Krieg und Kunst im 20. Jahrhundert* (Berlin, 1993), pp. 313–38.
69 *Ibid.*
70 S. Martin, 'Painting the end: British artists and the nuclear apocalypse, 1945-1970', in C. Jolivette (ed.), *British Art in the Nuclear Age* (Farnham, 2014), p.222
71 Seed, *American Science Fiction*, pp. 181–93.
72 M. Cox, 'Whatever happened to the 'second' Cold War? Soviet-American Relations: 1980-1988', *Review of International Studies* 16 (1990), pp. 155–72; O. Njølstad, 'The collapse of superpower détente, 1975-1980', in Leffler and Westad (eds), *Cambridge History of the Cold War*, volume III, pp. 135–55.
73 See the helpful discussion in H. Nehring, 'What was the Cold War?', *English Historical Review* 527 (2012), pp. 920–49, here p. 929.
74 Willis, 'The origins of British nuclear culture', pp. 59–89, here pp. 70, 79; see Seed, *Under the Shadow*, pp. 9–23.
75 See F. Coulmas, *Hiroshima. Geschichte und Nachgeschichte* (Munich, 2010), pp. 98–105. See also the chapter by Paul Boyer in this volume.
76 J. L. Gaddis, 'The long peace: elements of stability in the postwar international system', in J. L. Gaddis, *The Long Peace. Inquiries into the History of the Cold War* (New York. Oxford, 1987), pp. 215–45; J. L. Gaddis, 'The Cold War, the long peace, and the future', *Diplomatic History* 56 (1992), pp. 234–46.

2

The apocalyptic fiction: shaping the future in the Cold War

Eva Horn

The twentieth century was under the spell of an apocalyptic vision that was claimed to be both 'absolutely real' and 'quite close'. This vision found its expression in a single image: the nuclear explosion. The radiant flash of light, the mushroom cloud and a destroyed landscape reaching up to the horizon visualised the possibility of the extinction of all mankind, something neither traditional nor modern fantasies of the end of the world had ever pictured in this way. In this sense, the atomic bomb represented both an imminent future and the potential loss of all future. It represented the end of the world as being technically feasible, as a human option. In 1958, the German philosopher Karl Jaspers summarised the categories of this apocalyptic scenario:

> Today, the atomic bomb is more threatening to the future of mankind than anything else. Up to this point, irreal conceptions of an apocalypse existed … Yet right now we are facing the real possibility of an end of the world. Not any longer a fictitious apocalypse, actually not an apocalypse at all, but rather the killing of all life on the whole surface of the earth is the possible reality with which we have to reckon from now on, and that – given the increasing speed of all developments – already in the near future.[1]

Jaspers evokes a set of categories that shows the novelty and singularity of this kind of disaster: no longer an eschatological apocalypse with the Last Judgement, but biological extermination; no longer a distant end of times, but rather an imminent threat; no longer limited warfare, but total annihilation; and not a literary fiction but a 'real possibility'. Jaspers' formula is exemplary for the urgent diagnosis of the times of the 1950s (and later of the 1980s), in an era in which a disastrous end of the world was looming and yet had to be prevented at all costs. This is the spirit of the 'doomsday clock' suggested by Edward Teller, which showed initially seven, later two minutes to midnight, and which has been on the cover of the *Bulletin of the Atomic Scientists* since 1947.

In several ways, the discourse on 'the Bomb' is steeped in fictionality, a fictionality which is – as Jaspers' formula suggests – both present and hidden, a blind spot haunting the Cold War consciousness over and over again. Rarely has there been more talking about 'fiction' turned into 'reality' than during the Cold War, more debate about the fact that there were no 'real' experiences in dealing with a novel kind of weapon, and that it was impossible to gain experiences through experiments. Strategic planners thus had to rely on thought experiments, hypotheses, models and simulations – or on literature and films. Rarely ever has 'fiction' become as radically operative in politics than in the discourse on the Bomb. Literature and film therefore play a special, as it were 'meta-fictional' role here, as they produce reality, shape forms of thought and epistemological structures. However, fiction also ultimately provides a means of reflecting on and criticising the way in which the Bomb is understood in the Cold War era.

The weapon of the future

The nuclear apocalypse was dreamt about in literature and science decades before the first atomic bomb was ever built.[2] In the modern imagination, technological progress has often been thought of as a progression in weapon's technology, from Jules Verne and H. G. Wells to Stanislaw Lem or Michael Chrichton. The nuclear bomb is the epitome of the 'ultimate weapon', a weapon to win any war. As Thomas Brandstetter has shown, this dream inspired many of the scientists who in the 1940s put their basic research on nuclear physics into the service of the Manhattan Project. Yet, already in 1914, just before the start of the First World War, H. G. Wells published a novel, *The World Set Free*, about the future of the twentieth century, in which mankind makes nuclear fission accessible as an energy source, develops nuclear engines and finally builds and uses the nuclear bomb. With its 'continuous explosion', this bomb turns out to be a weapon against which no defence is possible. In the course of a world war during the 1950s, first Paris is destroyed, then in revenge Berlin is also demolished, and Holland gets flooded – until huge parts of Europe are ultimately reduced to rubble. With this vision of future weapons technology, Wells actually had his finger on the pulse of the contemporary research on radioactivity, boldly extrapolating its technological and military potential.

In fact, Wells owed the concept of nuclear power as both an infinite energy supply and a weapon of mass destruction to the chemist Frederick Soddy. In 1903, Soddy had published his research on radioactivity in a popular scientific treatise on 'The interpretation of radium'. In this early article, Soddy already pointed out the powerful, yet highly destructive potential of this new energy form. This potential has been part of the discourse on radioactivity right from the outset – long before nuclear fission was invented, atomic bombs exploded or accidents occurred in nuclear plants. As early as 1903, Soddy noted that the earth is 'a storehouse stuffed with explosives, inconceivably more powerful than any we know of, and possibly only awaiting a suitable detonator to cause the earth to revert to chaos'.[3] Accordingly, Wells' novel describes the uncontrollable power of destruction of the new decisive weapon in graphic fashion:

> Once launched, the bomb was absolutely unapproachable and uncontrollable until its forces were nearly exhausted, and from the crater that burst open above it, puffs of heavy incandescent vapour and fragments of viciously punitive rock and mud, saturated with Carolinum, and each a centre of scorching and blistering energy, were flung high and far. Such was the crowning triumph of military science, the ultimate explosive that was to give the 'decisive touch' to war.[4]

The bomb's disastrous power, however, eventually deploys a peace-making potential in Wells' novel that is prophetic of the Cold War's conflict structure. The war with the ultimate weapon turns into a 'war to end all wars'. Traumatised and disabused by the unprecedented destruction, the survivors of this war establish a global government and a regime of continuous peace. Wells drives home the message that the total weapon is part of the vision of the 'final' war. Even though the First World War – welcomed by Wells – proved this fantasy wrong, thirty years later it shaped the ideas about the use and function of the actual nuclear bomb. It is thus not a coincidence that the young Hungarian physicist Leo Szilard, who started to experiment with nuclear chain reactions in 1930s London, was a keen reader of Wells' novels and felt reminded of *The World Set Free* immediately after his first experiments on nuclear chain reactions.[5] Later Szilard became the main driving force behind the funding and development of the Manhattan Project in the 1940s, and thereby seems to have followed Wells's idea of a peace guaranteed by an ultimate weapon.

The nuclear bomb is thus science fiction. From its first inception on – and that is to say long before its actual realisation – the Bomb was considered an apocalyptic and global weapon. It epitomised both the possibility and the risk that by a single human decision – by pushing the famous button – all life on earth could be wiped out. 'Long before its actual impact was known', Thomas Brandstetter points out, 'absolute categories were used to assess the nuclear bomb. It was always about all or nothing.'[6] In 1946, Bernard Brodie, a strategist of the RAND corporation, a policy think tank for research and analysis, coined the expression 'absolute weapon', something that is no longer used as a decisive weapon to win wars, but to prevent them by deterrence.[7] In this sense, the Bomb is, from the outset, a fantasy about the end of the world – a fantasy that was then made operative to provide leverage in international politics. It is part of an apocalyptic rhetoric which never referred to anything less than 'the whole world', 'the survival of mankind' and the 'continued existence on earth'. In this sense, the nuclear bomb is in fact an 'imaginary bomb', as well as the Cold War is an 'imaginary war',[8] 'neither war nor peace',[9] frozen by weapons which could not reasonably be used. It is the dream of a super-weapon of an infinite energy supply, an instrument to rule the world and to guarantee eternal peace – or the button that, when pushed, means the end of mankind and the total loss of all future.

During the Cold War, this imaginary nature of the Bomb has been conjured up time and again, both in fiction and politics. It poses a challenge to a future of mankind (Günther Anders), it served to quantify mankind's extermination (Herman Kahn), it became the pivot of rational-choice strategies of security (Leo Szilard), and it became the chief metaphor of planned self-destruction (Stanley Kubrick, Sidney Lumet). Yet first and foremost it became instantly operative in political and military terms. In this context, 'the Bomb' has to be seen as a dispositive which is not limited to its mere technological and military nature. As a dispositive, 'the Bomb' operates on three levels, which cannot be seen separately and which constitute the intricate correlation of 'fiction' and 'political reality' at the heart of Cold War politics: The Bomb is (1) a weapons technology that is characterised by its unprecedented destructive potential; it designates (2) a political and military strategy of different options to use this weapon (deploying or not deploying); and it calls (3) for instruments to regulate and control the weapons technology, but also for communication structures within these political strategies.

The future with the Bomb

As much as the Bomb was imagined and fantasised about, contemporaries considered it as the unimaginable, the 'complete nothing', the 'unthinkable' and the unpredictable. In his *Theses on the Atomic Age* (1959), the philosopher Günther Anders, for instance, lamented man's inability to imagine the nuclear apocalypse, while at the same time dangerously being able to put it into action:

> The danger of an apocalypse which is dominating our lives reaches the pinnacle of its threat because we are not prepared and therefore incapable to *picture* the catastrophe ... Because we can create the complete nothing, our lack of imagination, our narrow-mindedness must not prevail. At least we have *to try to picture the nothing.*[10]

Thinking about the atomic bomb during the 1950s and 1960s produced formulas of a negative theology of destruction: the Bomb is the 'nothing', the 'end', 'total extermination' – the 'unthinkable' that nevertheless had to be thought, the unimaginable that needed to be imagined. In this sense, the nuclear apocalypse serves as a touchstone of a possible future of mankind. Günther Anders eloquently linked his diagnosis of the apocalypse to a general philosophical anthropology regarding the future viability of mankind. The possible collective self-destruction is the symptom of a 'Promethean gap'. This Promethean gap indicates the discrepancy between the human ability to produce technology and the inability to imagine the repercussions and consequences of these technologies, a gap between man's technological skills and impact assessment.[11] For Anders, this implies a specific modern relationship to the future, with its modernity based on this man-made apocalyptic potential. Precisely because mankind is able to design and choose its future, it is likely that it will ultimately destroy it.

> The future will not any longer just 'come' as we do not conceptualise it any longer as something that is just 'coming', but rather create it. And we do create it in such a manner that it includes its own alternative: the possibility of a rupture, of a potential lack of future. Even if this rupture does not already occur tomorrow – by the means of what we are doing today, it can occur the day after tomorrow, or in the generation of our grand-grandsons or in the 'seventh lineage'. As the effects of those things that we do today will persist, we already reach that future today: meaning that, in a pragmatic sense, this future is already present. Present in the sense in which an enemy is 'present' if he is, though absent in a formal sense, already in reach of our weapons, and hence can be hit by us. Thus we have power over a temporal structure that we usually do not consider to be a 'future' and cannot consider to be such a future. Our deeds accomplish more than our conception. We are throwing further than we can see, myopic as we are.[12]

The apocalyptic fiction

Thus, the Bomb as the symbol for what we are throwing is both project and projectile, and therefore the paradox of an attitude to the future that might destroy all future in a single blow. Anders' plea to imagine and to visualise the end draws on a very old role of the prophecy: the warning that ought to prevent the predicted disaster. Looking imaginatively ahead into the future (or, for that matter, into the apocalyptic lack of any future at all) is supposed to take over the role traditionally assigned to the prophecy: educate and warn, in order to change the society's attitude towards the deployment of the Bomb.

From this apocalyptic diagnosis, however, in the 1960s and 1970s a specific form of 'futurology' emerged especially in Europe – a form of research that, unlike that of Anders and Jaspers, faced the nuclear threat with cautious optimism. It shifted the emphasis from technological feasibility to social change and individual insight.[13] 'Fantasy', 'imagination' and 'creativity' became its keywords – yet this time not to picture the end of the world, but in service of its prevention. The German Robert Jungk was arguably the most prominent futurologist to follow Anders. He developed a futurology that emphasised a change in policy and social structure instead of technological and economic progress. According to Jungk, the malleability of the future should be switched from the apocalyptic to the utopian, by using 'social fantasy' and a 'futurology of mankind'.[14] During the 1960s, Jungk became the key spokesperson of a line of research into the future (*Zukunftsforschung*), which focused on 'peace research' instead of conflict modelling. It emphasised creativity instead of technological development and tried to assess the unintended consequences of technology instead of analysing technical feasibility.

Imagination and creativity could also be used in an entirely different vein. In the forms of strategic planning that American think tanks such as the RAND Corporation or the Hudson Institute pursued, imagination served mainly to picture the deployment of the Bomb in every conceivable detail. What would be the types of crises where a nuclear strike might become necessary? Which forms of deterrence are convincing enough, but would not lead to an escalation of the conflict? What health problems must be expected in the wake of a nuclear attack? What would the death toll look like? Which kind of civil defence would be reasonable? While German philosophers such as Anders criticised the 'blindness towards apocalypse', the US scientists tried to illuminate the catastrophe and its repercussions in all its lurid details. In 1960, RAND's chief strategist Herman Kahn published *On Thermonuclear War*, an extensive volume that contains his thoughts on strategic options, but also on possible consequences of a nuclear war.[15] Fred Kaplan quipped that the book looked as if a 'giant vacuum cleaner had swept through the corridors of RAND, sucking up every idea, concept, metaphor and calculation that anyone in the strategy community had conjured up over the previous decade.'[16]

A large section of the first chapter of *On Thermonuclear War* contains an apocalyptic thought experiment. It analyses the state of the world after being hit by an atomic bomb. 'Will the survivors envy the dead? How much tragedy is "acceptable"? What kinds of genetic damage will a nuclear strike cause? How long will it take to rebuild and restore everything? What kind of health problems will be caused by the radioactive fallout? What will be the degree of damage done to the infrastructure?' These are the questions Kahn asked. Some of these questions made Kahn famous and infamous: by calculating the differences of various scenarios of civil defence, he casually juggled with a death rate of between five and ninety million people.[17] Equally shocking was his frank admission, during a meeting of the RAND Strategic Objectives Committee to recommend a strategy, that it would involve a death toll of '*only* two million' people.[18] Yet, what sounds like callous cynicism is actually at the methodological core of Kahn's approach: he is interested in a quantification of the disaster, as he explains in the introduction of *On Thermonuclear War*.[19] Yet this quantification could only be completely hypothetical, because – apart from the bombings of Japan in 1945 and the H-bomb tests – no experience with the new nuclear weapons was available, and political experiments were unthinkable. For Kahn, that meant calculating the hypothetical damages, from the death toll and health issues to material damage, and gauging the risk of these damages. In one example, he compared the (hypothetical) genetic damage in the event of a radioactive contamination against the normal statistical frequency of inherited defects in the population – and came to the conclusion that the genetic effects of nuclear warfare are rather negligible. In this vein, he coined the often-quoted expression that the difference between war and peace was purely quantitative: 'War is a terrible thing, but so is peace. The difference seems to be a quantitative one of degree and standards.'[20]

Kahn's intention in fathoming the options and consequences of nuclear warfare are clearly anti-apocalyptic. He focused on the feasibility of a limited and limitable war which, under certain circumstances, could be accepted as a risk – just as he considered genetic damages merely as a quantifiable risk instead of something which was to be prevented at all costs.[21] He therefore not only calculated the hypothetical effects of nuclear weapons, but also the strategic options that would make it reasonable to use them, for instance in his thoughts about various types of deterrence and escalation.[22] Ironically, hardly any other planner of the nuclear war has fuelled apocalyptic visions more than Herman Kahn with his hypothetical death tolls in the millions. He became the model for the mad military scientists in *Dr. Strangelove* and *Fail-Safe*. Yet Kahn himself might have been closer to fiction than he himself was aware of. Especially in his methodological treatise on scenario planning, *Thinking about the Unthinkable*, he emphasised the fictionality of hypothetical scenarios, describing them as 'aids to the imagination'.[23]

The beginning of this way of exploring warfare through the development of fictional situations and narratives can already be found in *On Thermonuclear War*. In the third part of this book, Kahn (just like Wells in *The World Set Free*) tells a hypothetical history of the future anticipating innovations in the field of weapons technology. A brief sketch of technological developments during the First World War and the Second World War is followed by an account of two hypothetical wars which could have happened in the past (from the perspective of 1960, when *On Thermonuclear War* was published), that is to say, if a war had been fought based on the technological level achieved in 1951 (the Third World War) and in 1956 (the Fourth World War). Starting from this hypothetical history of would-be world wars, Kahn cheerfully moves to scenarios of future world wars (fifth to eighth), ending with the Eighth World War in 1973. It is obvious that he is dealing with possible futures – futures more and more shrouded by the unknown. In order to invent these hypothetical futures, Kahn calculates a small and constant amount of variables in several variations. Based on this hypothetical historiography of the future, he develops the methodical tools of his subsequent futurological research. He outlines what he calls 'scenario planning' by presenting various alternative developments in the future.

> A scenario results from an attempt to describe in more or less detail some hypothetical sequence of events. Scenarios can emphasise different aspects of future history ... The scenario is particularly suited to dealing with several aspects of a problem more or less simultaneously. By the use of a relatively extensive scenario, the analyst may be able to get a feel for events and the branching points dependent upon critical choices. These branches can then be explored more or less systematically. The scenario is an aid to the imagination. Thermonuclear wars are not only unpleasant events, they are, fortunately, unexperienced events, and the crises which threaten such wars are almost equally unexperienced.[24]

In the following decades, Kahn wrote several of those alternative histories of the future – about future disasters, their likeliness and the chance of forecasting them. In the 1970s and 1980s, he moved to more civilian topics, such as economic development, technological progress and the unstoppable spread of western lifestyles.[25]

Kahn's hypothetical method of scenario planning responds to the impossibility of gaining empirical experiences with the new weapon. 'How many thermonuclear wars have you fought recently?', the civilian Kahn used to ask military personnel who (often reluctantly) underwent his instructions on strategy.[26] In 1987, Theodore Draper summarised the paradox of weapons that cannot be used in one's own interest: 'Nuclear weapons are too effective to be used. This paradox is almost too much ... for the military mind to bear.'[27] For that reason, fiction – both as strategic scenario planning and as entertainment in the form of novels and films – became an integral part of the attempt to think about war with the new weapon. The scientists of the Hudson Institute founded by Kahn after his resignation at RAND read novels such as Peter George's *Red Alert* (1958), the novel on which *Dr. Strangelove* was based, 'to stimulate [their] reason and imagination to cope with history before it happens'.[28] Only through hypothetical narratives, such as Kahn's scenarios, can experimental knowledge on nuclear weapons be gained at all three levels of this dispositive: (1) on the level of impact assessment (how big is the destructive potential in what kind of landscape? How many children will be born with genetic defects after a nuclear strike?); (2) at the level of strategic options (which deterrence policies should be chosen?) and of tactical decisions (when to use nuclear and when conventional weaponry?); and (3) at the level of arms control (how to prevent an unintended war?). Kahn's line of reasoning is a 'what if ...?' approach that uses hypothesis and heuristic fiction to create thoughts which are actually 'unthinkable' in their materialisation.

Security through risk: MAD

Whereas Kahn's perspective on the feasibility of war was anti-apocalyptic in its intention (albeit not in its imagery), the apocalypse nevertheless served as a phantasm that, as it were, 'froze' the Cold War. As Jacques Derrida noted in 1984, the apocalypse is a 'rhetorical figure', an 'invention' or a 'fiction' – yet a fiction that reaches directly into the 'reality' of the conflict or, more precisely, one which constructs and formats this 'reality'.[29] Derrida suggested challenging this fiction with 'nuclear criticism', a rhetorical analysis of the textual nature of this fiction. However, the point was that this fiction *as* fiction (i.e. as narrative and hypothesis) was directly operational in political terms. The crucial doctrine of security and stability during the Cold War, the strategy of mutual deterrence, was based not on facts and reality, on existing stockpiles of weapons and on military supremacy, but on hypotheses about the enemy's options and potential actions or reactions in the future. It is not a coincidence that the doctrine of Mutual Assured Destruction (MAD) was not an idea developed by generals or diplomats, but by mathematicians. In 1953, Albert Wohlstetter designed the first draft of a strategy of 'second strike capability' for the RAND corporation. 'Second strike capability' was based on the possibility of deterring the enemy from an attack by maintaining the capability to strike back even after having suffered a disastrous attack.[30] Bernard Brodie who coined the phrase of the 'absolute weapon', elaborated this idea into a new strategy of deterrence.[31] The balance of MAD (i.e. the balance of terror) is based on the prospect of a retaliatory strike. Security is only possible when a first-strike strategy remains highly dangerous, in the sense that the retaliatory strike would still have devastating consequences for the aggressor. The notion that a future first strike can be prevented as long as one's own capability to retaliate is credible follows the abstract logic that it would be too great a risk for both enemies to attack first. Yet, this very logic also implies that it would be dangerous to disarm even when this might be reasonable in economic terms.

MAD is a strategic doctrine that is based on the assumption that both enemies are able to logically assess their own and their opponent's options, and that they will take their own decisions depending on the other side's options. The logical foundation for this approach was provided by game theory or rational choice theory. Game theory offers a model of conflict which assumes that both sides in fact look for a maximum profit in a given conflict, but are only willing to take a minimum risk. Game theory's most famous example, the 'prisoner's dilemma', is based on a situation in which both players must logically deduce their own and the opponent's possible course of action.[32] From this vantage point it is possible to extrapolate – at least in theory – the steps the opponent is likely to take. Does he expect a profit if he strikes first? Is the risk of a retaliatory strike low enough for him? A first strike is only profitable if the aggressor can expect to get away with it. This means that the opponent should be protected against an attack as efficiently as possible and, at the same time, should make the retaliatory strike as secure and fierce as possible (or at least make the aggressor believe in the inevitability of a second strike).

It was precisely at this point that the apocalyptic vision of nuclear war became directly operational in political terms. A doctrine in which political stability depends on the plausibility of a massive retaliatory strike tends to raise the stakes progressively. The more apocalyptic the consequences of a nuclear strike would look like, the more people would be killed for sure, the bigger the area that would be uninhabitable, the more effective is deterrence. Ironically, security and risk minimisation thus arise from maximising the destructive potential. This paradox is caused by the exclusively hypothetical nature of MAD. During the Cold War, imagination has had, indeed, no limits – yet in a quite different sense than that wished for by Günther Anders.

Tit for tat

This logic of deterrence created ever new and more fantastic suggestions. The most famous is certainly the 'Doomsday Device', a machine that, in the case of an attack, automatically triggers a devastating retaliatory strike. It became famous in Stanley Kubrick's satire on MAD, *Dr. Strangelove or: How I Learned to Stop Worrying and Love the Bomb* (1964). Yet the Doomsday Device was actually not an invention of Kubrick's fantasy. Herman Kahn, arguably the template for Dr. Strangelove, seriously thought about the notion of a Doomsday machine, but rejected the idea as too risky. The Soviet Union developed a system named 'perimeter', usually called 'the dead hand', and it has been speculated that it might be still in use or could at least be activated in times of international tension.[33]

Another suggestion along these lines came from Leo Szilard, the keen reader of Wells' novels, who, after having taken a leading role in developing the atom bomb, turned into one of the harshest critics of its political use. In 1955 and 1960, he published several papers in the *Bulletin of the Atomic Scientists*, promoting an idea of 'metastability' that was based on game theory, yet also went beyond it. Since the balance between the opponents can only be guaranteed by a credible potential of destruction on both sides, Szilard argued, an orderly 'tit-for-tat' should be put in place.[34] If the enemy destroys a city in the first line of attack, he must reckon that one of his own cities of equal size will be razed to the ground.[35] In his 1955 article, Szilard hoped that a treaty that settled these exchanges would gradually enable disarmament. In his 1960 article, he argued that a 'metastable' balance could be created by such an arrangement.[36] The problem of such an agreement is obvious: it must be 'credible', and it requires an enormous amount of mutual compromise and control – in short, communication. Herman Kahn noted the following on Szilard's suggestions: 'These current and somewhat bizarre sounding concepts have been extensively discussed. They now appear less bizarre than they seemed at first not because their nature has changed but as a logical consequence of the bizarreness of the balance of terror.'[37]

Szilard's idea was not heeded, however, which was reason enough for him to change the genre of his writing. In April 1961, Szilard published a collection of stories entitled *The Voice of the Dolphins*. Its title story is a partly ironic, partly affirmative engagement with precisely those hypothetic projections that futurologists such as Kahn elaborated. Nine months later Szilard wrote 'The mined cities', a story that outlines the model of tit-for-tat – a city for a city.[38] The first person narrator has gone into a frozen state of hibernation in 1962 for eighteen years in the hope that cancer treatment might be available in the future. He awakes in 1980. His doctor explains to him the era of world peace that has now lasted for decades. The basis of this peace, he explains, was the doctrine of the 'mined cities', an idea that is simple, democratic and surprisingly robust. Fifteen cities each in the United States and the Soviet Union have been mined with H-bombs that are controlled by troops from the respective opposite country. The bombs can be detonated in case of an attack on their own country, as a form of immediate and simple retaliation. All other nuclear bombs have been scrapped. With this security arrangement in place, the world has survived several serious international crises without one single city being destroyed.[39] The enemy troops that are based in each of the fifteen cities have their families in their respective twin city at home. In case of an emergency they would decide by a simple majority vote whether they would destroy the city (and themselves) in retaliation for the destruction of their home city. Obviously, this model of mutual assured destruction is game theory's dream: it is hyper-rational, easy to understand and – owing to the fact that the ultimate decision is being made by ordinary people – it is also democratic. Yet Szilard's model also succinctly reveals (apparently in affirmative fashion) that the *ultima ratio* of MAD is the willingness to commit suicide.

In its narrative form, Szilard's story, just like Kahn in *On Thermonuclear War*, writes a 'historiography of the future' which he borrows from Wells. From this viewpoint in the future, he is able to point out experiences with a system that has not yet been implemented. Just like Wells, he thinks about war as an orderly military conflict of strikes and counter-strikes. As soon as Paris is destroyed in *The World Set Free*, Berlin has its turn: 'Now', says the aircraft commander who is supposed to drop the Bomb on

Berlin, 'there's nothing on earth to stop us going to Berlin and *giving them tit-for-tat.*'[40] In his academic articles, Szilard had discussed and weighed up the pros and cons of a tit-for-tat model of sacrificed cities. In his fiction narrative, through the literary device of prolepsis, a look back from the vantage point of the future year 1980, he can give a clear description of this system, its background story and the experiences made with it. In times of crisis, Szilard suggests, the soldiers who control the H-bombs in the mined cities have proven themselves to be less prone to escalation than their governments. In Szilard's view, the tit-for-tat model will prevent the very escalation that Wells deemed to be inevitable.

Communication

In an ironic and self-reflexive fashion, Szilard refers to his own literary endeavours. The doctor in *The Mined Cities* explains: 'Incidentally, the whole sequence of events that I have just told you had been up to this point correctly predicted by Szilard in *The Voice of the Dolphins*. This is pure coincidence, of course, for nobody can correctly foretell the events of the future; few people can even correctly tell the events of the past.'[41] Writing fiction clearly allowed Szilard to take a complex attitude as both the creator and the critic of the bomb. This ambivalence has been analysed by Bernhard Dotzler as the core of his literary strategy: '[T]he latent inconsequence not to desist from doing what is clearly recognised as dangerous corresponds with the consequence to fathom this knowledge from the moment of its inception ... that is what truly deserves to be called science fiction.'[42]

For Szilard, unlike his academic publications, writing fiction had several advantages. His Wellesian 'historiography of the future' allowed for narrative omniscience, the knowledge of future outcomes of a political strategy, and for ironic self-reflexivity. Yet for Szilard, literature also served as a medium of communication in a political situation when communication was essential for survival. While his articles in the *Bulletin of the Atomic Scientists* went by and large unnoticed, he harboured big hopes for his stories: *The Voice of the Dolphins* contains a detailed and surprisingly accurate story of the future from 1960 to 1988. With its help, Szilard attempted to put himself forward as an advisor to the Kennedy administration. But he also tried to get in contact with the Soviet side. In preparation for a meeting with Nikita Khrushchev, during the winter of 1960 in Moscow, he had extracts from

The apocalyptic fiction

The Voice of the Dolphins translated into Russian, which he intended for the Soviet Prime Minister to read and which he wanted to explain to him.[43] Unfortunately, the meeting never materialised. For Szilard, literature was both applied futurology and political consultancy – but ultimately it was a privileged medium of communication, which in the context of the highly dangerous tit-for-tat of the MAD was all the more necessary. Szilard understood that each and every step in the speculative field of the mutual hyper-rational calculations – every scenario of conflict, every means of civil defence, every armament – always already was communication. In this sense, both Szilard's and Kahn's scenarios are messages to the enemy all along: we will strike if it is necessary; we build on civil defence and are therefore not as defenceless as it may seem, and so forth.[44] Yet these messages are easily trapped in the phantasmatic field of respective speculative projections.

In 'The mined cities', Szilard therefore invents a device that was supposed to prevent war much more effectively than the highly dangerous Doomsday Device, the famous 'red telephone': 'there ought to be a direct line installed between the White House and the Kremlin, so that in the case of an emergency President Kennedy could get through to Chairman Khrushchev without delay'.[45] In Szilard's story, the telephone is implemented, owing to a practical joke played by some students, who had sent a faked invitation to install this telephone line to both governments. Not surprisingly, the governments happily accepted. This step breaks open the paralysing stalemate of their game theory speculations. The telephone line between Washington and Moscow, well known from various films, was actually established two years later in the wake of the Cuban Missile Crisis. Initially, it was in fact not a telephone but a teleprinter, because it was expected that a written text was clearer, easier to translate and less likely to be impulsive than the spoken word.[46] In a way, the 'red telephone' is an allegory of what Szilard intended to do with his fiction. He wanted to establish communication in a situation that was frozen in hyper-rational, yet abstract speculations between the enemies. His ideas thus draw on the third dimension of the nuclear dispositive, on the question of control and communication within the strategic calculations of MAD. While Szilard's model of the mined cities is an extreme attempt to stabilise the spell by raising the stakes to the maximum, his invention of the 'red telephone' tries to lower the risk of an accidental war by establishing a medium of communication.

Eva Horn

The obscene desire for the Bomb: *Dr. Strangelove* and *Fail-Safe*

The apocalyptic spell was extremely fragile. The most pervasive fear was therefore that of an accidental war, a first strike caused unintentionally or unreasonably, which would then escalate into an all-out war owing to the logic of MAD. Not only strategists such as Kahn, but also films such as Stanley Kubrick's *Dr. Strangelove* and Sidney Lumet's *Fail-Safe* (both released in 1964 with a similar plot) focus on this type of worst-case scenario, since it reveals the blind spots of MAD. Both films are variations of the same topic – an unintended first strike, yet one as a tragedy (*Fail-Safe*), the other as a farce (*Dr. Strangelove*). It comes as no surprise that the farce was more successful with the audience.

Dr. Strangelove follows a precise composition that is confined to three settings (an air base, a B52 bomber and the War Room of the Pentagon), and has one single actor playing three different main characters (Peter Sellers as liaison officer at the air base, as US president and as his advisor Dr. Strangelove). Following the logic of scenario planning which focuses on single aspects of a potential conflict, Kubrick analyses a nuclear crisis on precisely three levels: the strategic level (at Burpleson Airbase from which the nuclear strike is being launched), the tactical level (the B52 bomber that actually delivers the Bomb to its target), and the political level (the War Room of the Pentagon, where the American president has gathered diplomats, generals and scientific advisors to discuss a solution for the imminent crisis). A paranoid US Air Force general single-handedly launches an attack on the Soviet Union; one of the B52 bombers with nuclear bombs is rushing towards Moscow and cannot be called back owing to a technical failure. In the War Room, a crisis management group consisting of the US president, military staff, the Russian ambassador and the inevitable mad scientist, Dr. Strangelove, tries to figure out a solution to avoid the imminent war. The US president calls the (not quite sober) Soviet prime minister. It turns out that the Russians got the Doomsday Device a while ago – but they forgot to inform the Americans.

No matter how ludicrous Kubrick's plot may seem, he nevertheless succinctly reveals the flaw of the hyper-rationalist doctrine of MAD. It lies in the possibility that the opponent does not act as reasonably as the rational choice conflict models suggest. His plot celebrates the victory of irrationality within the balance of terror. While on the part of the Americans it is madness, on the part of the Russians it is mere stupidity (or the fact that they did not read Kahn's works on the Doomsday machine), which ultimately brings about the end of the world. Kubrick's Russians simply did not understand that deterrence only works if the enemy knows about it. 'The whole point is lost if you keep it a secret!', Dr. Strangelove explains the logic of deterrence.[47] Kubrick lays bare the weak spot of the rational-choice type of conflict modelling: if both opponents lack the capability to analyse their options rationally, there is no point in applying rational choice theory. The existence of an enemy who is either too stupid (as the Soviets) or too crazy (as the Americans) to follow the optimal strategy ultimately causes the collapse of the system of MAD – and eventually brings forth the ultimate destruction. The nuclear apocalypse that the film celebrates gloriously at its end results from the clash between a highly rational security strategy that excludes human error and a complete failure of rationality. The sexual imagery pervading the entire film – from the copulation of aeroplanes to the intentionally silly names of the characters and places (such as General Jack D. Ripper, Burpleson Airbase, Ambassador de Sadeski and not least Dr. Strangelove himself) – reveals the obscenity underneath the rationalist calculation: an unavowable desire for the catastrophe to happen.

This suicidal tendency at the core of MAD becomes even more obvious in Sidney Lumet's attempt to stage the logic of nuclear deterrence as a tragedy. Walter Matthau plays the scientist Professor Groteschele – again a character based on Herman Kahn – who shocks the horrified guests of a party by explaining the advantages of a warfare that would cost 'only' sixty million lives instead of 100 million.[48] In a jovial mood typical for Kahn, he adds: 'It's all hypothesis of course, but fun to play around with.' A beautiful woman at the party comments: 'We all know we are going to die, but you make a game out of it, a marvellous game that includes the whole world.' This desire to play with apocalypse is, of course, unavowable for Kahn/Groteschele, and so he slaps the lady in the face. Nevertheless, in the course of the film, he eloquently advocates war, arguing that a limited, yet bold attack would start a war that can ultimately be won.

What warfare means in the age of nuclear weapons is demonstrated by the emerging crisis. An unknown airplane penetrates US air space. In response, 'Vindicator' bombers approach the Soviet Union; due to a technical defect a 'go code' is transmitted to six of these airplanes at the 'fail-safe' point. As a result, the planes set course for Moscow in order to bomb the city. While five of them can be ordered to return, one sets out to complete its mission of bombing the Soviet capital. A disastrous collapse of all communication and control follows: even a last telephone call between the US president and the Russian prime minister cannot prevent the bombardment of the city. The pilot of the fatal bomber cannot be called back since he has orders not to listen to any call-back once he has passed the 'fail-safe' point. Unlike Kubrick's film, which focuses on human irrationality overrunning the hyper-rational calculations of MAD, *Fail-Safe* demonstrates how human actors stick with the rational 'fail-safe' procedure of MAD, a course of action that ultimately ends in suicide.

In Lumet's scenario, the problem is not caused by a Doomsday Device, but by humans who follow defined procedures as if they were machines.[49] They refuse to communicate and can therefore run out of control just like machines.[50] The pilot carries out his instructions without wavering and eventually turns off the radio when his senior commanders and his wife implore him to return. In the end, war destroys the media of communication. The bombing of Moscow is transmitted to the United States in real time through the high-pitched whistling tone of the US ambassador's melting telephone. Ultimately, even the US president acts like a MAD automaton. Following the logic of 'tit-for-tat' he can see only one option to appease the Russians: he gives the order to bomb New York, although his wife is in the city. Tragically, the order has to be executed by a general whose family is also living in the city. With this plotline, Lumet follows precisely the logic of tit-for-tat that underpinned Szilard's 'mined cities', much more so than *Dr. Strangelove* does. Unlike Kubrick, Lumet interprets this logic as an allegedly tragic necessity of self-destruction, and not as a silly and obscene desire. But what both films unveil underneath the rationalistic doctrine of security as deterrence is a common suicidal wish, the unawowable desire for apocalypse.

The fiction narratives that we have discussed in this chapter present the unintended catastrophe in the calculus of nuclear deterrence during the Cold War not as an accident, but rather as a case of emergency that has been anticipated ever since the very inception of the Bomb. They reveal the nature of a security doctrine that is supposed to create security by mutually raising the stakes and increasing the risks. The apocalyptic fantasy that was at the heart of the idea of the 'ultimate weapon' long before its creation, reveals the blind spots of this hyper-rational, yet ultimately suicidal political logic. The Bomb does not guarantee stability. In this respect films such as *Dr. Strangelove* and *Fail-Safe* are lucid, meta-fictional comments on the fictions and hypothetical calculations that have been inherent in the political doctrines based on atomic weapons and nuclear deterrence. Kubrick and Lumet both demonstrate the political paradoxes in the logic of deterrence, exposing an obscene or tragic desire for the destruction of mankind at the hidden basis of that logic. At the heart of the Bomb, they argue, is not a desire for security, but a longing for collective death. In *Fail-Safe*, this is presented as the necessary decision to kill one's own people, that is the people of New York who have to die in order to save the rest of the country. The less tragic, more satirical *Dr. Strangelove* goes one step further. Accompanied by the tunes of the Second World War song 'We'll Meet Again', the film merrily celebrates the end of the world, brought forth by the detonations of the Soviet Doomsday Device. Kubrick satirically reveals a hidden desire for the catastrophe in Cold War thinking, a suicidal tendency that is obscenely enjoying the prospect of collective annihilation. Deterrence dreams of the catastrophe while actually claiming to prevent it. This strange desire for the apocalypse seems to be the reverse side of the totalising discourse on atomic bombs that started with its earliest inception: the notion that nuclear war was always about the 'entire humanity' and the 'whole world', that atomic bombs could actually destroy not a limited population of a given country or region, but all mankind. Seen as the 'ultimate weapon', the Bomb is also thought to be the final weapon, a weapon that is able to wipe out the entire human life on the planet. This, however, might actually be a human dream, not just a nightmare. For if all humans die at the same moment, death does not reduce the individual to his or her own mortality, but offers the somewhat consoling idea that the world will not go on after my or your personal end. In a global catastrophe, as the philosopher Hans Blumenberg has pointed out, 'life-time' and 'world-time' coincide, for once. Thus, one could interpret the unavowable desire for apocalypse that was inherent in the Cold War as the 'abolishment of the nuisance which is felt by the individual that the world does exist beyond the limits of his own lifetime … Not being outlived is the consolation caused by the idea that one will still lose the world and everything in it – as it always the case in the event of death – but just like everyone and with everything else.'[51] The Bomb might be a symbol for this secret fantasy and for the unacknowledged desire for collective death, a desire that pervades Günther Anders' urgent warnings as much as Herman Kahn's statistical calculations of mega-deaths. The vision of collective death celebrates a unity and equality that mankind only seems to find in the nuclear apocalypse.

Notes

1. K. Jaspers, *Die Atombombe und die Zukunft des Menschen. Politisches Bewusstsein in unserer Zeit* (Munich, 1962), pp. 21f. This book is the extended version of a radio essay that was broadcast in October 1956 in Germany.
2. See the excellent article by T. Brandstetter, 'Wie man lernt, die Bombe zu lieben. Zur diskursiven Konstruktion atomarer Gewalt', in G. Friesinger, T. Bauhausen and J. Grenzfurthner (eds.), *Schutzverletzungen. Legitimation medialer Gewalt* (Berlin, 2010), pp. 25–51. Early testimony on the apocalyptic discourse about radiation in S. R. Weart, *Nuclear Fear: A History of Images* (Cambridge, Mass., 1988), pp. 17–35.
3. F. Soddy, 'Some recent advances in radioactivity', *Contemporary Review* 83 (May 1903), pp. 708–20, quote p. 712.
4. H. G. Wells, *The World Set Free* (London, 1914), pp. 108f.
5. S. R. Weart and H. G. Szilard (eds), *Leo Szilard: His version of the Facts* (Cambridge, Mass., 1978), p. 18.
6. Brandstetter, 'Wie man lernt, die Bombe zu lieben', p. 39.
7. B. Brodie (ed.), *The Absolute Weapon: Atomic Power and World Order* (New York, 1946).
8. M. Kaldor, *The Imaginary War: Understanding the East-West Conflict* (Oxford, 1990).
9. H. Seton-Watson, *Neither War nor Peace: The Struggle for Power in the Postwar World* (New York, 1960).
10. G. Anders, 'Thesen zum Atomzeitalter [1959]', in G. Anders, *Die atomare Drohung. Radikale Überlegungen* (Munich, 1986), p. 96. (Emphasis added.)
11. G. Anders, *Die Antiquiertheit des Menschen. Über die Seele im Zeitalter der zweiten industriellen Revolution* (Munich, 1961 [first published 1956]), p. 16.
12. *Ibid.*, p. 283.
13. See G. Uerz, *ÜberMorgen. Zukunftsvorstellungen als Elemente der gesellschaftlichen Konstruktion der Wirklichkeit* (Munich, 2006), pp. 261–4.
14. For a programmatic statement on a type of futorology that was interested in 'social fantasy' and 'creativity', see R. Jungk, 'Die Entwicklung sozialer Phantasie als Aufgabe der Zukunftsforschung', in D. Pforte and O. Schwenke (eds.), *Ansichten einer künftigen Futurologie. Zukunftsforschung in der zweiten Phase* (Munich, 1973), pp. 121–35.
15. H. Kahn, *On Thermonuclear War* (Princeton, 1960). For an extensive biographical and intellectual assessment of Kahn's work and impact, see S. Ghamari-Tabrizi, *The Worlds of Herman Kahn* (Cambridge, Mass., 2007).
16. F. Kaplan, *Wizards of Armageddon* (Stanford, 1983), p. 227.
17. Kahn, *On Thermonuclear War*, p. 113.
18. Kaplan, *Wizards of Armageddon*, p. 222. (Emphasis in the original.)
19. Kahn, *On Thermonuclear War*, p. ix.
20. *Ibid.*, p. 228.

21 C. Pias, 'Abschreckung denken. Herman Kahns Szenarien', in C. Pias (ed.), *Abwehr. Modelle – Strategien – Medien* (Bielefeld, 2009), pp. 169–88, here p. 177.
22 See Kahn, *On Thermonuclear War*, Lecture II, pp. 190ff; and H. Kahn, *On Escalation: Metaphors and Scenarios* (New York, 1965).
23 H. Kahn, *Thinking about the Unthinkable* (New York, 1962), p. 143.
24 Ibid.
25 H. Kahn and A. J. Wiener, *The Year 2000: A Framework for Speculation on the Next Thirty-Three Years* (New York, 1967).
26 Cited in R. Kostelanetz, 'One-man think tank', *New York Times. Sunday Magazine*, 1 Dec. 1968, p. 105.
27 T. Draper, 'Nuclear temptations', in C. W. Kegley and E. R. Witt Kopf (eds.), *The Nuclear Reader. Strategy, Weapons, War* (New York, 1985), p. 27.
28 A. Herzog, 'Report on a think factory', *New York Times Magazine*, 10 Nov. 1963, p. 42.
29 J. Derrida, 'No Apocalypse, not now (Full Speed Ahead, Seven Missiles, Seven Missives)', *Diacritics* 14 (1984), pp. 20–31, here p. 23.
30 W. Poundstone, *Prisoner's Dilemma* (New York, 1992), pp. 91f.
31 B. Brodie, *Strategy in the Missile Age* (Princeton, 1959), chapter 8: 'The anatomy of deterrence', pp. 264–304.
32 See A. Rapoport, *Game Theory as a Theory of Conflict Resolution* (Dordrecht, Boston, 1974), pp. 17–34.
33 See www.wired.com/politics/security/magazine/17-10/mf_deadhand?current Page=all (accessed 7 July 2014).
34 Kahn discusses this type as 'Deterrence type III' in his *On Thermonuclear War*, pp. 126ff.
35 L. Szilard, 'Disarmament and the Problem of Peace', *The Bulletin of the Atomic Scientists* (Oct. 1955), pp. 295–307.
36 L. Szilard, 'How to live with the bomb – and survive. The Possibility of a Pax Russo-Americana in the Long-Range Rocket Stage of the So-Called Atomic Stalemate', *Bulletin of the Atomic Scientists* (Feb. 1960), pp. 59–73, p. 60.
37 Kahn, *Thinking About the Unthinkable*, p. 106.
38 L. Szilard, *The Voice of the Dolphins* (Stanford, 1992), pp. 153–67, 'The Mined Cities' was first published in the *Bulletin of the Atomic Scientists* (December 1961), and was later included in a new edition of *The Voice of the Dolphins*. On Szilard see the excellent article by B. Dotzler, 'Dr. Szilard Oder Wie man lernte die Apokalypse zu denken', in A. Wunschel and T. Macho (eds.), *Science & Fiction. Gedankenexperimente in Wissenschaft, Philosophie und Literatur* (Frankfurt, 2004), pp. 145–60.
39 L. Szilard, 'The mined cities', in Szilard, *Voice of the Dolphins*, pp. 153–67.
40 Wells, *The World Set Free*, pp. 98f. (Emphasis added.)
41 Szilard, 'Mined cities', p. 167.
42 Dotzler, 'Dr. Szilard', p. 154.

43 B. J. Bernstein, 'Introduction', in Szilard, *Voice of the Dolphins*, pp. 3–43, p. 40.
44 H. Kahn was well aware and even speculates that his book *On Thermonuclear War* could have and should have readers in Russia. Kahn, *On Thermonuclear War*, p. ix.
45 Szilard, 'Mined cities', p. 159.
46 On the media history and the fantasies surrounding the 'red telephone', see T. Nanz: 'Communication in Crisis. The "Red Phone" and the "Hotline"', *Behemoth. A Journal on Civilization* 3 (2010), online http://ojs.ub.uni-freiburg.de/behemoth/article/view/691 (accessed 17 June 2014); see also B. Kennedy: 'The Birth of the Hot Line', http://web.archive.org/web/20080923200642/http://www.cnn.com/SPECIALS/cold.war/episodes/10/spotlight/ (accessed 17 June 2014).
47 *Dr. Strangelove or: How I Learned to Stop Worrying and Love the Bomb* (dir. S. Kubrick, 1964); for a more detailed reading of Kubrick's film, see E. Horn, *The Secret War: Treason, Espionage, and Modern Fiction* (Evanston, 2013), pp. 238–50.
48 *Fail-Safe* (dir. Sidney Lumet, 1964).
49 Weart, *Nuclear Fear*, p. 276.
50 This uncontrollable nature of machines – or more precisely of the computers that govern them – is emphasised in the interpretation by T. Nanz of the novel that provided the narrative for Lumet's movie, authored by E. Burdick and H. Wheeler, *Fail-Safe* (New York, 1962). See Tobias Nanz, 'Bei Anruf: Apokalypse', in V. Wieser, C. Zolles, C. Feik and M. Zolles (eds), *Abendländische Apokalyptik. Kompendium zur Genealogie der Endzeit* (Berlin, 2013), pp. 227–38.
51 H. Blumenberg, *Lebenszeit und Weltzeit* (Frankfurt am Main, 1986), p. 78.

3

Building peace, fearing the apocalypse? Nuclear danger in Soviet Cold War culture

Miriam Dobson

There was no Soviet equivalent of *On the Beach*; no Russian Bill Haley hoping he would be the only man left with 'Thirteen Women' when the H-bomb went off. Before the Gorbachev era, few Soviet writers and film directors portrayed human civilisation on the brink of self-destruction, as in Nevil Shute's novel, or tried to conjure up a post-apocalyptic world. In the USSR, the first film to depict nuclear holocaust was Konstantin Lopushanskii's 1986 *The Letters of a Dead Man*.[1] Imagining the destructive power of atomic weapons was antithetical to the forward-looking spirit of the communist project. As Viacheslav Molotov, Stalin's right-hand man, put it: 'How can it be asserted that civilization could perish in an atomic war? … Can we make the people believe that in the event of war all must perish? Then why should we build socialism, why worry about tomorrow? It would better to supply everyone with coffins now.'[2]

Over the last thirty years, historians have studied how a 'nuclear consciousness', to borrow Paul Boyer's term, developed to the west of the Iron Curtain.[3] In many countries, this body of work suggests, governments tried to restrain discussion of the danger posed by the bomb and to reassure the public.[4] But newspapers, novels, film, comics and fine art provided imaginative spaces in which to reflect on the how the Bomb changed the world.[5] Some of these, such as Shute's novel, portrayed humankind's final moments. Others explored the new world generated by the destruction of civilisation: as a site of regeneration and renewal; as a paradise of new freedoms, sometimes sexual; or a hellish landscape inhabited by mutants.[6] For some, Christianity offered a means of interpreting the nuclear threat: from the first explosion at Hiroshima some fundamentalist Christians interpreted the Bomb as a sign that Armageddon was at hand, and 'apocalyptic fantasies' began to move from the margins of society into the mainstream.[7]

These Cold War cultures were, of course, neither uniform across the Western bloc, nor monolithic within a single country.[8] Visions of nuclear apocalypse led some to pacifist positions, others to restate their commitment to fighting communism. It is difficult to know, moreover, how far audiences responded to what Jacques Derrida called the 'fabulously textual' nature of full-scale nuclear war.[9] Writing about disaster films as early as the mid-1960s, Susan Sontag suggested that they were 'one of the ways of accommodating to and negating … the perennial human anxiety about death'; this anxiety was intensified by the mid-twentieth-century 'trauma' of realising that 'collective incineration and extinction [...] could come at any time, virtually without warning'. Although she saw them as an 'inadequate response', Sontag believed that these fantasies nonetheless distracted people from both real and anticipated terrors and helped to normalise, or neutralise, the unbearable.[10] For Sontag and others, the nuclear culture of the West – which, as we shall see, the Soviet authorities were to so deride – was a coping mechanism for what one historian has called 'a man-made threat of unprecedented magnitude'.[11] At the same time, of course, the movies, books and art produced could also help to conjure up new fears.[12]

As Peter Schmelz recently argued, it is often assumed that a 'Cold War culture' did not exist within the USSR.[13] He quotes from the work of anthropologist Nancy Ries, who suggested in 1997 that 'the kind of consciousness of the nuclear arms race that from 1945 on inspired Western war fantasies and peace movements, and their thousands of cultural productions, had hardly taken place in Russia'.[14] Like Schmelz, I argue here that a Cold War culture of sorts did exist, but that it was one very different in terms of scope and content from its counterparts in the West.

In the USSR, as elsewhere, the government was keen to prevent the escalation of nuclear fears and the party-state was far more able to restrict public access to cultural forms which they thought would stimulate anxiety. This is not to say that the Cold War was absent from Soviet culture. Since the Russian Revolution, the spectre of the enemy, intent on overturning the revolution, had loomed large: not only internal enemies (the Whites, Trotskyists, kulaks, etc.), but also foreign foes, from the foreign interventionists of the Civil War period to the fascists of the 1930s and 1940s. Now the prime aggressor became the USA. Rich and exploitative, war-mad, but also weedy, American capitalists and commanders were a regular feature in the Soviet press, particularly on the pages of the satirical magazine, *Krokodil*. Their presence made for effective binaries: capitalist aggression contrasted with the communist love of peace;

Nuclear danger in Soviet Cold War culture

American cowardice was the inverse of Soviet courage. The Soviet peace campaigns, launched in the late 1940s, may have been intended in large part for fellow travellers overseas but they were also meant for internal consumption. In terms of the domestic response, Timothy Johnston calls it 'an unusually successful political campaign'.[15] The crusade for peace, launched early in the Cold War, certainly became a central component of Soviet rhetoric.

In the mid-1950s, the death of Stalin and the advent of thermonuclear weapons coincided. There was no radical departure, and the atomic anxieties that characterised the 1950s elsewhere were more contained in the realm of mainstream Soviet culture: the dangers posed by nuclear weapons – for example, radiation dangers – were discussed, but in a more sober manner. As we shall see, the notion that a third world war would could spell the end of 'civilisation', or perhaps even of human life itself, was rarely articulated. Fears about the 'end of the world' were repeatedly presented as anathema to the Soviet spirit: it was only in the benighted climate of the USA that such depressing ideas could take root. Nonetheless, a Soviet nuclear culture of sorts had developed. And when Cold War tensions reignited in the early 1980s, the party leadership, and with it the Soviet media, became more ready to admit the scale of devastation that nuclear war could render, although Soviet citizens were still expected to fight actively for peace, rather than neurotically dread the end. If we understand the Cold War as a sustained attack on the collective imagination, then Soviet citizens were certainly under siege, with firm directives about how they were not only to behave but also feel during this (prolonged) period of national crisis.[16]

In this chapter, I use the press to explore three features of Soviet nuclear culture: first, the notion of the war-mongering enemy versus the Soviet desire for peace, a binary established in the late Stalinist era; second, the problematic nature of imagining conflict itself, particularly atomic warfare, even for Stalin's successors, who, by the 1950s, admitted to some of the dangers of radiation; and third, Soviet condemnation of anyone who feared global self-annihilation as religious fanatics, charges which became particularly prevalent in the 1980s when Ronald Reagan had taken up residency in the White House. The final section of the chapter turns its attention to the audience for these texts and images, asking why the authorities felt it necessary to remind Soviet citizens that they were not fearful of nuclear war with such dogged insistence: were people perhaps unable to control their emotions in the manner expected?

Miriam Dobson

Lampooning the enemy; constructing peace

In 1945, the Soviet Union was a country in ruins. In these immediate post-war years, a weekly magazine, *Ogonek*, provided readers with optimistic stories of how cities, town and villages were 'raising themselves from the ashes' (*podnimat'sia iz pepla*).[17] These heroic narratives of reconstruction were, however, complicated by the beginnings of the Cold War. Lampoons of the US 'imperialists' were particularly suited to the traditions of Soviet political satire. Kevin McKenna notes that following a Central Committee decree in September 1948 a new propaganda offensive was launched, leading to a significant increase in the number of political cartoons criticising the USA by the following year.[18] On 10 May 1952, the front cover of *Krokodil* was typical of the kind of binary of which early Soviet Cold War culture specialised: the brightly coloured page of a Soviet calendar, fluttering high in the picture, depicts fireworks shooting through the sky above the Kremlin as the nation celebrates Victory Day on 9 May; underneath, US politicians and military commanders cluster together, faces green with fear, heads grasped in anguish and yellowed teeth clenched on tremulous hands. Festive celebration in Moscow contrasted with wretched fear on the other side of the Atlantic.[19]

Despite these vivid depictions of the enemy, the Soviet government always presented itself as the reluctant participant in the Cold War: while the USA stoked the flames of war, the USSR desired only peace. This was an international campaign meant to shore up communist support across the globe, but it also had a domestic audience. The press celebrated the 1948 World Congress of Intellectuals for Peace in Wrocław, the World Congress of the Partisans of Peace in 1949 (held jointly in Paris and Prague), the launch of the Stockholm 'peace petition' in March 1950, and – after it was called off in Sheffield – the Second World Peace Congress in Warsaw in November 1950.[20] In terms of press coverage, 1950 was the peak year, and in the early spring editions of *Pravda* were full of references to the peace campaign. Given the Soviet commitment to developing its own atomic and thermonuclear weapons at this time, it is easy to write these pieces off as mere 'propaganda'.[21] But it is perhaps more pertinent to ask why 'peace' became so integral to Soviet rhetoric in these years and what it meant in the lexicon of the late Stalinist period.

Peace meant not repeating the war that had just ended. Alongside cultural luminaries, scientists and religious leaders, veterans of the last conflict were regular speakers at peace events. At the Paris Congress of Partisans for Peace in April 1949, for example, the delegation included the mother of Zoia Kosmodem'ianskaia, the young partisan girl executed by the Germans in 1942, and Aleksei Mares'ev, a war hero, who, after losing both legs in combat, adapted his bomber plane and continued flying. He spoke as follows to the Congress: 'we war veterans will never allow war to be unleashed again. During the battle against fascism we made huge sacrifices in order to save mankind, for the sake of peace and freedom.'[22] Later that year, *Ogonek* printed letters from concerned citizens who voiced their support for the peace cause, often mentioning their war service, or the loss of children. Yet they were laconic in their invocation of the past.[23] References to the past conflict were ubiquitous, but concise. Visually, the simple insertion of the swastika on to images of American aggression was an effective form of shorthand. The Soviet authorities were reluctant to allow physical and emotional pain to saturate the post-war world; in the world of fine art, for example, images of serious disability amongst veterans were taboo until at least the mid-1960s, when the twentieth anniversary of the war's end saw the damaged soldier appear more frequently, and more graphically, in paintings.[24]

Peace was not primarily about the past, but was written into the Soviet narrative of progress.[25] Take, for example, this definition of peace provided by a delegate at the 1949 Moscow peace conference:

> For us, Soviet people, peace is inspired labour, it is new homes, new cities and villages. For us peace is wooded strips in the field and new works of literature and art. For us peace is high harvests and plump livestock, it is citrus fruits in the far north and the irrigation of deserts in the south. Peace is the friendship of the people.[26]

The juxtaposition of seemingly unrelated phenomena – the planting of 'natural' windbreaks in open grasslands listed in the same exhilarated breath as the composition of new paintings or books – served to demonstrate the scope of Soviet progress. Here peace was not just about reconstruction, but about building the better future the Revolution had promised. This required not only the construction of cities, but also the transformation of the natural world: the extreme climates of both north and south could be brought under Soviet mastery.[27] Peace was not just the absence of war; it was the future that revolution was meant to bring. The concept of peace became a metonym for communism itself. As was the case with communism, peace was a cause that required a fighting spirit. Long deployed to describe the revolutionary struggle against capitalism, military metaphors were introduced into the peace rhetoric: Soviet citizens would always 'fight for peace' (*borot'sia za mir*) and there was confidence that 'the peace cause will conquer in the whole world' (*delo mira pobedit vo vsem mire*).[28]

In his exploration of diplomatic overtures between the USSR and the USA in the months following Stalin's death, Jeffrey Brooks has argued that the Soviet leadership was locked into its own peace rhetoric and was unable to communicate effectively a genuine desire to reduce hostilities.[29] Although such rhetoric may have proven confusing on the international diplomatic stage, it appears to have been powerful at home. Johnston has suggested that the movement found resonance for its domestic audience, even if many actually articulated positions closer to genuine pacifism than to the Soviet version of peace.[30] In the shadow of the Second World War, this yearning to avoid further conflict was harnessed to a brand of patriotism which – embedded in the rhetoric of 'peace' – could claim to be universalistic rather than jingoistic.

An unimaginable war

As demonstrated above, satirical cartoons, such as the kind favoured by *Krokodil*, lent themselves well to the depiction of the American capitalist, exploiting his workers to maintain wealth and weapons. US society, as imagined on the pages of the Soviet press, was a highly polarised one, the ordinary worker a victim of the capitalist/imperialist, and a potential ally for the Soviet Union. Andrey Shcherbenok has argued that this made depicting a war with the USA difficult, suggesting that in contrast to American cinema, Soviet films contain relatively few scenes showing actual combat with the Cold War enemy and that they failed 'to foster fear and hatred towards the United States'.[31] He proposes two key reasons: first, the Marxist underpinnings of Soviet culture meant that American society could not be essentialised as an homogenous enemy, but was instead painted as a site of ongoing class (and racial) conflict; second, the very recent experience of invasion and occupation made actual depictions of a US attack on Soviet territory too raw and painful. In addition, portraying a third world war would require the visualisation of atomic warfare.

Within days of the attack on Hiroshima, 'imaginative speculation' was rampant in the US popular press: pride in the American triumph rubbed shoulders with fears about what a nuclear future would hold. Photographs of the nuclear cloud over Hiroshima appeared, and terrifying visions of a nuclear holocaust far exceeded the actual destruction that atomic weapons could inflict at that time.[32] In contrast, over the course of 1945 *Pravda* and *Izvestiia* each devoted a single article to the advent of atomic warfare. Buried on their fourth page, both newspapers carried an identical report on Truman's 6 August announcement. Soviet readers learnt from Truman that a bomb had been dropped which was 2,000 times more powerful than the Grand Slam (a highexplosive bomb first used by the RAF in 1945) and heard how the Allies had collaborated throughout the war in order to master atomic weaponry before the Germans.[33] The Soviet articles offered little extraneous commentary, and omitted Truman's famous claim that 'the force from which the sun draws its power has been loosed against those who brought war to the Far East'.[34] There were no pictures.

Even as the Cold War, and the accompanying peace campaign, gathered strength towards the end of the 1940s, the destructive power of nuclear weapons received relatively little attention.[35] In 1950, the Stockholm Peace Appeal demanded 'the unconditional prohibition of the atomic weapon' and branded the first government to use atomic warfare 'a war criminal';[36] yet the extensive coverage given to the Appeal in the press largely centred on the claim that the USA wanted to unleash a new war, rather than on the unique nature of the technology it would deploy. There was relatively little coverage of why atomic missiles represented more of a threat than previous weapons. In the press, one of the strongest expressions of concern regarding nuclear weapons came from N. S. Tikhonov, chairman of the Soviet Committee for the Defence of Peace, who called the bomb 'this weapon of aggression and of the mass destruction of people' (*eto oruzhie agressii i massovogo unichtozheniia liudei*).[37] Reports from the US embassy suggested that when the Soviet government let it be known that the USSR also had atomic weapons in the autumn of 1949, the public responded with 'little excitement, some pride in Soviet achievement'. This calm reaction was explained as follows: 'Soviet press has never whipped up apocalyptic hysteria about [the] importance of [the] bomb as has [the] US press since 1945.'[38]

Ten years after Hiroshima, the anniversary coverage offered criticism of the US decision to deploy atomic bombs (absent in 1945), but there was still little appetite for depicting the full horror of nuclear conflict. In an opening paragraph, *Izvestiia* spoke of the 200,000 deaths as an abuse of mankind's scientific discoveries, but by the second paragraph moved to admonish readers: 'The ten-year anniversary of the Hiroshima tragedy is not only a day for remembering the victims of atomic bombings. It is above all a day of battle (*bor'ba*), a battle against the atomic arms race, a battle for the peaceful use of atomic energy in order that it can serve mankind.'[39] The article went on to describe the peace conference being held in Hiroshima and the leading role played by Soviet representatives in discussions about arms reduction at the Geneva summit.[40] As was the case with the peace coverage of the late Stalinist era, fear remained a taboo emotion: 'The tragedy of Hiroshima has not frightened people, no, it inspired in them a determination which grows daily that the atomic bomb will fall on no other city, that atomic energy will be used only for peaceful ends.'[41]

Although it was neither dramatic, nor clear-cut, a shift of sorts was occurring in the mid-1950s. Stalin's death was in part responsible for an increased awareness of nuclear danger because it ended an era of secrecy in which even Stalin's closest colleagues were ignorant about the effects of nuclear weapons.[42] But it also reflected a global wave of concern internationally about the nuclear threat, beginning in 1954, which was sparked by images and newsreel of the H-bomb tests.[43] With the advent of thermonuclear tests and the well-publicised poisoning of the *Lucky Dragon* fishing boat after the Bikini Atoll test in March 1954, the dangers of radiation became a major concern.[44] Although, in the USSR, party leaders still resisted discussion of civilisation's destruction, the Soviet press did alert readers to the dangers of radioactive fallout, particularly in the wake of H-bomb tests. Rather than suppressing reports of radiation sickness, the Soviet leadership deployed them as part of its rhetoric against the USA: in July 1954, for example, attentive *Izvestiia* readers could learn that the Supreme Soviet of the USSR was discussing a Japanese petition for nuclear tests to be banned following the *Lucky Dragon* death;[45] in August of the same year a more sensationalist *Pravda* feature reported on US solders being used as 'human guinea pigs' in experiments to measure the effect of food carrying high doses of radiation.[46] Such reports might seem an obvious means of attacking the USA, but it was a departure from the rhetoric of the earlier peace campaigns in which atomic weapons had been treated as essentially the same as any other kind of warfare, but simply on a grander scale.

Even though Khrushchev did not favour some of the more explicit statements that his predecessor Georgii Malenkov had made, the cessation of tests became an important issue for him.[47] From the mid-1950s, Soviet scientists were granted permission to participate in the Pugwash conferences, a movement initiated by Bertrand Russell and Albert Einstein, figures once both reviled in the Stalinist press. Now the Pugwash initiative was even given positive coverage in the Soviet media.[48] After returning from the first conference in August 1957, A. V. Topchiev, an academic, authored an article under the headline 'To eliminate the threat of atomic war'. The conference had recognised, he explained, that in the case of a nuclear war millions of people could die directly from the blast, high temperatures and radiation, that large areas of the world's surface would become inhospitable to life (*neprigodonyi dlia zhizni*) for long periods, and that millions would be contaminated by radioactive fallout. Those who survived would pass on genetic flaws, causing high mortality and abnormalities in their offspring.[49] Despite the reservations of leaders already noted, *Pravda* readers were thus made aware of many of the key issues which were to fuel protest movements elsewhere in the world. Topchiev noted that the situation would provoke 'legitimate alarm' (*zakonnaia trevoga*) amongst people, especially scientists 'who know better than most what disaster atomic war would bring'. In 1958, nuclear physicist and future dissident, Andrei Sakharov, wrote an article that calculated the numbers of deaths which would result from genetic mutations caused by radioactive fallout; Khrushchev gave personal approval for its publication (although not in the daily press).[50]

Soviet citizens were still discouraged, however, from imagining the bleak future Topchiev and Sakharov had posited. In 1959, Moscow leaders watched the film adaption of *On the Beach,* but decided it unwise to show it publicly.[51] In the following year, Alfred Schnittke's oratorio, *Nagasaki,* was played on Radio Moscow for a Japanese audience, but attracted considerable criticism back home, with an article in *Pravda* arguing that 'gloomy, psychologically exaggerated suffering' of works like this 'overshadowed' the 'optimistic purposefulness' of Soviet aesthetics.[52] In the 1950s, information about the dangers of nuclear tests and nuclear war were more available to Soviet citizens than under Stalin, but people were discouraged from contemplating its full destructive potential. The bomb did not have the ubiquitous presence it did in the West, and visually its presence was far more restricted.

The images of atomic war, commonplace in the American media since August 1945, had been absent from Soviet culture.[53] Now in the mid-1950s, the mushroom cloud made its debut but it rarely appeared in an unmediated form. Aerial photographs of nuclear tests remained exceptional.[54] When the atomic cloud was featured, it was often in images of clearly foreign provenance (see, for example, coverage of German peace protests in 1957).[55] Otherwise cartoon clouds became incorporated into the tradition of lampooning US and German aggression.[56] In October 1960, *Ogonek* played on a weak pun between the words Bonn and bomb with the caption 'How far might the atomic rearmament of Bonn go?', under a sketch of Adenauer morphing into an atomic missile, and then a mushroom cloud, with all four images bearing the Nazi insignia.[57] A simple *Krokodil* cartoon from 1962 depicted the New York skyline, the Statue of Liberty holding aloft a torch, out of which rose an atomic cloud.[58] In the same year, another showed a US waiter carrying a tray towards the door of a meeting room where members of the UN-sponsored Eighteen Nation Committee on Disarmament met; his offering was a tin, labelled 'atomic mushroom', out of which rose a vertical column of smoke.[59] By privileging the satirical lampoon over the truth-asserting medium of the photograph, the 'mushroom cloud' was neutered.

In the USA, in contrast, the cloud developed a powerful aesthetic and, as Peter Hales suggests, quickly became 'the only accepted visual sign' of the atomic bomb.[60] Although for peace activists it invoked fear, for others the explosion was a sublime and thrilling display of power testifying to the raw energy of the world.[61] This second response seemed both to intrigue and horrify Soviet editors. In 1962, *Ogonek* ran a story entitled 'The Bomb and the dollar', which were the two things Americans allegedly loved best.[62] Pictures of atomic explosions were apparently amongst those collected by long-wave radio aficionados in the USSR. They exchanged postcards with fellow amateurs, with whom they had successfully been in contact over the airwaves. Another had received a postcard depicting a dollar. 'Perhaps', the journalist worried, 'they will succeed in frightening somebody'. Images of the nuclear cloud were thus not only distanced, but rejected as an alien part of the US's war-mongering propaganda machine. To imagine annihilation was not Soviet. Nor was falling victim to fear; alarm, perhaps, but not fear.

Atomic Armageddon

In October 1953, the doyen of the peace movement, Il'ia Erenburg, wrote a long *Pravda* feature about nuclear culture in the USA and Western Europe.[63] Two weeks earlier the newspaper had informed the public that the USSR had tested a hydrogen bomb; now Erenburg gloated that US diplomats had been foolish to believe their country would keep a monopoly for long.[64] He mocked the West's nuclear culture: the poems and sermons devoted to the bomb; and the clever businessmen who named coffee houses, pens and even bras as 'atomic'. But it was particularly the anxiety it generated which Erenburg targeted. Newspaper editorials were, he observed, starting to sound like the charlatans in the year 999 who predicted the end of the world. Hearing that the USA was no longer the only one to have the bomb, panic and hysteria had seized the nation, and those Americans who yesterday worshipped 'Gilda' were now suffering from neurasthenia, with some even contemplating suicide.[65] Seven years later, as Khrushchev's 'peaceful coexistence' project ran aground, another *Pravda* article described a new wave of panic allegedly seizing the USA.[66] This time, the trigger was extreme weather conditions: alarmed by the early start to the hurricane season, 'religious sects' had spread rumours that the end of the world was coming.[67] Once again, these eschatological fears were linked to the Soviet nuclear arsenal, with *Pravda*'s Washington correspondence writing that 'in the city of Benson, in the state of Arizona, hundreds of evangelists locked themselves into their homes, bricked up the windows, tightly sealed the doors and announced that on 9 July America will perish … from the Soviet hydrogen bomb'. In New Jersey, 200 evangelical families moved to an abandoned railway tunnel in order to shelter from Soviet missiles.[68]

During the build-up to the Cuban Missile Crisis, US society was once more presented as a society at war with itself, the exploitative ruling class consciously instilling panic in ordinary citizens. Religious leaders were often portrayed as instrumental in stirring this fear. One long piece in *Ogonek*, for example, described how a priest encouraged Americans to keep a gun in their bomb shelter so they could stop those without shelter from seeking refuge in the wake of an atomic attack. The piece, a column by the American journalist and World Peace Council member, Albert Kahn, was also striking for the graphic description of the whirlwinds of fire and the macabre assertion that the bomb shelters only had one purpose – as crematoria for the dead. Kennedy had apparently admitted that atomic war would leave 70 million Americans dead.[69]

Tensions lessened in the wake of the Cuban Missile Crisis, but escalated once more in the late 1970s. In terms of Soviet rhetoric, this new wave of the Cold War saw an important shift: the Soviet government became more ready to admit the idea that death was not only an American fate. In 1977, Brezhnev took what was, for a Soviet leader, the unprecedented step of declaring that neither side would be victorious in a nuclear war.[70] During the following year, he attacked the concept of 'limited war', noting that although the West accepted the death of 10 per cent of the planet's population, the Soviet government could never condone any loss of life.[71] Other pieces in the press also condemned the concept of a limited war.[72] Yet, despite the increased readiness to admit to nuclear war's destructive potential at the very highest level, the denunciation of fear as the emotional preserve of the capitalist west continued to be an integral part of Soviet Cold War culture, as it had been since the late 1940s. Echoing Stalin's statement over thirty years earlier that 'atomic bombs are intended for intimidating weak nerves', Brezhnev stated that 'Soviet people have strong nerves. They have never fallen into panic and never will.'[73] The portrayal of Westerners as morbidly fearful became especially pronounced in the following years. In particular, the notion that fears of the end of the world were incited and exploited by religious leaders, already pre-empted in Erenburg's article of 1953, was to become a dominant feature in the early 1980s.

The Reagan admission gave the Soviet press ample material with which to work, particularly the rise of the religious right, and the USA was portrayed as a country where the beliefs and superstitions of the Middle Ages still prevailed.[74] In July 1982, a *Pravda* article repeated the claim that the US military–industrial complex had no concerns about the deaths that would arise from any kind of atomic war, and compared its leaders to medieval crusaders, the only difference being their attacks would not be limited to holy places.[75] A senior military official in the Pentagon, it was reported, had recently reproached Americans and Western Europeans for worrying too much about the end of the world; after all, only 500 million would die.[76] In general, though, it was this anxiety about the End that was targeted by the Soviet press. Later in the same year, *Pravda* reported on an interview in *People* which Reagan was questioned about his belief that Armageddon would happen in his lifetime; subsequent pieces repeated his eschatological predilections.[77] Evangelical leaders, such as Jerry Falwell, were a gift to Soviet journalists. A. Tolkunov reported that while he was waiting to interview Falwell, he was given a pamphlet with the preacher's most recent sermon; the front cover pictured a mushroom cloud across which were printed the words 'Armageddon and the future war with Russia'.[78] Tolkunov quoted from the sermon as follows: 'And Satan will come out and seduce people. But fire fell from heaven and consumed them. Rejoice, my children. Holy fire will destroy the communist threat!' In the interview that followed, Falwell apparently said that America would perish if the supporters of a nuclear freeze were successful, and he finished off with the cliché 'better dead than red'.[79]

The discussion of nuclear weapons and their dangers, which had started in the 1950s, was far more pervasive by the early 1980s.[80] There was greater recognition of the threat atomic weapons posed. But condemnation of fear, and the insistence on 'fighting' for peace, remained a central theme in the Cold War culture of the USSR. There was striking similarity in the way the potential for nuclear war was depicted visually on the pages of *Krokodil*. In one cartoon from 1982, for example, the US commander stretches out towards the nuclear button a spindly limb, wrapped in an armband which at once conveys both fascist and capitalist proclivities, only to be stopped by three strong proletarian arms, sleeves rolled up as if off to work.[81] This established repertoire was augmented by new plays on the notion of 'crusade'.[82] The rise of the religious right in the USA added a new dimension and allowed fears of nuclear annihilation to be associated not only with the negative values firmly attributed to the US since the inception of the Cold War, but also with the rejected values linked with religious 'obscurantism'.

Popular reactions

Opinion polls and sociological investigations were thin on the ground in the USSR, particularly before the 1960s, and this makes the task of surveying the emotions and beliefs generated by the Cold War even harder than elsewhere. Some resources do exist, however. One of the early sociological ventures of the post-Stalin era was the Institute of Public Opinion, organised under the auspices of the youth newspaper *Komsomol'skaia pravda* and headed by Boris Grushin.[83] The very first survey was carried out by the Institute in May 1960 a few days prior to the Paris summit at which the heads of the Soviet, US, British and French governments met to discuss the 'problem of peace'.[84] The survey's purpose was to gauge the public's confidence that a new world war could be prevented and the headline numbers are striking: 968 of the 1000 respondents answered 'yes' to the first question: 'Will mankind avert war?'[85] The survey also included open-ended questions: On what did you base your answer to the first question? What must be done first and foremost to strengthen peace? Many of the answers echo the language of the press. One 58-year-old male from the town of Nikel' on the Kola peninsula, not far from the Norwegian border, said the following: 'Peace has become different since the Second World War. The forces for peace are growing and strengthening, the militarists' powers are in decline [*driakhleiut*].'[86] A 24-year-old soldier explained his confidence in the peace cause as follows: 'The peoples of the world don't want war. With each year the peace movement broadens. The might of the socialist camp is growing. The alignment of forces is now such that any attempt at aggression is doomed to failure.'[87]

A retrospective survey of attitudes conducted after the demise of Soviet power gives very different results. Whereas almost all of Grushin's respondents were hopeful that war could be averted, a poll carried out in the late 1990s suggested that many people remembered feeling fear – that most taboo of emotions. Iurii Aksiutin found that when asked about their reactions to the Cuban Missile Crisis, almost half of respondents claimed they had believed the world was on the brink of a third major war. One worker said: 'Everyone was afraid that the USA would unleash a nuclear conflict.' Aksiutin noted that the idea that everyone was 'afraid' [*boialis*'] recurred quite frequently.[88]

With one suggesting almost universal optimism, the other at least reasonably widespread fear, these two surveys preclude easy conclusions about the levels of nuclear anxiety within Soviet society in the early 1960s. Both methodologies have their problems, however. When he published a collection of the surveys in the post-Soviet period, Grushin offered a subtle and thoughtful commentary, arguing that the answers embodied a genuine Soviet patriotism, resting on a strong sense of 'us' and the enemy 'other', not least because of the depth and complexity of the answers given.[89] Yet, it is difficult not to wonder, as Grushin himself does, whether at least some of the respondents stuck close to the script provided by the Soviet media because they knew what was expected of them. With Aksiutin's respondents, the passage of a half-century would surely have clouded their recollections, particularly in terms of recalling emotions.[90] Further research is certainly needed to understand more fully the impact of the 'attack on the imagination' within Soviet society. But there is some evidence to suggest that there were those who felt the mainstream texts and images – which had first alerted them to the dangers of nuclear war – were inadequate, giving little guidance in terms of imagining how this future conflict might look and feel. Some citizens looked outside the interpretative framework offered by the state.[91]

In her *Stories of the Soviet Experience: Memoirs, Diaries, and Dreams*, Irina Paperno offers a close reading of the notebooks kept by Evgeniia Grigor'evna Kiseleva (1916–90). Hoping that her life story could be the subject of a film, Kiseleva sent the first of her notebooks to a Moscow studio in the 1970s, and they were later published. Born in a Ukrainian village, Kiseleva received five years of schooling before moving to a nearby town at the time of the famine; during, and after, her two failed marriages, she made a living taking in lodgers, and working as a security guard and cleaning woman. Her texts provide, Paperno suggests, 'a window into the world of a semiurbanised Soviet peasant' and show 'how Soviet power shaped Kiseleva's life and how it inspired her to tell her life story'.[92] In the later Brezhnev era, when Kiseleva was an old and lonely woman, television played a key role in her life; but she proved less obedient in her reproduction of Soviet rhetoric than Grushin's informants. Throughout the notebooks, the fear of war is repeated time and again and engenders emotional responses to the threat of a third world war. In response to seeing President Reagan on the screen, the semiliterate Kiseleva wrote the following:

> I can not look at his mug he thinks he'll survive or rather his people will stay alive no, if the War comes to us everyone will die just the same, on the whole earth. They say that in the USSR we've got 45 nuclear stations we will fight to the last we too can fight we can we're already wise to it. But he thinks he's got these underground cities in his country but I've heard that they can't live long first the earth will be barren for 10 years what will people live on they'll beg for death, them that remain living there won't be nothing no more, no life how stupid them leader of the USA they should have thought with their clever head, why War but our leader Gorbachev fights with all his strength so that there aren't no Wars.[93]

Here she shares the government's assumption that the Soviet Union is the superior force and echoes the derision of US attempts at self-protection discussed above. But although she does adopt and adapt terms and phrases from the official lexicon (Paperno notes in another diary entry, for example, an improvisation on the 'ne dopustim' formula common in Soviet antiwar discourse), her writing is a long way from the texts found in the media, and not just because of her limited literacy.[94] As Paperno notes, the picture of a devastated land 'clearly operated with the biblical apocalyptic imagery'.[95] She also observes that Kiseleva herself draws attention to the oral sources which provided this imagery ('I've heard it such'). Through television, the state addressed Kiseleva and, writes Paperno, its 'appeals found an echo in the traditional beliefs and images, in the folk religious culture, whose apocalyptic tendency proved well fitted to express the political concerns of the day – nuclear proliferation'.[96] Writing in 1987, Kiseleva was not alone in making connections between the dangers of the atom and apocalyptic fears and the Chernobyl disaster fed into a religious revival that was underway.[97] One child who survived Chernobyl later remembered: 'There was a black cloud, and hard rain. The puddles were yellow and green, like someone had poured paint into them. They said it was dust from the flowers. Grandma made us stay in the cellar. She got down on her knees and prayed. And she taught us, too. "Pray! It's the end of the world. It's God's punishment for our sins."'[98]

Although the media coverage, and then Chernobyl, ratcheted up the tensions in the 1980s, this need to look outside the explanatory frameworks offered by the Soviet media was not in itself new. Christian culture, particularly the images provided in the Book of Revelations, offered an alternative vision of the future, which allowed fears of terrible devastation to be articulated. In the first half of the twentieth century, rumours of the anti-Christ's imminent return had spread during times of crisis: the Civil War, the early collectivisation campaigns, the military build-up of the late 1930s.[99] They also returned in the post-war years, and apparently intensified as the Cold War escalated.[100] Between 1948 and 1950, with media coverage of the peace campaign at its peak, observers noted widespread fears that the end of the world was nigh.[101] In May 1950, Karpov, the chairman of the Council of the Affairs of the Russian Orthodox Church reported to the party's Central Committee on a wave of rumours claiming that war would begin in 1950, a prediction in part based on the fact that the sum of the figures (1 + 9 + 5 + 0) came to 15, as had the fateful years of 1914 and 1941. Karpov also reported that the dissemination of 'holy letters' had been noted and provided an example which included the following prophecy: 'Christ said: "Half of the people will perish on the 12th June 1950 and on the 15th all the rivers and lakes will fill up [*napolniatsia*] and the sun will grow dark and will stop shining."'[102] Apocalyptic fears seemed to continue into the fall of that year, and in a subsequent report Karpov noted that in the Voronezh region some collective and state farms' work had been seriously disrupted as people began to prepare for the end of the world.[103] It is certainly tempting to see a correlation between these waves of eschatological fear and the escalation of the aggressive peace campaigns which began in 1948, intensified in the spring of 1950, and reached their apotheosis with the outbreak of the Korean War in June 1950. As the rhetoric of 'peace' intensified on the pages of the Soviet press, some readers realised this in fact signalled its fragility. And they seemingly found that biblical texts, with which many were still (if hazily) familiar, allowed articulation of emotions such as fear and anxiety that were explicitly taboo in the muscular world that Soviet ideologues sought.

Conclusion

Over a number of decades, the Soviet press gradually increased the information provided to its audience. In the late 1940s, the goal of 'peace' almost seemed to overshadow everything, even the concept of communism itself, but there was relatively little discussion of nuclear weapons *per se*. In the 1950s and early 1960s, the dangers of radiation became more widely recognised in the world and some of these concerns filtered through to Soviet readers, although normally in relatively sober tones; the more sensationalist invocations of nuclear war were reserved for the effect of the conflict on US territory, but never imagined on Soviet ground. In the final wave of the Cold War, the danger of a nuclear war to all of humanity became a more frequent theme. Yet throughout it all, Soviet audiences were expected to keep their emotions in check. Anger was required; alarm sometimes expected; but fear was taboo – an unworthy and un-Soviet emotion. According to Soviet depictions of US society, in contrast, the ruling classes there incited fear and hysteria, sometimes for material gain (the sale of bomb shelters or atomic-themed toys, for example).[104] Religious leaders were often portrayed as complicit in this. The association repeatedly made between fears of the end of the world and America's religious culture was an important rhetorical device that was used to reaffirm the negative value of both.

Yet, paradoxically perhaps, religious culture also helped at least some Soviet citizens to find a language to talk about their anxieties. Although in the earlier years of the Cold War, the Stalinist authorities criminalised such thinking, it did not necessarily entail hostility or resistance to Soviet power; Kiseleva, for example, praised Soviet leaders, considering them her protectors against outside threat.[105] Yet, the appearance of apocalyptic thinking in the margins of Soviet culture – in the notebooks of a semi-literate pensioner watching the Reagan–Gorbachev summit on TV, or in the 'holy letters' circulated in 1950 – is significant. It points to the limitations of a secular culture that allowed some knowledge of the nuclear threat to be disseminated, but at the same time stigmatised attempts to engage imaginatively with its consequences.

Notes

1 A. Shcherbenok, 'Asymmetric warfare: the vision of the enemy in American and Soviet Cold War cinemas', *KinoKultura* 28 (2010). Available at www.kinokultura.com/2010/28-shcherbenok.shtml.
2 Quoted in D. Holloway, *Stalin and the Bomb: The Soviet Union and Atomic Energy, 1939–1956* (New Haven and London, 1994), pp. 338–9.
3 P. S. Boyer, *By the Bomb's Early Light: American Thought and Culture at the Dawn of the Atomic Age* (Chapel Hill, 1994), pp. xviii.

4 Civil defence propaganda, for example, was one way to prevent fear from becoming debilitating by assuring the public that a nuclear attack could be survived. G. Oakes, 'The family under nuclear attack: American civil defence propaganda in the 1950s', in G. D. Rawnsley (ed.), *Cold-War Propaganda in the 1950s* (Basingstoke, 1999), pp. 67–85. In the UK, the 1966 BBC film *The War Game* was not broadcast because its vision of a war fought with H-bombs was considered too gruesome. In the USA, the government released very few pictures of the wounded at Hiroshima in the 1950s and 1960s. S. Weart, *Nuclear Fear: A History of Images* (Cambridge, Mass., 1988), pp. 236–7.

5 Adrian Bingham shows how the British popular press, despite being largely in favour of nuclear weapons, often allowed 'sceptical voices' to disrupt 'official narratives'. A. Bingham, '"The monster?" The British popular press and nuclear culture, 1945–early 1960s', *The British Journal for the History of Science* 45 (2012), pp. 609–24 (p. 623).

6 Weart, *Nuclear Fear*, pp. 215–40.

7 'Apocalyptic fantasies' comes from Weart, *Nuclear Fear*, p. 106. See also P. Boyer, 'The growth of fundamentalist Apocalyptic in the United States', in B. McGinn, J. J. Collins and S. J. Stein (eds), *The Continuum History of Apocalypticism* (New York, 2003), pp. 516–44.

8 On the specific nature of German anxieties, see M. Geyer, 'Cold War angst: the case of West German opposition to rearmament and nuclear weapons', in H. Schissler (ed.), *The miracle years: A Cultural History of West Germany, 1949–1968* (Princeton, 2001), pp. 376–408. On differences between British and American beliefs about the possibility of surviving a nuclear war, particularly in terms of the legacy of the Blitz, see M. Grant, 'The imaginative landscape of nuclear war in Britain', in this volume.

9 Jacques Derrida, 'No Apocalypse, not now (full speed ahead, seven missiles, seven missives)', *Diacritics* 14 (1984), pp. 20–3, p. 23.

10 S. Sontag, 'The imagination of disaster', in *Against Interpretation and Other Essays* (New York, 1966), pp. 209–25.

11 J. Hogg, '"The family that feared tomorrow": British nuclear culture and individual experience in the late 1950s', *The British Journal for the History of Science* 45 (2012), pp. 535–9 (p. 539).

12 Weart, *Nuclear Fear*, p. 192.

13 Schmelz, 'Alfred Schnittke's *Nagasaki*', pp. 413–14. Kate Brown's recent work shows how productive thinking comparatively about the Cold War experience can be. See K. Brown, *Plutopia: Nuclear Families, Atomic Cities, and the Great Soviet and American Plutonium Disasters* (New York, 2013).

14 N. Ries, *Russian Talk: Culture and Conversation During Perestroika* (Ithaca, 1997), p. 7.

15 T. Johnston, *Being Soviet: Identity, Rumour, and Everyday Life under Stalin, 1939–1953* (Oxford, 2011), p. 152.

16 Michael Geyer's notion of an attack on the collective imagination is discussed in the introduction to this volume. I am grateful to the editors for explaining the ideas presented in Geyer's article: M. Geyer, 'Der kriegerische Blick. Rückblick auf einen noch zu beendenden Krieg', *Sozialwissenschaftliche Informationen* 19 (1990), pp. 111–17.
17 See, for example, I. Erenburg's article in *Ogonek*, no. 16–17, Apr. 1946.
18 K. J. McKenna, *All The Views Fit To Print: Changing images of the U.S. in Pravda political cartoons, 1917–1991* (New York and Oxford, 2001), p. 78. See also R. Stites, 'Heaven and hell: Soviet propaganda constructs the world', in Rawnsley (ed.), *Cold-War Propaganda*, pp. 85–104; A. V. Fateev, *Obraz vraga v sovetskoi propagande: 1945–1954 gg* (Moscow, 1999).
19 *Krokodil*, 10 May 1952 (no. 13), p. 1.
20 On the development of the peace congresses: P. Deery, 'The dove flies East: Whitehall, Warsaw and the 1950 World Peace Congress', *The Australian Journal of Politics and History* 48 (2002), pp. 449–68; W. Ullrich 'Preventing "peace": the British Government and the second World Peace Congress', *Cold War History* 11 (2011), pp. 341–62; L. S. Wittner, *One World or None: A History of the World Nuclear Disarmament Movement Through 1953* (Stanford, 1993), pp. 175–86.
21 For a searing attack on the dupes in the West who were taken in by the Soviets' peace campaigns, see V. Bukovsky, *The Peace Movement and the Soviet Union* (London, 1982).
22 'Vsemirnyi kongress storonnikov mira', *Izvestiia*, 24 Apr. 1949, p. 3.
23 'Moskva, ulitsa Kropotkina, 10': Pis'ma sovetskikh liudei v podgotovitel'nyi komitet po sozyvu Vsesoiuznoi konferentsii storonnikov mira', *Ogonek*, Aug. 1949 (no. 34), pp. 2–3.
24 C. McCallum, 'The fate of the new man: reconstructing and representing masculinity in Soviet visual culture, 1945–1965', PhD thesis, University of Sheffield, 2011.
25 Benjamin Ziemann notes the 'future orientation' in his study of images of peace in West Germany and attributes this to the 'future-oriented nature of modern society'. It is probably fair to say that Soviet culture was even more fixated on forward movement than other modern societies. B. Ziemann, 'The code of protest: images of peace in the West German peace movements, 1945–1990', *Contemporary European History* 17 (2008), pp. 237–61.
26 M. Tursun-Zade, 'My otstoim delo mira', *Ogonek*, 4 Sept. 1949 (no. 36), p. 12.
27 On Stalin's plans for transforming nature, the most recent work is S. Brain, 'The Great Stalin Plan for the transformation of nature', *Environmental History* 15 (2010), pp. 670–700.
28 Letter from M. Grebenshchikov, *Ogonek*, Aug. 1949 (no. 34), p. 3.
29 J. Brooks, 'When the Cold War did not end: The Soviet peace offensive of 1953 and the American response', *Kennan Institute Occasional Papers*, 278 (2000).

30 Johnston, *Being Soviet*, pp. 154–60.
31 Shcherbenok, 'Asymmetric warfare'.
32 The phrase 'imaginative speculation' comes from Timothy Garvey, 'László Moholy-Nagy and atomic ambivalence in post-war Chicago', *American Art* 14 (2000), pp. 22–39, 36–7. See also Boyer, *By the Bomb's Early Light*, pp. 3–26; Weart, *Nuclear Fear*, chapter 6.
33 'Zaiavlenie Trumena o novoi atomnoi bombe', *Izvestiia*, 7 Aug. 1945, p. 4; 'Zaiavlenie Trumena o novoi atomnoi bombe', *Pravda*, 8 Aug. 1945, p. 4.
34 Weart, *Nuclear Fear*, p. 103.
35 Some historians suggest that this reflected Stalin's personal position. Campbell and Radchenko argue that, in part because reports from Soviet diplomats suggested that the Japanese press was exaggerating the destructive power of the bomb, Stalin concluded that the effect of atomic weapons was not dissimilar to the devastation wrought on many Soviet cities by traditional warfare during the battles of the Second World War. Others attribute to Stalin more significant concerns about nuclear weapons, either before 1945 (Tyuoshi Hasegawa), or after Hiroshima (David Holloway). C. Campbell and S. Radchenko, *The Atomic Bomb and the Origins of the Cold War* (New Haven, 2008), pp. 93–110.
36 On the Stockholm Peace Appeal, see Wittner, *One World or None*, pp. 182–4.
37 'Sovetskii narod edinodushno podpishet Stokgol'mskoe Vozzvanie: Beseda s predsedatelem Sovetskogo komiteta zashchity mira', *Pravda*, 29 June 1950, p. 1.
38 Wittner, *One World or None*, p. 147. For the roundabout way in which the Soviet public was informed that the USSR also had atomic weapons, see 'Soobshchenie TASS', *Izvestiia*, 25 Sept. 1949, p. 2, and further coverage *Izvestiia*, 29 Sept. 1949, p. 3.
39 'Eto ne dolzhno povtorit'sia!', *Izvestiia*, 6 Aug. 1955, p. 10.
40 At the summit in July 1955, Khrushchev and Eisenhower discussed the Soviet proposal put forward on 10 May 1955. Despite US support for an earlier memorandum, which had included similar points, no agreement was reached. M. Evangelista, *Unarmed Forces: The transnational movement to end the cold war* (Ithaca, 1999), pp. 91–3.
41 'Eto ne dolzhno povtorit'sia!', *Izvestiia*, 6 Aug. 1955, p. 10.
42 D. Holloway, *Stalin and the Bomb: The Soviet Union and Atomic Energy, 1939–1956* (New Haven and London, 1994), pp. 336–40.
43 In terms of the USA, Weart attributes particular importance to the Operation IVY film viewed by TV audiences in April 1954, which gave a 'real sense of the scale of destruction possible'. Weart, *Nuclear Fear*, pp. 183–4. See also, Brown, *Plutopia*, p. 226. On the impact of the hydrogen bomb in Britain, see Grant, 'The imaginative landscape'; on West Germany, see Ziemann, 'The code of protest', p. 245.
44 Weart, *Nuclear Fear*, p. 185; J. Suri, *Power and Protest: Global Revolution and the Rise of Detente* (Cambridge, Mass., 2005), p. 9.

45 'Obrashcheniem Iaponskogo parlamenta po voprosu o zapreshchenii iadernogooruzhii i prekrashchenii ego ispytanii', *Izvestiia*, 17 July 1954, p. 6.
46 'Podarki Amerikanskim iunosham', 4 Aug. 1954, *Pravda*, p. 3.
47 Evangelista, *Unarmed forces*, p. 46 and p. 58. Khrushchev announced a unilateral moratorium on testing in 1958. See coverage in *Izvestiia*, 1 Apr. 1958, p. 5; *Pravda*, 1 Apr. 1958, p. 4.
48 On Khrushchev and the cessation of tests, see Evangelista, *Unarmed forces*, pp. 25–44. On the different positions taken by Malenkov and Khrushchev, see Holloway, *Stalin and the Bomb*, pp. 320–46.
49 A. V. Topchiev, 'Ustranit' ugrozu atomnoy voiny', *Pravda*, 16 Aug. 1957, p. 4.
50 Evangelista, *Unarmed Forces*, p. 58, and J. Bergman, *Meeting the Demands of Reason* (Ithaca: Cornell University Press, 2009), pp. 82–7. The article was published in *Atomniia energiia* and then republished the following year in a collection: A. V. Lebedinskii, *Sovetskie uchenye ob opasnosti ispytanii iadernogo oruzhiia* (Moscow, 1959).
51 Weart, *Nuclear Fear*, p. 217.
52 Schmelz, 'Alfred Schnittke's *Nagasaki*'.
53 Boyer notes that it was in the 20 August 1945 edition of *Life* that 'many Americans encountered for the first time the towering mushroom-shaped cloud that would become the quintessential visual symbol of the new era'. Boyer, *By the Bomb's Early Light*, p. 8. With regard to the USSR, Kate Brown writes: 'In general, Moscow propagandists left the veneration of the mushroom cloud to the Americans and instead trumpeted the "peaceful atom".' Brown, *Plutopia*, p. 133.
54 For an exception, see *Ogonek*, 20 Feb. 1955 (no. 8), pp. 18–19.
55 E. Pral'nikov, 'Pered vyborami', *Ogonek*, Sept. 1957 (no. 38).
56 In its first appearances in the mid-1950s, the atomic cloud did not have the pure form familiar to the West. It either lacked the vertical column (see, for example, the billowing black cloud in *Krokodil*, 10 Sept. 1955 (no. 25), p. 16); or was on the periphery of the image, half-hidden (*Krokodil*, 30 May 1958 (no. 15), p. 8).
57 'Zapadnogermanskaia BONNba', *Ogonek*, 16 Oct. 1960 (no. 42), p. 7.
58 G. Iorsha, 'Vot on – novyi svet!', *Krokodil*, 20 May 1962 (no. 14), p. 11. McKenna notes that in the 1960s *Krokodil* sought to undermine the idea of the US as a land of 'freedom' and the Statue of Liberty often became the target of satirical images. McKenna, *All The Views*, p. 113.
59 *Krokodil*, 30 Mar. 1962 (no. 9), p. 10.
60 P. B. Hales, 'The atomic sublime', *American Studies* 32 (1991), pp. 5–32 (p. 10).
61 *Ibid.*; P. Rosenthal, 'The nuclear mushroom cloud as cultural image', *American Literary History* 3 (1991), pp. 63–92; B. Taylor, 'Nuclear pictures and metapictures', *American Literary History* 9 (1997), pp. 567–97.
62 'Bomba i dollar', *Ogonek*, July 1962 (no. 31), pp. 2–3.
63 I. Erenburg, 'Tupik v Vashingtone', *Pravda*, 2 Oct. 1953, p. 4.

64 For the announcement, see 'Pravitel'stvennoe soobshchenie ob ispitanii vodorodnoi bomby v Sovetskom Soiuze', *Pravda*, 20 Aug. 1953, p. 2.
65 Weart notes that the bombs tested in 1946 were reportedly named 'Gilda' and 'Bikini Helen'. See Weart, *Nuclear Fear*, pp. 146–7.
66 B. Strel'nikov, 'Trevozhnoe leto', *Pravda*, 6 Aug. 1960, p. 3.
67 Weart notes that from 1951 the Atomic Energy Commission had been receiving letters from all over the world saying that bomb tests were upsetting weather patterns. He also suggests such concerns could come from Moscow. Weart, *Nuclear Fear*, p. 187.
68 Strel'nikov, 'Trevozhnoe leto'.
69 'Pis'mo professora Iks', *Ogonek*, 8 July 1962 (no. 28), pp. 9–12.
70 L. S. Wittner, *Confronting the Bomb: A Short History of the World Nuclear Disarmament Movement* (Stanford, 2009), p. 134.
71 'Otvety tovarishcha L. I. Brezhneva na voprosy ezhenedel'nika Sotsial-demokraticheskoi partii Germanii "Forverts"', *Izvestiia*, 3 May 1978, p. 1.
72 'Otstoiat' mir na planete', *Pravda*, 5 Apr. 1982, p. 5.
73 Stalin made the comment in September 1946 to a London *Times* correspondent. See Evangelista, *Unarmed Forces*, p. 287. The quotation from Brezhnev is taken from 'Otvety tovarishcha L. I. Brezhneva'.
74 McKenna notes a rise in the proportion of political cartoons which were related to the USA in 1981–82. McKenna, *All The Views*, p. 147.
75 McKenna also notes that *Pravda*'s lead editorials and commentaries characterised US foreign policy in terms of an anti-Soviet 'crusade'. *Ibid.*, pp. 147–51.
76 V. Korionov, 'Krestonostsy XX veka', *Pravda*, 14 July 1982, p. 4.
77 'Fatalist' iz Belogo doma', *Pravda*, 22 Dec. 1982, p. 5. See also 'Kuda idet dela Vashington', *Izvestiia*, 15 Apr. 1984, p. 3.
78 A. Tolkunov, 'Naedine s 'prorokom', *Pravda*, 3 Aug. 1984, p. 4.
79 On the concept of nuclear freeze, see Wittner, *Confronting*, p. 123.
80 See, for example, the prominence of nuclear issues in the articles devoted to *Ogonek*'s sixtieth anniversary: Nov. 1982 (no. 47); Dec. 1982 (no. 51).
81 *Krokodil*, Feb. 1982 (no. 6), p. 1.
82 *Ogonek*, Oct. 1982 (no. 44), 4; *Ogonek*, Nov. 1982 (no. 45), p. 4.
83 B. A. Grushin, *Chetyre zhizni Rossii v zerkale oprosov obshchestvennogo mneniia. Ocherki massovogo soznaniia rossiian vremen Khrushcheva, Brezhneva, Gorbacheva i El'tsina v 4-kh knigakh, vol. 1: Zhizn' 1-ia: Epokha Khrushcheva* (Moscow, 1998). See also S. Huxtable, 'A Compass in the Sea of Life: Soviet Journalism, the Public, and the Limits of Reform after Stalin, 1953–1968', PhD thesis, Birkbeck College, University of London, 2013, chapter 4.
84 The Paris summit brought together the heads of state of the USA, Britain, France and the Soviet Union with the hopes of resolving differences, particularly with regard to nuclear testing and on-site inspections. Matthew Evangelista suggests that several members of the Soviet delegation anticipated agreement on at least a partial test ban but that their hopes were dashed by Khrushchev's reaction to the American U-2 spy plane incident. Evangelista, *Unarmed forces*, pp. 78–80.

85 Grushin, *Chetyre zhizni Rossii*, vol. 1, p. 84.
86 *Ibid.*, pp. 75–6.
87 *Ibid.*, p. 82.
88 Iu. V. Aksiutin, *Khrushchevskaia 'ottepel'' i obshchestvennye nastroeniia v SSSR v 1953-64 gg.* (Moscow: Rossiiskaia politicheskaia entsiklopediia, 2004), pp. 304–10.
89 Grushin, *Chetyre zhizni Rossii*, vol. 1, p. 108.
90 P. Jones, review, *Kritika: Explorations in Russian and Eurasian History* 8 (2007), pp. 695–704.
91 These ideas are explored more fully in M. Dobson, '"This Hellish Atomic Technology": Peace, Pacifism and Soviet Evangelicals in the Early Cold War', work in progress.
92 I. Paperno, *Stories of the Soviet Experience: Memoirs, Diaries, Dreams* (Ithaca, 2009), pp. 118–58.
93 *Ibid.*, p. 143.
94 *Ibid.*, p. 145.
95 *Ibid.*, pp. 143–4.
96 *Ibid.*, p. 146.
97 In her study of apocalyptic tropes in the religious subcultures in post-Soviet Russia, Mariia Akhmetova notes that the fears of atomic war were rare and she suggests that Chernobyl 'supplanted fear of the atomic war in late Soviet culture'. M. Akhmetova, *Konets sveta v odnoy otedel'no vziatoi strane: religioznye soobshchestva postsovetskoi Rossii i ikh eskhatalogicheskii mif* (Moscow, 2010), pp. 113–14.
98 S. Alexievich, *Voices from Chernobyl: The Oral History of a Nuclear Disaster*, trans. K. Gessen (New York, 2006), p. 217.
99 L. Viola, *Peasant Rebels Under Stalin: Collectivization and the Culture of Peasant Resistance* (New York, 1996), chapter 2; N. Werth, 'Rumeurs defaitistes et apocalyptiques dans l'URSS des années 1920 et 1930', *Vingtième Siècle* 71 (2001): 25–35; S. Smit [S. Smith], 'Nebesnye pis'ma i rasskazy o lese: 'sueveriia' protiv bol'shevizma', *Antropologicheskii forum* 3 (2005), pp. 280–306.
100 On this point, my argument differs from that of Johnston, who argues that 'the religious language of apocalyptic transformation' typical of the 1920s and 1930s was not present in the post-war period. See Johnston, *Being Soviet*, p. 137.
101 Russian State Archive of Social and Political History (hereafter RGASPI), f. 17 (Central Committee of the Communist Party of the Soviet Union), op. 132 (Propaganda and agitation section, 1948–53), d. 6 (memos, letters, articles, 1948–49), ll. 177–82.
102 RGASPI f. 17, op. 132, d. 285 (memos and information, 1950–51), ll. 96–9.
103 *Ibid.*, ll. 198–9.
104 A 1950 article by D. Zaslavskii piece compared American toy manufacturers to cannibals and invited Soviet readers to recoil in horror at the kind of

toys given to children in the USA, particularly a model city, which the child could destroy with the accompanying airplane and 'atomic bombs'. At least, Zaslavskii concluded bathetically, there are no Auschwitz or Majdanek gas chambers on sale yet. D. Zaslavskii, 'Igrushki Amerikanskikh gangsterov', *Pravda*, 21 Mar. 1950, p. 4.

105 Paperno, *Stories of the Soviet Experience*, p. 146.

4

Sixty years and counting: nuclear themes in American culture, 1945 to the present*
Paul Boyer (†)

In his 1978 autobiography, Arthur Koestler, author of the anti-Communist classic *Darkness at Noon*, wrote the following: 'If I were asked to name the most important date in the history and prehistory of the human race, I would answer without hesitation 6 August 1945. The reason is simple. From the dawn of consciousness until 6 August 1945, man had to live with the prospect of his death as an *individual*; since the day when the first atomic bomb outshone the sun over Hiroshima, mankind as a whole has had to live with the prospect of its extinction as a *species*.'[1] Today, more than sixty years after Hiroshima, we still grapple with the meaning of August 6, 1945, and all that followed.

The sixtieth anniversary of Hiroshima and Nagasaki found Americans at a disorienting moment in their long encounter with nuclear weapons. On one hand, nostalgia for the atomic age was everywhere. In 2004, Columbia Pictures released a special fortieth-anniversary DVD of the film *Dr. Strangelove*. 'Atomic Bomb' rings, offered for fifteen cents and a Kix cereal boxtop in 1947, were fetching fifty or sixty dollars on eBay, and the web site Conelrad.com featured an array of atomic age memorabilia. In what *Preservation* magazine in 2005 called a good example of 'survivalist chic', a Kansas couple converted a decommissioned Atlas E missile silo into an underground residence. A travel agency advertised a week of scuba diving off Bikini Atoll to explore the ships sunk in the 1946 atomic tests.[2]

Yet nuclear reality stubbornly resisted all efforts to relegate it to the past. Even under America's 2002 treaty with Russia, the United States will still possess six thousand nuclear warheads in 2012, twentytwo hundred of them fully armed – a total that would have horrified the atomic scientists of 1945. The George W. Bush administration, meanwhile, sought funds for 'robust nuclear earth penetrators', also known as 'bunker busters.' If the ultimate nightmare of global thermonuclear war had faded, nuclear proliferation remained a grave danger. Even as Americans grappled with post-September 11 fears of terrorists acquiring nuclear weapons or knowhow, concerns about aging nuclear reactors and how to dispose of tons of radioactive waste that will remain lethal for millennia added to citizens' nagging if ill-focused anxieties.[3]

So Americans felt ambivalent as they marked another anniversary of the fateful events of August 1945, longing to put the nuclear threat behind them yet uneasily aware that it remained a part of their present reality. Unsurprisingly, then, I have never been able to file away this topic, which I began to research in 1980. It still engages me, in all its chameleon-like variety. As I explore some of the ways the nuclear reality has shaped our culture over the years, I will advance two simple arguments. First, post-1945 American culture makes no sense without taking into account the atomic bomb. Second, this cultural impact has not been a constant. Over this sixty-year period it has waxed and waned, reflecting differing levels of public anxiety and political activism. Broadly speaking, our nuclear history falls into three cycles, each marked by a surge of political activism and cultural expression, followed by an interval of comparative quiescence and diminished attention.

The first cycle runs from August 6, 1945, to the mid-1950s. President Truman's announcement of the atomic bombing of Hiroshima – which he misleadingly called a 'military base' – and his revelation of the Manhattan Project unleashed a torrent of excited commentary. As a kid growing up in Dayton, Ohio, I recall reading aloud the newspaper headline about the 'A-*tome*-ic bomb' – mispronouncing the new word that would soon become very familiar. Amazement turned to celebration when Japan's surrender quickly followed the dropping of a second atomic bomb on Nagasaki on August 9. Truman and other high officials reinforced the natural conclusion that the atomic bomb had won the war and saved countless American lives. So did *The Beginning or the End*, a 1946 Hollywood film that purportedly revealed the story of the Manhattan Project and the decision to drop the bomb. Though increasingly questioned by historians, the belief that only the A-bomb had forestalled an inevitable invasion of Japan became an article of faith for millions, particularly veterans of the Pacific war.[4]

With the jubilation and relief, however, also came a surge of fear. The same weapon that had devastated two Japanese cities might one day be turned against the United States. Radio news commentators compared Hiroshima to U.S. cities of similar size, such as Denver and New Haven. Newspapers printed maps of their cities with concentric circles showing

Nuclear themes in American culture, 1945 to the present

the levels of destruction at Hiroshima and Nagasaki.⁵ Partially masking the terror was a surge of nervous humor and marketing hype – a predictable response to mortal danger. A radio comedian joked that Hiroshima looked worse than Ebbets Field after a game between the Giants and the Dodgers. Headline writers punned about Japan's 'atomic ache.' *Life* magazine named a sexy Hollywood starlet the '*anatomic* bomb.' In 1946, launching one of the atomic age's more enduring legacies, a French fashion designer christened his skimpy new bathing suit the bikini, after the Marshall Island atoll that was site of that year's U.S. atomic tests. By 1947, some forty businesses in New York City alone had appropriated the potent new word, including the Atomic Underwear Company.⁶

Beneath the surface froth, however, fear and sober second thoughts intruded. John Hersey's *Hiroshima*, published in the *New Yorker* in August 1946 and then in book form, reduced the abstraction of a devastated city to human terms by telling of six survivors and what they had witnessed. Hundreds of letters from shaken readers poured in.⁷ Radio networks devoted air time to uninterrupted readings of the work. In November 1946, *Life* magazine ran an illustrated feature, 'The Thirty-Six Hour War,' picturing New York City reduced to rubble by rocket-delivered atom bombs. *Life* and other media also warned that terrorists could smuggle in the components of an A-bomb, secretly assemble the bomb in a major city, and force the government to accept their demands.⁸

Atomic fear even surfaced in country music. The Buchanan Brothers' 1946 hit 'Atomic Power' begins, 'Oh, this world is at a tremble with its strength and mighty power/They're sending up to heaven to get the brimstone fire.'⁹ Indeed, many believers found atomic war foretold in Bible prophecies of the end times, such as in 2 Peter: 'The heavens shall pass away with a great noise, and the elements shall melt with fervent heat, the earth also and the works that are therein shall be burned up.'

Such fears fueled support for the Acheson-Lilienthal plan for the international control of atomic energy, presented to the United Nations in June 1946. Atomic scientists, capitalising on their newfound prestige, campaigned for international control as the only alternative to atomic war. The Federation of American Scientists made the case in *One World or None*, a collection of essays sold for a dollar. Some activists went further, arguing for world government. Hollywood belatedly promoted the cause with *The Day the Earth Stood Still*, a 1951 film in which space visitor Michael Rennie warns earthlings to form a global union to enforce peace or face annihilation, since their atomic tinkering threatens not only Earth but also the cosmos itself.¹⁰

By 1947, this initial wave of fear-driven activism and cultural attention was fading. As the Cold War began, Washington shifted from international control to building more bombs. With the Russian A-bomb test in 1949, Truman authorised development of the hydrogen bomb, a thousand times more powerful than the 1945 bombs. The public supported Truman's decision. Communisation had replaced vaporisation as the urgent threat. In 1951, as the Korean War dragged on, a majority of Americans favored dropping atomic bombs on 'military targets' in that Asian nation.[11]

The federal government, meanwhile, contributing to what psychiatrist Robert Jay Lifton would later call the process of 'nuclear numbing', promoted a two-pronged propaganda effort promising safety through civil defense and touting the atom's peacetime uses. Civil-defense handbooks such as the reassuring *You Can Survive an Atomic Bomb* (1950) insisted that with timely preparation, atomic war might not be so bad. At the same time, encouraged by David Lilienthal, head of the new Atomic Energy Commission (AEC), science writers and journalists glowingly described the atom's potential to heal the sick, produce bumper crops, control the weather, provide electricity too cheap to meter, and fuel cars, ships, and planes for pennies a year. Privately, Lilienthal brooded about the nuclear arms race; publicly, he played the cheerleader role.[12]

In 1947, CBS radio broadcast an hour-long program called 'The Sunny Side of the Atom.' In 1948, the AEC, General Electric, and Westinghouse organised a 'Man and the Atom' show in New York's Central Park featuring eye-catching exhibits and free propaganda, including a comic book called *Dagwood Splits the Atom*. The National Education Association pitched in with *Operation Atomic Vision*, an upbeat high school study unit.[13] By 1950, then, thanks to various developments, atomic fear was muted, the international control campaign was dead, and cultural attention to the bomb had faded.

The second cycle of nuclear history extends from the mid-1950s through the late 1970s. This cycle, too, saw an initial wave of fear, political activism, and cultural attention followed by an interval of diminished awareness. By the mid-1950s, Cold War hostilities, the deployment of Nike Hercules missiles around U.S. cities, and the race for more powerful intercontinental ballistic missiles (ICBMs) and more sophisticated warheads had reawakened fears of nuclear war. The 1961 Berlin crisis, not to mention the 1962 Cuban Missile Crisis, terrified millions. In this climate, the 'peaceful atom' and civil defense seemed cruel hoaxes. Indeed, the evidence suggests that civil-defense drills, fallout-shelter campaigns, and school films such as *Bert the Turtle*, far from offering reassurance, actually *heightened* anxiety.[14]

Along with generalised anxiety about nuclear war came a new and urgent cause for fear: radioactive fallout. The March 1954 U.S. H-bomb test at Bikini Atoll contaminated a wide area of the Pacific and brought radiation sickness and death to a Japanese fishing crew eighty miles away. As Strontium-90 and other blast byproducts dispersed through the atmosphere, radiation levels over North America increased. With its calcium-like properties, Strontium-90 concentrates in bone and teeth, especially in children. Scientists warned of contaminated rivers and pasture lands. Official denials failed to ease the public's fears. A *McCalls* article warned of 'Fallout, the Silent Killer.' The title of a *Saturday Evening Post* article minced no words: 'Radioactivity Is Poisoning Your Children.'[15]

A broad test-ban campaign soon arose. At Washington University in St. Louis, Barry Commoner organised the 'Baby Tooth Survey' to promote both medical research into radiation hazards and the test-ban cause. Children whose baby teeth were mailed in for analysis received a pin that read, 'I Gave My Tooth for Science.' The leading test-ban organisation, SANE, the National Committee for a Sane Nuclear Policy, was founded in 1957. In one memorable SANE ad, captioned 'Dr. Spock Is Worried,' the famed baby doctor peers with a worried expression at a winsome little girl. The text explained his concern: fallout threatened America's children.[16]

Once again, nuclear fear gripped the culture. Science fiction stories such as Walter Miller's 1959 novel *A Canticle for Leibowitz* explored post-nuclear war scenarios. Alain Resnais's 1959 movie *Hiroshima Mon Amour* intercut the wartime memories of a French actress making a film in Hiroshima, with grainy footage of the city after the A-bomb attack, reminding a new generation what the bomb could do. Stanley Kramer's 1959 film *On the Beach*, based on a novel by Nevil Shute, imagined the after-effects of a global thermonuclear war as a deadly radioactive cloud drifts towards Australia, where a few survivors await the end.[17] Government officials feared the political power of such cultural productions. A 1959 cabinet meeting presided over by Vice-President Richard Nixon discussed *On the Beach* and reviewed a memo sent to all U.S. embassies, advising them how to refute the film's antinuclear message.[18]

But the output continued. Sidney Lumet's *Fail-Safe* (1964), starring Henry Fonda and based on a novel by Eugene Burdick and Harvey Wheeler, somberly explored a scenario of accidental nuclear war. Stanley

Kubrick, with the help of writer Terry Southern and an inspired cast headed by Peter Sellers, treated the same subject as black comedy in *Dr. Strangelove*, also in 1964. With deadly serious intent, Kubrick satirised the strategic thinking of Herman Kahn of the RAND Corporation, a U.S. Air Force think tank. Some lines in *Strangelove* come directly from Kahn's 1960 book *On Thermonuclear War*. The gung-ho bluster of George C. Scott's Gen. Buck Turgidson eerily evoked the bombastic Curtis LeMay, head of the Strategic Air Command.[19] This cycle of nuclear fear inspired some of the most memorable songs of Tom Lehrer, a young Harvard mathematician turned satirist, such as 'We Will All Go Together When We Go':

> We will all go together when we go.
> What a comforting fact that is to know.
> Universal bereavement,
> An inspiring achievement,
> Yes, we will all go together when we go.

And who can forget the line from Lehrer's song 'Wernher von Braun'? "Once the rockets are up, who cares where they come down? That's not my department,' says Wernher von Braun.'[20]

Mad magazine in the late 1950s introduced a 'post-nuclear war hit parade' with the comment, 'These are the songs young couples of the future will hum as they walk down lovers' lane arm in arm *in arm*.' Several episodes of Rod Serling's TV series *The Twilight Zone* dealt with a post-nuclear war society or the social effects of nuclear fear.[21] In 1955, Ralph Edwards's popular TV show *This is Your Life* featured the so-called Hiroshima Maidens, twenty-five young women severely disfigured by the atomic blast, brought to the United States for cosmetic surgery. An *Enola Gay* crew member appeared on the show to present a check for the cause, and some twenty thousand viewers mailed in contributions.[22]

These years also saw a wave of mutant creature movies, beginning in 1954 with *Them!* and including such camp classics as *The Creature from the Black Lagoon*, *The Incredible Shrinking Man*, and *Attack of the Crab Monsters*. The Japanese contributed *Godzilla*, also in 1954. Typically, the mutants are the product of exposure to an atomic blast or nuclear radiation. The monster ants of *Them!* crawl from the Alamogordo test site. The 'incredible shrinking man' begins to shrivel after his sailboat encounters a glowing radioactive cloud. Godzilla is jolted from his slumber in Tokyo Harbor by the atomic bomb.[23] The link between this genre and the era's pervasive nuclear fear is obvious.

Nuclear themes in American culture, 1945 to the present

As in 1945–46, marketers exploited the revived nuclear awareness. In 1954, amid news of H-bomb tests, Chicago's Ferrara Pan Candy Company launched a new product called the Atomic Fireball. Responding to my query, President Nello Ferrara wrote, 'Our candy piece known as the 'Atomic Fireball' was first introduced as a penny item in 1954. We have many letters [from] … university campuses, such as 'You get a better blast out of atomic fireball than … from a puff of marijuana.' We make no claims of preventing the use of marijuana, but I am personally quite confident that many young people went the fireball route who might have gone the marijuana route. I trust this answers your inquiry, and trust you are enjoying atomic fireballs as millions of Americans are presently doing.'[24]

This second wave of political activism and cultural attention to the bomb faded after 1963, when the United States, Russia, and Great Britain agreed to ban atmospheric nuclear tests. Underground testing continued, and the treaty certainly did not end the danger of nuclear war. But it did address fallout fears and signaled that the superpowers were at least trying to subject the arms race to rational control. The 1972 Strategic Arms Limitation Treaty (SALT I) and Anti-Ballistic Missile Treaty held out further hope that Washington and Moscow were cautiously cooperating to avoid nuclear catastrophe. As fears of fallout and of nuclear war diminished, other issues assumed more urgency, most notably, of course, the Vietnam War and the domestic unrest it unleashed. In the mid-1970s, the Watergate crisis and soaring fuel prices further absorbed the nation's political attention. Once, again, however, the tide turned and nuclear dangers again rose to prominence in the public's awareness.

The final cycle of nuclear activism and cultural attention arose in the late 1970s. Once again, as in the mid-1950s, this cycle had specific causes, now including rising fears of nuclear proliferation. As early as 1965, after France and China had conducted nuclear tests, Tom Lehrer in his song 'Who's Next?' had speculated that Alabama might become the next nuclear power. By the late 1970s, despite the 1970 Nuclear Non-proliferation Treaty, India had tested a 'nuclear device' and Israel, Libya, Pakistan, South Africa, South Korea, and other nations harbored nuclear ambitions. As for the superpower arms-control process, it stalled in 1979, when President Jimmy Carter withdrew the SALT II agreement from the Senate after the Soviet invasion of Afghanistan.

Also worrisome was the safety of the nuclear-power industry, once the poster child for the promise of atomic energy. In 1974, in a dramatic act of civil disobedience, young Sam Lovejoy toppled a five-hundred-foot weather tower in western Massachusetts erected as part of a planned nuclear-power plant. By the late 1970s, protests against nuclear power erupted from coast to coast. The movement gained momentum in 1979, when an accident at the Three Mile Island nuclear-power plant in Pennsylvania coincided with the Jane Fonda film *China Syndrome*, featuring the meltdown of a California nuclear-power plant following an earthquake.[25]

With this background, Ronald Reagan's election as president in 1980 proved the tipping point for a renewed round of activism against nuclear weapons. To many citizens, Reagan's first term seemed a return to the darkest days of the Cold War. The arms-control process languished, Reagan denounced the Soviet Union as an 'evil empire,' and Secretary of State Alexander Haig warned of 'nuclear warning shots' if Russia menaced Western Europe. In addition, civil-defense officials pushed the idea of crisis relocation, whereby city dwellers would descend on designated small towns in a nuclear emergency. As before, the more the government talked of civil defense, the more nervous people became.

The predictable result was yet another wave of political activism and cultural attention addressing nuclear threats. On the political front, millions rallied to the nuclear weapons freeze campaign, urging the nuclear powers to halt all nuclear weapons research and development while seriously pursuing arms-reduction talks. Beginning in New England town meetings in the winter of 1981, the freeze idea spread rapidly. Half a million people attended a freeze rally in New York's Central Park, and Wisconsin, California, and other states passed nuclear-freeze referenda in November 1982.[26]

As before, the popular culture quickly reflected and amplified the new mood. *Time* magazine featured a mushroom cloud on its cover for the first time in years. A 1982 episode of CBS's popular *Lou Grant* show, set in a Los Angeles newspaper office, challenging the administration's vision of orderly crisis relocation, portrayed the panic and chaos that even a *rumor* of nuclear attack would likely unleash in a crowded metropolis. At least nine novels and some forty science fiction stories of the early 1980s explored themes related to nuclear war.[27]

In the 1983 movie *War Games*, a Pentagon computer misreads incoming data, nearly triggering nuclear war. In Tom Clancy's 1984 novel *The Hunt for Red October*, made into a film starring Sean Connery, the captain of a Soviet nuclear sub, Marko Ramius tries to defect rather than launch his missiles against the United States as ordered. Ramius himself becomes the target when the KGB feeds misleading information to Washington. These popular-culture products both reflected and intensified the public's sense that the combination of massive nuclear arsenals, human fallibility, and error-prone technology created a high risk of nuclear disaster – the same fear that had inspired *Fail-Safe* and *Dr. Strangelove* twenty years earlier.

The Day After, a 1983 ABC-TV special starring Jason Robards and watched by millions of viewers, portrayed the after-effects of a nuclear strike on a Kansas missile base (Senator Barry Goldwater complained that *The Day After* had shown only 'the negative side of nuclear weapons.') Jonathan Schell's 1982 bestseller *The Fate of the Earth* first serialised in the *New Yorker*, imagined a post-nuclear war planet where only insects survive.[28]

Nuclear fear seeped into early 1980s pop music. In 'Walking in Your Footsteps' (1983), the British rock star Sting (Gordon Sumner) compared the dinosaurs' fate to that of the human race if nuclear war broke out:

> Hey mighty Brontosaurus,
> Don't you have you a message for us?
> ...
> Walking in your footsteps.

Sting's 1984 song 'Russians' included the line 'How can I save my little boy/from Oppenheimer's deadly toy?' For early 1980s culture producers, the winning weapon of 1945 had become a fearsome menace. Like the first two cycles of America's nuclear history, however, this one also proved short lived, thanks in part to President Reagan. In March 1983, to the surprise of the Pentagon, Reagan proposed his Strategic Defense Initiative, a seductive vision of rendering nuclear weapons 'impotent and obsolete' by a network of detection satellites, space-based lasers, and computer-guided antimissile missiles. Scientists derided Reagan's 'Star Wars' proposal as a Buck Rogers fantasy, and indeed, the seventy billion dollars spent on SDI research since 1983 has produced little.[29] But his speech proved a brilliant move politically, neutralising the freeze campaign by shifting the debate from *eliminating* nuclear weapons to defending *against* them. Even more important, the world situation changed dramatically as the 1980s wore on. With Mikhail Gorbachev in charge in Moscow, the Berlin Wall came down in 1989 and the Soviet empire collapsed. The Cold War had ended with breathtaking suddenness, and with it, the threat of global thermonuclear war dramatically diminished.

Under these radically altered circumstances, nuclear themes did not disappear from the culture, but they took new forms, including a kind of nostalgia. As Harry Angstrom muses in John Updike's 1990 novel *Rabbit at Rest*, 'I miss it, the Cold War. It gave you a reason to get up in the morning.' In Don DeLillo's sprawling 1997 novel *Underworld*, which one reviewer called 'a wake for the Cold War,' the bomb, nuclear tests, and the Cuban Missile Crisis are revisited in a great bouillabaisse of atomic age memories. In one vivid passage, DeLillo writes of the metal tags that were issued to schoolchildren: 'The tags were designed to help rescue workers identify children who were lost, missing, injured, maimed, mutilated, unconscious or dead in the hours following the onset of atomic war ... Now that they had the tags, their names inscribed on wispy tin, the [civil defense] drill was not a remote exercise but was all about them, and so was atomic war.'[30] The video-game industry clung to the Cold War. Several urban-combat video games of the 1990s were set in cities devastated by nuclear attack. Ads for MDK, a popular game of the later 1990s, featured images of blasted cities and grimly proclaimed, 'On a good day, only 1.5 billion people will die.'[31]

A gentler kind of nostalgia emerged in the TV series *The Simpsons*. In a 1991 episode recalling the once-urgent issue of nuclear-power safety, Homer Simpson manages by sheer dumb luck to prevent a meltdown at the nuclear power plant where he works. (He plays 'eenie-meenie-miney-moe' to decide which button to push.) In a 1995 *Simpsons* episode called 'Sideshow Bob's Last Gleaming,' an embittered former TV clown discovers a discarded nuclear warhead in a trash can during a U.S. Air Force base open house. Furious that his show has been cancelled, he threatens to detonate the bomb unless all TV is eliminated. When Lisa Simpson pleads, 'Don't do it. That would be taking the easy way out,' he replies, 'I quite agree' and pulls the pin. But nothing happens. Bob has missed the consumer-advisory notice pasted on the bomb: 'Best if used before 1959.'[32]

This episode offered an array of atomic age memories. In a world without TV, one character mutters, 'The survivors will envy the dead' – Nikita Khrushchev's much quoted comment about nuclear war. As Sideshow Bob tries to detonate the bomb, he whistles, 'We'll Meet Again,' the World War II song Stanley Kubrick recycled in *Dr. Strangelove*. As the episode unfolds, little Maggie Simpson plucks petals from a daisy, evoking the famous anti-Goldwater TV campaign commercial of 1964. Along with Cold War nostalgia, the popular culture of the 1990s also addressed – or exploited – nuclear issues that still remained, including terrorism and instability in the former Soviet Union. The 1995 movie *Crimson Tide*, for example, dealt with chaos in post-Cold War Russia, as ultranationalists seize the nuclear submarine base at Vladivostok and threaten to nuke the United States. When garbled orders reach a U.S. nuclear sub, conflict erupts between the by-the-book captain, played by Gene Hackman, who is determined to launch a nuclear counterattack, and his executive officer, Denzel Washington, who urges caution. Other nuclear-themed mass-culture products of the 1990s focused on rogue states and terrorist groups. In Tom Clancy's 1991 novel *The Sum of all Fears*, Palestinians funded by Iran set off a nuclear blast at the Denver Skydome during the Super Bowl, hoping the United States will blame Russia and revive the Cold War. In the 1994 Arnold Schwarzenegger action film *True Lies*, Islamic fundamentalists acquire a nuclear warhead and threaten to obliterate Florida unless their demands are met. Needless to say, Ah-nold saves the day. In the 1997 film *The Peacemaker*, George Clooney and Nicole Kidman outwit a Croatian Muslim terrorist who steals a nuclear missile from a Russian military train.

In other post-Cold War cultural products, home-grown loners threaten nuclear destruction. In the 1992 film *Under Siege*, a disgruntled former CIA agent commandeers a U.S. Navy ship transporting nuclear missiles headed for deactivation. In *Broken Arrow* (1996), John Travolta, an air force pilot embittered by low pay and lack of respect, takes off with two nuclear warheads and threatens to obliterate Denver. As Americans coped with the mysterious Unabomber and the bombing of the Oklahoma City federal office building, this theme touched a nerve.[33]

Indeed, the shadowy menaces that loom large in the nuclear-themed cultural products of the 1990s mirrored the mood of the decade. During the Cold War, the adversary was at least a nation-state headed by rational leaders with whom one could negotiate. In the volatile and destabilised post-Cold War world, lethal menace could lurk anywhere, and the popular culture reflected the resulting anxieties. Another characteristic of the nuclear-themed cultural material of the 1990s is its exploitive, opportunistic quality. Many of the earlier cultural products we have noted – *Hiroshima*, *A Canticle for Leibowitz*, *On the Beach*, *Fail-Safe*, *Dr. Strangelove*, *The Day After*, the songs of Tom Lehrer and Sting – were serious in intent, addressing the bomb's awesome destructive power and the threat to human survival itself.

The movies and mass-market novels of the 1990s that appropriated nuclear themes lack this dimension for the most part. The nuclear threat in movies such as *True Lies* or *The Peacemaker* is a cheesy plot device, not a viscerally felt reality. Nuclear danger in video games was simply a gimmick for pumping up the adrenaline of those too young to remember the real fears of the early 1980s, let alone the 'duck and cover' years of their parents' generation.

This triviality is particularly evident in such blockbuster movies as *Independence Day* (1996), in which scientists try to use nuclear explosions to destroy an alien spaceship hovering over Washington, D.C., or *Armageddon* (1998), in which Bruce Willis is rocketed up to plant a thermonuclear bomb on an asteroid to deflect it from a collision course with Earth. With movies such as these, the mushroom cloud becomes simply another special effect, not a cautionary warning. One exception to this rule was the 1991 film *Rhapsody in August* by the venerable Japanese director Akira Kurasawa. As an old woman of Nagasaki tours the city with her grandchildren, she suddenly relives the moment of the atomic-bomb blast, when she herself was young. But the experience seared in her memory is lost on the carefree, uncomprehending children.

Despite the fading of nuclear fear in the 1990s, the events of August 1945 could still rouse deep emotions, as in the 1995 dispute over the Smithsonian Institution's planned exhibit of the *Enola Gay* – a controversy that pitted many historians against politicians and veterans' organisations.[34] As William Faulkner once said, 'The past is not dead; in fact, it is not even past.'

Then came September 11, not the all-out nuclear attack Americans had long feared, but an assault involving the most mundane weapons imaginable: box cutters available in any hardware store and commercial aircraft turned into death-dealing missiles. Later attacks hit Bali, Madrid, and London, all employing similarly lowtech weaponry, including homemade bombs carried in backpacks. After September 11, the nuclear awareness that had persisted in the popular culture through the 1990s largely faded. The nuclear issues of the early twenty-first century, though menacing enough, lacked the mind-concentrating clarity and emotional power of 'global thermonuclear war' – the nightmare that, with good reason, so terrified Cold War Americans. By contrast, the nuclear realities of the early twenty-first century were confusing and murky: Pakistan, whose top nuclear scientist admitted to funneling vital information to Iran, Libya, and other states, stood as America's staunch ally in the 'war on terror.' Iran and North Korea used their on-again, off-again nuclear programs as bargaining chips, symbols of national pride, or proof of their determination to stand up to America. Experts even puzzled over Brazil's secretive uranium-enrichment program.[35]

As for U.S. nuclear weapons policy, the United States (along with Russia) still stockpiled many thousands of nuclear warheads, and as we have seen, the George W. Bush administration pushed for new tactical nuclear weapons for actual battlefield use and pursued a determined and extremely costly missile defense program, including not only long-range research on space-based system – Reagan's original dream – but also actual land-based deployment of anti-missile-missiles in Alaska and Eastern Europe, with all its destabilising potential.[36] And the debate over nuclear-waste disposal dragged on, involving mind-numbing technical studies about rates of water seepage in the Nevada desert.

Serious as these issues were, they hardly stimulated the apocalyptic, gut-churning sense of menace that had once gripped the imagination of a John Hersey, a Stanley Kubrick, or a Rod Serling. They remained the arcane preoccupation of diplomats, agency bureaucrats, technical experts, and think-tank intellectuals, largely below the general public's cultural radar. In the build-up to the Iraq war, the administration deliberately played the nuclear card. National Security Advisor Condoleezza Rice, justifying the pre-emptive invasion of Iraq, warned ominously, 'We don't want the smoking gun to be a mushroom cloud.'[37] As the manipulative aim of that strategy became evident, and Iraq's current nuclear program proved largely illusory, the task of focusing public attention on *actual* nuclear dangers grew more difficult. Citizens jaded by the propagandistic use of imagined nuclear stockpiles and 'mushroom cloud' imagery grew blasé about nuclear issues that did cry out for attention. John Kerry in the 2004 campaign called nuclear proliferation the gravest danger the nation faced, but the public mood did not reflect a similar sense of urgency. In the frustrating aftermath of September 11, Americans' fears of 'terrorism' and 'weapons of mass destruction' were both real and amorphous, undermining citizens' ability to focus clearly on specific issues.

In such uneasy times, the nation's culture producers had difficulty finding ways to deal imaginatively with shadowy and complex threats. In contrast to earlier eras, a fundamental disconnect arose between politics and the popular culture. While the administration sternly called upon Americans to fight the 'War on Terror' at home and abroad, the mass culture offered mainly escapist fare. The *Left Behind* series of prophecy novels, envisioning an apocalyptic end of history in which Christ will gather up the righteous into the heavens and annihilate the evildoers at Armageddon, sold tens of millions of copies.[38] A vogue of so-called reality TV programs studiously avoided reality. The most popular movies in the four years after September 11 included *Finding Nemo*, an animated cartoon of a fish who survives various dangers as he finds his way home to the Great Barrier Reef; *Revenge of the Sith*, the conclusion of George Lucas's Star Wars epic; the *Harry Potter* and *Lord of the Rings* fantasies; and films featuring animated comic-book superheroes: *Spider Man*, *Batman*, the *Incredibles* and the *Fantastic Four*. This process of cultural avoidance and displacement came full circle with Steven Spielberg's *War of the Worlds* (2000), an update of H. G. Wells's tale of Martian invaders that had so terrified radio listeners in 1938. In Spielberg's version, the government is no help; like Kevin McCarthy at the end of *Invasion of the Body Snatchers* (1956), Mr Everyman, Tom Cruise, is on his own.

The era when the popular culture offered entertainment while addressing serious issues, including nuclear dangers, seemed remote indeed. But if the past offered any guidance, the nation's culture creators could be expected to again find their voice, once more devising imaginative ways to address the nuclear dangers that still hovered ominously on the broader landscape of menace that is the contemporary world. Whatever the future holds, one thing is clear about the past: If we are to understand the full meaning and impact of the nuclear weapons created more than sixty years ago at Los Alamos, Hanford, Chicago and Oak Ridge, we must look at more than the actions of scientists, politicians, generals, strategists, and diplomats. We must also extend our horizon to include the arts and the humanities, and even the raucous arena of mass entertainment. Attention to the culture, as well as to politics and strategy, is essential to understanding how the Manhattan Project changed America.

Notes

* Paul Boyer's "Sixty years and counting: nuclear themes in American culture, 1945 to the present" originally appeared in *The Atomic Bomb and American Society: New Perspectives*, edited by Rosemary B. Mariner and G. Kurt Piehler. Copyright © 2009 by The University of Tennessee Press. Reprinted by permission.

1 A. Koestler, *Janus. A Summing Up* (New York, 1978), p. 1.
2 C. Le Beau, 'Down home: converted Cold War missile sites combine brilliant adaptive use with Survivalist Chic', *Preservation* (2004), pp. 33–37; E. Hanauer, 'Return to Bikini', *EScuba*, 15 Aug. 2005, www.escuba.com/articles/index.asp?WCI=Articler&WCE=7 (accessed 9 March 2008).
3 The literature on post-Cold War nuclear dangers and controversies is vast. For an introduction, see G. Allison, *Nuclear Terrorism: The Ultimate Preventable Catastrophe* (New York, 2004); R. E. Powaski, *Return to Armageddon: The United States and the Nuclear Arms Race, 1981-1999* (New York, 2003); B. R. Schneider and W. L. Dowdy, eds., *Pulling Back from the Nuclear Brink: Reducing and Countering Nuclear Threats* (London, 1998); B. Phelan, 'Buried truths: debunking the nuclear 'bunker buster', *Harper's Magazine*, Dec. 2004, pp. 70–72; 'Trouble in the nest: George Bush's nuclear plans', *Economist*, 30 Apr. 2005, pp. 26–27; 'Still the stuff of nightmares: securing Russia's loose nukes', *Economist*, 18 June 2005, p. 29; and 'Who scares the rest? See bottom left', *New York Times*, 8 May 2005, News of the Week in Review, 4 (chart of world's nuclear weapons arsenals, arranged by nation); B. Keller, 'Nuclear nightmares', *New York Times Magazine*, 26 May 2001, pp. 22–29, p. 51.

Nuclear themes in American culture, 1945 to the present

4 J. G. Shaheen, ed., *Nuclear War Films* (Carbondale, 1978), pp. 3–10; P. Boyer, *By the Bomb's Early Light: American Thought and Culture at the Dawn if the Atomic Age*, 2nd ed. (Chapel Hill, 1994), pp. 185–87, pp. 194–95; P. Boyer, 'Whose history is it anyway? Memory, politics, and historical scholarship,' in E. T. Linenthal and T. Engelhardt (eds), *History Wars: The Enola Gay and Other Battles for the American Past* (New York, 1996), pp. 115–39.

5 D. Goddard, CBS radio news broadcast, 6 Aug. 1945, in *Atomic War/Atomic Peace: Life the Nuclear Age* (Princeton, 1975), cassette 2, side 2; [N. Cousins], 'Modern man is obsolete,' *Saturday Review of Literature*, 18 Aug. 1945; *Milwaukee Journal*, 8 Aug. 1945, p. 12; Boyer, *By the Bomb's Early Light*, pp. 12–16.

6 'Gags away,' *New Yorker*, 18 Aug. 1945, p. 16; *Life*, 3 September 1945, p. 53 ('anatomic bomb' photo); Boyer, *By the Bomb's Early Light*, pp. 12–16.

7 M. Yavenditti, 'John Hersey and the American conscience: the reception of Hiroshima,' *Pacific Historical Review*, 43 (1974), p. 32, p. 34; Boyer, *By the Bomb's Early Light*, pp. 203–10.

8 'The 36-Hour War,' *Life*, 19 Nov. 1945, pp. 22ff.

9 C. Wolfe, 'Nuclear country: the atomic bomb in country music,' *Journal of Country Music*, 7 (1978), p. 11.

10 Boyer, *By the Bomb's Early Light*, pp. 27–81, p. 104.

11 *Ibid.*, pp. 337–40.

12 R. J. Lifton, *Death in Life: Survivors of Hiroshima* (New York, 1967); R. H. Gerstel, *How to Survive an Atomic Bomb* (Washington, D.C., 1950); Boyer, *By the Bomb's Early Light*, pp. 109–21 (hopeful visions atomic future), pp. 294–95, p. 349 (Lilienthal).

13 'The Sunny Side of the Atom,' CBS radio broadcast, 30 June 1947, transcript, Folder 14, Box 19, Papers of the Atomic Scientists of Chicago, Regenstein Library, University of Chicago; J. Musial, *Learn How Dagwood Splits the Atom!* (New York, 1949); H. M. Evans et al., *Operation Atomic Vision* (Washington, D.C., 1948); Boyer, *By the Bomb's Early Light*, pp. 296–97 ('Man and the Atom' exhibit). For a somewhat later example of similar reassuring material, see H. Haber, *The Walt Disney Story of Our Friend the Atom* (New York, 1956).

14 D. Garrison, *From Duck and Cover to Duct Tape: The Myth of Civil Defense in the Nuclear Age* (New York, 2005); K. D. Rose, *One Nation Underground: The Fallout Shelter in American Culture* (New York, 2001). The 1982 documentary film *Atomic Café* by Jayne Loader and Kevin Rafferty offers a rich array of archival film and music relating to the civil-defense activities of the late 1950s and early 1960s, as does the Internet web site Conelrad.com.

15 Boyer, *By the Bomb's Early Light*, pp. 352–53.

16 P. Boyer, *Fallout: A Historian Reflects on America's Half Century Encounter with Nuclear Weapons* (Columbus, 1998), pp. 83–84.

17 M. Broderick, *Nuclear Movies: A Filmography* (Northcote, 1988), pp. 56–57; J. F. Shapiro, *Atomic Bomb Cinema: The Apocalyptic Imagination on Film* (New York, 2002), pp. 89–94 (On the Beach).

18 Cabinet Meeting, 11 Dec. 1959, p. 2, Eisenhower Presidential Library, Abilene, Kans., cited in Boyer, *Fallout*, p. 110. At this cabinet meeting, Leo Hoegh, director of the Office of Civil Defense Management, denounced *On the Beach* as 'very harmful because it produced a feeling of utter hopelessness, thus undermining OCDM's efforts to encourage preparedness on the part of all citizens.'
19 Broderick, *Nuclear Movies*, p. 65, p. 66; Shapiro, *Atomic Bomb Cinema*, pp. 147–48, pp. 143–53, pp. 158–60, pp. 166–68; P. Boyer, 'Dr. Strangelove,' in *Past Imperfect: History According to the Movies*, ed. M. C. Carnes (New York, 1995), pp. 266–69; L. Menand, 'Fat Man: Herman Kahn and the Nuclear Age,' *New Yorker*, 27 June 2005, p. 96.
20 'We Will All Go Together When We Go,' on the album *An Evening (Wasted) with Tom Lehrer*, Lehrer Records, 959; 'Wernher Von Braun' on the album *That Was the Year That Was*, Reprise/Warner Brothers, 1965. For lyrics, see 'Tom Lehrer Song Lyrics,' http://members.aol.com/quentncree/lehrerl (accessed 9 March 2008).
21 *Like Mad* (New York, 1973), p. 16 (paperback collection of *Mad* magazine features from 1956 to 1960); M. S. Zacree, *The Twilight Zone Companion* (New York, 1982). For episodes dealing with nuclear-war themes see pp. 66–70, pp. 72–73, pp. 90–92, pp. 226–27, and pp. 263–65.
22 R. Barker, *The Hiroshima Maidens: A Story of Courage, Compassion, and Survival* (New York, 1985).
23 Shapiro, *Atomic Bomb Cinema*, pp. 111–12, pp. 225–27 (*Godzilla*); Boyer, *Fallout*, p. 110, p. 200.
24 Nello V. Ferrara to author, 6 March 1985.
25 J. S. Walker, *Three Mile Island: A Nuclear Crisis in Historical Perspective* (Berkeley and Los Angeles, 2004).
26 M. Kazin, 'The freeze: from strategy to social movement,' in P. Joseph and S. Rosenblum (eds), *Search for Sanity: The Politics of Nuclear Weapons and Disarmament* (Boston, 1984), pp. 445–61; F. Butterfield, 'Anatomy of the nuclear protest,' *New York Times Magazine*, 11 July 1982, pp. 14–17, pp. 32–39; Boyer, *By the Bomb's Early Light*, pp. 359–61.
27 *Time* cover and lead story, 29 March 1982; P. Brians, *Nuclear Holocausts: Atomic War in Fiction, 1895–1984* (Kent, Ohio, 1987), pp. 362–64; Boyer, *By the Bomb's Early Light*, pp. 361–62.
28 J. Schell, *The Fate of the Earth* (New York, 1982); Boyer, *By the Bomb's Early Light*, pp. 361–62.
29 'Defense missile for U.S. system fails to launch,' *New York Times*, 16 Dec. 2004, p. 1; F. Fitzgerald, 'Indefensible,' *New Yorker*, 4 Oct. 2004, pp. 33–34; D. G. Kimball, 'The nuclear arms control legacy of Ronald Reagan,' *Arms Control Today*, July/Aug. 2004. For the text of Reagan's March 23, 1983, address proposing the Strategic Defense Initiative, see P. Boyer (ed.) *Reagan as President: Contemporary Views of the Man, His Politics, and His Policies* (Chicago, 1990), pp. 207–8.

30 D. DeLillo, *Underworld* (New York, 1997); quoted passage cited by M. Amis in *New York Times Book Review*, 5 Oct. 1997, p. 12.
31 P. Boyer and E. Idsvoog, 'Nuclear menace in the mass culture of the late Cold War era and beyond,' in Boyer, *Fallout*, pp. 208–10, p. 214 (MDK quote on p. 209). See also P. Boyer, 'Apocalypse now,' *Washington Post Magazine*, pp. 14–18, p. 31, for a more extended discussion of nuclear themes in post-Cold War video games.
32 Boyer and Idsvoog, 'Nuclear menace,' p. 217, p. 219.
33 M. Broderick, 'Is this the sum of our fears? Nuclear imagery in post-Cold War cinema,' in S. C. Zeman and M. A. Amundson (eds), *Atomic Culture: How We Learned to Stop Worrying and Love the Bomb* (Boulder, 2004), pp. 125–48; Boyer and Isdvoog, 'Nuclear menace,' pp. 210–25.
34 Linenthal and Engelhardt (eds), *History Wars*.
35 'If Brazil wants to scare the world, it's succeeding,' *New York Times, News if the Week in Review*, 31 Oct. 2004.
36 See note 3 above, and P. Boyer, 'Selling star wars: Ronald Reagan's Strategic Defense Initiative,' in K. Osgood and A. K. Frank (eds), *Selling War in a Media Age: The Presidency and Public Opinion in the American Century* (Gainesville, 2010), pp. 196–223.
37 CNN.com, 'Top Bush officials push case against Saddam,' 8 Sept. 2002. http://archives.cnn.com/zooz/ALLPOLITICS/o9/o8/iraq.debate (accessed 19 March 2008).
38 T. LaHaye and J. B. Jenkins, *Left Behind: A Novel if the Earth's Last Days* (Wheaton, Ill., 1996). This was the first of a twelve-volume series of end-of-the world novels loosely based on Bible prophecy. The final volume, *Glorious Appearing: The End if Days*, was published in 2004. All told, the *Left Behind* books had sold in excess of sixty million copies by late 2000s, plus many spin-off products, including aversion for young people, CDs, DVDs, a movie, and Internet web sites.

5

The imaginative landscape of nuclear war in Britain, 1945–65

Matthew Grant

The prospect of nuclear destruction was a central, defining part of the British experience in the years following the Second World War. Fighting the Cold War was not solely the task of diplomats, spies, or even 'cultural front' organisations. Fighting a third total war in the lifetime of many in Britain seemed a very real prospect. At the heart of Britain's Cold War was the risk of being attacked with nuclear weapons. The diplomatic and military strategy of Britain throughout the conflict concentrated on an openness to negotiation which often outpaced its allies, and a belief that Soviet aggression could only be fully curtailed through armed strength and diplomatic will.[1] Nuclear weapons were central to this strategy, enshrining the nation's ability and willingness to risk a nuclear confrontation. From the mid-1950s, Britain's possession of the deterrent amounted to virtually its only military strategy, and ever since it has been safeguarded by successive governments more mindful of its symbolic prestige than of its actual military worth.[2] Deterrence through nuclear strength may have been official British policy, but it was one actively resisted by sections of the British public, with a mass protest mobilised by the Campaign for Nuclear Disarmament from 1958.[3] The history of nuclear weapons in Britain is the history of a nation preparing for a war that never came: but its absence was far from inevitable, and the anxieties and fears – the expectations, even, for some – about a future war were a real and deep-seated part of post-war British life. These responses to the threat of nuclear war, ranging from cultural anxiety and protest to political and military decisions about deterrent strategy, relied on and were shaped by ideas about the nature of nuclear war that were rooted not only in scientific and technical knowledge but in deep-seated cultural, social and political assumptions. The entire history of the British experience of nuclear weapons, from Cabinet discussions to street-level demonstrations, was determined by how nuclear war was imagined.

The imaginative landscape of nuclear war in Britain, 1945–65

For many, the process of mentally mapping nuclear destruction was a relatively straightforward one: there would be nothing to map – such was the destructiveness of these weapons. This was a vision of the nuclear future that was often put forward by opponents of nuclear weapons. In *Has Man a Future?*, Bertrand Russell noted 'I am writing at a dark moment (July 1961), and it is impossible to know whether the human race will last long enough for what I write to be published.'[4] This apocalyptic imagining of nuclear war was widespread in the years following the hydrogen bomb, characterising debate about 'mutually assured destruction'. It was used by proponents of deterrence as much as by opponents of the policy, with former Chief of the Air Staff John Slessor arguing in 1957 that as a war fought with hydrogen bombs would cause a 'global holocaust', it was 'arguable that the deterrent would even be strengthened by the knowledge that nuclear war would have such appalling results'.[5] The belief that a future war would obliterate all life was also prevalent in the years immediately following Hiroshima, when a stream of politicians, journalists and thinkers all joined the chorus calling for a revolution in human affairs to stop the world from being obliterated by the new weapon.[6]

Such ideas dominated the way in which nuclear destruction has been understood throughout most of the 'nuclear era'. Yet this was not the only manner in which nuclear war was imagined. The certainty expressed by some masks the fact that the 'reality' of nuclear destruction was contested throughout the Cold War by variety of groups and individuals who believed that nuclear war would not destroy the world, or eliminate civilisation, but would be survived by millions of people. Many of these people were associated with civil defence in some form. The government actively promoted civil defence as a means by which nuclear attack could be survived, founding the Civil Defence Corps in 1949 to recruit and train volunteers. It had half a million members at its peak in 1955, and still retained in excess of 120,000 when it was scrapped in 1968.[7] The belief in the ability of the nation and individuals to survive an attack was especially marked after 1948, in the years following the initial wave of atomic bomb pessimism. This view was promoted in government civil defence propaganda, but was also firmly rooted in an immediate frame of reference that struck deeply in the British public's imagination: namely the legacy of the Second World War. Atomic destruction was elided with the effect of the Blitz on British cities in political and popular culture in complex ways, linking contemporary issues with the mental and physical landscape of the 'people's war'. Although based on a narrative of victory rather than of defeat and occupation, the memory of the war is equally as essential to early history of Britain's Cold War as it is to the history of the conflict in continental Europe.[8]

As we shall see, this vision of atomic bomb warfare as a repeat of the Blitz was not sustained in the thermonuclear era, but even after 1954 there were people happy to argue that it was possible to survive all-out thermonuclear war. These views, although held by an increasingly small, civil defence-led minority, were nevertheless common into the 1960s. Thus, when nuclear war was imagined in the first decade and a half of the Cold War, it was not automatically assumed that it would lead to the destruction of the world, humanity or even necessarily the individual. After 1954, however, narratives that emphasised the impossibility of survival dominated discussions of nuclear issues, influencing social and political choices about the conflict and Britain's role in it. This chapter focuses on how nuclear war was imagined from 1945 until the 1960s, analysing an enormous shift in the place of nuclear weapons in British culture – from a contested and complex mixture of ideas to the increasingly prevalent and monolithic view of nuclear weaponry as a potentially world-ending phenomenon.

The debates were based on contrasting ways of imagining nuclear conflict: on whether it could be survived or whether it would destroy civilisation. In 1946, the scientist Jacob Bronowski argued that after Hiroshima 'there has been a danger of drifting into arguments in which exaggerated rumours are countered by equally wild understatements'.[9] Such oscillations between exaggeration and understatement typified ways of seeing nuclear war between 1945 and the mid-1960s, a result of the centrality of imagining nuclear war within political discourse. At the same time, however, there was a genuine difficulty in conceptualising destruction. There was undoubtedly a struggle to imagine the bomb's impact on the British physical and social landscape: those that attempted it seemed consciously or unconsciously to either map the experience of the Second World War onto the atomic future, or else struggle with an imaginative void which could be filled only by imagining the end of the world. Analysing the results of such attempts to imagine nuclear war helps us confront several key issues in the history of the Cold War. First, the difficulties in confronting the issue of nuclear war and the problematic nature of 'imagining' it created opposing visions of nuclear war which were equally 'imagined' and removed from the truth. This bifurcated way of imagining nuclear war underpinned political choices made about nuclear deterrence. Second, imaginings of nuclear war explain the development of

The imaginative landscape of nuclear war in Britain, 1945–65

government policies on nuclear deterrence and civil defence, especially the belief that nuclear weapons enhanced British power and prestige in an age of 'superpowers'. Finally, the very difficulties in imagining nuclear war may help explain the paucity of attempts to conceptualise the issue, as people turned away from the prospect of destruction. Overall, the nuclear conflict was at its heart an imaginary war, based on contested symbols and ideas. But it was also very real: the mental landscape of nuclear destruction was rooted in the lived experience of a population that had experienced the Second World War. It also shaped real actions in the Cold War, influencing politics and strategy at the highest level, and inspiring both protest and anxiety throughout British society. By the 1960s, it can be seen as a structural factor in how the Cold War was understood and fought – by disarmament campaigners who saw in nuclear weapons the potential end of civilisation, and by the politicians and strategists who argued that such destruction could only be avoided through deterrence. Both standpoints relied on a shared vision of nuclear weapons that imagined those weapons as apocalyptic and world-ending.

The atomic bomb

The difficulty people had imagining atomic warfare was noticeable from the first discussions of it within British political and popular culture. In the first few months after Hiroshima and Nagasaki, the bomb dominated the press – hundreds of thousands of words were spent repeating stories and seemingly endlessly debating the bombs' consequences at a time when newsprint was still severely restricted.[10] The mid-market *News Chronicle*, breaking the story to its readers, outlined the difficulty in taking in the news: it was 'so staggering that not even a people which has had much experience of bombs can form any sort of picture of them', but 'presumably a few such bombs might, in a matter of minutes, wipe a city the size of London off the face of the earth'.[11] The *Yorkshire Post* stressed that 'now the peril is such that imagination baulks at its contemplation ... the maintenance of peace has become the most vital of all human issues, for the next war may in very truth be Armageddon'.[12] A short story in the mass-market *Daily Mirror* attempted to dramatise this future in November 1945. Set in a post-war future, among 'bleak vistas' and the 'smoke ... from a ruined, burned-out town', it features the 'Leader' of the nation and the 'Scientist' responsible for the weapons that were launched forty-eight hours previously: 'Only two days and we have wiped out the world', cries the Leader, 'wiped out civilisation. You and I between us, and you and I are the only living creatures left.'[13] Such reactions were widespread: a sense of bewilderment at the scale of the weapon, an admission of the difficulty in imagining the weapon's effects, and the immediate impulse to translate the bomb's power into terrifying visions of total destruction.

This process of coding the bomb as a harbinger of civilisation-ending cataclysm was exacerbated by uncertainty concerning the future of the world order, and Britain's place in it. The absence of any concrete plan for future world peace and co-operation after the end of the Second World War heightened the fears surrounding the release of atomic energy. As people confronted with the bomb imagined the future, they saw the new destructive force coupled with the anarchy of international competition – a state of affairs which had seen Britain fight two world wars in the last thirty years. Other commentators concentrated on the economic and technical promise of atomic energy, from free electricity and atomic cars to the ability to alter Britain's grey and rainy climate.[14] Atomic energy's revolutionary and utopian potential if harnessed for good went hand-in-hand with its apocalyptic and dystopian consequences if harnessed for evil. Yet it is clear that anxiety about the atomic bomb declined markedly after the first months following Hiroshima: writing in January 1946, Leonard Woolf thought the debate about the atomic bomb had been 'short-lived and in effect transient and abortive'.[15]

Two developments help explain this decline in discussions of what an atomic war might be like. The first was the growth of attempts to secure international control of atomic energy. This would not have changed the way atomic warfare was imagined as such, but crucially it had the potential to allay fears about the *likelihood* of war. International control was a major global political issue in the 1945–48 period, waning only when it had become clear that the Soviet Union would never agree to limitations on sovereignty contained in the proposals emanating from the West. British opinion was enthusiastic for international control. From the prime minister, Clement Attlee, to the tabloid newspapers, the topic was attributed near-millenarian importance. Attlee would go on to invest a great deal of time and effort in order to secure his aims,[16] and the widespread commitment to the initiative was a direct result of the way in which atomic war was initially constructed within British culture. For most of its supporters, international control seemed the only choice open to the world in the face of the atomic bomb's power.[17] Furthermore, it was hoped that the prospect of catastrophe would force nations to co-operate, with the atomic bomb becoming the catalyst for a sustained era of peace.[18] As such, the pessimistic imagined future of atomic destruction was the driving force behind an international initiative that in many ways embodied the best hopes and dreams of a generation of internationalists. Support in Britain did not reach the organisational heights seen in America,[19] but it was a notable feature of public discussion of post-war international affairs. Of course, in making their case for the necessity of international control, advocates of the scheme actually dramatised the consequences of atomic attack – ramping up the rhetoric of destruction to provide the greater contrast with peaceful co-operation.

Hopes of international control were comparatively long-lived. As late as the autumn of 1949, when news broke of the Soviet Union's atomic bomb test, it was flagged as a necessary step on the road to peace.[20] This may help to explain why reaction to this news was so muted. The prime minister announced that the Soviet bomb had long been expected, and an article in the *Economist* similarly suggested that the development would have little effect on Soviet policy or on the chances of war.[21] The daily press was equally keen to play down the risks of disaster, with the *Daily Mail* arguing that the bomb would contribute to a new 'balance of power' that would aid the preservation of peace.[22] The *Times* joined the chorus of voices hoping this would give a fresh impetus to talks concerning control. The *Daily Mirror* added that 'while the British people took the A-bomb news calmly, there was great excitement in America',[23] and the round-up of BBC broadcasts printed in the *Listener* also preferred to discuss the rather more anxious American reaction to events.[24]

The news of the Soviet bomb coincided with the second, and more important, development explaining the decline of visible nuclear anxieties in the late 1940s: the beginning of a government scheme of civil defence designed to prepare Britain for war. The government's civil defence schemes included a great deal of work to ensure that Britain would be able to resist atomic attack and continue to prosecute a European war.[25] A key element of this policy was its public promotion, in particular the task of securing recruits for the new Civil Defence Corps. Central to such efforts were arguments focusing on the utility of civil defence, the lives it could save, and the fact that atomic destruction had been exaggerated by many. Annual nationwide campaigns featuring ministerial speeches, poster campaigns, cinema shorts and demonstrations publicised the utility of civil defence and the survivability of atomic war, all reinforced by a supportive and largely deferential mass media.[26] In all its forms, civil defence was designed to reshape how the atomic war was imagined. Surveys suggested that the intense government propaganda efforts were successful in convincing people that the government would be able to save lives in a future war: in 1951 only one-fifth of the sample did not believe that civil defence would save lives in an atomic attack.[27]

These reports also revealed that deep-seated anxieties about the destructiveness of atomic war remained. Some were expressed by pacifist opinion, at times dramatically illustrating the bomb's destructive power, such as the powerful pamphlet *If It Fell on Hampstead*, which used official government data on the effects of atomic bombing to graphically highlight the consequences for the local urban space, imposing concentric circles of destruction onto a map of local streets.[28] More generally, the atomic bomb also entered British culture as a rich repository of allusion and metaphor for the powerful or shocking. Reviewing a landmark Picasso retrospective, which opened in London in December 1945, the BBC radio reviewer said that 'he has a power that does not seem so strange now in a world trembling at the liberation of atomic force'.[29] Rhetorical flourishes also continued to emphasise the enormous destructiveness of the weapon. This was no more evident than when Britain's first atomic bomb was successfully exploded in 1952. The press responded with an orgy of destructive symbolism, with Britain's own might and prestige being linked to the destruction it could wreak on its enemies. As a caption in the *Illustrated London News* put it, this was a 'blast which revises Britain's place in the hierarchy of nations'.[30]

Fears, though, were clearly reduced and to a degree contained, albeit uneasily, in the atomic period. Hopes for international control during 1945–49 and around the ability of civil defence to save lives after 1949 are obvious reasons for this, as is the growing belief in the rationality, if not the peaceful intent, of the Soviet Union, and the concomitant belief that an atomic attack was not on the immediate horizon, even in moments of crisis such as the outbreak of the Korean War. There is a deeper reason, however, which explains why atomic war was imagined the way it was, and why civil defence narratives both took the form they did and received support. This is the enduring cultural power of the Second World War and the imaginative difficulties people had in separating out atomic war from conventional war. Geoff Eley has argued that after 1945 the memory of the war pervaded official and popular cultures, becoming 'worked into public discourse in inspiring, insidious, and enduring ways, making an active archive of collective identification'. This memory was dispersed and reinforced by a wide chain of associations built not just on films and novels set during the war, but a 'promiscuous melange of imagery and citation' and – crucially – the associations it triggers.[31]

The imaginative landscape of nuclear war in Britain, 1945–65

The way in which atomic war was imagined was undoubtedly part of this process, shaped by direct evocations of the previous war as comparator, by ideas of resilience and unity becoming rooted in assumptions about the nature of British society, and by the physical and mental landscape of post-war Britain.

From the very beginning of attempts to imagine atomic war, the memory of the previous war was a central shaping factor. A scientific mission was sent to study the ruins of Hiroshima and Nagasaki by the government in 1945,[32] and although this provided detailed knowledge about the physical nature of destruction, when the government deliberated on the social consequences of atomic war it was guided virtually exclusively by the experiences of the Second World War, and the public's reaction to enemy bombardment in particular. For example, the investigation of issues such as public morale and how the population would respond to widespread evacuation were cursory at best. In a secret 1946 study, it was assumed that the 'will' of the British public would be 'highly resistive' because of its experience of bombardment. The Soviet Union would be the same, but America's lack of a collective history of a 'blitz' experience meant less damage would be needed before a devastating collapse in morale. As such, it was assumed that the morale and behaviour of the population in an atomic war would be little different from 1940–41.[33] These assumptions translated into evacuation and dispersal plans, the building blocks of the nation's strategy for fighting a future war: the government assumed a quiescent population would not only leave or stay in urban areas at the state's command, but that the industrial workforce would be happy to be transported into attacked areas for work. By assuming that the population would respond in this way, maintaining economic production and morale, the government convinced itself from 1947 to 1951 that Britain would be able to prosecute a future atomic war.

We can compare the scanty British efforts to understand the social consequences of nuclear attack with the enormous sums spent by the American government on the same issue. Vast projects were set up in the United States, using an enormous array of scientific, architectural and psychological knowledge, to imagine an atomic attack on American cities.[34] British efforts instead relied on basic assumptions derived from the quasi-mythical memory of public behaviour in the Blitz of 1940–41. Such staunchness was assumed when the government imagined atomic war, and was used to reassure people about civil defence. When Clement Attlee called for recruits to the new volunteer civil defence force in broadcasts in 1950, he asked: 'How did we defeat the blitz in the last war?

By the skill, devotion, courage and self-sacrifice of thousands of ordinary citizens. If war should come again … we must be ready. Good civil defence can do much to enable the population to endure the strain of attack and mitigate its effects.'[35] This link was continually stressed in press advertisements for the Corps, emphasising the ability of veterans of the Blitz to save lives in any atomic war.[36] For Attlee and his government, the link between the Blitz and the atomic bomb was designed to allay public fears. It was not empty propaganda, however, as the government itself understood the legacy of the Blitz as a real threat linking the experience of the last war with the ability of the nation to resist atomic aggression.

The role of the memory of the Second World War in shaping the imagined atomic conflict reached its apogee in the Boulting Brothers' popular 1950 thriller, *Seven Days to Noon*, in which an atomic scientist disappears with a bomb and holds the nation to ransom – either renounce such weapons or face the destruction of London.[37] The film's treatment of the subject is typical of the contradiction at the heart of British imaginative responses to the bomb at the end of the 1940s and the early 1950s: great emphasis was placed on the bomb's destructive power, but central to the film was an extended sequence demonstrating how the authorities – with the help of the public – would minimise the destruction. Volunteer civil defence workers organise the total evacuation of London in a matter of days, and the population patiently queues in the capital's railway stations. Here the government's civil defence planning was brought to life, and its origins in the previous war laid bare, literally in the case of *Seven Days to Noon*, as archive footage of the 1939 evacuation of children was interpolated into the film.

When attempting to imagine atomic destruction, the public had pointers not only from the government and popular culture, but also from the physical landscape surrounding it. Reconstruction of bombed cities advanced slowly after 1945, and for those living in towns and cities the reality of war surrounded them.[38] The reality of bomb damage, its representation and its legacy had been part of British life since 1940, and there can be little surprise that it shaped ideas of a future war. Post-atomic London, as featured in Orwell's *Nineteen Eighty-Four*, for example, was recognisably post-Second World War London, with its landmarks and topographies unchanged. It was part of the curious mental landscape of atomic destruction that emerged from British culture after 1945 – one which largely understood what atomic attack would mean, but believed that Britain would absorb it and fight on. It was based on an experience of wartime destruction that was barely comparable with that experienced by Germany in 1944–45, let alone a future atomic war.[39] This memory pervaded the government's civil defence plans, and created the cultural context in which they could be positively received. After all, the public and the government shared many of the same assumptions. It was an unstable way of imagining the atomic future, however, which was reliant on the belief that the atomic bomb was not radically different from the bombs which rained down on British cities from 1940, and on the assumption that the British public could rise to any challenge. It was not a mechanism for imagining nuclear war that bore a great deal of scrutiny, and it certainly would not last long into the thermonuclear era.

The hydrogen bomb

Although a hydrogen bomb had been exploded by the United States as early as 1952, it made relatively little impact within political or popular culture. Coming just a few days after Britain's successful atomic test, the new weapon was largely ignored amid the celebratory coverage. As late as Christmas Eve 1953, the government's chief civil defence planner believed that the hydrogen bomb required 'no special studies'.[40] The hydrogen bomb seized the British imagination only during the Pacific tests in March 1954.[41] News came that tests had contaminated a Japanese fishing-boat some 82 miles away from the blast, signalling both the bomb's enormous destructive power and the new phenomenon of deadly and widespread radioactive fallout.[42] The shock the bomb caused was palpable. The *Daily Mirror* christened the weapon 'the monster' and 'the horror bomb'.[43] That weekend, the popular Sunday tabloid the *News of the World* put the bomb in stark context: 'A hydrogen bomb war would wreck civilisation and might well destroy the world.'[44] The implications of the bomb for Britain were obvious: the new bomb could destroy every town and city in the United Kingdom.

If the initial reaction to the hydrogen bomb resembled the immediate response to Hiroshima less than a decade previously, a result both of the real shock both weapons caused and the relatively limited lexicon of destruction available to commentators, the lasting consequences were very different. The belief that the hydrogen bomb could and indeed might bring about the 'end of the world' did not peter out after 1954. Instead, this belief was maintained and strengthened within British culture, becoming the dominant mode of imagining nuclear weapons and decisively shaping political choices in Cold War Britain. In mid-1950s popular culture, there was a basic understanding of the hydrogen bomb as a uniquely apocalyptic weapon. Anglo-Australian author Nevil Shute's *On the Beach* (1957) depicted nuclear war as leaving no survivors in the northern hemisphere, and the book largely concerned the slow wait for radioactivity to wipe out the southern hemisphere too. *On the Beach*, partly through the Hollywood adaptation which followed in 1959, became synonymous with the idea of the eradication of humanity – although one review noted that as 'the characterization is so weak, the reader, faced with the extinction of the human race as represented by Mr Shute's characters, is left comparatively unmoved'.[45] John Wyndham's *The Chrysalids* (1955) is set in a post-nuclear future with no understanding of its own past. Reduced to a state of religious fundamentalism from ignorance of the causes of the widespread genetic mutations, the society depicted in the novel is pieced together after a war which has truly destroyed Western civilisation as it was known.[46] On British screens, the same assumptions were rife. From the experimental animation of *A Short Vision* (1955), which depicted the world as a light that would be extinguished, to the science fiction film *X the Unknown* (1956), which conveyed the sinister powers of radiation, the nuclear future was imagined as all-destructive.[47] When Britain tested its first thermonuclear device in 1957, the news bulletin on one of Britain's two television channels pointed out that 'another world conflict would almost certainly mean the end of our civilisation'.[48] These assumptions about nuclear war were reflected in opinion polls. In May 1954, only 24 per cent of those polled believed that civilised life would not be destroyed in a nuclear war;[49] and in March 1958 only 13 per cent believed that a nuclear war would leave up to half the British population alive.[50]

After 1954, the imaginative landscape of nuclear war was largely denuded of survivors. Instead, there was an imaginative void – the world largely ceasing to exist. As such, the nuclear future was perhaps 'unimagined' rather than imagined. From the late 1960s, the horrors of actually surviving such an attack provided a rich imaginative seam for discussing the nuclear future. In the second half of the 1950s, however, the British imagination struggled to confront seriously this prospect, instead focusing on symbolising nuclear war through absence, empty spaces and the language of apocalypse. For any sense of what would happen to individuals, recourse was still taken to the stories and images of Hiroshima. In 1960, James Cameron, a journalist and peace campaigner, counterpoised the banality of optimistic civil defence prognoses of the effects of nuclear war with stories from his visit to Hiroshima in 1945.[51] This imaginative absence may be explained by a literal inability to imagine nuclear destruction.[52] The struggle in conceptualising nuclear war was admitted by both defence planners and opponents of nuclear weapons. Defence planners declared it was 'beyond the imagination' in 1955,[53] and the literary critic Philip Toynbee, writing in 1958, explained that 'perhaps it is an event which is beyond the powers of the human mind to contemplate'.[54]

Yet despite the struggle to conceptualise the impact of the hydrogen bomb, a clear picture did emerge of its apocalyptic consequences. This reaction was shaped by a complex set of historical, geographical and cultural factors, and not by any deep-seated understanding of the 'reality' of nuclear weapons. In the United States, in contrast to British pessimism, nuclear war was often imagined as a survivable, though terrible, event. The sheer size of the nation, the sprawling nature of suburban development, and the existence of ample space in gardens and housing plots meant that middle-class Americans believed they and their families would be able to survive a nuclear attack.[55] Private companies sold domestic fallout shelters, and the issue reached such heights that there was a genuine moral panic during 1960 and 1961.[56] Nothing comparable happened in Britain, and a domestic shelter market failed to materialise. The divergent histories of shelters were symptomatic of the specific ways nuclear war was imagined in British and American popular culture, and remind us of the key role played by cultural specificity in shaping responses.

British pessimism can be explained by the immediate belief that the bomb was able to destroy all British cities in their entirety (and that radioactivity would kill those outside the cities), and the lack of credible alternatives to the idea of the destructive nuclear war. After Hiroshima, Bertrand Russell said the following: 'As I go about the streets and see St Paul's, the British Museum, the Houses of Parliament and the other monuments of our civilization, in my mind's eye I see a nightmare vision of those buildings as heaps of rubble with corpses all round them.'[57] After 1954, people did not envisage nuclear destruction as leaving such recognisable traces. Britain was highly urbanised, with compact towns and cities, and two-thirds of the population lived in towns of more than 50,000 people. It seemed axiomatic that Britain's large cities would be obliterated. Nor was there any confidence in survival beyond the city, with the spectre of radioactivity spilling all over the countryside. Combined, these dangers shattered the link between the experience of the Second World War and contemporary nuclear reality, removing a key way in which anxiety about the atomic bomb had been contained in the years before the hydrogen bomb, and cutting the imagined nuclear war adrift from the anchorage of lived or remembered experience. Essentially, these dangers destroyed the ability of people to imagine a post-nuclear world.

The pessimism that dominated the mental landscape of nuclear war after 1954 did not go unchallenged, however, but attempts to discuss how nuclear war could be survived failed to make headway against the enormous discursive power of destructive visions of the bomb. The government, for example, struggled to present a coherent picture of the difference civil defence might make in the thermonuclear era.[58] They suffered a blow when Coventry City Council announced in April 1954 that it would cease funding civil defence measures, as it was a waste of time and money, considering the bomb's 'devastating effects'.[59] Coventry's actions were particularly damaging for the prestige of civil defence, considering that city's iconic status as a blitzed area. In response to these views, the government did attempt to maintain the view that nuclear war could be survived along old lines. The Home Secretary declared that 'we must not lose our nerve in the face of this fresh potential horror. To suppose that one such bomb could destroy the world or even kill everyone in this country is a sign of ignorance, hysteria and panic.' In an attempt to continue the façade of civil defence, the government argued that the increased scale of destruction made trained civil defence volunteers more, not less, necessary and continued to downplay the effects of radiation.[60] Those who did support the ability of civil defence to save a significant number of lives increasingly found themselves in the minority, a trend which only accelerated after the Campaign for Nuclear Disarmament (CND) was formed in 1958. Discussions of nuclear war featured more heavily in the media from this point, and included more critical depictions of civil defence. By 1960, civil defence was increasingly portrayed in the media as misguided, naive, or an outright government lie.[61] The assumptions surrounding the hydrogen bomb in British culture were left largely untouched by the government's civil defence propaganda, a result of the difficulty in imagining nuclear survival in British popular culture.

The collapse in the concept of nuclear survival and the dominant tendency for individuals to imagine nuclear war as an apocalyptic event in which they and others would perish had profound consequences for how the Cold War was understood and fought from 1954 until the end of the conflict. First, it shaped attitudes towards Britain's possession of nuclear weapons, helping to underpin belief both in the concept of deterrence and the nation's own capacity to deter nuclear attack from the vastly more powerful Soviet Union. Second, it inspired CND to mobilise a section of the population to protest against Britain's possession of such weapons. These opponents of the bomb believed that only by actively campaigning for peace and disarmament could the disastrous effects of war be avoided. Such a war, they seemed sure, was inevitable given the rapid build-up of weapons and antagonism. Support for both deterrence and disarmament was underpinned by the process of imagining nuclear war as all-destructive, and the rhetorical strategies of both positions reinforced and deepened this mode of understanding nuclear war.

There were times when politicians and officials appeared to revel in the bomb's destructive power, celebrating Britain's own hydrogen bomb capacity. When the decision to build a British hydrogen bomb was announced to the public, it was argued that the destructive power of the thermonuclear weapon 'has significantly reduced the risk of war on a major scale'. The meaning of deterrence was also spelt out: Britain would be determined 'to face the threat of physical devastation, even on the immense scale which must be foreseen' rather than adopt 'an attitude of subservience to militant Communism, with the national and individual humiliation that this would bring'.[62] The government's tendency to stress the bomb's power in order to bolster its own deterrent policy, at the expense of its civil defence message, reached its apogee with the famous statement in the 1957 Defence White Paper. This document signalled Britain's full adoption of a deterrent strategy in which conventional troop numbers would be cut, with a nuclear 'tripwire' deterring conventional as well as nuclear attacks. It stated that 'it must be frankly recognised that there is at present no means of providing adequate protection for the people of this country against the consequences of an attack with nuclear weapons'.[63] This form of words may have been the result of a clumsy redrafting of the section that was meant to explain the impossibility of fighter aircrafts preventing nuclear attack, but it was widely accepted as a damning admission that nothing could mitigate the effects of attack.[64] It was rapidly seized on by the government's opponents, who quoted the admission back to make their point about the bomb's all-destructive power.[65] Yet the idea that there was no defence against the hydrogen bomb was central to both the exponents and opponents of the bomb.

Revelling in the power of the bomb tapped into a deep British desire to 'sit at the top table' (as Churchill thought it would allow Britain to do).[66] The news bulletin announcing Britain's hydrogen bomb declared that 'in the belief that possession of the great deterrent is the only way to ensure world peace, Britain has become joint custodian of the deadliest weapon yet devised by man'.[67] From the 1950s onwards, there was an obsession with maintaining a 'credible' and 'independent' deterrent,[68] a posture based on the assumption that these weapons were so destructive as to eliminate virtually the possibility of survival, allowing a handful of British warheads to ensure continuing British world power, and the belief that British custody of the bomb has provided a calming influence on the nuclear world. Yet the destructive power of the bomb sat uneasily with official narratives which promised the ability of civil defence to ameliorate some of the effects of nuclear attack. This conflict was only resolved when civil defence was essentially scrapped in 1968 and it reveals the problematic way the government fought the Cold War, the imaginary war on the home front. Cabinet policy, only secretly acknowledged of course, was that civil defence was a 'façade' designed to bolster public support for the deterrent policy. In short, it was a propaganda exercise, an imaginative assault on the public designed to convince them to support the state's Cold War policies. But it was not solely this: civil defence policy grew out of the state's own difficulty in imagining nuclear war. For every cynic in the Air Ministry treating civil defence as a fig leaf, there was an earnest advocate in the Home Office desperately seeking additions to the medical, food and equipment budgets for the post-nuclear emergency.

Fighting the logic of deterrence was a key aim for the members and supporters of CND. Founded, after it had become clear in the autumn of 1957 that the Labour Party would disarm only as part of a global settlement, CND was inspired by moral revulsion. The CND stance was built on assumptions of the apocalyptic nature of nuclear war which had been circulating widely after 1954, and contributed enormously to entrenching them still further within popular culture. Their arguments concentrated on the immorality of weapons, on their enhancing the chances of war, and Britain's chance to set a leading example to the world.[69] What nuclear war would be like was taken for granted and used as a building block in rhetoric. As Benn W. Levy put it in an early CND pamphlet, 'sober opinion holds that we have now mastered powers of destruction (or they have mastered us) to the point where we may, without intending it, put an end to all human life. Certainly our own country would, on present prospects, be the earliest and easiest area for obliteration.'[70] This belief in the apocalyptic nuclear war and the call to individuals to do something about it was CND's hallmark, featured on news items and on television, inspiring its leaders and followers alike.

The imaginative landscape of nuclear war in Britain, 1945–65

People of pro- and anti-deterrent opinions shared the same inability to see beyond the 'emptiness' of the post-attack world, or rather the lack of a post-attack world. Indeed, commentators, politicians and artists alike relied on it in when arguing for or against the bomb. The anti-CND Denis Healey, later to become a staunchly pro-deterrent Defence Secretary in the 1964 Labour Government, declared that 'the very magnitude of the danger [nuclear weapons] represent may evoke a response of comparable grandeur – if it does not, the species *homo sapiens* may disappear for failing to live up to its name'.[71] Likewise, the more sympathetic Philip Toynbee argued, 'if an "incident" should happen on the present frontier between America and Russia it must lead not only to war but to the total destruction of this country and perhaps of the human race'.[72] None of these figures attempted to picture, let alone successfully fill the imaginative emptiness. People were, however, acutely aware of that emptiness, and of the difficulty in either filling it or of understanding the imaginative consequences of its horror. D. N. Pritt argued that 'the advocates and manufacturers of hydrogen bombs hope that the mere idea may paralyse all our minds and lead us to remain idle, thinking that no one will use so terrible a weapon'.[73] As Ted Hughes put it in his 1959 poem 'A Woman Unconscious', the bomb would ensure 'all mankind wince out and nothing endure – / Earth gone in an instant flare'.[74] But 'flitting thought / (Not to be thought ridiculous) / Shies from the world-cancelling black / Of its playing shadow'.

It can be argued, however, that this way of imagining nuclear war, dramatised by both sides but more so by CND, helped the government's case for deterrence rather more than it helped CND's aims. Indeed, we could go so far as to say that CND's activities unconsciously underpinned deterrence. Certainly, while CND's assumptions about the nature of nuclear war were widely shared by the public, its advocated course of action to prevent it was not. Public opinion appeared to be firmly behind the deterrent strategy. In April 1958, only 22 per cent of the public indicated their support for CND's aim of unilateral disarmament, and in opinion polls support never rose above 30 per cent.[75] Perhaps the more catastrophic nuclear war seemed, the less likely it seemed that such a war would occur. This was bolstered both by assumptions about nuclear war and assumptions about the broader deterrent effect of diplomatic and military strength and political will, assiduously promoted by Western governments throughout the 1950s. The peaceful resolution of the Cuban Missile Crisis in 1962, seen as a key reason for the decline in the peace movement, further enhanced this idea of the 'rationality' of the Cold War.[76] By the end of 1963, perhaps as a result of Cuba, only 16 per cent of poll respondents believed that nuclear weapons would be used in their lifetime.[77]

CND's difficulties were neatly encapsulated in the satirical early 1960s revue *Beyond the Fringe*. It mercilessly attacked both civil defence advocates and disarmament campaigners. Peter Cook, posing as a civil defence volunteer, may have declared 'there's nothing like a good old paper bag for protecting you' in a nuclear war, but CND also came in for attack. Alan Bennett, posing as an activist, informed the audience that all local Labour branches were asked 'Would you like to see your wife and kids go up in smoke? Ninety-four per cent of the replies said "*no*". If that is not a mandate for unilateral nuclear disarmament I do not know what is.'[78] Civil defence was openly ridiculed for its inability or refusal to grasp the basic truth of nuclear war: that there would be no survival. At the same time, CND was criticised for assuming that this knowledge would ensure support for its views. As Denis Healey made clear, it was easy to oppose CND while sharing its basic assumptions about the nature of nuclear war. Quite simply, these views about nuclear war were widespread throughout British culture, and underpinned not only CND, but the whole basis of deterrence and the nuclear policies it was attempting to reverse.[79]

Of course, anxiety about nuclear war continued to run very deep. In the 1960s, there were growing fears about the basic irrationality of nuclear war, and the prospects of miscalculation or accident triggering global conflagration. The plot of *Dr. Strangelove* was only the most famous scenario of people who feared a war might come despite the apparent rationality of Cold War leaders. Furthermore, the 1960s was the key decade in which people began to seriously confront the idea of nuclear *survival* and what that might actually mean. Disarmers turned to openly challenging the policies of civil defence and nuclear survival in 1962, especially in the Peace News pamphlet *H-Bomb War: What It Would Be Like*,[80] and CND's FALLEX '63 campaign, publicising the consequences of survival for the first time.[81] *H-Bomb War* began to explore what life in Britain might be like after a nuclear attack, telling its readers that 'if war broke out tomorrow, most of us on this island could be dead within a few hours ... and those of us alive might well wish they had died.'[82] Peter Watkins' *The War Game* (1965), which was kept off British television screens owing to its controversial mixture of distressing images and forthright opposition to nuclear weapons, attempted to destroy any vestige of faith in civil defence, bringing home to those who viewed it in special screenings what nuclear war might actually be like.[83] Throughout the 1970s and 1980s, depictions of nuclear war plumbed more imaginative depths than previously, and the horrors of survival became a standard way of depicting war, such as in the BBC drama *Threads* (1984), or Russell Hoban's novel *Riddley Walker* (1980).

The imaginative landscape of nuclear war in Britain, 1945–65

Much more concern was also given to the emotional consequences of living in the shadow of such destruction. As Jonathan Hogg has noted, in 1957 the *Daily Mirror* was greatly exercised by the tragic suicide of a couple apparently driven to despair by the threat of nuclear war.[84] In the early 1960s, Doris Lessing and Arnold Wesker both wrote plays for television detailing the emotional and psychological strain involved in the 'pre-war' state that Britain was in. Wesker's *Menace* depicted the fraught interaction of a group of bed-sitters,[85] while Lessing's *The Truth about Billy Newton* portrayed an elderly radical and his disintegrating family.[86] Lessing's play was produced in the same year in which her landmark novel *The Golden Notebook* was published, yet takes a very different stance to it. *Billy Newton* takes place against the backdrop of anti-nuclear marches, which provide a solution just off-screen to the sense of powerlessness that pervades the characters in the drama. *The Golden Notebook*, however, is set in the mid-1950s, and highlights the difficulty people had in conceptualising nuclear weapons. Lessing's novel focuses on the interior life of Anna Wulf, who details her thoughts, emotions and experiences on a range of issues in a set of coloured notebooks.[87] Her disillusionment with the Communist Party of Great Britain is brilliantly chronicled as a gradual process of self-doubt and antagonism. The nuclear threat, however, is conveyed through a series of newspaper pieces, apparently 'pasted' into the notebook unmediated by the narrator.[88] In a novel all about the self and its interactions with the world, the inability of the main character to process information about nuclear weapons and the threat of war is eloquent testimony to the struggle involved in imagining nuclear war.

Both Lessing and Wesker were associated with CND, and were clearly attempting to counter the fact that the imagined nuclear future was deliberately shut out of the minds of people who could or would not confront the psychologically troubling prospect of the future being anything less than an open horizon. A similar process is on display in John Schlesinger's 1965 cinematic critique of the selfish values of 1960s celebrity, *Darling*. The central character Diana has the following exchange with her friend Malcolm:

Diana: (despairingly, drunkenly): Oh, my life is a pisspot.
Malcolm: Well, you see, I have the answer to that (pause). It's the bomb, lovey. It must be.
Diana: (building to a shout): That's right, it's the GREAT BIG BOMB.
Malcolm: THE NASTY, NASTY BOMB.

The exchange can be read in two ways: as the bitter cry of two people with little meaning in their hedonistic lives lived under the shadow of the bomb, or as the ironic jeers of people seeking some excuse for their plight, but mocking the idea that the bomb has an impact on their lives – here, the bomb would be a mere backdrop to their lives or a meaningless symbol. Either way, *Darling* illustrates a longer-term impact of nuclear weapons that needs excavating: with the collapse of CND's popularity, the bomb became part of the seemingly unchangeable backdrop of British lives, and the majority of people accepted it either by rationalising it as an important component in process of maintaining 'peace', or as something to ignored, relegated to the liminal spaces of the imagination. It is in these spaces we will find the deeper history of the nuclear age.

Conclusion

Britain's Cold War was indelibly marked by the peculiar way in which nuclear war was imagined after 1945. From Hiroshima to Cuba, there was deep-seated anxiety about the future of the nation and of humanity. This anxiety was to a great extent contained in the atomic age, a testament both the vigour with which the government pursued civil defence and the enormous legacy of the Second World War on both the physical and mental landscape. Imagining atomic war as destroying parts, but not all, of urban areas was initially central to its containment. People could imagine living through an attack, imagine being rescued and imagine the nation pulling together as it did in 1940. The memories of the last conflict helped to underpin these assumptions, as did the rhetoric of the government and the empty, bombed-out spaces that remained a fixture of towns and cities in the first post-war decade. That such a mechanism of containment could not outlive the atomic age is by no means remarkable – the noteworthy point was that British depictions of atomic warfare could be so sanguine in the first place. After 1954, the assumption that all cities would be destroyed, that the countryside would be irradiated, and that all civil defence was useless became dominant. This led to nuclear war being imagined as completely destructive and apocalyptic. The prospect of millions of survivors living a grim existence and struggling to keep a hold on life was rarely confronted. As such, the 'truth' about nuclear war so firmly expounded in the 1950s, above all by the supporters of CND, was often anything other than this. Like the derided supporters of civil defence, they based their opinions on an imagined nuclear reality. It was one widely shared in Britain, linking CND and pro-deterrent opinions.

The annihilatory view of nuclear war prominent after 1954 was, to some extent, a reaction to the overly sanguine assumptions that were common before. Both reactions were firmly rooted in wider British culture, and both were shaped by the manifest difficulties people had in 'imagining' nuclear war. People confronting the bomb naturally built a composite picture from the elements available around them, firmly tethering their idea of atomic warfare in the memory and experience of the Blitz. The difficulties caused by the step-change in destructive technology from conventional to atomic weapons were essentially side-stepped by this process; the scale of the bomb became linked to remembered and visible destruction, and the ability of the state to help linked to a remembered and mythical national effort. The containment of atomic anxiety, and the belief that the nation could survive a future war, became overly reliant on these mental processes for imagining atomic war. After 1954, these processes were no longer tenable. It was not possible to believe in a city damaged but not destroyed, or that the state would be able to help everyone. This rupture was complete, and the wartime anchor no longer secured the imagination. Yet, British culture was seemingly not ready for the grim depiction of survival, of literally imagining the lives of those not killed in the first waves of nuclear attack. Instead, people focused on nothingness, on complete destruction – they could not imagine their own survival. Perhaps it was easier to imagine nothing than to piece together the catastrophic consequences of the bomb. This apocalyptic bomb provided rather neater certainties – of the simple moral imperative to fight against the bomb, of the rationality of deterrence, of the maintenance of British power, or even of the wisdom of ignoring it. These were the certainties that became established in the mid-1950s and dominated British culture and politics in the rest of the Cold War, and which drove the imaginary war on the home front. Civil defence measures and propaganda and anti-nuclear protests highlighted the very real dangers of the Cold War, and made a mockery of the concept of a long peace in these decades.[89] The imaginary war, as much as anything, was a fight that was not about what nuclear weapons would do to Britain, but what they had already done. As such, we can see that the true nuclear revolution in British politics and culture occurred not in 1945, but in 1954, when the imaginative landscape of nuclear war in Britain was changed forever.

Notes

1. For a succinct account of British strategy in early Cold War period, see A. Deighton, 'Britain and the Cold War, 1955', in M. P. Leffler and O. A. Westad (eds), *The Cambridge History of the Cold War, vol. I: Origins* (Cambridge, 2010), pp. 112-32.
2. See P. Hennessy, *The Secret State: Preparing for the Worst, 1945-2010* (London, 2011).
3. R. Taylor, *Against the Bomb: The British Peace Movement, 1958-65* (Oxford, 1988); and H. Nehring, *The Politics of Security: British and West German Protest Movements and the Early Cold War, 1945-1970* (Oxford, 2013).
4. B. Russell, *Has Man a Future?* (Harmondsworth, 1961), p. 120.
5. J. Slessor, *The Great Deterrent* (London, 1957), pp. 184, 193.
6. See, for instance, E. L. Woodward, 'Has all this happened before?', *The Listener*, 28.3.1946.
7. M. Grant, *After the Bomb: Civil Defence and Nuclear War in Britain, 1945-68* (Basingstoke, 2010).
8. R. Bessel and D. Schumann, 'Violence, normality and the construction of postwar Europe', in Bessel and Schumann (eds), *Life After Death: Approaches to a Cultural and Social History during the 1940s and 1950s* (Cambridge, 2003), pp. 1-14.
9. J. Bronowski, 'Mankind at the crossroads', *The Listener*, 4 July 1946, p. 7.
10. See, for example, M. Gowing, *Independence and Deterrence: Britain and Atomic Energy, 1945-52. Volume I: Policy Making* (Basingstoke, 1974), chapter 2; Grant, *After the Bomb*, chapter 1; and C. Laucht, '"Dawn - or dusk?": Britain's *Picture Post* confronts nuclear energy', in D. van Lente (ed.), *The Nuclear Age in Popular Media: A Transnational History, 1945-65* (Basingstoke, 2012), pp. 117-48.
11. 'Red light', *News Chronicle*, 7 Aug. 1945, p. 2.
12. 'An immense discovery', *Yorkshire Post*, 7 Aug. 1945, p. 2
13. E. Brookes, 'World without end', *Daily Mirror*, 20 Nov. 1945.
14. See Gowing, *Independence and Deterrence*, pp. 52-5.
15. L. Woolf, 'Britain in the atomic age', *Political Quarterly* 17:1 (1946), p. 13.
16. See R. Smith and J. Zametica, 'The cold warrior: Clement Attlee reconsidered, 1945-1947', *International Affairs* 61:2 (1985), 237-63.
17. See A. Salter, *The United Nations and the Atomic Bomb* (Oxford, 1945); L. Curtis, *World War: Its Cause and Cure* (second edn, Oxford, 1945); H. E. Wimperis, *World Power and Atomic Energy: The Impact on International Relations* (London, 1946).
18. See the special issue of *The Listener*, 13 Mar. 1947, for reprints of a series of BBC radio broadcasts in March 1947.
19. P. S. Boyer, *By the Bomb's Early Light* (New York, 1985), pp. 68-79.
20. 'Atomic echoes', *The Times*, 27 Sept. 1957, p. 5.
21. 'Back to the atom', *The Economist*, 1 Oct. 1949, pp. 706-8.

22 'Comment: the Russian bomb', *Daily Mail*, 24 Sept. 1949.
23 'Atomic blast in Russia', *Daily Mirror*, 24 Sept. 1949.
24 Erwin Canham, 'The atomic state of mind in U.S.A.', *The Listener*, 6 Oct. 1949.
25 Grant, *After the Bomb*, pp. 36–57.
26 M. Grant, '"Civil defence gives meaning to your leisure": citizenship, participation and cultural change in Cold War recruitment propaganda, 1949–53', *Twentieth Century British History* 22:1 (2011), pp. 52–78.
27 D. L. Lambeth, *Recruitment to the Civil Defence Services – II* (London, 1951).
28 Hampstead Peace Council, *If It Fell on Hampstead* (London, 1949).
29 P. James, 'Picasso and Matisse', *The Listener*, 13 Dec. 1945.
30 'Fission or fusion?', *Illustrated London News*, 11 Oct. 1952.
31 G. Eley, 'Finding the People's War: film, British collective memory, and World War II', *American Historical Review* 106:3 (2001), pp. 819–20.
32 Published as Home Office and Air Ministry, *The Effects of the Atomic Bombs at Hiroshima and Nagasaki: Report of the British Mission to Japan* (HMSO, 1946).
33 The National Archives [hereafter TNA], CAB 121/272. TWC(46)1, 'Likely morale effect of atomic bombs', 12 Jan. 1946.
34 See G. Oakes, *The Imaginary War: Civil Defense and American Cold War Culture* (New York, 1994), pp. 47–51.
35 'Appeal for civil defence recruits: Mr Attlee's broadcast', *Manchester Guardian*, 16 Oct. 1950.
36 Grant, 'Civil defence gives meaning to your leisure'.
37 M. Grant, 'Images of survival, stories of destruction: nuclear war on British screens from 1945 to the early 1960s', *Journal of British Cinema and Television* 10:1 (2013), pp. 7–26.
38 C. Flinn, '"The city of our dreams"? The political and economic realities of rebuilding Britain's blitzed cities', *Twentieth Century British History* 23:2 (2012), pp. 221–45.
39 For the way in which the disruptive image of the 'atom' was contained within discourses of reconstruction, see R. Hornsey, *The Spiv and the Architect* (Minneapolis, 2010).
40 TNA, CAB 134/791. CD(O)(53)29, 'Civil defence planning policy to take account of development of atomic weapons', Note by General Irwin, 24 Dec. 1953.
41 A. Bingham, '"The monster"? The British popular press and nuclear culture, 1945–early 1960s', *British Journal of the History of Science* 45:2 (2012), 609–25.
42 'Radioactive fish alarm in Japan', *The Times*, 20 Mar. 1954; the story of the boat was graphically told in the best-selling R. E. Lapp, *The Voyage of the Lucky Dragon* (Harmondsworth, 1958).
43 'The monster', *Daily Mirror*, 2 Apr. 1954; 'The horror bomb', *Daily Mirror*, 2 Apr. 1954.
44 'Bomb, budget and bewilderment', *News of the World*, 4 Apr. 1954.

45 A. Calder-Marshall, 'Setting the pace', *Times Literary Supplement*, 14 Jun. 1957.
46 D. Ketterer, 'John Wyndham's World War III and his abandoned *Fury of Creation* trilogy', in D. Seed (ed.), *Future Wars: the Anticipations and Fears* (Liverpool, 2012), pp. 103-29.
47 Grant, 'Images of survival'.
48 'H-Bomb exploded', *ITN Late Evening News*. Transmitted 18 May 1957. Available at http://jiscmediahub.ac.uk/record/display/039-00042140 (accessed 15 February 2016).
49 G. C. Gallup, *The Gallup International Public Opinion Polls: Great Britain, 1937-1975* (New York: Random House, 1977), p. 25.
50 *Ibid.*, p. 454.
51 J. Cameron, *One in Five Must Know* (London, 1960).
52 P. Schwenger, 'Writing the unthinkable', *Critical Inquiry* 13:1 (1986), pp. 33-48.
53 Grant, *After the Bomb*, pp. 77-98; J. Hughes, 'The Strath Report: Britain confronts the H-Bomb, 1954-55', *History and Technology* 19:3 (2003), pp. 257-75.
54 P. Toynbee, *The Fearful Choice* (London, 1958).
55 On American responses, see Oakes, *The Imaginary War*; L. McEnaney, *Civil Defense Begins at Home* (Princeton, 2000); and D. Garrison, *Bracing for Armageddon* (Oxford, 2006).
56 M. A. Henriksen, *Dr Strangelove's America: Society and Culture in the Atomic Age* (Berkeley, 1997), pp. 87-111.
57 Earl Russell, *House of Lords Debates*, vol. 138, 28 Nov. 1945, c.89.
58 Grant, *After the Bomb*, pp. 107-13.
59 TNA, HO 322/136. Letter from the Town Clark, Coventry, to the Home Secretary, 7 Apr. 1954.
60 House of Commons, *Official Report*, 27 May 1954, cols 41-4W.
61 See NA, CAB 21/4762. 'Motivational Factors and Recruitment to the Civil Defence Corps', report by Market Research Department, F.C. Pritchard, Wood & Partners Ltd, October 1960.
62 Ministry of Defence, *Statement on Defence, 1955*, Cmd 9391 (London: HMSO, 1955).
63 Ministry of Defence, *Defence: Outline of Future Policy*, p. 2.
64 M. Grant, 'Home defence and the Sandys defence White Paper, 1957', *Journal of Strategic Studies* 31:6 (2008), pp. 925-49.
65 B. Russell, *If Man Is to Survive* (London, 1958); Atomic Sciences Committee of the Association of Scientific Workers *Nuclear Nightmare* (Association of Scientific Workers, 1958).
66 Hennessy, *The Secret State*, pp. 57-8.
67 'H-Bomb Exploded', *ITN Late Evening News*.
68 M. Grant, 'Upgrading Britain's nuclear deterrent: from V-Bombers to Trident Replacement', *History & Policy*, Paper No. 91 (2009).

69 J. Burkett, 'Re-defining British morality: Britishness and the Campaign for Nuclear Disarmament, 1958-68', *Twentieth Century British History*, 21:2 (2010), pp. 184-205.
70 B.W. Levy, *Britain and the Bomb: the Fallacy of Nuclear Defence* (London, 1958).
71 D. Healey, *The Race Against the H-Bomb* (London, 1960), p. 20.
72 Toynbee, *The Fearful Choice*, p. 11.
73 D.N. Pritt, *Ban the Bomb: Start the Talks* (London, 1955), p. 4
74 The poem was first collected in T. Hughes, *Lupercal* (London, 1960).
75 Gallup, *Gallup International Public Opinion Polls*, pp. 449.
76 Taylor, *Against the Bomb*.
77 Gallup, *Gallup International Public Opinion Polls*, pp. 716-17.
78 R. Wilmut (ed.), *The Complete Beyond the Fringe* (London, 1987), pp. 82, 93. (Emphasis in the original.)
79 Healey, *Race Against the H-Bomb*.
80 *H-Bomb War: What it Would be Like* (London, 1962).
81 Taylor, *Against the Bomb*, p. 99.
82 *H-Bomb War: What It Would be Like*, p. 2.
83 For more on *The War Game*, see the introduction to this volume, pp. 6-9.
84 J. Hogg, '"The Family that feared tomorrow": British nuclear culture and individual experience in the late 1950s', *The British Journal for the History of Science* 45:4 (2012), 535-49.
85 The script is in A. Wesker, 'Menace', in his *Six Sundays in January* (London, 1971), pp. 61-98.
86 Harry Ransom Center, University of Texas at Austin. Lessing Papers, Box 33, folders 1-4.
87 D. Lessing, *The Golden Notebook* (London, 2007 [1962]).
88 Lessing, *Golden Notebook*, pp. 119-227.
89 J. L. Gaddis, *The Long Peace. Inquiries into the History of the Cold War* (New York, 1987), pp. 215-45.

6

German angst? Debating Cold War anxieties in West Germany, 1945–90

Benjamin Ziemann

In the early 1980s, many leading US newspapers commented on a strange malady that had the largest Western European country firmly in its grip: German angst. American journalists noted that the people in West Germany seemingly relished their feelings of anxiety.[1] To some extent, this could be simply seen as an expression of the dark side of Teutonic romanticism. But these expressions of angst had a serious backdrop: the dual-track solution. This was a decision taken by NATO in December 1979 to offer negotiations between the superpowers over the mutual reduction of intermediate-range nuclear missiles, but to deploy 572 US Pershing II and cruise atomic missiles in Belgium, Germany, Italy, the Netherlands and the UK in case these negotiations failed. In their collective obsession with the potential results of an all-out nuclear war, the angst-ridden people in West Germany were a crucial factor in the complicated negotiations that followed the dual-track decision. Richard Perle (who, as US undersecretary of defence from 1981 to 1987, was a constant participant in the talks that formed the negotiating track of the 1979 NATO decision), later commented that the Germans were 'deeply neurotic on security issues'.[2] One could argue that the use of such rhetoric was driven by the vested interest of portraying the Germans as notoriously unreliable partners in the framework of NATO, compared to the sober realism of the US administration. Yet German angst was not only a label that was attached from the outside; it was also part and parcel of self-descriptions in the West German media in the 1980s.[3]

In this chapter, I will discuss nuclear anxieties in Germany from the end of the Second World War to the end of the Cold War. As a closer examination reveals, angst had already been an underlying motif in debates about German rearmament, war and peace during the 1950s. Yet anticipations and imaginations of the effect of nuclear weapons did not have a fixed and stable presence in West German society. While the 1950s and the 1980s were marked by intensive attempts to come to grips with the effects of nuclear weapons, the intensity of these endeavours receded during the fifteen years from the early 1960s to the mid-1970s. When the domestic conflict over the deployment of cruise missiles reached its apex, from 1981 to 1983, the earlier debates from the 1950s were by and large forgotten, and it could appear as if the West German public confronted the prospect of nuclear war for the first time.

Any consideration of the nuclear fantasies of the German public must consider two fundamental points. It has been – first of all – argued that many descriptions and imaginings of an impending nuclear apocalypse were only 'secularised' versions of older Christian millenarian hopes for a survival of the 'few righteous' believers in the wake of the apocalypse.[4] According to this argument, the possibility of nuclear war in the post-war period was a mere extension of an older tradition of apocalyptical thinking.[5] This interpretation, however, rests on shaky ground, as descriptions of a post-nuclear future in the Federal Republic were based on the fundamental insight that nuclear death was man-made, and not simply a teleological continuation or even fulfilment of history. It was seen as a leap into an unknown future, depending on contingent decisions taken by human beings, even if these human beings were effectively only appendices of the machines they struggled to control. This was a man-made future. It is precisely for this reason that imaginings of a nuclear apocalypse were part and parcel of the battlefield of the Cold War in Germany: conflicts over the rationale for nuclear deterrence, as well as anticipations of its potentially disastrous outcomes, were essentially political conflicts in the sense that they rested on competing notions and visions of human agency in regard to the use of the bomb. Visions of a nuclear apocalypse also differed from the Christian tradition in that they lacked 'a vision of salvation' – the firm expectation of a new perfect world that 'gave meaning and purpose to the end of the world'. In that sense, it was only a 'docked' or arrested apocalypse, one that was bereft of a crucial part of traditional thinking about the end of the world.[6]

While we try to emphasise that the contested imaginations of nuclear war have to be seen as a crucial battlefield of the Cold War, it is important to note – secondly – that Germany itself was perceived to be that battlefield. As in other countries, perceptions of the atomic bomb were deeply entwined with recollections of the bombing war of 1939–45. The imaginary battlefield of nuclear warfare was thus articulated and perceived against the backdrop of the real devastation that the Allied bombing campaign had brought to German cities during the Second World War.⁷ But throughout the intensive debate over nuclear armaments from the 1950s to the 1980s, Germany was also perceived as the main battlefield of a future nuclear war. Hence, there was a specific sense of urgency in the German discourse about the bomb that added heightened controversy and a sense of *Betroffenheit* – the feeling of being personally concerned, an important catchword of the 1970s and 1980s – to the German debate.

When US Air Force planes dropped atomic bombs on the Japanese cities of Hiroshima and Nagasaki in August 1945, these cataclysmic events barely registered among the German public. At this point, the military governments of the three Allies that controlled the Western zones of occupation had licensed only a fairly limited number of newspapers. Their coverage of the impact of the bombs was fairly limited and focused on the great extent of the devastation of the two cities, and on the great number of fatalities. Newsreel footage was not available before the autumn of 1945, and the effects of radiation were not discussed at all at this point.⁸ The lack of precise information was, however, only one of the factors that shaped German perceptions at this point. Even when the German media finally published images of the devastated cityscape of the two Japanese cities, they did not provoke outrage or moral revulsion. In the immediate post-war period, the citizens of many German cities lived amidst the ruins that the Allied bombing campaign during the Second World War had produced. If anything, the firestorms produced by the bombing of Hamburg in July 1943 and of Dresden in February 1945 were for them more potent symbols of large-scale destruction. Memories of the bombing during the war strongly resonated among the West German population well into the 1950s and beyond.⁹ When the first more extensive reports on Hiroshima appeared in the German media in 1947, a Catholic journal tried to take stock of the attitudes that had prevailed among the German public in the immediate aftermath of the attack on the Japanese city. 'Not for the first time', the author argued, 'had we heard of 200,000 dead people who had been carried off within a few hours.' People had 'shivered for a short moment' in the face of the ease with which destruction of this magnitude had been achieved. Then they moved on, facing a 'daily fight for their naked continued existence' and forgetting about Hiroshima amidst a plethora of other things that were 'closer to our conscience'.¹⁰

As the article demonstrates, large segments of German society were at this point still firmly in the grip of Nazi propaganda, as they apparently believed in the grossly exaggerated numbers of German victims in

Dresden and Hamburg that the regime had circulated. Only the belief in these inflated numbers allowed them to compare their own plight with that of the hibakusha, the survivors of the US atomic bombs in Hiroshima and Nagasaki. The economic hardship of the rubble society in the immediate post-war years fed into the perception that the Germans were victims of the bombing campaign. It was part of a broader victimisation discourse that emerged in the late 1940s and continued well into the 1950s, sustained both by the governing Christian Democrats and by many associations of Wehrmacht veterans. Images of emasculated German POWs in Soviet captivity were another important part of this discourse.[11] Against this backdrop, there were only scattered attempts to politicize the meaning of Hiroshima and to alert the Germans about the potential consequences of a nuclear war during the late 1940s. One of them was a radio play by journalist Axel Eggebrecht, broadcast in 1947. It featured an 'atomic blues' that included the lines: 'Einstein says he is anxious, and when Einstein is anxious, so am I. And if you are anxious about the A-bomb, then listen to what you have to do: band together with the whole of humankind.' The short text ended with the chorus: 'Hiroshima, Nagasaki, Bikini'.[12] The latter was a nod to the public interest in the atomic test the US military had conducted at Bikini Atoll in July 1946. It had received widespread coverage in the German media, and many comments stressed what they perceived as the apparent limits of destruction on the islands. There was also an ambiguous fascination with the mushroom clouds over Bikini Atoll. This was just one part of an important current in German engagement with nuclear technology from the late 1940s, which highlighted the seemingly boundless possibilities of the new nuclear technology and stressed that its civilian, peaceful uses were welcome. Even activists of the left-wing Social Democratic Party (SPD) perceived the 'atomic age' as positive, as a future characterised by a limitless supply of cheap electric energy.[13]

The prospect of nuclear destruction became a hotly contested topic in West German politics only in the wake of German rearmament. Public debate on this issue had started in 1950, and until the founding of the *Bundeswehr* rebuilt German armed forces within the framework of NATO in 1955. A crucial prerequisite of Germany's return to (still limited) sovereignty, and its rearmament, was Chancellor Konrad Adenauer's public waiving of any German intention to produce atomic weapons during the London Nine Power Conference in September 1954.[14] In the middle of the 1950s, strategic debates in US military and NATO circles about the use of atomic weapons shifted. Tactical atomic warheads with a lower yield and destructive capacity than strategic intercontinental missiles were now available. With their limited range, typically between fifteen miles for the 'Honest John' rocket and 110 miles for the Nike Hercules missiles, they could be used on the battlefield against enemy troops with conventional weaponry. That made a limited nuclear war in the European theatre more likely, as the need to respond immediately to any Soviet aggression through massive retaliation receded. It was against this backdrop that the main governing party, the Christian Democratic Union, the government itself and top-brass *Bundeswehr* officials pursued the option of equipping the German military with weapons systems that would carry American nuclear warheads – having the key to the warheads in German hands was never considered as a serious option.[15]

For Chancellor Adenauer, supplying the *Bundeswehr* with nuclear weapons systems had a clear rationale that was based on his notion of responsible statesmanship: only with them, Germany could regain full national sovereignty and acknowledgement as a major power among its Western allies.[16] Rather unclear and highly ambiguous, however, were the specifications of these warheads and their actual impact. Since 1954, the party executive committee of the CDU had repeatedly discussed the prospect of a nuclear war, and Adenauer himself, usually the main speaker, had described its effects in no uncertain terms. He explained in June 1955 that a city like New York could be 'completely terminated' by a single hydrogen bomb, not necessarily through total physical destruction, but in the sense that all 'organic life' would be 'killed' through radiation. In November 1956, Adenauer described the result of an all-out war with H-bombs as the 'doom of all humankind'.[17] Yet Adenauer and his colleagues struggled to find an appropriate terminology for an understanding of the technology of tactical nuclear warheads. In September 1956, he described it as something that could be fired from a 'regular cannon' or potentially even from a 'handgun'. Adopting another phraseology, he used – 'in want of a better expression' – the distinction between 'large and small nuclear weapons'. Theodor Blank, however, the minister of defence, interjected 'miracle weapon' into the debate. That was, in the German context, a clear allusion to the V-2 long-range missiles that the Wehrmacht had used to terrorise civilians in Belgian and British cities in 1944–45. Blank's use of this analogy created 'unrest' in the committee, and led Eugen Gerstenmaier, a leading CDU-functionary with a background in the Confessing Church and resistance against the Third Reich, to oppose the use of such terminology.[18]

Some historians have read these internal debates over the terminology of tactical nuclear weaponry as a cynical ploy, as a deliberate political attempt for the 'belittlement' of the potential devastation created by atomic warheads.[19] Yet this is not really plausible if we take the whole conduct of the meetings of the CDU party executive into account, including the rather desperate attempt by Blank to use the *Wunderwaffe* V-2 as a point for comparison. Adenauer and his colleagues were clearly struggling to understand how regular – in terms of their delivery – battlefield weapons could inflict devastation on such a vast scale. It was not (yet) the aim of political scheming, but rather a fundamental lack of knowledge, and a concomitant lack of imagination, that made these party debates so incoherent, despite the fact that Adenauer had consistently used every opportunity to be briefed on details in meetings with Allied diplomats and generals.[20] Able to obtain more specified knowledge were those *Bundeswehr* officers who worked in liaison with NATO staff or were for other reasons able to observe NATO war games that operationalised the use of nuclear warheads in Central Europe. Yet not all of this knowledge remained confidential. Already in the summer of 1955, news coverage of the NATO exercise Carte Blanche had shocked the German public. As a result of air force battles over six days, 268 atomic bombs were dropped during the war game on Germany alone, leading to 1.7 million dead and 3.7 million injured people. And that was only the lower end of possible fatalities, as the *Spiegel* magazine reported dryly, as the main focus of the bombings had been to destroy military airfields, not cities.[21] These disastrous consequences were widely read as a confirmation of the prediction of military writer Adelbert Weinstein that the first major consequence of nuclear warfare would be to turn Germany into the main battlefield.[22]

Projections such as Carte Blanche did not only shock the German public. They also disturbed the participating German officers. Particularly worrying was the fact that most of the tactical nuclear warheads that were hitting German cities in these simulations were fired by Allied and not by Soviet troops. In operation Lion Noir, for instance, a war game conducted in the spring of 1957, 108 Western and only twenty enemy nuclear weapons impacted on German targets. This simulation was based on the insight that the conventional troops NATO had at its disposal in Germany would not be able to withstand a major Soviet attack. Thus, tactical nuclear weapons were considered as the main instrument for stopping a projected advance of the Red Army at the Rhine at the very latest. From the perspective of the *Bundeswehr*, the 'primary aim' in such war games was thus to secure the 'survival of the German population'. That the Allies would 'have that always in mind' was rather doubtful to the German military.²³

For the German military, a rapid expansion of their own conventional territorial forces was the best bet to alleviate this problem, as it might help them to withstand a Soviet conventional attack eventually. But those German generals who knew NATO thinking realised that this was a futile hope, given the slow progress of training in the *Bundeswehr*, the overall balance of troops in Europe, and Western strategic thinking. In 1960, the German general Albert Schnez visited the SHAPE headquarters of the Allied forces in Europe at Fontainebleau. Reporting back to the minister of defence, Franz Josef Strauß, he could confirm that members of staff at SHAPE were indeed studying the results of a defensive use of tactical warheads with 'scientific rigour'. Yet the practical implementation of any such strategy, Schnez concluded, would lead to a truly 'paradoxical' result: the Western Allies would 'extinguish' the very country that had to be defended, Germany. The victory of the 'free world' over 'bondage' in the East, as Schnez formulated in a juxtaposition that used liberal Cold War thinking, could only be achieved over a 'Golgotha of the German people'.²⁴ Conjuring up the notion of the German people crucified by atomic blasts, Schnez' metaphor tapped into a victimisation discourse that saw the Germans not only as the victims of the previous, but also as those of a future world war.

As NATO implemented the use of tactical nuclear warheads as a default option in its planning for the European theatre, and the Adenauer government aimed to make these weapons available to its military, anxieties about the potential consequences of their use were articulated even among those *Bundeswehr* officers who had to implement these policies. These anxieties were articulated only in confidential meetings and classified documents. Yet in 1956–57, plans to provide the German army with nuclear equipment broke into the open and became a battleground for domestic politics. Incidentally, it was Adenauer himself who provided the debate with an important catchphrase, when he argued as follows in a press conference on 4 April 1957: 'Tactical atomic weapons are basically nothing else than an advancement of artillery ... these are special yet normal weapons in the normal armaments.'²⁵ Basically, Adenauer only reiterated a terminology that was used by US officials whom he had met in the past year. Yet because any of these 'normal weapons' had an explosive power that equalled or exceeded that of the Hiroshima bomb, Adenauer had opened himself up to accusations of hypocrisy.²⁶

Already on 12 April 1957, eighteen leading atomic physicists, including many of those who had worked on a project to develop the atomic bomb for the Wehrmacht, stepped into the public limelight by publishing their 'Göttingen declaration'. In this short text, they explained the distinction between tactical and strategic weapons (hydrogen bombs in particular), and highlighted the tremendous destructive power the former already had. They invoked their professional responsibility in 'pure science and its application' to recommend that Germany should relinquish any possession of atomic weaponry. As far as this group was concerned, Adenauer was able to defuse their protest by inviting some of the physicists to the Chancellery shortly after they had voiced their concerns.[27] But Adenauer's slip and the declaration of the nuclear physicists triggered a much larger protest movement. It comprised a number of left-wing intellectuals, artists and writers as well as significant groups and leading theologians within the Protestant churches in West Germany, namely in the Rhineland and in Hesse-Nassau. By far the largest constituent of this movement, however, were Social Democratic members of the trade union movement and of the SPD itself, acting with support of the leadership of both organisations. The movement gathered some momentum ahead of the Federal elections on 15 September 1957, which returned the Christian Democrats with an absolute majority. After that setback, it regrouped and established a more formal structure with the founding of a steering committee in February 1958, which issued a public appeal 'Fight against Atomic Death' on 10 March 1958.[28]

In the first half of 1958, the campaign 'Fight against Atomic Death' organised a large number of mass rallies across Germany. It campaigned for a referendum over the question of whether the *Bundeswehr* should be equipped with nuclear weaponry and launching sites for nuclear missiles built in Germany. Yet, on 30 July 1958, the Federal Constitutional Court, called upon by the government, ruled that such a referendum was unconstitutional. After the ruling, SPD and the trade unions called off the campaign.[29] Even though it was only a short-lived campaign, followed by the Easter March movement of the 1960s that gained considerably less traction throughout the decade, 'Fight against Atomic Death' was remarkable for its interventions in the battle over imagining nuclear war in Germany. At least three points should be mentioned. First, 'Fight against Nuclear Death' entailed some of the first substantial attempts in Germany to make the devastation caused by nuclear war visible and hence knowable. In many ways, these endeavours were incoherent, yet also remarkable in that they used different media of visual communication. Posters were one of them.[30] Artists also rallied to the cause. From 1958 to the end of 1962, a touring exhibition with 100 paintings and other pieces of graphic art was on display in various German cities, in support of the 'Fight against Atomic Death' campaign even after it had been called off. The subjects of the woodcuts, etchings and pencil drawings varied as widely as their visual codes, ranging from irony – with the line 'do not throw anything on the ground' above a bin, against the backdrop of bombs falling to the ground in a woodcut by Frans Masereel – to the grotesque, as the mutated 'nuclear waste frogs' in a gouache by Heinrich Eugen.[31]

The campaign used also short documentary films, released in cinemas ahead of the main feature. One example was 'Key to Hell', funded and produced on behalf of one of the German Deutscher Gewerkschaftsbund (DGB) trade unions, and released in the spring of 1958.[32] The central premise of the short film is the ambivalence of modern technology: it can build and nourish affluence, but can also destroy, and thus offers the 'key to hell' that the title metaphor invokes. In one sequence, footage of a mushroom cloud emanating from one of the nuclear tests was cut against a pan shot over the ruins of a bombed-out West German city, implying that this was the safest way to make Germans able to relate to the prospect of mass destruction. Another sequence tried to drive home the dangers of radiation, using footage that showed the burned and scarred skin of – in all likelihood Japanese, although this was not made explicit – people who had been exposed to nuclear fallout.

A second important aspect of the campaign against nuclear death was the new inclusive language that it brought to the fore. A speech by Martin Niemöller demonstrates this point. Niemöller, Church President of the Protestant Church in Hesse-Nassau, was one of the signatories of the 'Fight against Atomic Death' appeal and a leading figurehead of German pacifism more generally. As a former submarine captain during the First World War who had spent eight years in Nazi concentration camps for being the most outspoken voice of the Confessing Church, Niemöller was better placed than anyone else to signify the pacifist consciousness of the Germans and their turn away from militarism post-1945.[33] In his speech, delivered in 1958, he reiterated some of the hallmark arguments of his nuclear pacifism, and detailed the campaigning of the ecumenical World Council of Churches – of which he was a leading member – against nuclear testing. He ridiculed Adenauer's statement about tactical nuclear weapons as a 'mere advancement' of conventional artillery. 'Carpet bombing' during the Second World War, Niemöller stated, had already been a 'crime against humanity'. New and decisive, however, was the point that politicians could now destroy 'life altogether' on the planet Earth with the H-bomb. This 'totally new situation' also had an impact on the concepts used to describe war and peace, which had lost their previous meaning as 'war is not any longer war', and what was called peace 'was already war'.[34] Thus, Niemöller not only demonstrated a fine sense for the inversion of concepts in the shadow of the bomb that the philosopher Günter Anders analysed so sharply at the same time. Without using that precise terminology, he also echoed Anders' point that nuclear war differed fundamentally from past atrocities or genocides, even those of the Second World War, as it had to be understood as an omnicide, a killing of all humankind.[35]

The third pertinent issue in this context is the notion of angst. When the campaign against atomic death rallied hundreds of thousands of people across Germany in 1957–58, it was already the third wave of mobilisation against the military in that decade alone, after the protests against German rearmament in the years from 1950 to 1952, and the subsequent campaigning against the reintroduction of general conscription in 1955–56. The overwhelming rejection of nuclear arms for the *Bundeswehr* in 1957–58 stood in a stark contrast with the astounding majority the Christian Democrats achieved in the 1957 Federal election. Yet as Michael Geyer has argued, the Cold War angst of the Germans actually preceded the debate over nuclear equipment for the German military. As early as 1954, an opinion poll revealed that a majority of the Germans believed that their country would be 'the target of atomic bombs'. Neither the introduction of nuclear-free zones – widely debated in 1957–58 in the guise of the Rapacki-plan that the Polish foreign minister, Adam Rapacki, had presented to the UN in October 1957 – nor the prospect of sustained air defence systems made any difference to that perception. The main fear of the Germans was not that the *Bundeswehr* might be equipped with nuclear weapons systems. Rather, amidst the space of experiences that the past war had marked in their perception, and set against the expectation of an unstable future, they feared imminent death.[36] It was the link between the scars of the past and the prospect of nuclear missiles raining down on their country that deeply engrained angst in the collective mentality of the West Germans. Chancellor Adenauer, who showed throughout these debates what a canny political operator he was, knew as much. In May 1957, he instructed his party executive to take these emotions seriously: '[b]elieve me, the *Angst* for the atomic bomb is something emotional, and in order to master this emotional situation, after the German people had to endure the last war, will be very difficult'.

Adenauer was also determined to impress on his party colleagues the need not to misinterpret the Social Democrats as the main enemy in this political battle. The battle was not against the opposition, he insisted, it was rather a 'fight against the angst', which also haunted the followers of his own party. The only way to combat this angst, Adenauer concluded in a strikingly honest formulation, was to 'banish it with an even bigger angst'.[37] The German Chancellor was well aware that fear of the Soviet Union was not big enough to accomplish this feat, in spite of the fierce and often hysterical anti-communism in 1950s Germany. Without giving names – although he clearly alluded to Niemöller, at this point the nemesis of the Adenauer government – he referred to those who would 'rather be red than dead'.[38] Nevertheless, during the 1957 federal election campaign the CDU used a poster that showed a mushroom cloud behind hammer and sickle, admonishing against 'red atomic death'.[39]

Throughout the 1960s, angst about the prospect of nuclear annihilation was not a prominent feature of West German political culture. To be sure, the anti-nuclear pacifism of the Easter march movement emerged out of the remnants of 'Fight against Atomic Death'. In 1960, it staged its first event over the Easter weekend, inspired by CND's Aldermaston marches. Yet the Easter march movement had a rather marginal presence in German politics, bringing only between 100,000 and 150,000 people to the streets in the years 1964–68.[40] As historian Frank Biess has observed, other factors compounded so that nuclear angst received increasingly scant attention. International factors such as the resolution of the Cuban Missile Crisis and the Nuclear Test Ban Treaty in 1963 had an impact, as they made the prospect of imminent nuclear war less likely. Changing perceptions of the US were also crucial. More positive attitudes towards America implied that West Germans increasingly trusted that the US nuclear shield might protect them effectively.[41]

Yet new departures in NATO strategy and policy from the late 1960s changed the ways in which West Germans perceived the dangers of nuclear weapons, and refreshed their feelings of angst vis-à-vis an invisible threat. In its nuclear strategy, NATO had formally adopted the notion of 'flexible response' in 1967–68. Thus, it had opened up a scenario in which the use of nuclear weapons would not automatically lead to an all-out, global nuclear war, but would be restricted to the European theatre of operations.[42] And as a Soviet attack with conventional forces in Central Europe was the starting point for NATO planning in these simulations, West Germany was easily identifiable as the main target for the first wave of nuclear warheads. Thus, it was by all chance the first country to be totally destroyed in a future nuclear war. It was precisely this perception of the potential shortcomings of 'flexible response' from a European perspective which had led Social Democratic German Chancellor Helmut Schmidt to call for a Western response to the deployment of Soviet SS-20 intermediate missiles in his talk at the London International Institute of Strategic Studies in October 1977.[43] This response was meant to fill the gap that had been opened up by the recent changes in US strategic thinking. Ironically, Schmidt, who advocated and in fact instigated the NATO dual-track solution, and the millions of Germans who took to the streets over the coming years in protests against it, were driven by similar worries about a country devastated by nuclear war.

The conflicts over the approval and the subsequent implementation of the NATO dual-track solution during the years from 1979 to 1985 were momentous events in the history of the Federal Republic. They not only led to the downfall of the coalition government between the SPD and the Liberals in 1982, ushering in sixteen years of stable Christian Democratic governments, and changing the German party system for good in establishing the Greens as the fourth major nationwide party. Through intensive debates that involved all political currents and groups, the conflict over cruise missiles also worked as a 'catalyst' for a renegotiation of crucial parameters of West German citizenship, of its transatlantic orientation, and of conceptions of nationhood.[44] Not least, a new culture of mass protest emerged. During the early 1980s, no less than 2.7 per cent of the West German population described themselves as active members of the anti-nuclear peace movement, and 45 per cent as potential activists. It is fair to assume that the overall number of participants in protest events during the 1980s was more than twice that of the 1960s, although these are only informed estimates based on the compilation of newspaper reports. The total during the 1980s stood at about 21 million participants. Almost half of these took part in peace protests.[45] Key protest events were the *Hofgartendemo* in Bonn on 10 October 1981 with 300,000 people and the human chain that an estimated 400,000 protesters formed on 22 October 1983 across a 67 mile stretch between the cities of Stuttgart and Neu-Ulm. They have become landmark moments in the history of the Federal Republic, captivated in iconic photographs and a recurring talking point for participants even more than three decades later.[46]

The conflict over the dual-track solution – known as 'Nachrüstung' or an 'up-grading of armaments' in German parlance, a government term that the peace movement consistently refuted – conjured up a plethora of images of nuclear destruction. Given the sheer scale of its support among the population, the peace movement was the most important stakeholder of attempts to sketch out the immediate consequences of a nuclear war for Germany.[47] Compared with debates in the late 1950s, a more general feature of these attempts was that they were based on efforts to gather and extrapolate more detailed knowledge about the sites of impact and, once they had been identified, develop war games and scenarios on the basis of that knowledge. The first strategy in that respect was to map nuclear militarisation. Activists tapped into publicly available information mostly of American provenance and learned to identify the technical and geographical features that suggested that a US military facility either held nuclear ammunition or was a potential launching site for Nike Hercules missiles and other types of nuclear weapons. Based on the exchange of this information, various atlases of the nuclear threat were published. They included detailed maps of the Federal Republic with information on confirmed and suspected nuclear sites. The key aim of this strategy was to lift the 'veil of secrecy' that covered nuclear missiles and made them 'invisible', as one booklet stated in 1983. Photographs of guarded entry points to the facilities were often added to make the eerie emptiness of these sites more tangible.[48]

In a second step, local peace initiatives tried to make the prospect of nuclear war tangible by developing worst-case scenarios of a potential impact. Most of these texts were based on the premise of a war by mistake, based on the malfunctioning of technology or erratic behaviour by mid-level military personnel. Another core feature of these narratives was to stress the short-term nature of the threat, or, in other words, that everything would be finished within hours, if not moments. Mapping was used as a visual aid, outlining the circles of devastation around the epicentre of an atomic blast. The key point of these scenarios was to drive home the message that nuclear devastation was coming to the doorstep of German citizens, and that is was not a remote or abstract probability, but something that would hit their local environment. The epitome of atomic war in the neighbourhood was the small village of Hattenbach in Hesse. It was part of the so-called 'Fulda gap', the most extended protrusion of GDR-territory into the Federal Republic, and thus the first gateway of a Soviet attack in all war games since the 1950s. Hattenbach rose to prominence after it was featured in a 1981 CBS documentary on the defence of the US as the most likely place for the first 'ground zero' – being hit by US warheads to stop the Soviet advance across Germany. The German media picked up on this story, and print media, public broadcast television (which did not show the CBS documentary, as it was only broadcast on Austrian television) and publications of the peace movement were quick on their feet to use Hattenbach and the 'Fulda gap' as signifiers for the first place to be wiped out in a nuclear war.[49]

Hattenbach is a striking example for the dual structure of the imaginary war: the duplicity of simulation and case of emergency, of the imaginary and its embodiment, and the links between the two. As both the CBS documentary and German media reports highlighted, Hattenbach did in fact exist twice. At the US Army Combined Arms Center at Fort Leavenworth, Kansas, a facility for the training of army leadership candidates, Hattenbach existed as a sandpit model, that is, as a plastic replica of the original village and the relief in which it was situated. As such, it was a teaching aid that was used to familiarise US army officers with the terrain in which a war with tactical nuclear weapons in Central Europe would be fought in all likelihood. As the CBS voice-over clarified, it was easy to forget for the US officers that they engaged with what was at the same time a real village, which the CBS team visited to get a sense of the place that was bound to be wiped out first in a nuclear war. When local village folk insisted that the documentary should be shown in Hattenbach, the mayor, a Social Democrat, opposed such a move, arguing that 'one would not tell a pig in advance that it is going to be slaughtered'.[50] Through coverage of topics such as the Fulda gap, a significant cross-circulation of signifiers between the peace movement and the mass media took place, in which the latter used some of the key tropes of the threat scenarios of the former and adopted them to frame the public debate over the dangers of the dual-track solution.[51]

The fictitious nuclear war scenarios that the peace movement publicised were fairly simple and lacked more elaborate narratives. These were provided by the many books published during the 1980s that offered a detailed scenario of an impending nuclear catastrophe. Established novelists and playwrights in both East and West Germany made many original contributions to the literary imagination of a nuclear war during the 1980s, and found novel artistic solutions to the problems of depicting nuclear devastation. They also developed an anti-nuclear activism of their own, not least through high-profile meetings between authors from the GDR and the Federal Republic.[52] In some respects, more pertinent are the books by those authors who were not professional fiction writers, and whose books straddled or deliberately blurred the distinction between the genres and narrative modes of non-fiction and fiction. This was an international genre that included German translations of titles by authors such as Sir John Hackett, a retired British army general who had served as commander of the British army of the Rhine from 1965 to 1968, or Brian Harris.[53]

Yet German authors also had a prominent voice in this type of literature, and their books quickly shifted hundreds of thousands of copies. One example is the 'Diary from the Third World War' that the left-liberal journalist Anton Andreas Guha (1937–2010) published in 1983.[54] Guha had already made a name for himself as a staunch critic of Western security policy with previous non-fiction releases. He explained his move to a portrayal of nuclear war through the means of fiction as a result of the need to make the unimaginable available to 'sensual experience'.[55] Guha's account of an all-out nuclear war – triggered by the mobilisation of US troops in East Asian military bases, and the subsequent Soviet retaliation – is organised as a first-person narrative of an alter ego of Guha, a newspaper journalist who lives in Frankfurt. In terms of emplotment, nuclear war is portrayed as an inevitable tragedy. While politicians pretend to act and speak with reason, they are only cogs in a drama that unfolds with necessity. Yet at the root of this catastrophe is the ultimate 'failure of the fantasy and of the capacity for imagination' by actors on all sides to make the wanton destruction caused by nuclear bombs tangible. Guha himself does not try. As the narrative unfolds, the utter anomy, the total breakdown of societal structures caused by the blast, takes centre stage. At the end, after his partner has died, the narrator commits suicide.[56]

Guha made it clear that there were no survivors and used the form of a fictitious diary to create suspense as the events unfolded. Horst Eberhard Richter took a different approach. A renowned psychologist and therapist, Richter was a leading member of the German section of IPPNW. In his 1981 book 'Everyone talked about Peace', which had a particularly large audience owing to its serialisation in the *Spiegel* magazine, he told the story of nuclear annihilation from the perspective of a team of scientists from a distant star who tried to unravel the causes of global destruction on earth.[57] At the beginning, Richter tapped into traditional notions of pacifism. He quoted a line from French novelist Henri Barbusse, popular among German war veterans in the 1920s, according to which 'two belligerent armies are in fact one that is committing suicide'.[58] Yet his subsequent plot offered a more dystopian vision. Scrutinising the surviving papers of one of its agents, the future scientists uncovered that 'HERMES', a clandestine board of intelligence service agents from the East and the West, had conspired to prepare governments and populations on both sides of the Iron Curtain for the actual use of nuclear weapons in a co-ordinated master-plan. Nuclear war was, in fact, the result of assisted suicide. Aside from the portrayal of spies as the masterminds behind the war, Richter suggested a catastrophic failure of a technocratic form of rationality that was dominant in the West and the East as the reason why the masses where so easily lulled in submission. An additional factor was that not even Hiroshima had been able to inspire the fancy of politicians and ordinary people and to make them think about the potential recurrence of such a disastrous event.[59]

During the 1980s, expressing subjective and highly intimate anxieties about nuclear catastrophe was not any longer deemed to be an offence against the code of personal conduct, but rather as a necessity for both one's own wellbeing and the survival of humankind. Angst did not appear to be a debilitating and paralysing emotion, but as something that could have a liberating effect and spur individuals into action. 'The audacity of angst' (*Mut zur Angst*) was a popular slogan among peace movement supporters that encapsulated this new emotional regime.[60] This new understanding of angst that the peace movement of the 1980s brought to the fore was firmly contextualised in the 'psycho-boom' of the 1970s, a widespread interest in therapeutic forms of self-understanding and life-reform that had captured the imagination of the left-alternative milieu in the wake of the 1968 revolt.[61] In the context of the conflict over the dual-track solution, the readiness of peace activists to own up to personal anxieties about impending nuclear destruction fulfilled a number of functions, as historian Susanne Schregel has demonstrated. To highlight subjective emotions in public could serve a political purpose, as it was used to counter the 'cold', instrumental rationality of politicians and the military that was the root cause of the 'death-inducing arms race'.[62] Showing emotions was thus not irrational, as conservative politicians claimed, but could foster a new type of rationality that was needed to unmask the pitfalls of nuclear deterrence. Confessing to angst about cruise missiles could, second, also be used to deflect the charge that in reality West Germans had to fear the Soviets first and foremost. Among the many activists of the peace movement, opinions differed about the extent to which the Soviet Union was to blame for the nuclear arms race. Yet there was widespread consensus that 'Russenangst', an emotion that had been nurtured and propagated since 1945, should not any longer distract the Germans from taking a critical stance towards nuclear weapons.[63]

The third and most important point, however, was that confessing to feelings of angst about an impending nuclear war was an act of self-authentication.⁶⁴ Therapists were confronted with clients who recalled extensive and repeated dreams about their own actions as one of the few survivors of an all-out nuclear war. From the perspective of the psychotherapists, the nightmarish visions their clients had in their dreams circled around questions about the meaning of their personal life, the problem of an 'apocalyptic mood' that prevailed in their social circles, and obviously about 'angst about an atomic war'.⁶⁵ More than anything else, the nightmares of ordinary Germans who anticipated their own death or their own survival in an imminent nuclear war during those fleeting traces of their own subconscious activity confirmed that the imaginary war had in fact a reality. In an article published in 1986, Ernst Tugendhat, professor of philosophy in Berlin, offered his own reflections on the contested issue of angst. Tugendhat was one of the few philosophers who took the dual-track solution as a challenge to reflect on the limits of instrumental rationality. His conclusion was that those anxieties 'were adequate to reality'. The real question was not, he argued, why large numbers of Germans confessed to their feelings of angst, but rather why the 'great majority' of them did not seem to have these feelings.⁶⁶

Contrary to what the international media reported in the early 1980s, the anxiety of many Germans about nuclear armaments had not just emerged in the wake of the decision on the dual-track solution. Angst about nuclear war had already gripped the Germans throughout the 1950s and in the early 1960s, largely irrespective of political orientation or social standing. At this point, however, angst was not yet a matter of public discourse. In the anonymous setting of opinion polls, respondents were free to voice their fear that a nuclear destruction of Germany seemed to be imminent. Yet in public discourse, the protest against nuclear weapons was framed as a fight against death, and only a few members of the Easter march movements openly expressed their feelings of anxiety. One of the few prominent figures during the 1950s who not only spoke openly about nuclear angst, but also analysed the ways in which it blocked political progress was Martin Niemöller. To some extent, however, this only confirmed his role as a maverick who was confronting post-war Germany with all sorts of radical arguments.⁶⁷ Only the therapeutic culture of confession that emerged during the 1970s made it possible for individuals and groups to speak openly about their nuclear anxieties, and they could consider these feelings as the very basis for a new form of political rationality that was urgently needed amidst the renewed Cold War tensions of the time. Discursive frameworks such as the psycho-boom were thus an important external condition of the ways in which the imaginary nuclear war was articulated. In 1981, even the inspector general of the *Bundeswehr* could admit in an interview that he had sleepless nights when he considered the potential implications of his professional work on nuclear weapons systems.[68] In his 1960 book on thermonuclear war, Herman Kahn had famously asked whether the survivors of a nuclear war might perhaps envy the dead. In the Federal Republic of the 1980s, many people were probably inclined to answer this question in the affirmative.[69]

Both during the 1950s and the late 1970s and 1980s, the prospect of nuclear destruction was for many Germans not a distant apocalyptical vision that might lead to a final reckoning. Rather, it was a short-term expectation – something that people thought could and indeed would occur at any moment.[70] This perception requires an explanation, and the charge, brought by some foreign observers during the 1980s, that the Germans were naturally prone to self-pity and a form of black romanticism, does not really suffice. It is impossible to give a single straightforward answer, and the issue still requires much further research for both periods. An important point was without doubt the knowledge (which was shared by officers and planners in the ranks of the *Bundeswehr* as well as by politicians, peace activists and ordinary people) that Germany would be the primary battlefield of a 'limited' nuclear war with tactical warheads – a scenario that seemed to be the most likely outcome from the point at which these weapons were available in the 1950s. During the 1950s, this knowledge was rather sketchy and tentative even among the German military who had yet to be inducted into the details of NATO nuclear target planning.

No elaborate knowledge of military planning was needed, however, in order to figure out the consequences of nuclear deterrence for the German people. This can be gleaned from the diaries of Franz Göll (1899–1984), who lived all of his rather unassuming life in the same flat in the western part of Berlin, working as a night-watchman in the post-war years. Yet while he lacked any higher education, Göll was a keen and apt observer of contemporary affairs. From the 1950s to the early 1980s, the proliferation of nuclear weapons and their inherent risks occupied Göll more than any other of the many 'dramatic episodes' in Berlin's Cold War, including the 1953 uprising in East Berlin and the student riots in 1967–68.[71] Göll objected to Adenauer's policy of using nuclear weapons as a bargaining chip for acceptance in the Western alliance. He was highly sceptical of the deployment of nuclear warheads on German soil, not only because it brought the world closer to a 'Third World War … "by the hour", but much more so, as he well understood the underlying weaknesses of nuclear deterrence: 'To be sure', he mused in a diary entry in March 1958, 'a zone that is not secured *can* be attacked without risk', but hastened to add that 'a zone that is secured [with nuclear weapons] will be attacked with *certainty*'. He also doubted the logic of mutually assured destruction, calling it 'frivolous' and 'barbaric' 'to use words like courage and cowardice in connection with the atomic threat'.[72]

During the 1950s and 1960s, Göll's level of insight may have been exceptional among ordinary Germans. Yet in the 1980s, with a much more proactive and knowledgeable peace movement, many details about military planning that were in the open domain were pieced together and produced more elaborate knowledge about the impending destruction that people as the village folk in Hattenbach were facing right at their doorstep. The anxieties that spurred German into anti-nuclear action were not based on deep-seated ideological commitments or the effect of sinister machinations by the Stasi and the West German fellow-travellers of Soviet Communism. These anxieties emanated in those many neighbourhoods in which Germans noted that the threat of nuclear devastation was not confined to some distant islands in the South Pacific, but could happen right where they lived, or, as historian Susanne Schregel has called it, as 'nuclear war in front of the apartment door'.[73] There is an important parallel that can be drawn here to anti-nuclear protests in the United States during the 1970s and 1980s, which have been aptly described as a form of 'front porch politics'.[74]

The perception of many West Germans that nuclear war could happen right on their own doorstep revealed one of the fundamental paradoxes of the Cold War as a nuclear conflict: that the spatial dimension of war, so crucial for military strategy in all previous wars, had become largely meaningless for the conduct of nuclear war. One of the first German officers to recognise this paradox fully was Wolf Count von Baudissin (1907–93). He had been among the group of officers who built up the *Bundeswehr* behind the scenes since 1951, and was instrumental in developing the notion of 'inner leadership' that should prevent an ideological abuse of the military as it had happened during the Third Reich. In the summer of 1962, Baudissin (who was then serving at the NATO headquarters in Fontainebleau as deputy chief of AFCENT) gave a public lecture in Germany that outlined his thinking on nuclear war. A front-line in the traditional sense would not exist in such a war, Baudissin argued, as any larger gathering of troops would come under immediate fire from tactical nuclear warheads. As a consequence, also the distinction between the centre, left and right wing, so crucial for traditional strategy, would disappear, and armies would not any longer fight to conquer space. In a nuclear war, Baudissin opined, 'space would only be a medium of warfare, within which a certain purpose of battle' should be achieved.[75] It was precisely because nuclear war could be fought everywhere that so many Germans imagined it could happen right on their doorstep.

Notes

1. F. Brühöfener, '"Angst vor dem Atom": Emotionalität und Politik im Spiegel bundesdeutscher Zeitungen 1979–1984', in P. Bernhard and H. Nehring (eds), *Den Kalten Krieg denken. Beiträge zur sozialen Ideengeschichte nach 1945* (Essen, 2014), pp. 285–306, p. 285.
2. Interview with Richard Perle, 25 February 1988, online at: http://openvault.wgbh.org/catalog/wpna-f03bb6-interview-with-richard-perle-1988 (accessed 16 February 2016).
3. Brühöfener, 'Angst'.
4. P. Gassert, 'Popularität der Apokalypse: Zur Nuklearangst seit 1945', *Aus Politik und Zeitgeschichte* 61:46/7 (2011), pp. 48–54, p. 50.
5. K. Vondung, *The Apocalypse in Germany* (New York, 2000).
6. *Ibid.*, p. 5.
7. J. Arnold, '"Kassel 1943 mahnt..." Zur Genealogie der Angst im Kalten Krieg', in B. Greiner, C.T. Müller and D. Walter (eds), *Angst im Kalten Krieg* (Hamburg, 2009), pp. 465–94.
8. I. Stölken-Fitschen, *Atombombe und Geistesgeschichte. Eine Studie der fünfziger Jahre aus deutscher Sicht* (Baden-Baden 1995), p. 23.
9. D. Süss, *Death from the Skies: How the British and Germans Survived Bombing in World War II* (Oxford, 2014), pp. 455ff.
10. *Herder-Korrespondenz* 1 (1947), p. 306, quoted in Stölken-Fitschen, *Atombombe*, p. 24.
11. R.G. Moeller, 'War stories: the search for a usable past in the Federal Republic of Germany', *American Historical Review* 101 (1996), pp. 1008–48.
12. 'Das Fräulein und die Weltgeschichte. Refrain: Hiroshima, Nagasaki', *Der Spiegel*, 3 May 1947, p. 18.
13. Stölken-Fitschen, *Atombombe*, pp. 32–6, 148–87.
14. M. Knoll, *Atomare Optionen. Westdeutsche Kernwaffenpolitik in der Ära Adenauer* (Frankfurt, 2013), pp. 127–34.
15. The most comprehensive study of these debates is B. Thoß, *NATO-Strategie und nationale Verteidigungsplanung. Planung und Aufbau der Bundeswehr unter den Bedingungen einer massiven atomaren Vergeltungsstrategie 1952 bis 1960* (Munich, 2006), pp. 68–198.
16. H.-P. Schwarz, 'Adenauer und die Kernwaffen', *Vierteljahrshefte für Zeitgeschichte*, 37 (1989), pp. 567–93.

17 G. Buchstab (ed.), *"Wir haben wirklich etwas geschaffen." Die Protokolle des CDU-Bundesvorstandes 1953 bis 1957* (Düsseldorf, 1990), p. 120, quotes pp. 506 (3 June 1955), 1117 (23 November 1956).
18 *Ibid.*, quotes pp. 1029, 1073, 1078 (20 September 1956).
19 D. Bald, *Die Atombewaffnung der Bundeswehr. Militär, Öffentlichkeit und Politik in der Ära Adenauer* (Bremen, 1994), pp. 22–9, quote p. 25.
20 Schwarz, 'Adenauer und die Kernwaffen', p. 574.
21 'Überholt wie Pfeil und Bogen', *Spiegel*, 13 July 1955, pp. 7–10.
22 *Ibid.*; Thoß, *NATO-Strategie*, pp. 106f.
23 Thoß, *NATO-Strategie*, pp. 344ff., 352f. (quotes), 414f.
24 Quoted *ibid.*, p. 727.
25 Extract from a press conference with Adenauer, 5 Apr. 1957, cited in: 'Die Bombe im Schiff', *Spiegel*, 15 May 1957, p. 12.
26 Knoll, *Atomare Optionen*, pp. 146–52.
27 R. Lorenz, *Protest der Physiker. Die "Göttinger Erklärung" von 1957* (Bielefeld, 2011), pp. 31f.
28 A. Schildt, '"Atomzeitalter." Gründe und Hintergründe der Proteste gegen die atomare Bewaffnung der Bundeswehr Ende der fünfziger Jahre', in *"Kampf dem Atomtod!" Die Protestbewegung 1957/58 in zeithistorischer und gegenwärtiger Perspektive* (Munich. Hamburg, 2009), pp. 39–56; see also H. Nehring, *Politics of Security. British and West German Protest Movements and the Early Cold War, 1945–1970* (Oxford, 2013), chapters 2–4.
29 Schildt, '"Atomzeitalter"', pp. 46–51.
30 B. Ziemann, 'The code of protest: images of peace in the West German peace movements, 1945–1990', *Contemporary European History* 17 (2008), pp. 237–61.
31 A. Jürgens-Kirchhoff, 'Artists against Nnclear war' (1958–1962). A touring exhibition at the time of the Cold War', in B. Ziemann (ed.), *Peace Movements in Western Europe, Japan and the USA during the Cold War* (Essen, 2007), pp. 211–36, pp. 220f., 234.
32 'Schlüssel zur Hölle. Ein dokumentarischer Filmbeitrag zum Kampf gegen den Atomtod.' Cassiopeia Film, 16mm, b/w, 12 minutes, n.d. [1958]: Archiv für soziale Bewegungen, Bochum, Altsignatur 61.
33 The standard account, now somewhat dated, is J. Bentley, *Martin Niemöller* (Oxford, 1984), pp. 199–218.
34 *Martin Niemöller zur atomaren Rüstung. Zwei Reden* (Darmstadt, 1959), p. 13f.
35 This crucial distinction is missed in the analysis of this passage by Nehring, *Politics of Security*, p. 56.
36 M. Geyer, 'Cold War angst: the case of West-German opposition to rearmament and nuclear weapons', in H. Schissler (ed.), *Miracle Years. A Cultural History of West Germany, 1949–1968* (Princeton, 2001), pp. 376–408, pp. 397f.
37 Buchstab (ed.), *"Wir haben wirklich etwas geschaffen"*, quotes pp. 1229, 1236 (11 May 1957).

38 *Ibid.*, p. 1129.
39 H. Löttel, 'Des "Emotionalen Herr werden." Konrad Adenauer und die "Angst vor der Atombombe" im Jahr 1957', in P. Bormann, T. Freiberger and J. Michel (eds), *Angst in den Internationalen Beziehungen* (Göttingen, 2010), pp. 205–25, p. 223.
40 Nehring, *Politics of Security*, pp. 230–58.
41 F. Biess, '"Jeder hat eine Chance." Die Zivilschutzkampagnen der 1960er Jahre und die Angstgeschichte der Bundesrepublik', in Greiner, Müller and Walter (eds), Angst im Kalten Krieg, pp. 61–93, pp. 89–91.
42 Knoll, *Atomare Optionen*, pp. 95–107.
43 H. Haftendorn, 'Das doppelte Mißverständnis. Zur Vorgeschichte des NATO-Doppelbeschlusses von 1979', *Vierteljahrshefte für Zeitgeschichte* 33 (1985), pp. 244–87; T. Geiger, 'Die Regierung Schmidt-Genscher und der NATO-Doppelbeschluss', in P. Gassert, T. Geiger and H. Wentker (eds), *Zweiter Kalter Krieg und Friedensbewegung: Der NATO-Doppelbeschluss in deutschdeutscher und internationaler Perspektive* (Munich, 2011), pp. 95–122.
44 The two most important edited collections are C. Becker-Schaum, P. Gassert, M. Klimke, W. Mausbach and M. Zepp (eds), *"Entrüstet Euch!" Nuklearkrise, NATO-Doppelbeschluss und Friedensbewegung* (Paderborn, 2012); Gassert, Geiger and Wentker (eds), *Zweiter Kalter Krieg und Friedensbewegung*, here the chapter by P. Gassert, 'Viel Lärm um Nichts? Der NATO-Doppelbeschluss als Katalysator gesellschaftlicher Selbstverständigungin der Bundesrepublik', pp. 175–202, quote p. 176.
45 D. Rucht, 'Peace movements in context: a sociological perspective', in Ziemann (ed.), *Peace Movements*, pp. 271–83, pp. 276, 279.
46 Based on a personal communication in December 2013 with Ute Finckh-Krämer, who participated in the 1983 human chain and was a member of the Bundestag for the SPD since 2013.
47 For the following, see the important study by S. Schregel, *Der Atomkrieg vor der Wohnungstür. Eine Politikgeschichte der neuen Friedensbewegung in der Bundesrepublik 1970–1985* (Frankfurt am Main, 2011).
48 *Ibid.*, pp. 78–136, quote 108.
49 *Ibid.*, pp. 137–84.
50 *Ibid.*, p. 167; 'Ich sag' dem Schwein nicht, wann es stirbt', *Spiegel*, 1 Mar. 1982, pp. 105–8.
51 For this important point see Schregel, *Atomkrieg vor der Wohnungstür*, p. 184.
52 A.M. Stokes, *A Chink in the Wall. German Writers and Literature in the INF-Debate of the Eighties* (Bern, 1995).
53 W. v. Bredow, 'Unernste Rechtfertigung, apokalyptischer Protest: Nukleare Kriegs-Szenarien', in M. van der Linden and G. Mergner (eds), *Kriegsbegeisterung und mentale Kriegsvorbereitung* (Berlin, 1991), pp. 279–94.
54 A.A. Guha, *Ende. Tagebuch aus dem 3. Weltkrieg* (Königstein, 1983).

55 Quoted in P. Baur, 'Nukleare Untergangsszenarien in Kunst und Kultur', in Becker-Schaum *et al.* (eds), *"Entrüstet Euch!"*, pp. 325–38, p. 330.
56 Guha, *Ende*, pp. 23, 35, 123ff., 180f., quote p. 89.
57 H.E. Richter, *Alle redeten vom Frieden. Versuch einer paradoxen Intervention* (Reinbek, 1981). See *Spiegel* issues 39/1981 to 43/1981.
58 Richter, *Alle redeten vom Frieden*, p. 20; B. Ziemann, *Contested Commemorations. Republican War Veterans and Weimar Political Culture* (Cambridge, 2013), p. 162.
59 Richter, *Alle redeten vom Frieden*, pp. 35–8, 45, 50, 53, 72.
60 Baur, 'Nukleare Untergangsszenarien', p. 332.
61 F. Biess, 'Die Sensibilisierung des Subjekts: Angst und »Neue Subjektivität« in den 1970er Jahren', *Werkstatt Geschichte* 49 (2008), pp. 51–71; S. Reichardt, *Authentizität und Gemeinschaft: Linksalternatives Leben in den siebziger und frühen achtziger Jahren* (Frankfurt am Main, 2014), pp. 782–807.
62 For the following see Schregel, 'Konjunktur der Angst. "Politik der Subjektivität" und "neue Friedensbewegung", 1979–1983', in Greiner, Müller and Walter (eds), *Angst im Kalten Krieg*, pp. 495–520, quote p. 501.
63 Schregel, 'Konjunktur der Angst', pp. 508–11.
64 *Ibid.*, pp. 511–15.
65 H. Dieckmann, 'Angstträume und Wirklichkeit. Reaktionen unseres Unbewußten auf Atomkrieg und ökologische Krise', in K. Horn and E. Senghaas-Knobloch (eds), *Friedensbewegung- Persönliches und Politisches* (Frankfurt am Main, 1983), pp. 62–71, quotes p. 62.
66 E. Tugendhat, *Nachdenken über die Atomkriegsgefahr und warum man sie nicht sieht* (Berlin, 1986), p. 106.
67 M. Niemöller, 'Unser Glaubenskampf gegen die Angst', in M. Niemöller, W. Lüthi, G. Casalis and D. van der Meulen (eds), *Frieden. Der Christ im Kampf gegen die Angst und den Gewaltgeist der Zeit* (Zurich, 1954), pp. 11–30, pp. 13–16.
68 H. Nehring and B. Ziemann, 'Do all paths lead to Moscow? The NATO dual-track decision and the peace movement – a critique', *Cold War History* 12 (2012), pp. 1–24, p. 13.
69 Based on arguments developed by US senator Edward Kennedy: 'Die Überlebenden werden die Toten beneiden', *Der Spiegel*, 26 Apr. 1982, pp. 149–70.
70 On this distinction, see the chapter by Eva Horn in this volume.
71 P. Fritzsche, *The Turbulent World of Franz Göll. An Ordinary Berliner Writes the Twentieth Century* (Cambridge, Mass. and London, 2011), p. 204.
72 Quoted *ibid.*, p. 207 (emphasis in the original).
73 See Schregel, *Atomkrieg vor der Wohnungstür*.
74 M.S. Foley, *Front Porch Politics: The Forgotten Heyday of American Activism in the 1970s and 1980s* (New York, 2013).

75 W. Count v. Baudissin, *Das Kriegsbild* (Bad Godesberg, 1962), cited in A. Gablik, '"... von da an herrscht Kirchhofsruhe". Zum Realitätsgehalt Baudissinscher Kriegsbildvorstellungen', in M. Kutz (ed.), *Gesellschaft, Militär, Krieg und Frieden im Denken von Wolf Graf von Baudissin* (Baden-Baden, 2004), pp. 45–60, p. 52.

7

After Hiroshima: Günther Anders and the history of anti-nuclear critique

Jason Dawsey

The rich scholarship on the worldwide anti-nuclear movement has not yet been matched by comparable work on the history of anti-nuclear thought. With regard to the long and unfinished struggle to abolish the Bomb, a rigid division of labour between social historians and intellectual historians can only perpetuate the classic (and flawed) bifurcation of activists and theorists. Many of the critiques of the atomic threat produced after 1945 yielded extraordinary ideas linked to questions of praxis.[1] Among them were compelling notions of citizenship and internationalism, a rethinking of the imperatives directing the use of science and technology, and reflections on the ethics of political violence. This essay contributes to a more integrated history of the insurgency against the atomic menace by examining the case of the German-Jewish intellectual and anti-nuclear militant Günther Anders (1902–92).[2]

Until recently, Anders' remarkable life and writings have been largely neglected in the Anglophone academic world. The only monograph on his thought available in English is still a translation of the study by the Dutch philosopher Paul van Dijk.[3] Since the late 1980s, though, there has been a steady release of books and articles on Anders by German and Austrian scholars, mostly in the fields of philosophy and *Germanistik*.[4] Burgeoning Italian and French discussions have followed.[5] In the last decade, several historians have finally begun to take note of Anders. Mainly drawing from his astonishing writings on the nuclear age, they have appropriated aspects of his later thought for analyses of the Western European peace and ecology movements – movements with which Anders was directly engaged for many years.[6] This wave of historical research connecting Anders to the central political struggles of the Cold War should be supplemented with a more sustained engagement with his oeuvre and an evaluation of his place in the history of anti-nuclear critique.

After Hiroshima

For the purposes of this volume, Anders is especially important. He was one of the first thinkers to conceptualise the nuclear age as a distinct world-historical epoch where the future of humankind as a whole had become precarious. More rigorously than his contemporaries, he attempted to think through the prospects of a nuclear conflict between the superpowers. For Anders, this entailed accepting, as a principal philosophical and political task, the challenge to imagine the 'imaginary war'.[7] According decisive importance to the faculty of 'imagination' (*Vorstellung*) in meeting this challenge, he sought to bind his chilling speculations on a likely Third World War to the existing Ban-the-Bomb mobilisations of his time. Theory and practice were always intertwined for Günther Anders.[8]

This essay is an interrogation of the crucial concept of 'after Hiroshima' in Anders' philosophy, how the obliteration of Hiroshima and Nagasaki signalled for him the advent of a new and final era of global history. I rely primarily on Anders' multi-volume *magnum opus*, *Die Antiquiertheit des Menschen* (*The Obsolescence of Human Beings*), a series of other works Anders produced between 1955 and 1965, during the first phase of his involvement in the anti-nuclear movement, and a selection of interviews he gave between 1979 and 1987, when he became involved, though much less directly because of his advanced age, with another round of mobilisation against nuclear armaments. Three interrelated topics are highlighted: (1) Anders' transition to the nuclear question; (2) his argument that Hiroshima symbolised our 'world condition' after 1945; (3) Anders' startling attempts to envision the consequences of a future nuclear conflict between the Cold War blocs. In the process, I make the case for Anders' importance as a serious political thinker and theorist of the Atomic Age, in fact our most salient theorist of omnicide.[9]

The making of an anti-nuclear militant

In his publications, speeches, and interviews, Günther Anders often identified with the desperate, prophetic persona of a Noah or a Cassandra, and called himself a 'panic-maker' or a purveyor of 'warning images'.[10] His philosophical labours were organised, he asserted, around a 'main theme', the 'destruction of humanity and the possible self-eradication of humanity', and his thinking (along with that of Theodor W. Adorno) comprised 'something like an encyclopaedia of the apocalyptic world'.[11] Despite the emphasis Anders placed on his activism, he actually joined the opposition to the Bomb relatively late, first becoming involved only in the mid-1950s. Once he embraced the cause of nuclear abolitionism, however, he wholly dedicated himself to it as long as his health permitted. Anders' entry into the struggle to eliminate the Bomb marked a new, long and final phase of an extraordinary twentieth-century life.

In 1962, reflecting back on his own very difficult period of emigration and exile, Anders urged that '*Vitae*, not *vita*', should apply to the biographies of people like himself.[12] He had lived several 'lives' already. Born Günther Stern (he adopted Anders as a pseudonym in the early 1930s), he was the son of the eminent psychologist William Stern. He was also Hannah Arendt's first husband (they were married from 1929 to 1937), a student of Edmund Husserl and Martin Heidegger, an exponent, along with Max Scheler and Helmuth Plessner, of a current in German philosophy known as philosophical anthropology, a participant in Weimar leftist circles that included Bertolt Brecht and George Grosz, a distant cousin of Walter Benjamin, and a fellow-traveller of the Frankfurt School of Critical Theory. Anders, too, must be counted as part of the exodus of artists, scientists, writers and political radicals who emigrated from Germany after Hitler assumed power. He found refuge in Paris for three years after fleeing Berlin in the aftermath of the February 1933 Reichstag fire, before relocating to the United States. After spending fourteen years in New York City and southern California, Anders and his second wife, the Austrian writer Elisabeth Freundlich (they were married from 1945 to 1955), relocated to Vienna in 1950. Living in Vienna as an independent, left-wing writer for the remainder of his life, he won there an international reputation as a critic of modern technology, an advocate of Holocaust remembrance and a tireless voice against the Bomb.[13]

Hiroshima and the revelations about the Nazis' destruction of European Jewry comprised the final 'caesuras' in Anders' life.[14] By his own recollection, Anders heard the news of the dropping of the atom bomb on Hiroshima over the radio in New York. The announcement struck him dumb. He experienced a total inability to respond to the 'monstrousness' of the news.[15] Anders claimed that several years passed before he summoned the requisite concentration to begin a philosophical analysis of nuclear weapons. Stalin's acquisition of the Bomb in August 1949 and the concomitant anti-communist hysteria in the United States helped to convince him and Freundlich that it was time to return to Europe.[16] Following their move to Vienna in 1950, he succeeded in working out some preliminary reflections on the nuclear threat.[17]

The American and Soviet race to create the first hydrogen bomb, undoubtedly, motivated him to try again. A short text, with the provocative title, 'Faust is Dead', indicated the direction he would take in the following decade. There, he proclaimed the death of a figure regarded, especially in German cultural history, as representative of the modern age. Unlike our ancestors who reached, in futility, for the 'infinite', human beings, with the invention of atomic and hydrogen bombs, were now 'effectively capable of the boundless', and, having seen the fruits of this capability, were 'demi-gods who desperately wanted to be humans again'.[18] Anders wondered if a suitable replacement could be found for Faust and whether the legend of the ill-prepared 'sorcerer's apprentice' might epitomise better the condition of modern humanity.[19]

In 1956, Anders offered his readers a much lengthier and more imposing essay, 'On the Bomb and the Roots of our Blindness to Apocalypse'. The closing piece in the first volume of his radical critique of technology, *The Obsolescence of Human Beings*, the ninety-page essay was one of the first systematic philosophical analyses of the nuclear menace. It appeared at the time of the Suez Crisis, when the Soviet Union threatened Britain and France with nuclear strikes and shortly before the fierce controversy in 1957–58 in the Federal Republic of Germany over the nuclearisation of the country's recently created armed forces.[20] In the essay, Anders contended, 'as philosophical terrain the Bomb – or more accurately: our Dasein under the sign of the Bomb ... is a completely unknown land. To map it out right away is not possible.'[21] The text, he hoped, might provide a 'cartographic image' of this landscape.[22] In a later work, Anders recalled how he assumed, during these years, the task of overcoming the 'spreading speechlessness', similar to his own, about nuclear weapons and 'to find or invent a somewhat adequate vocabulary and a way of speech worthy of the enormity' of the peril.[23]

What separated *The Obsolescence of Human Beings* from so much of the contemporary philosophical literature on the nuclear question was its extremely complex philosophical anthropology of the human condition in an epoch of technological dominance. In the book's opening pages, Anders declared, 'in no different sense than Napoleon had asserted it 150 years ago of politics, and Marx 100 years ago of the economy, technology is now our fate (*Schicksal*).'[24] In the second volume of *Obsolescence*, he expanded this radical argument, insisting that 'technology has now become the subject of history with which we are only still "co-historical" ('*mitgeschichtlich*').'[25] The technological sphere of contemporary society had acquired the qualities of agency and self-determination, inexorably subjected men and women to its dictates, and steadily reduced their role. According to Anders, there was a 'principle' or 'tendency' governing modern life discernible in the production of those 'instruments (*Geräte*), which through their functioning, we make ourselves superfluous, we exclude ourselves, we "liquidate" ourselves'.[26] Thus, the fundamental tendency driving technological development could be expressed by means of the motto 'without us'.[27]

Under the rubric of 'technology', Anders included the assembly-line, the Taylorist model of 'scientific management', robotics and automation, mass adverting, radio and television, nuclear reactors, aviation, space travel and genetic engineering.[28] The impact of these phenomena transcended the Cold War divisions between the superpowers. What Anders called, in one instance, *Technifizierung* (technologisation or technification) transformed life regardless of political or economic differences and did not respect national boundaries.[29]

At the centre of Anders' post-1950 work was a set of claims about the 'obsolescence (*Antiquiertheit*)' of certain essential qualities of being human. He tapped the rich Greek myth of the Titan Prometheus, who had created the human race, stolen fire from the gods to give to people, and suffered terrible punishment for it, to signify the predicament of a global humanity in servitude to technology. Attracted to the mixture of the divine and the human in Prometheus, Anders decided on the vivid term 'Promethean gap (*prometheisches Gefälle*)' as the most adequate characterisation of the situation faced by men and women after 1945.[30] The concept encompassed 'gaps' that had arisen (1) between 'making and imagining/representing'; (2) between 'doing and feeling'; (3) between 'knowledge and conscience'; (4) finally and above all, that 'between the produced instrument and the (not suited to the "body" of the instrument) body of the human being'.[31] The argument about this discrepancy between our basic human faculties was so salient to his critique of technology that he agreed, in a 1985 interview, that the phrase 'philosophy of discrepancy' captured his philosophical outlook.[32] In these formulations of his theory of human obsolescence, Anders always prioritised the gulf that had grown between a deficient 'imagining/representing (*Vorstellen*)' and an out-of-control 'producing (*Machen* or *Herstellen*)'.[33] A philosophical–anthropological position attuned to this dilemma would have to concentrate on determining and, if possible, overcoming the 'limits' of our *Vorstellung*.

Anders understood the industrialised murder process implemented during the Holocaust and the looming possibility of nuclear annihilation as the most extreme instantiations of modern technology's fundamental tendency to liquidate the human element as well as the most profound challenges to our existing capacities for imagination. Social critique had to be reoriented in order to fully confront Auschwitz and Hiroshima. The scientific, technological and socio-psychological conditions of possibility for both horrors persisted. Therefore, their 'repeatability' concerned him above all.[34]

Although the Shoah and the nuclear threat formed an essential binary in Anders' later philosophical thought, they did not hold equal weight. Hiroshima was, he made clear, the 'sharpest' of the 'caesuras' that divided his life.[35] The magnitude of the problem of the Bomb caused him to devote far more of his time and energy into disrupting the 'preparation of tomorrow's global Hiroshima'.[36] After 1956, he decided to bind his talents to the burgeoning worldwide peace movement.

Two episodes are particularly noteworthy from his involvement with anti-nuclear politics. In the summer of 1958, Anders travelled to Japan and served as a delegate at the Fourth World Conference Against A and H Bombs and for Disarmament. During this truly transformative journey, Anders visited with survivors from the bombings of Hiroshima and Nagasaki and took part in a peace procession from Hiroshima to Tokyo. The account of his trip there, published a year later as *Der Mann auf der Brücke* (*The Man on the Bridge*), is extremely moving reading and shows his excitement at the possibility of non-violent resistance across national borders to the escalating arms race.[37]

The most important aspect of Anders' participation in the anti-nuclear resistance, though, was his communications with Claude Eatherly, the American pilot of the B-29, the *Straight Flush*, who gave the 'go-ahead' signal to the *Enola-Gay* to drop the atomic bomb on Hiroshima on the morning of 6 August 1945. After learning of Eatherly from a *Newsweek* article passed to him by his third wife, Charlotte Zelka, Anders started a correspondence in June 1959 with Eatherly, then held at a Veterans Administration hospital in Waco, Texas.[38] Over the next few years, Anders became a public advocate for Eatherly, attested to the pilot's remorse over his role in Hiroshima's destruction, and argued that Eatherly embodied our basic moral conundrum – how to reassert the right to a conscience when the division of labour under mechanisation obviated any inclination to take responsibility for our deeds. The record of his correspondence with Eatherly, *Burning Conscience*, strengthened Anders' stature as a leading figure in the international Ban-the-Bomb movement.[39]

Subsequently, Anders aspired to be the movement's leading theoretical voice, much as Herbert Marcuse tried to guide the New Left and Jean-Paul Sartre the struggles against European colonialism. Within the

Central European context, Anders, looking back on the decade between 1955 and 1965, considered the anti-nuclear campaigns there as the 'first great moral movement after the collapse of National Socialism'.[40] The confrontation with atomic death could be a place where Germans started the work of redeeming their failure to prevent the Judeocide. Confronting the Nazi genocide and stopping global nuclear omnicide were fused in his political work.

Two decades later, in the wake of NATO's 1979 dual-track decision, a second generation of opponents of the Bomb eagerly sought out Anders' works. He had lived long enough to watch a new escalation of Cold War sabre-rattling, but, also, thankfully, to see a new insurgency arise, a 'second crusade' as he dubbed it, against the reactionary and dangerous policies of Ronald Reagan, Margaret Thatcher and Helmut Kohl.[41] This final phase of engagement with the anti-nuclear movement proved to be much less convivial than its antecedent, however. Anders' rejection of non-violence as a viable form of dissent and demand for 'counter-violence' strained his ties to the peace movement.[42] Once tensions between the superpowers eased after 1986 Reykjavik negotiations between Reagan and Mikhail Gorbachev, the controversy over his support for violence subsided. Soon thereafter, Anders' writings finally began to receive attention from scholars.

Conceptualising the atomic age

What Anders contributed to the international peace movement, in addition to his organising talents and uncompromising moralism, was a formidable philosophical-anthropological analysis of the contemporary world under the shadow of the Bomb. His books from *The Obsolescence of Human Beings* forward constantly raised the question of how to grasp history 'after Hiroshima'.[43] The approach Anders utilised relied on the essay or, in the case of *The Man on the Bridge*, the journal entry, as the primary forms of critical exposition. It is Anders' theory of the nuclear menace that I address in the remainder of this piece.

In *Obsolescence*, Anders embedded the atomic bomb within his theory of the 'Promethean gap'. Not the A-bomb itself, but the broader course of mechanisation in the twentieth century had brought about this ominous cleft between industrial production and our imagination, emotions and sense of conscience. While not the original source of the discrepancy, the splitting of the atom and the new super-weapons resulting from it marked, in Anders' interpretation, a limit-case for the *Gefälle*.

'We as feeling beings are still always stuck at the stage of the rudimentary homeworker', while 'we as killing beings or as corpse-producers have already reached the proud stage of industrial mass production', Anders contended.[44] 'Today', he went on, 'we can plan and implement the annihilation of a large city without further ado with the aid of the means of annihilation we have produced. But in imagining this effect, we can only comprehend it entirely inadequately.'[45] Compared to the scale of devastation, the 'smoke, blood, and ruins' that had resulted and would result again from the use of such weapons, we could muster merely a 'tiny quantum' of genuine empathy and understanding.[46] At the very most, Anders explained, men and women could imagine ten dead, but could only sincerely mourn one deceased person.[47]

Hiroshima, then, represented the ultimate, decisive instance of the Promethean gap. Consequently, Anders fashioned a universal moral history around the Japanese city's destruction. This new philosophical perspective adumbrated a very different conceptualisation of the twentieth century and a radically new historical consciousness. In Anders' hands, 'Atomic Age (*Atomzeitalter*)' designated a distinct and unprecedented historical epoch. As he interpreted it, Hiroshima was not only the constitutive event of the second half of the twentieth century but a complete rupture with all previous history. If the Holocaust exhibited that 'all people are killable (*tötbar*)', then Hiroshima and Nagasaki ushered in a new era of where 'humanity as a whole is killable'.[48] For Anders, 'killability' denoted a stage in the history of barbarism where the human species in its entirety could be eliminated through catastrophic violence.

In other passages, Anders concluded that 'killable', as evocative as the term was, still did not sufficiently grasp humanity's status after Hiroshima. Already in the first volume of *Obsolescence*, he described his contemporaries as those who 'have not yet been murdered'.[49] In the second volume, he elaborated, 'we living today are not mortal but rather primarily the murderable (*Ermordbare*)'.[50] Similarly, Anders came to repudiate phrases defining nuclear annihilation as the human race's 'suicide', choosing 'atomic murder' as far more precise.[51] Eventually, as weapons of mass destruction became ever more destructive, he settled on the concepts of 'annihilism' and 'globocide', categories to grasp the looming eradication of all planetary life.[52] With 'globocide' actually feasible technologically, the Second World War, with the staggering numbers of killed and wounded, the Nazi genocide, and the first uses of the Bomb, could be viewed, for Anders, in retrospect, as the 'classical years of annihilation'.[53]

In his universal moral history of the twentieth century, Anders transformed Hiroshima into the essential symbol for late technological modernity. Hiroshima was our 'world condition', he proclaimed. Explaining what he meant by this claim, Anders wrote, 'with 6 August 1945, the Day of Hiroshima, a New Age began: the age in which at any given moment we have the power to transform any given place, on our planet, and even our planet itself, into a Hiroshima'.[54] Later, he compressed his thesis into a simple slogan: 'Hiroshima is everywhere'.[55] Elsewhere, Anders spoke of the day the first A-Bomb was dropped as the 'Day Zero' the day 'in which was demonstrated that perhaps world history no longer continues'.[56] 'Day Zero' indicated that a separate chronology for post-Hiroshima history was needed. In his 1958 *The Man on the Bridge*, Anders tried to do just that. 'We live', he proclaimed, 'in the Year 13 of the Calamity. I was born in the Year 43 before. Father, who I buried in 1938, died in the Year 7 before'.[57] In the second volume of *The Obsolescence of Human Beings*, the invention of the atom bomb marked the advent of what Anders called the 'Third Industrial Revolution', the most radical revolution in human history, where human beings had acquired the means 'to produce their own demise' as a species.[58] This revolution led to a definitive, irreversible change in the historical condition of humanity. 'Since 1945', since Hiroshima, 'the epoch of epochal change is over', he announced.[59] There would be no post-nuclear age. Humanity's only way out from under this 'definitive mark of Cain our existence' was nuclear immolation.[60] The very categorisation of historical time that Anders' remarks outlined pivoted around the ur-event, the fateful 'Day of Hiroshima'.

According to Anders, Auschwitz and Hiroshima, the former transformed as well by Anders into a symbol for the Holocaust as a whole, had also refuted the old Biblical conception of a good, just, and almighty God. If such a deity did exist, he proclaimed, 'then he is one who did not prevent Auschwitz and Hiroshima'.[61] Similarly, Anders declared that traditional ethics had been totally overturned by the Holocaust and the advent of the Atomic Age. 'The previous religious and philosophical ethics, without exception and without pause, have become obsolete; they have also been co-exploded in Hiroshima (*mitexplodiert*) and co-gassed (*mitvergast*) in Auschwitz. We stand in the Year Zero of a new morality'.[62] To Anders, nothing was left untouched by Hiroshima (and Auschwitz).

Yet, in a few quite noteworthy instances, Anders expressed unease with the elevation of Hiroshima into a master metaphor. During his stay in Nagasaki, he became especially troubled by the tendency 'to understand Hiroshima as the symbol', 'thus to say "Hiroshima and Nagasaki"'.[63]

Anders accounted for the 'universal usage' of this phrase 'partially from chronological reasons, partially because the number of dead here [at Nagasaki], by a geographical accident, remained 'limited' to 70,000'.[64] No matter how understandable it was that people continued to utter 'Hiroshima and Nagasaki', the phrase had to be roundly criticised. 'This usage is not justified', Anders insisted. 'For the moralist, Nagasaki should stand in the first place, it thus should be called: "Nagasaki and Hiroshima".'[65] Such a claim, believed Anders, should not be in the least controversial. 'Even those of my friends from Tokyo', he noted, 'who, from exaggerated fairness, attempt to find Hiroshima still strategically understandable, or who trouble themselves as Christians to justify this strike as "deserved", fall silent when the name Nagasaki is heard and then remain petrified'.[66] There could be no room for debate about the morality of Nagasaki's destruction. Anders became convinced that the Truman Administration actually unleashed a 'bloodbath' in Nagasaki on 9 August 1945 in order to intimidate Joseph Stalin.[67] In other words, for Anders, Nagasaki's dead needlessly perished in the initial phase of a new conflict, the Cold War. Two decades after he authored this commentary, he still considered the atomic assault on Nagasaki to be an 'absolutely unforgivable' act.[68]

Despite these strong reservations, Anders' philosophy of the Bomb nonetheless prioritised Hiroshima. As the first victim of atomic armaments, Hiroshima always symbolised, for him, the fate of the human race. It was Everycity, a model necropolis for a future constantly imperilled by the threat of nuclear war. To Anders, the 'Hiroshima-Event' heralded a new, final epoch and a new categorisation for humans.[69]

In *The Obsolescence of Human Beings* and its sequels, Anders clarified for his audience the essential features of this new epoch. He did so by adopting terminology from Jewish and Christian apocalyptic eschatology. As a passionate unbeliever, he nonetheless judged these traditions to be most adequate for the danger posed by the Bomb.[70] Recasting eschatological ideas for his philosophy of a man-made apocalypse, he categorised history since 6 August 1945 as the *Endzeit*. Literally translated as 'End Time', 'Final Age' or 'Last Age' also approximate Anders' intent with this word.[71] As was noted above, Anders proclaimed that this era would not give way to a subsequent, different era, just as recorded history had always done. That traditional understanding of historical change had expired in the ruins of Hiroshima.

The duration of the *Endzeit*, Anders contended, would depend on the success of global civil society in preventing nuclear war. To accent this epoch's uncertain length, Anders relied on the term *die Frist* ('respite' or 'grace period').[72] Any changes in social life could only play out within *die Frist*. For Anders, the overarching *Endzeit* or *Atomzeitalter*, the socio-temporal structure which enveloped our civilisation, was not amenable to fundamental transformation.

Equally constant was the possibility that, if the 'fight against this man-made Apocalypse' failed, the 'End Time' would 'turn into The End of Time (*Zeitenende*)', Anders warned.[73] The concept of *Zeitenende* showed Anders at his most pessimistic. A potential immanent to our technological way of life, this definitive 'End' would haunt every generation of human beings and would not be completely extirpated even if nuclear disarmament were achieved. The Bomb would always threaten humanity, since the matrix of scientific–technical knowledge which had spawned it could not be abolished. 'From now on', Anders stated, mankind will always and for eternity live under the dark shadow of the monster. 'The apocalyptic danger is not abolished by one act, once and for all, but only by daily repeated acts … For the goal that we have to reach cannot be not to have the thing; but never to use the thing, although we cannot help having it; never to use it, although there will be no day on which we couldn't use it.'[74] There could never be a return to a pre-nuclear era. At best, the Final Age might continue indefinitely, if humanity successfully stemmed nuclear war.

At the limits of the imagination

In *The Obsolescence of Human Beings*, Anders deplored the existing lack of recognition of and effective resistance to the nuclear peril. He credited Albert Einstein with being among the very few who really understood the monstrousness of the situation.[75] Why were so many indifferent to the impending apocalypse? Why were there not huge crowds in cities around the world clamouring for disarmament? He accounted for this shocking absence of panic with his concept of 'blindness to apocalypse'. According to Anders, this widespread and disastrous ailment had 'historical' as well as 'philosophical-anthropological roots', he wrote.[76] Among the former, he referred to the absorption of eschatological impulses by movements of the radical Left (the Jacobins' proclamation of 1792 as the Year One, the idea of the classless society in Marxism) and of the radical Right (the 1,000-year Reich in National Socialism). Their profoundly incongruent visions of a millennium did share an indifference to 'an apocalyptic end' and concern only for the 'situation *after* the end'.[77]

Other factors, thought Anders, contributed to this indifference. While he readily acknowledged the salience of Jewish and Christian eschatology, the oldest and most powerful apocalyptic traditions available, the 'replacement of an eschatological Christianity by an existential one', undertaken by German theologian Rudolf Bultmann immediately after the First World War, represented 'the last formulation of a neutralisation of apocalypse'.[78] Theologians of apocalypse had become minoritarian figures. In the years since 1945, a very different, socio-economic source for lack of belief in an Endtime emerged. For Anders, the stunning and unwelcome 'robust resurrection of the concept of progress' amidst the massive post-war economic boom promoted a faith that 'history was a priori without end'.[79] Mustering an oppositional consciousness to the Bomb was steadily hampered by the distracting comforts of the new 'standard of living' in Western Europe and North America.[80]

Anders made it clear, though, that the 'main root' of the 'blindness' was not these ideological forms, pernicious as they were, but the 'Promethean gap', the fundamental dilemma of our 'being human'.[81] This predicament was the most difficult barrier for contemporary humanity to surmount, since its source lay in the human constitution itself. For Anders, then, the given state of the 'imagination' decisively limited recognition of the nuclear danger. How then could the 'eschatological' be filled again with its original dread, a dread before the end of the world? One example illustrates Anders' answer to this problem extremely well.

In *The Dead*, Anders cited a speech by André Malraux that he heard in Paris in 1936, which was probably given immediately after Hitler had ordered German troops into the demilitarised Rhineland in March of that year. What he most recalled from the address was how Malraux suffered from 'impatience and despair over the blindness and the spiritual laziness of those who did not yet recognise or did not want to recognise that Hitler meant war'.[82] Anders greatly admired the 'means' Malraux 'improvised' in order to 'open the eyes' of those in attendance. Gesturing with his finger at the crowd, he said '*Mort* (dead)' for every tenth person he counted.[83] Those were 'good times', Anders stressed, when only one in ten would die in an impending war.[84] Attempting to fill a similar role as an 'eye-opener', Anders also 'improvised' his own techniques to dispel the 'blindness' and 'indifference' to a coming Third World War.[85]

The most significant technique Anders devised was his remarkable proposal for overcoming the 'Promethean gap' by strengthening the faculty of *Vorstellung*. To Anders, the ability to imagine, to form and hold images in the mind that overshot the given reality, was indispensable in the anti-nuclear struggle. The 'decisive moral task' was the 'formation of the moral imagination', Anders declared.[86] In a letter to Claude Eatherly, he spoke of

> bridging the gap that exists between your two faculties: your faculty of making things and your faculty of imagining things; to level off the incline that separates the two: in other words: you have to violently widen the narrow capacity of your imagination (and the even narrower one of your feelings) until imagination and feeling become capable to grasp and realise the enormity of your doing; until you are capable to seize and conceive, to accept or reject it – in short your task is: to widen your moral fantasy.[87]

Many years later, he repeated that 'imagination, the power of imagination (*Vorstellungskraft*)', 'is the most necessary thing today'.[88] Behind these utterances stood a central claim about the mutability of this basic human faculty. From his work in the area of philosophical anthropology, Anders believed that our imagination was indeed pliable enough that it could be deliberately broadened and bolstered.[89]

In the first volume of *Obsolescence* and in subsequent essays, Anders demonstrated his commitment to this 'decisive moral task' by attempting to envision a future nuclear conflict. Representing a 'fictional apocalypse' raised the most extreme problems for anyone willing to attempt it, however.[90] How could one conceive something that seemed so patently inconceivable? How could one adequately and ethically depict the deaths of millions or billions of people?

Responding to these dilemmas, Anders modelled a type of 'radical imagining' in his writings on the atomic peril between 1956 and 1965, reminiscent of the most powerful works in the genre of Holocaust literature.[91] Depicting nuclear warfare, he knew, would require the highest exertion of imaginative thought. During his trip to Japan, Anders demanded of his listeners that they 'try to actually visualise the effects of an atomic war instead of just using the word like the words "car" or "toothpaste". And don't be discouraged when you fail in your attempt at picturing it. Even this defeat will be a "sound" defeat, for it will give you an idea of the immensity of the effects we can cause.'[92] Such 'productive frustration', as he phrased it elsewhere, worked 'against our initiating further actions whose effects transcend our capacity to fear.'[93] For Anders, no matter how strenuous and discouraging its results might be, the 'imperative' to 'expand the capacity of your imagination' should operate as an absolute obligation guiding one's actions.[94]

Anders did not concern himself in these speculations with the possibility of 'limited' nuclear conflicts waged by political elites in the name of 'small presumptions or partial goals'.⁹⁵ The idea of 'limited' or 'tactical' nuclear strikes or counter-strikes attributed far too much wisdom to politicians. Anders criticised those who believed that the ruling classes would shrink from utilising nuclear arms in their possession from fear of their own destruction. Since the 'imagination-deficit of these omnipotent fools is far greater than their cowardice', he wrote to Erwin Schrödinger, citizens of the nuclear states should not feel confident that their leaders would, for reasons of self-preservation, abstain from using the Bomb.⁹⁶ Such confidence was based on the delusional premise that politicians knew how to manage the godlike power they wielded.

As part of his efforts to overcome this 'imagination-deficit', Anders conducted a series of thought experiments about a third and final world war. Even if the post-1945 world had not yet seen a 'hot war' between the superpowers and their satellites, Anders rightly directed his audience to the ceaseless preparation for a new conflict on both sides.⁹⁷ Because of this situation, Anders spoke, unambiguously, of the 'gloomy likelihood of the catastrophe' that would engulf every country.⁹⁸ Quite controversially, he also argued that Earth as a whole had become a concentration camp with no possibility for its inmates to get away.⁹⁹ Like the Third Reich's mode of waging war, nuclear warfare 'would make no distinction between civilian and military', but '*would take place as the mechanised production of corpses, thus as a war of liquidation*', a war, he did not hesitate to add, that, unlike the previous global conflicts, '*could liquidate the whole of humanity*'.¹⁰⁰ Unique in the annals of military history, this would be a war where human extinction was at stake.

In Anders' thought experiments, a terrible irony emerges. Nuclear warfare, the most destructive form of violence in human history, might not ensue from a deliberate act of aggression but might be precipitated, instead, by an action he dubbed 'triggering (*Auslösen*)'.¹⁰¹ 'Triggering' covered, for Anders, the vast majority of labouring activities under conditions of industrialism.¹⁰² With mechanisation, the individual simply initiated a process and the machine(s) did the rest. According to Anders, this subsumption of labouring activity by machinery, long underway, culminated in what he termed the '"push-button'-epoch"', where the diminution of human agency had reached such an extent that, in wartime, the mere pressing of a button could quickly unleash devastation on the other side of the globe.¹⁰³ 'It can even happen', he wrote, 'that one first push of a button sets in motion a whole chain of secondary triggerings – till the end-result – never intended, never imagined, by the first button pusher – consists of millions of corpses.'[104] Here, Anders pointed to the terrifying endgame of hi-tech warfare. Technological mass annihilation on a global scale did not require declarations of war and carefully managed onslaughts utilising men and *matériel*. An accident or momentary lapse of judgment sufficed to instigate Armageddon.[105]

As Anders portrayed it, this future conflict would not be a war with any battlefields, but a 'war of remote murder (*Fernmord-Krieg*)'.[106] Consequently, animosity towards an enemy one sees and kills, a constant feature of warfare since ancient times, would be definitively replaced by impersonal, machine-executed acts of mass destruction. The Third World War, this 'coming remote war, will be the most hateless war there has ever been in history', Anders predicted.[107] Although the complete mechanisation of warfare had accomplished the 'macabre abolition of hatred', this development could scarcely be celebrated.[108] Nuclear war would not be fought as a 'war between enemies', and the 'effect of atomic war will show no duality, since the enemies will run together into a single defeated enemy. Truly, 'fission has, in hindsight, led to "fusion"'.[109] Anders contended that, strictly speaking, the Third World War should not be titled a war at all. For the perverse 'abolition of war' facilitated by nuclear proliferation the word 'extermination (*Vertilgung*)' was far more adequate.[110] With every point on the globe within their range, the 'tens of thousands of stationed rockets and warheads' could achieve the 'manifold extermination of humanity' with minimal human intervention.[111]

Once hostilities started, the combatants in the Third World War would consist, Anders forecast, almost solely of 'automatic systems of apparatuses, of robots and rockets'.[112] A fully computerised 'struggle of things against one another' would ensue, where 'rockets will battle rockets and apparatuses will rise as opponents of apparatuses in battle' across the planet.[113] Anders thought that, from the perspective of the human beings overtaken by this global nightmare, the missile strikes by one nation and counter-strikes of the other(s) would merge, would destroy in unison. Opposing nuclear apparatuses would form a 'single apparatus', a 'combined whole', scorching and irradiating Earth.[114] If anyone was left to declare victory, how many would survive to celebrate and monumentalise it? And for how long could any survivors endure?[115]

In this final, 'globocidal' war of liquidation between the nuclear states, the only role granted to human beings by machines was victimhood. Anders' speculations led, almost inexorably, to the darkest of meditations, to peering beyond the veil that screened the mind from the aftermath of a nuclear apocalypse. Such a war would bring about the *Zeitenende*, the termination of the collective life of the human species, perhaps of all life. History would lie buried under the ruins with all the remnants of civilisation.[116] Anders implored his readers to survey with him the expanse of human history from the vantage point of a post-Third World War future. Stretching from our pre-human origins, from 'total animality', to a 'post-human' desolation, his vision placed 'the human between two (at least similar in the negative) phases of inhumanity'.[117] Elsewhere, Anders confronted his audience with the finality of humanity's destruction. He wrote as follows:

> And 'humanity' doesn't mean only today's humanity, not only humanity spread over the provinces of our globe, but also humanity spread over the provinces of time. For if the humanity of today is killed then that which has been, dies with it; and the humanity to come too. The humanity that has been because where there is no one who remembers, there will be nothing left to remember; and the humanity to come, because where there is no today, no tomorrow can become a today.[118]

The civilisation erected by *Homo sapiens* would appear then as an 'episode' 'between two nothingnesses': 'between the nothingness of that which, remembered by no one, will have been as though it had never been, and the nothingness of that which will never be. And as there will be no one to tell one nothingness from the other, they will melt into one single nothingness.'[119] For Anders, if there was any phenomenon that deserved the moniker 'totalitarian', it was the atomic threat. The Bomb, Anders emphatically stated, was a 'total weapon' that could lay waste our world and inflict irreparable devastation upon humanity's past, present and future.[120]

What Anders' writings foregrounded and modelled, to pull together the material examined in this section, was the act of imagining a world humanless and adrift in the aftermath of nuclear cataclysm. In fact, if one evaluated his writings after the Second World War as a whole, this envisioning of a 'world without human beings (*Welt ohne Menschen*)', as Anders himself made clear, was its principal theme.[121] Here we can see why Anders bestowed so much significance on the capacity of *Vorstellung*. Only the most concentrated, strenuous labours of imagining could ensure that we fully comprehended the likelihood of the death of the human race, maybe of all life. Human beings might thus reclaim a genuine fear of dying – as individuals and as a species. In a 1982 interview he asserted, 'the task for the imagination, which we have to fulfil daily, consists therein that we imagine the image of a lifeless, bare planet which was once called "Earth".[122] Anders' terror-inspiring speculations about universal death, then, might be accurately defined as forays into the 'necrological'.[123]

Through encounters with such frightful 'warning-images', people, Anders hoped, would be terrified, shaken from their torpor, their 'blindness to apocalypse', and compelled to save their world from nuclear destruction. Taking precedence over the Biblical commandment about love for one's neighbour was a new imperative to 'frighten thy neighbour as thyself'.[124] Our neighbours encompassed all of our contemporaries, however, since 'we are all on the same boat', he reminded.[125] None of the old internationalisms, including the most progressive of them, the Marxist conception of working-class solidarity, sufficed. Consequently, Anders replaced Marx and Engels' exhortation for workers of the world to unite with the slogan – 'Imperilled of all lands, unite (*Gefährdete aller Länder, vereinigt euch!*)!'[126] The living, united against impending apocalypse, would have to accept the Atlas-like burden of protecting the dead and the unborn. Thus, he called as well for an 'International of Generations' to replace the older socialist and communist Internationals.[127] This new International Anders envisioned would integrate humanity across geographical and temporal boundaries. Only through such a radical broadening of the 'horizon of responsibility' could people respond to the prospect of nuclear cataclysm.[128] The international peace movement, Anders believed, prefigured this new ideal of human unity.

In conjunction with this rethinking of Marxian internationalism, Anders also revised Marx's eleventh thesis on Feuerbach to fit the impetus for this new, post-Hiroshima solidarity: 'It is not enough to change the world. That we do anyhow … We have, then, to interpret this change. And, indeed, in order to change this change. Thereby, the world itself does not change without us. And not, eventually, to a world without us.'[129] The focus on changing the world had to be rethought. Hence forward, for Anders, theorising and abolishing the preconditions for the Third World War had to command the attention of the Left.

Conclusion

For historians of the Cold War, the nuclear arms race, and peace movements, Günther Anders' powerful philosophy of the atomic age should become a central point of reference. His ideas could be appropriated for theoretically sophisticated histories of resistance to the Bomb. These ideas, most of which were explicated in the late 1950 and early 1960s anticipated or directly influenced some of the most incisive critical thinking on the nuclear threat during the second major wave of international protest against the spectre of nuclear war in the late 1970s and early 1980s.

Anders set forth his concept of 'annihilism' long before historian E. P. Thompson depicted the 'last stage of civilisation' as 'exterminism'.[130] His approach to Auschwitz and Hiroshima as a binary that defined the second half of the twentieth century prefigured the excellent essay by philosopher Berel Lang on genocide and omnicide.[131] Robert Jay Lifton and Eric Markusen drew on Anders' work when they elaborated their idea of a species mentality in their important book, *The Genocidal Mentality*.[132] *New Yorker* staff writer Jonathan Schell's much-discussed envisioning of nuclear extinction as a 'second death' in his 1982 *The Fate of the Earth* redounded, to a striking degree, with Andersian themes. The resemblances were so strong that Anders accused Schell of plagiarising his writings.[133] These publications, some of the most significant in the humanities during these two decades, really were catching up to Anders' insights, whether they knew of him or not.

Anders' conception of history 'after Hiroshima' could also inform investigations of the history of anti-nuclear critique and might serve as the basis for comparative reflection on the problem of 'after Auschwitz' in contemporary philosophy and theology. Moreover, as Michael Geyer has pointed out, Anders' works after 1956 suggest fruitful ways to reconsider the relationship between modern technology and mass annihilation, and the question of how to link the Cold War to the two world wars.[134] Finally, he is an indispensable thinker for coming to terms with, as the present volume thematises, the remarkable array of attempts to 'imagine the unimaginable', the prospect of global nuclear devastation. Thus, Anders' philosophical thought has much to offer for any critical history of the twentieth century.

The atomic age endures, if in a different form than Anders confronted, and is still an enormous problem for social theory and political praxis. In the struggle to ensure that, in the twenty-first century, the 'twilight of the Bombs' turns into a world without such weapons, Günther Anders' books can still throw light on the past century when the Inhuman became the measure of all things.[135]

Notes

1 For attempts to consider questions of theory and praxis together, see these two fine studies: M. Bess, *Realism, Utopia, and the Mushroom Cloud: Four Activist Intellectuals and Their Strategies for Peace, 1945–1989: Louise Weiss (France), Leo Szilard (USA), E.P. Thompson (England), Danilo Dolci (Italy)* (Chicago, 1993); I. Stölken-Fitschen, *Atombombe und Geistesgeschichte: Eine Studie der fünfziger Jahre aus deutscher Sicht* (Baden-Baden, 1995).

2 This essay overlaps with and expands upon the analysis of Anders' philosophy in my dissertation, 'The limits of the human in the age of technological revolution: Günther Anders, post-Marxism, and the emergence of technology critique'. Unpublished PhD thesis, University of Chicago, 2013.

3 P. van Dijk, *Anthropology in the Age of Technology: The Philosophical Contribution of Günther Anders*, trans. F. Kooymans (Atlanta, 2000). The Dutch original appeared in 1998.

4 For some good general studies of Anders in German, see K. P. Liessmann, *Günther Anders zur Einführung* (Hamburg, 1988); E. Schubert, *Günther Anders: Mit Selbstzeugnissen und Bilddokumenten* (Reinbek bei Hamburg, 1992); K. P. Liessmann (ed.), *Günther Anders kontrovers* (Munich, 1992); M. Lohmann, *Philosophieren in der Endzeit: Zur Gegenwartsanalyse von Günther Anders* (Munich, 1996); C. Dries, *Günther Anders* (Paderborn, 2009); R. Bahr, *Günther Anders: Leben und Denken im Wort* (Vienna, 2010); G. Bischof, J. Dawsey and B. Fetz (eds), *The Life and Work of Günther Anders: Émigré, Iconoclast, Philosopher, Man of Letters* (Innsbruck, 2014).

5 For some examples, see P. P. Portinaro, *Il principio disperazione: Tre studi su Günther Anders* (Turin, 2003); C. David and K. Parienti-Maire (eds), *Günther Anders: Agir pour repousser la fin du monde* (Paris, 2007); É. Jolly, *Nihilisme et Technique: Étude sur Günther Anders* (Lille, 2010).

6 For this excellent new research, see H. Nehring, 'Cold War, apocalypse and peaceful atoms: interpretations of nuclear energy in the British and West German anti-nuclear weapons movements, 1955–1964', *Historical Social Research* 29:3 (2004), pp. 150–70; B. Ziemann, 'The code of protest: images of peace in the West German peace movements, 1945–1990', *Contemporary European History* 17:2 (2008), pp. 237–61; B. Ziemann, 'Introduction', in B. Ziemann (ed.), *Peace Movements in Western Europe, Japan and the USA during the Cold War* (Essen, 2007); A. Jürgens-Kirchhoff, '"Artists against nuclear war" (1958–1962): a touring exhibition at the time of the Cold War', in *ibid.*; C. Dries, '"Zeitbomben mit unfestgelegtem Explosionstermin": Günther Anders und der kalte Krieg', in P. Bernhard and H. Nehring (eds), *Den kalten Krieg denken: Beiträge zur sozialen Ideengeschichte* (Essen, 2014).

7 M. Kaldor, *The Imaginary War: Understanding the East-West Conflict* (Cambridge, 1990).

After Hiroshima

8 For more on Anders' involvement with the peace movement, see E. Röhrlich, 'To make the end time endless: the early years of Günther Anders' fight against nuclear weapons', in *The Life and Work of Günther Anders* (hereafter *LWGA*).
9 Philosopher John Somerville coined the term 'omnicide' in the early 1980s. For Somerville's invention of the word, see M. Granberry, 'Octogenarian coined "Omnicide" during lifelong push for peace', *Los Angeles Times*, 30 Nov. 1986.
10 For these characterisations, see O. G'schrey, *Günther Anders: 'Endzeit' Diskurs und Pessimismus* (Cuxhaven, 1991), p. 96. Anders' 1961 reworking of the Noah story, 'Die beweinte Zukunft', is in his *Die atomare Drohung: Radikale Überlegungen* (Munich, 1981) (hereafter *DaD*). Anders' interest in the Cassandra figure is already evident in his 1939 poem 'Aus: "Kassandra"' in his *Tagebücher und Gedichte* (Munich, 1985), pp. 312-15. For Anders' notion of 'warning-images', see his 'Warnbilder' in *Das Tagebuch und der moderne Autor*, ed. Uwe Schultz (Munich, 1965).
11 *Die Antiquiertheit des Menschen*, vol. 2: *Über die Zerstörung des Lebens im Zeitalter der dritten industriellen Revolution* (Munich, 1980), p. 11 (hereafter *AM*, vol. 2). The quotation about the 'encyclopedia of the apocalyptic world' is taken from Anders' speech upon receiving the Theodor W. Adorno Prize from the city of Frankfurt am Main in 1983, 'Gegen ein neues und endgültiges Nagasaki' in *Günther Anders antwortet: Interviews & Erklärungen*, ed. Elke Schubert (Berlin, 1987), 174 (hereafter *GAa*). This comment is the starting point for B. Wiesenberger's *Enzyklopädie der apokalyptischen Welt: Kulturphilosophie, Gesellschaftstheorie, und Zeitdiagnose bei Günther Anders und Theodor W. Adorno* (Munich, 2003).
12 See his 1962 'The Émigré', trans. O. Binder, in *LWGA*, p. 171.
13 For more biographical information, see Bahr, *Günther Anders*; van Dijk, *Anthropology*, chapter 2; Dawsey, 'The limits of the human', chapter 1.
14 *Ibid.*, pp. 41-2. Anders related four 'caesuras' in his life: (1) the First World War; (2) Hitler's assumption of power; (3) knowledge of the Nazi genocide; (4) the dropping of the atomic bomb on Hiroshima. The second and third made him a 'political writer'.
15 See Anders' 1979 interview with Mathias Greffrath, 'Wenn ich verzweifelt bin, was geht's mich an?' in *GAa*, p. 42.
16 E. Freundlich, *The Traveling Years*, trans. E. Pennebaker (Riverside, Calif.: Ariadne Press, 1999), pp. 97-8. There were personal reasons for the move too. Freundlich strongly wanted to return to her home city of Vienna.
17 See Anders' introduction to his *Hiroshima ist überall* (Munich, 1982), pp. xi-xii (hereafter *Hiü*). There, he noted that a three-page text resulted in 1952 or 1953 from his first successful effort to write something about the atom bomb. See also 'Wenn ich verzweifelt bin', in *GAa*, pp. 42-3, where he gave 1950 or 1951 as the date for his first success in this endeavour.

18 'Faust ist tot', *Aufbau*, 27 Nov. 1953. A few years later, Anders resumed his commentary on the death of Faust in *Die Antiquiertheit des Menschen*, vol. 1: *Über die Seele im Zeitalter der zweiten industriellen Revolution* (Munich, 1956), pp. 239–42 (hereafter *AM*, vol. 1).
19 'Faust is tot'.
20 For these overlapping crises, see J. Dülffer, 'Die Suez-und Ungarn-Krise', in M. Salewski (ed.), *Das Zeitalter der Bombe: Die Geschichte der atomaren Bedrohung von Hiroshima bis heute* (Munich, 1995); M. Cioc, *Pax Atomica: The Nuclear Defense Debate in West Germany during the Adenauer Era* (New York, 1988); M. Geyer, 'Cold War angst: the case of West German opposition to rearmament and nuclear weapons', in H. Schissler (ed.), *The Miracle Years: A Cultural History of West Germany, 1949–1968* (Princeton, 2001), pp. 376–408.
21 See *AM*, vol. 1, p. 235.
22 *Ibid.*, p. 236.
23 Introduction, *Hiü*, p. xi.
24 *AM*, vol. 1, p. 7.
25 *Ibid*. For more of Anders' argument about technology as a historical Subject, see *AM*, vol. 2, pp. 279–80.
26 'Die Frist', in *DaD*, pp. 198–9.
27 *Ibid.*, p. 199.
28 For a slightly different list of these developments, see G. Althaus, *Leben zwischen Sein und Nichts: Drei Studien zu Günther Anders* (Berlin, 1989), pp. 38–9.
29 See Anders' usage of this word in *AM*, vol. 2, p. 397. His statements on technological domination in both the capitalist and communist blocs are in *AM*, vol. 1, p. 3, p. 7. For his argument about the "obsolescence of boundaries," see *AM*, vol. 2, pp. 208–9.
30 *AM*, vol. 1, p. 16.
31 *Ibid.*
32 'Brecht konnte mich nicht riechen', in *GAa*, p. 104. See also Introduction, *Hiü*, p. xii.
33 'Brecht konnte mich nicht riechen', in *GAa*, p. 104. There, Anders accented the 'fact that we can produce more than we can imagine'. (Italics in the original.)
34 *AM*, vol. 2, p. 405.
35 'Wenn ich verzweifelt bin', in *GAa*, p. 42.
36 'Der hippokratische Eid: Erwägungen zum Problem des "Produktstreiks"', in *DaD*, p. 140.
37 *Der Mann auf der Brücke: Tagebuch aus Hiroshima und Nagasaki* (Munich, 1959). The book was also reprinted in *Hiü*. It is the latter that I use in the following section (hereafter *MadB* in *Hiü*).
38 For the article Zelka gave to Anders, see 'The "curse" of Hiroshima', *Newsweek* (25 May 1959), p. 112. The piece appeared in the 'Science' section of the magazine.

39 Anders translated his correspondence with Eatherly into German. It appeared as *Off Limits für das Gewissen: Der Briefwechsel zwischen dem Hiroshima-Piloten Claude Eatherly und Günther Anders 1959–1961* (Reinbek bei Hamburg, 1961). The following year, the correspondence was published in the United States as *Burning Conscience: The Case of the Hiroshima Pilot, Claude Eatherly, Told in His Letters to Günther Anders* (New York, 1962) (hereafter *BC*). For extensive analyses of the correspondence, see G. Geiger, *Der Täter und der Philosoph-der Philosoph als Täter: Der Begegnung zwischen dem Hiroshima-Piloten Claude R. Eatherly und dem Antiatomkriegphilosophen Günther Anders oder Schuld und Verantwortung im atomaren Zeitalter* (Bern, 1991); C. Biladt, *Günther Anders und der 'Antipode Eichmanns': Briefwechsel Günther Anders & Claude Eatherly* (St. Wolfgang, 2008).
40 Introduction, *Hiü*, p. x.
41 *Ibid.*, p. xxx.
42 The most detailed exposition of Anders' critique of non-violence (with responses from figures in the West German and Austrian public spheres) appeared in *Gewalt – ja oder nein? Eine notwendige Diskussion*, ed. M. Bissinger (Munich, 1987). For several considerations of Anders' views on violence, see the special issue of *Ethica & Politica/Ethics & Politics* XV:2 (2013).
43 It must be kept in mind that Anders embedded both Auschwitz and Hiroshima within his critique of technology. For comparable ideas on 'after Auschwitz' see T. W. Adorno, *Negative Dialectics*, trans. E. B. Ashton (New York, 1973), pp. 361–5; D. LaCapra, *History and Memory after Auschwitz* (Ithaca, 1998).
44 *AM*, vol. 1, p. 271.
45 *Ibid.*, p. 267.
46 *Ibid.*
47 *Ibid.*
48 *Ibid.*, p. 243.
49 *Ibid.*, p. 257.
50 *AM*, vol. 2, p. 247.
51 See his incisive essay, 'Atomarer Mord – kein Selbstmord', in *DaD*.
52 For 'annihilism' see *AM*, vol. 1, pp. 294–306, and the 1981 foreword to *DaD*, p. x. For 'globocide' see *AM*, vol. 2, p. 410.
53 *AM*, vol. 2, pp. 281–2.
54 'Theses for the atomic age', in *LWGA*, p. 187. This English translation, done by Anders himself, first appeared in *The Massachusetts Review* 3:3 (Spring 1962), pp. 493–505. The German original, written in 1959, is available in *DaD*.
55 I am referring here to Anders' choice of title for his collection *Hiü*.
56 *MadB*, in *Hiü*, p. 66.
57 *Ibid.* Anders' father, William Stern, having lost his faculty position at the University of Hamburg during the Nazis' purge of the German civil service, left Germany in 1935. He secured a professorship in psychology at Duke University and died following a heart attack in 1938.

58 *AM*, vol. 2, p. 19. (Italics in the original.) In Anders' philosophical understanding of modernity, the two previous industrial revolutions consisted of, first, the classic Industrial Revolution of the eighteenth and nineteenth centuries and, second, the impact of technology, especially mass media and advertising, on the psyche. See *ibid.*, pp. 15–16. For Anders' critique of mass media, see his essay on radio and televison in *AM*, vol. 1, pp. 97–211.
59 *AM*, vol. 2, p. 20.
60 *Ibid.*
61 See *Ketzereien* (Munich, 1982), p. 33. See also pp. 35–6, 82–3, 103–4.
62 For this remarkable statement, see Anders' essay 'Nach "Holocaust" 1979', in *Besuch im Hades* (Munich, 1979), p. 195. For more on Anders' extremely provocative attempts to think Hiroshima with Auschwitz, see Dawsey, 'The limits of human', chapter VI.
63 *MadB*, in *Hiii*, p. 110.
64 *Ibid.*
65 *Ibid.*
66 *Ibid.*
67 *Ibid.*, pp. 111–12. The atomic bombing of Nagasaki was, to Anders, a '*threat-gesture*' and the 70,000 killed (his number) '*threat-material*'. See *ibid.*, p. 112.
68 'Wenn ich verzweifelt bin', in *GAa*, p. 42.
69 'Die Frist', in *DaD*, pp. 170–1.
70 'Der Sprung', in *ibid.*, p. 20.
71 For *Endzeit*, see 'Thesen zum Atomzeitalter', in *ibid.*, pp. 93–4. Anders translated the term as 'Time of the End' and 'End Time' and also used 'Last Age' as a synonym. For his translation, see 'Theses for the atomic age', in *LWGA*, p. 187.
72 Anders translated *die Frist* as 'respite' in 'Theses for the atomic age', in *LWGA*, p. 187. In 1960, he produced a lengthy essay on this concept, titled 'Die Frist' and available in *DaD*, that I draw on extensively in this piece.
73 He utilised *Zeitenende* in 'Thesen zum Atomzeitalter', in *DaD*, pp. 93–4. For his translation of the word as 'The end of time', see 'Theses for the atomic age', in *LWGA*, p. 187.
74 'Commandments for the atomic age', in *BC*, p. 20.
75 *AM*, vol. 1, p. 263.
76 *Ibid.*, pp. 266–7.
77 *Ibid.*, p. 277. (Emphasis in the original.)
78 'Die Frist', in *DaD*, p. 216. To be sure, Anders, while drawing on the language of these traditions, carefully separated man-made apocalypse from Jewish and Christian representations.
79 *AM*, vol. 1, p. 4, p. 278.
80 See 'Die Wurzeln der Apokalypse-Blindheit', in *DaD*, pp. 119–21.
81 *AM*, vol. 1, p. 267.

82 *Die Toten*, in *Hiü*, p. 392.
83 *Ibid.*, pp. 392–3.
84 *Ibid.*, p. 393.
85 For one example, see his 1983 interview with Wolfgang Bogensberger and Robert Zadra, 'Ich bin nur ein Augenöffner', in *GAa*, pp. 71–8.
86 *AM*, vol. 1, p. 273. (Emphasis in the original.)
87 'Commandments for the atomic age', in *BC*, p. 13.
88 See Anders' 1982 interview with Hans-Horst Skupy, 'Vorstellungskraft ist das Notwendigste', in *GAa*, p. 56.
89 *AM*, vol. 1, p. 282.
90 I take the term from Raimund Kurscheid, *Kampf dem Atomtod! Deutsche Schriftsteller im Kampf gegen eine deutsche Atombewaffnung* (Cologne, 1981), pp. 58–61.
91 This phrase is taken from Sara Horowitz's excellent *Voicing the Void: Muteness and Memory in Holocaust Fiction* (Albany, 1997).
92 See Anders' 'Moral code in the atomic age', Typoskript, Österreichisches Literaturarchiv der Österreichischen Nationalbibliothek, Vienna, Nachlass Günther Anders 237/04, 3 (hereafter ÖLA-ÖNB, NGA 237/04).
93 'Theses for the atomic age', in *LWGA*, p. 190.
94 *Ibid.*
95 'Der Sprung', in *DaD*, p. 20.
96 Günther Anders to Erwin Schrödinger, 26 July 1960, ÖLA-ÖNB, NGA 237/04.
97 See Anders' 'Unmoral im Atomzeitalter: Warnung während einer Windstille', in *DaD*, p. 68.
98 'Theses for the atomic age', in *LWGA*, p. 194.
99 *Ibid.*, p. 188. There is an extensive treatment of this claim in C. Dries, *Die Welt als Vernichtungslager: Eine kritische Theorie der Moderne im Anschluss an Günther Anders, Hannah Arendt und Hans Jonas* (Bielefeld, 2012).
100 *Die Toten*, in *Hiü*, p. 365. (Emphasis in the original.)
101 'Theses for the atomic age', in *LWGA*, pp. 191–2.
102 *Ibid.*, p. 192.
103 *AM*, vol. 2, p. 70.
104 'Theses for the atomic age', in *LWGA*, p. 192.
105 For more on this, see 'Über Verantwortung heute', in *DaD*, pp. 38–9.
106 *MadB*, in *Hiü*, pp. 112–14.
107 *Ibid.*, p. 114.
108 'Theses for the atomic age', in *LWGA*, p. 193.
109 'Die Frist', in *DaD*, pp. 202–3.
110 *MadB*, in *Hiü*, p. 113.
111 'Der hippokratische Eid', in *DaD*, p. 163.
112 'Unmoral im Atomzeitalter', in *ibid.*, p. 91.
113 *Ibid.*

114 'Die Frist', in *ibid.*, p. 202.
115 *Ibid.*, pp. 199–200.
116 *AM*, vol. 1, p. 263.
117 'Die Frist', in *DaD*, p. 201.
118 See 'Commandments in the atomic age', in *BC*, p. 11. Translation modified.
119 *Ibid.*
120 See *AM*, vol. 1, p. 258.
121 See Anders' introduction to his *Mensch ohne Welt: Schriften zur Kunst und Literatur* (Munich, 1984), p. xi.
122 'Vorstellungskraft ist das Notwendigste', in *GAa*, p. 60.
123 I borrow this term from T. W. Adorno, *Aesthetic Theory*, trans. R. Hullot-Kentor (Minneapolis, 1997), p. 4. Adorno applied it to debates in the late 1960s over the purported 'death of art'.
124 'Theses for the atomic age', in *LWGA*, p. 190.
125 *MadB*, in *Hiü*, pp. 20–1.
126 *Die Toten*, in *ibid.*, p. 381.
127 'Thesen zum Atomzeitalter', in *DaD*, p. 95. Anders rendered '*Internationale der Generationen*' as '*League of Generations*' in 'Theses for the atomic age', in *LWGA*, p. 188, effectively removing the Marxist associations of the former.
128 'Theses for the atomic age', in *LWGA*, p. 188.
129 *AM*, vol. 2, p. 5.
130 E.P. Thompson, 'Notes on exterminism: the last stage of civilization', in New Left Review (eds), *Exterminism and Cold War* (London, 1982).
131 B. Lang, 'Genocide and omnicide: technology and the limits of ethics', in his *The Future of the Holocaust: Between History and Memory* (Ithaca, 1999).
132 R. J. Lifton and E. Markusen, *The Genocidal Mentality: Nazi Holocaust and Nuclear Threat* (New York, 1990), p. 260, pp. 261–2.
133 J. Schell, *The Fate of the Earth* (New York, 1982). For the charge of plagiarism against Schell, see Anders' 'Brief zur Plagiat-Affaiäre (Schell-Anders)', *Die Zeit* (11 Feb. 1983). Schell vigorously denied the accusation.
134 M. Geyer, 'Humanity in an age of total destruction: Friedrich Georg Jünger: *Die Perfektion der Technik* (1939/1946)', in U. Jensen, H. Knoch, D. Morat and M. Rürup (eds), *Gewalt und Gesellschaft: Klassiker modernen Denkens neu gelesen: Bernd Weisbrod zum 65. Geburtstag* (Göttingen, 2011), p. 173.
135 R. Rhodes, *Twilight of the Bombs: Recent Challenges, New Dangers, and the Prospects for a World without Nuclear Weapons* (New York, 2010).

8

Hiroshima/Nagasaki, civil rights and anti-war protest in Japan's Cold War

Ann Sherif

Twenty years after the Hiroshima and Nagasaki bombings, the rest of the world had come to regard nuclear destruction as a function of the imagination, visually and rhetorically preparing for apocalypse, defining the looming threat as a permanent feature of modern life. In Hiroshima and Nagasaki, that global imagination co-existed uncomfortably with the living memories, the social challenges, and visible and hidden scars of the hibakusha (survivors of the atomic bombings).[1] During the 1960s, many people who had experienced the Hiroshima and Nagasaki atomic bombings, along with other residents of those cities, participated with fervour in the anti-nuclear movement. Hiroshima and Nagasaki, self-designated as the Cities of Peace, became destinations for anti-bomb political protestors from around the world, an odd sort of Cold War pilgrimage. The mantra-like threat of nuclear annihilation due to the Superpower's development and stockpiling of the next generation of nuclear weapons made a visit to Hiroshima strangely alluring.[2]

Throughout the Cold War, did a shared atomic moment remain the most pressing mutual concern between the Japanese people and the Americans, between Hiroshima and Nagasaki and the outside world? This chapter examines the political and cultural dynamics of social movements that converged in Hiroshima and were transformed by its Cold War inflections, as they built on dynamic currents of Cold War discourse distinct from the bomb. In contrast to well-known debates about nuclear weapons among political parties and nations that raged from the 1950s and well into the 1960s, diverse grass-roots groups that converged in Hiroshima during the 1960s articulated an emerging global norm: a fresh articulation of the notion of human rights.[3] This chapter uses a case study to explore significant new articulations of the discourse of human rights during the Cold War that emerged as America's legitimacy shifted during the Vietnam War and transnational dialogues among social movements became tremendously influential. Specifically, in 1966, five Hiroshima anti-nuclear activists and two Americans involved in the anti-Vietnam War and civil rights movements sat together as presenters at an anti-Vietnam War teach-in at Hiroshima University attended by three hundred students and local residents. Why did the transnational group of anti-war protestors come to Hiroshima? How did they find common cause with the hibakusha and activists in Hiroshima? Was the Vietnam War their only concern?

One of the hibakusha representatives at the 1966 Hiroshima teach-in was Professor Moritaki Ichirô, a philosopher and the head of the Japan Confederation of A- and H-Bomb Sufferers Organisations (Hidankyô). Moritaki was well known in Hiroshima, frequently appearing in the local media and at events as an advocate for hibakusha and as an opponent of nuclear weapons. In recent years, Moritaki had also gained a national reputation for speaking out on behalf of Hiroshima survivors when he was featured in novelist Ôe Kenzaburô's reportage *Hiroshima Notes*. In what is arguably one of the best known non-fiction works about Hiroshima, Ôe describes a classical Cold War scene, in which Moritaki is booed when he steps up to 'say words of remembrance for the dead and the surviving A-bomb victims' in front of some 20,000 anti-nuclear protestors, who gathered in the Peace Park in August 1963. Some of those in the crowd had no patience for his tales of the hibakusha's plight and messages of peace from Hiroshima; they were instead interested in the neo-imperialism implied when Moritaki brought up the topic of bombers that took off from US bases in Okinawa and Polaris missiles.

In the 1960s, social protest in Japan shifted its gaze to a distinctly Cold War issue: the Vietnam War. One of the most significant anti-Vietnam War events of the era was the 1966 teach-in series organised by the anti-war coalition Beheiren (the Citizens' Alliance for Peace in Vietnam).[4] The ambitious programme, which included numerous lectures, debates and symposia, took place in nine different cities and at least fourteen different venues throughout Japan, from Hokkaido in the north to Kyushu and Okinawa (then still occupied by the United States). Notably, Beheiren decided to include Hiroshima on the tour, despite any misgivings over the possibility of a replay of the kind of East Bloc–West Bloc dispute and communist–socialist fracture over the huge topic of nuclear weapons. Such debates had the potential to become mired in the sore subject of Japan's own militarist and imperialist past and the way it perched under the US nuclear umbrella.

Although the organisers might have chosen other leaders from the burgeoning American anti-war protest movement as guest presenters at the teach-ins, Beheiren decided to feature Howard Zinn and Ralph Featherstone, who were better known for their civil rights activism in the Student Non-Violent Coordinating Committee. What would they talk about in Hiroshima, usually crowded with anti-nuclear and hibakusha groups? What objectives, ideas and language did these disparate groups share? Were the encounters solely focused on the way of abolishing violence and war itself? Or were there other pressing Cold War issues that could serve as common ground among hibakusha and other Hiroshima activists and the visitors from afar?

This chapter proposes ways to understand the anti-nuclear movement and the anti-war movement of the 1960s as part of related currents in Cold War discourse, by revealing the ideas and rhetoric that closely linked groups as seemingly disparate as the anti-nuclear movement, the American and Japanese anti-Vietnam War movements, the civil rights movement, national liberation movements, and black activism. The struggle that compelled politically engaged people was that of ensuring human rights – the rights of the Vietnamese people to self-determination, the rights of the hibakusha to health and happiness, the rights of blacks to vote, to dignity. The stated purpose of the events organised by Beheiren was to interrogate and protest against the Vietnam War, and not to address human rights *per se*. However, the discourse of human rights as articulated in the international community since the war's end underlay most of the assumptions about the goals of these diverse groups' activism.[5] This case study allows the foregroundings of the knowledge building and political transformation that transpired on the ground among historical actors who were political activists but also ordinary 'Free World' citizens in the Cold War. The connections forged between local, national, and transnational politically engaged citizens illuminate larger dynamics in the diverse and vibrant social activism of the 1960s. Featherstone and Zinn's visit to Hiroshima also provided a fresh context for anti-nuclear and hibakusha protest, by shifting it from a dogmatic bipolar framework to a humanist discourse focusing on human rights.

The core group of presenters who made this extensive anti-war tour around Japan included the co-organisers of Beheiren, along with Featherstone and Zinn. The Beheiren leaders were all prominent writers and activist intellectuals who appeared frequently in the public media and on the streets: novelist Oda Makoto (1932–2007), critic and philosopher Tsurumi Shunsuke (1922–2015), novelist and communist Iida Momo (1926–2011). Beheiren was accustomed to inviting speakers from abroad: in 1966 alone they hosted socialist and pacifist Dave Dillinger (then associated with the Students for Democratic Society or SDS), a number of American GIs resisters, and, from Europe, Jean-Paul Sartre and Simone de Beauvoir, among others. It was through Harvard connections that Oda Makoto and Tsurumi Shunsuke knew Boston University professor and activist Howard Zinn (1922–2010). Zinn had worked with Student Non-Violent Coordinating Committee (SNCC) and through it met SNCC staff member Ralph Featherstone (1937–70).[6]

Many members of the audience at the lectures and teach-in participants in the June anti-war tour were university students – not surprising in the 1960s when such networks of students, formal and informal, spread around the globe, culminating in the influential student protests of 1968.[7] The teach-in format itself was inspired by events on US college campuses organised by the SDS and others. Co-organiser Iida Momo estimated that nearly 10,000 people participated in the nationwide events.[8] In many student protest groups, such networking facilitated the exchange of information, ideas and strategies and encouraged the participants to join together with the goal of outlining 'transnational solutions for global problems and to prepare a global revolutionary strategy that would result in the transformation of the Cold War system'. At the same time, older participants in the Japanese teach-in such as Tsurumi Shunsuke, who experienced political repression in wartime Japan, were acutely aware that the freedom to conduct this tour and to assert their critical political positions in public rested on rights guaranteed by Japan's post-war constitution (modelled closely after the US Constitution and promulgated as part of the Allied Occupation), as well as on the rise of capitalist Japan's economic power during the era's high economic growth.

The mid-1960s was a period of rapid change in the Cold War owing to factors distinct from the nuclear arms race: the civil rights movement; proxy wars, such as the Vietnam War; and national independence movements in non-aligned countries across the globe. These urgent issues, along with the first moves towards international nuclear arms controls in the aftermath of the Cuban Missile Crisis, altered perceptions of nuclear weapons and of the atomic-bombed cities. Despite Hiroshima and Nagasaki's passionate devotion to abolishing the bomb, by the mid-1960s, some members of the high-profile, long-standing anti-nuclear movement in Japan expressed opposition to the Vietnam War.[9] The discussions and debates at the Beheiren-sponsored Hiroshima teach-in reveal that, in this period, anti-nuclear activists were actively searching for new means of contextualising their movement through studying the relationship of the past to the present, and learning about the ways that the discourse of human rights related to the hibakusha's lives in the changing context of war and peace.

Before Ralph Featherstone visited Hiroshima, he was likely not aware of the extent to which American views of the bomb differed from those in Japan, where a vast majority of citizens believed that nuclear weapons should be eliminated, nor that the anti-nuclear movement had established legitimacy across a broad political spectrum in Japan, and even in party politics. In 1966, Featherstone and Zinn sat face to face with the people of Hiroshima, at the boundary between the now entrenched imagination of apocalypse and the site where nuclear weapons had been first deployed. It was the face of the city of Hiroshima – and Nagasaki too – that manifested the nuclear allergy of Japan, even as that country joined the new global nuclear regime and submitted itself to economic and psychological dependency on nuclear technologies peaceful and military. With their experience in confronting the legacies of violence and racism at home, Featherstone and Zinn sat down to exchange ideas with people in this city. Could they find common ground?

Japan's Hiroshima: domestic politics and space for criticism

On 10 June 1966, 300 people – including many hibakusha – gathered in Hiroshima to discuss, not nuclear weapons, but the war in Vietnam with Zinn and Featherstone, citizens of the nation that was waging that war. Along with A-bomb survivor and leader Moritaki Ichirô, the Hiroshima organising committee included hibakusha, professors and well-regarded local journalist Kanai Toshihiro. The regional newspaper *Chûgoku Shinbun* where he worked was listed as a co-sponsor with Hiroshima University. The tour organisers' media savvy can be seen in their enlistment of local newspapers with large circulation in other cities as well, including Sapporo and Naha.

Domestic politics and activism in Japan and in the United States are important contexts for Featherstone and Zinn's visit. In Japan, the pro-US conservative base represented by the Liberal Democratic Party (LDP) promoted rapid re-industrialisation, a focus on consumerism and economic growth. Tokyo-based Beheiren organisers Oda Makoto and Tsurumi Shunsuke represented progressive citizen activists and intellectuals who were deeply engaged with participatory politics and frequently critical of the status quo. Tsurumi Shunsuke and Oda Makoto knew in considerable detail about the American civil rights movements.

The Japanese hosts had a sophisticated, first-hand understanding of contemporary America. Therefore their choice of Featherstone and Zinn, rather than other Vietnam War activists, was intentional. While not flamboyant revolutionaries, Featherstone and Zinn had proven themselves by dedicating themselves to activism in the Deep South, and thus were ideal partners.[10] On the tour, Oda, knowing well that many in the audience had a negative view of the American War in Vietnam and of the USA's imperialist aims, was careful in his introduction of Featherstone and Zinn.[11] First of all, Oda made sure to inform the audience that he himself had travelled through Europe and in the Soviet Union in order to meet anti-war activists, including Viet Cong (National Liberation Front of South Vietnam) representatives.[12] The US anti-war movement, Oda told them, was the strongest of all, and therefore indispensable to a global coalition. And Zinn and Featherstone were the 'conscience of America'.

Ralph Featherstone was the only African-American who participated in the tour as a core presenter. Featherstone and Zinn stood at the forefront of the protracted struggle for civil rights and the opposition to the Vietnam War, both defining movements of America's Cold War. Neither of them were active in SANE, the 'largest, best-known anti-nuclear movement' in the United States with a membership of only about 25,000 at its peak in 1958.[13] The distance between the Americans' frames of reference and those of Japanese participants at the teach-ins is indicated by the numerous questions about the relationship between the civil rights movement and the anti-war movement, and about Americans' awareness of Japanese protest movements.

Historical contexts of nuclear discourse in Hiroshima and Nagasaki

The Hiroshima and Nagasaki atomic bombings in August 1945 bound Japan to the Cold War in general and most specifically to nuclear inflections of that rivalry. These events are entangled with national identity and memory in Japan in myriad complex ways, coinciding as they did with Japan's defeat in the Asia–Pacific War (1931–45) and the commencement of a long military, economic, and political alliance with the United States. While the atomic bombings resonate so profoundly with the horrific violence of the Second World War on all sides, Hiroshima and Nagasaki remain alive in the imagination because they also signify the start of the nuclear age.[14]

From 1949, with the revelation of Soviet possession of nuclear devices, a fierce arms race was accompanied by bizarre public atmospheric tests of thermonuclear weapons by the superpowers and then by other possessor nations. In March 1954, media coverage brought world attention to the toxic fallout from a US hydrogen bomb test at Bikini Atoll that rained down on a Japanese fishing boat called the *Lucky Dragon*. The *Lucky Dragon* or Bikini Incident sparked widespread protest in Japan, and the resulting awareness that radioactive particles from H-bomb tests could enter the food chain and be detected in children's teeth in any country provoked anti-nuclear sentiment around the world. The superpowers promised peace and security to their own citizens and allies by means of their technological achievements. The fallout issue raised international concern about the hubris of two Superpowers as they willingly exposed their citizens – and people around the globe – to radioactive fallout. Evident in letters to the editor and anti-nuclear petitions in Japan are the simultaneous currents of so-called victim consciousness (Japan as victim) and political awareness of the need to acknowledge Japan's militaristic past and also to deal constructively with social issues in the Cold War present.

From soon after the August 1945 atomic bombings, people in Hiroshima and Nagasaki had engaged in various ways with discourses of the Bomb. The Allied Occupation identified the atomic bombings with 'peace'. With its gradual emergence as the Asian 'economic miracle' after its defeat and destruction in the Second World War, Japan appeared to have regained the authority to advance its national interest and priorities on the world stage. Important aspects of that identity included the public's nuclear allergy and the tension between victim consciousness and the struggle to understand and ethically position Japan's militarist past.

After global public pressure contributed to the ratification of the first international control on nuclear weapons, the Nuclear Test Ban Treaty (1963), the hibakusha gained a new visibility as witnesses to weapons deemed by the world to be in need of policing. The claim of a globalised Hiroshima's moral authority, however, was contradicted in several ways, with discrimination against and lack of support for hibakusha continuing, and the arms race raging on, with underground nuclear testing. By the mid-1960s, the anti-nuclear movement in Japan had become a major 'pressure group', which was so varied and broad that it encompassed everyone from student radicals to moderates. Even the LDP 'announced that they were forming their own nuclear disarmament organisation'.[15]

From the 1960s, domestic criticism of US bombing raids in the Vietnam War lead to new debates about the meanings of the Hiroshima and Nagasaki bombings, as it had in the United States.¹⁶ Prime Minister Sato Eisaku's administration, under public pressure about American military bases on Japanese soil, declared in a parliamentary resolution (1967) its adherence to three non-nuclear principles: 'Japan shall neither possess nor manufacture nuclear weapons, nor shall it permit their introduction into Japanese territory'. The United States–Japan Security Treaty had long before brought Japan under America's nuclear 'umbrella'.

Freedom of movement in the free world?

The global Cold War dynamic played decisive roles in making possible the 'unlikely encounter' between a range of moderate, progressive, and radical Japanese and Americans in 1966 Hiroshima. Featherstone and Zinn's trip to Japan was entangled in the US government's effort to bolster its international legitimacy and downplay domestic racism. Japan, bound to the United States by the controversial security treaty, was also compelled to uphold the ideals of the American Founding Fathers, on which the post-war Japanese Constitution was based. The ruling political party (Liberal Democratic Party) co-operated extensively with US Cold War aims, at cultural, political economic and military levels.

During the 1950s and 1960s, the US State Department and White House struggled to uphold a positive image as a means of fighting Soviet criticisms of the rampant violation of racial and economic equality and rights in America. As Mary Dudziak explains about the 1960s, the 'focus of American foreign policy was to promote democracy and to "contain" communism, but the international focus on US racial problems meant that the image of American democracy was tarnished … The Soviet Union capitalised on this weakness.' As a result, 'U.S. government officials realised that their ability to promote democracy among peoples of colour around the world was seriously hampered by racial injustice at home.'¹⁷ The superpowers vied to assert their moral superiority vis-à-vis race and rights in order to influence and bring into their own sphere non-aligned nations, especially recently independent states.

At the same time, the FBI closely monitored civil rights and anti-war movements, wary that public protest or statements would bring unwanted attention to racist practices and further compromise America's international reputation. SNCC, both then and now regarded by many as the most 'revered' of all civil rights organisations, was an organisation of particular interest to the FBI.¹⁸ Ralph Featherstone and Howard Zinn were well known to the FBI and local authorities in the South for their political organising and sharp criticism of the government. Even so, the State Department decided to permit the trip of these outspoken critics of the government to Japan. Their elite credentials and connections with intellectuals in Japan, along with their philosophy of non-violence, made them palatable.[19] In this way, both governments guarded their reputations as Free World nations, conscious of criticism from their Cold War rival, the USSR, and from emerging Third World nations that the United States hoped to pull into its sphere.

Human rights as a Cold War concept: the search for a shared language

The encounter between Zinn/Featherstone and Japanese people from a broad political spectrum, from moderates to radicals, tapped into an important transnational discourse of human rights. It was in the concept of universal human rights, articulated formally by the United Nations in the early years after the end of the war, that the American visitors and hibakusha from Hiroshima and Nagasaki, along with the rest of the politically diverse Hiroshima audience, found a common language and common ground. It was through the concept of universal human rights that they forged connections in their opposition to the ongoing Vietnam War, the plight of the hibakusha and the nuclear age.

During the 1966 teach-in, Ralph Featherstone engaged with the Hiroshima audiences, as he sat shoulder to shoulder with various local people, including atomic bomb survivors.[20] The inclusion of hibakusha speakers on the part of political movements was a long-standing practice; many hibakusha groups organised testimonial activities for various political and social ends. Yet the hibakusha presenters at the 1966 teach-in did not talk about their own experiences of the bombing, and instead maintained a focus on the Vietnam War, foreign policy and the contemporary geopolitical contexts of the anti-nuclear movement.

Hiroshima teach-in participant Moritaki Ichirô did not preach a simplistic message of hibakusha as victims of war and the bomb. He, along with other experienced hibakusha activists, were well aware of the contingent nature of their witnessing and political presence, as they struggled to make their voices heard in rapidly changing geopolitical hierarchies. In the 1960s, their activities and thinking were informed as much by the concept of universal human rights, one of the most prominent currents of Cold War discourse, as they were by the particular historical circumstances of the bombing.[21]

How did the notion of universal human rights rise to such prominence during the Cold War? In 1946, the United Nations Commission on Human Rights was founded, motivated by the need to investigate means of establishing international standards for human rights and civil liberties in the aftermath of the horrific abuses of the 1930s and 1940s in Nazi Germany, among others. International deliberations, such as the Nuremberg Trials, employed the concept of human rights in its prosecution of war crimes. However, the eyes of the world rested not only on past abuses, but also contemporary practices.

Unable to find adequate support in the US government for the project of eliminating racist discrimination, violation of rights and violence, Dr W. E. B. DuBois and the NAACP in 1947 formally protested to the international Commission that 'U.S. discrimination' was '"not only indefensible but barbaric"', and furthermore that it 'is not Russia that threatens the United States so much as Mississippi … The disenfranchisement of the American Negro makes the functioning of all democracy in the nation difficult; and as democracy fails to function in the leading democracy in the world, it fails the world.'[22]

In 1948, the 'Universal Declaration of Human Rights' was adopted by the United Nations General Assembly. The Declaration crystallises myriad ideas and discourses about justice, economic rights and social rights that emerged in the aftermath of the world wars, and during a period of intense decolonialisation and ending of empires, not to mention the global sensation created by the NAACP's appeal.[23] The UN aimed at 'giving the individual human being standing in international law', apart from the state, because the 'horrors of the Nazi regime had created a consensus around the need to shift the balance of power away from the state and towards civil society and the individual'. By the 1960s, this valorisation of the rights of all individuals continued to exert authority in an institutionalised and legal form, but also much more broadly in popular discourses around the globe. In the 1960s, powerful movements, including the US civil rights movements and the anti-Vietnam war protests, mobilised the notion of human rights fully. The language of protest in the Vietnam War asserted the rights of the people of Vietnam to determine their own future, and to safety and security.[24]

These articulations of human rights – the United Nations' explicit articulation of the need for the state to protect human rights for all people, everywhere, and a more general discourse of human rights disseminated through the media and civil society – strongly informed post-war world public opinion, and in turn the dialogue among anti-war activists, civil rights activists, intellectuals, artists, journalists and scholars at the Hiroshima symposium. It was such a concept of human rights that allowed for common ground among participants at the Beheiren teach-ins along a broad range of the political spectrum, polarised and fractured by Cold War tensions as it was.

Civil rights, one the most pressing issues in the United States during the 1960s, is often understood as primarily a domestic concern. By silencing certain voices and by promoting a particular vision of racial justice, as Mary Dudziak notes, the Cold War led to a narrowing of 'acceptable civil rights discourse' and 'kept discussions of broad-based social change, or a linking of race and class, off the agenda'.[25] Critical voices within the United States, however, looked to the United Nations, which had articulated an ideal of equality and rights that could be claimed by people everywhere. SNCC's dispatch of its members internationally, such as Featherstone's trips abroad, was a means of forging bonds with like-minded people and organisations and enlisting international support for its goals and ideas.

Ralph Featherstone: civil rights and Vietnam

In Ralph Featherstone, the Japanese participants were encountering one of the most respected and effective SNCC leaders. Although he did not rise to the media fame of SNCC colleagues like Stokely Carmichael, Featherstone exemplified the spirit of SNCC in his formidable contributions to political mobilisation and organisation, as well as education, in Southern communities. Featherstone had, in fact, only rather recently expressed public opposition to the Vietnam War.

Discussions with college students all over Japan were likely to have been eye-opening for Featherstone and Zinn. Japanese university student participants in the teach-ins exhibited a sophisticated awareness of the ideological and economic currents of the Cold War Western bloc. A Nagoya University student compared the strong anti-communism of the United States that forms the context of student activism there with the predominance of Marxist thought in Japanese academia, while lamenting the complacency of many young people in the era of consumerism and high economic growth.[26] College students tended to critique the Vietnam War through a Marxist lens. He asked Featherstone 'are college students' ideas about the Vietnam War in the U.S. influential outside of the universities?' Featherstone turned his question around, and pointed out how much American college students learned from leaving their campuses and working on the Freedom Rides and Freedom Schools in the South. 'That is a tremendous education for the students who come down, and for all students ... and a chance for them to test their commitment to social justice.'[27] Implied in Featherstone's advocacy of direct action is the issue of the violations of human rights in these communities, and grass-roots strategies for fighting for those rights alongside working-class and poor people.

Although Vietnam War protest was the stated purpose of the Japan teach-ins, the presence of a core member of the American civil rights movement like Featherstone lent tremendous legitimacy to the American delegation of two. In contrast with SNCC leaders such as Stokely Carmichael and controversial Black Power activist H. Rap Brown, Featherstone was not a media star. But he was a key member of SNCC, internationally known as one of the groups that energised and transformed the civil rights movement.

At the Hiroshima teach-in, Featherstone explained to a university student that SNCC sent him to Japan in order to forge solidarity with Japanese anti-war groups and carry on the struggle together.[28] Featherstone represented SNCC at demonstrations across the United States, and also in Congress, testifying in from on before the House Judiciary Subcommittee on the Voting Rights Bill in 1965.[29] As did other SNCC workers, Featherstone travelled to other parts of the world. His trip to Cuba in 1968 was 'part of SNCC's effort to identify itself with the world's emerging nations and revolutionary movements'.[30]

Dudziak notes that, in regard to civil rights, the Cold War was 'simultaneously [an] agent of repression and an agent of change ... Struggles in the streets of American cities continually pushed the boundaries and redefined the narrative. The government's inability to control the story forced American leaders to promote stronger civil rights reform. When the international gaze later shifted to Vietnam and to civil unrest, the international leverage for civil rights reform receded.'[31] Early in the Beheiren tour, Featherstone emphasised to his audience at Tohoku University that SNCC's activities did not simply focus on access to the voting booth:

> Early on, SNCC focused on protesting discrimination in public places, such as segregated restaurants and city buses. But we realised that if we just concentrated on these rather narrow instances of discrimination, we would never be able to address the fundamental issues, such as poverty and other economic and social problems.[32]

Featherstone explained to the Japanese audience other achievements of the civil rights movement, such as advocating for equality in education for black children, and teaching them about black history. Featherstone was a key member in the implementation of SNCC's Freedom Schools in Mississippi and other parts of the South, where many African-American children attended underfunded and under resourced schools, and learned nothing of their own heritage or black history. He even explained that 'we are going to create a political party' where blacks can represent their own opinions and beliefs.[33]

Given the horrific deprivation of African-American's human rights that continued in the United States well after the Second World War, it is worth mentioning the reasons that advocacy for civil rights (right to participate in the political system) in America is often regarded as distinct from a human rights agenda. There are historical reasons for this separation of categories. During the 1930s groups such as the NAACP sought to bring international attention to flagrant violations of the human rights of African-Americans, culminating in its petitions to the UN soon after the war. A focus on civil rights became the politically safe path, because citizen access to the voting booth could be defined in terms of the values of the American Revolution and the Constitution, without reference to categories such as class and economic rights that suggested socialist and anti-imperialist discourses in the red-baiting context.[34] Thus, Featherstone and SNCC more broadly engaged with a New Left critique of capitalism and American society and did not subscribe to a constricted definition of 'civil rights'.

Oda and other teach-in participants spoke with admiration for the New Left and the general trend towards the valorisation of youth culture in the Western bloc since the 1950s. The New Left advanced the idea of young people and students in the vanguard of political protest and engagement, rather than traditional cohorts of political activists, such as labour union members and established intellectuals.[35] In the United States, the New Left rose as part of student protest and the civil rights movement. Considering the courage of SNCC and some other New Left groups who fought not only the horrific deprivation of voting rights, but also sought to forefront human rights (rights to safety, economic and social equity, and education, among others) of African-American and other minorities, it is fair to regard the civil rights movement in the United States as part of human rights advocacy.

Featherstone illuminated the complex currents of race, ideology and power that fuelled America's war in Vietnam. A Hiroshima teach-in participant asked Featherstone whether US actions in Vietnam were primarily motivated by race and whether he considered it a race war.

While acknowledging that the Vietnamese are an 'Asian people' and the American leaders are white, Featherstone emphasised the Cold War ideological rationale of battling communism as the primary rationale. He despaired at the lack of knowledge about communism and Marxism among American citizens and leaders, even as thousands of lives were being sacrificed.[36]

In Hiroshima, as at multiple other stops on the tour, participants asked Featherstone for clarification about the connection between the civil rights movement and the anti-war movement. Featherstone pointed out the realisation among civil rights activists about the disproportionate percentage of African-American military personnel fighting in Vietnam. Although the Vietnam War was not a race war per se, Featherstone noted, racial injustice and discrimination played a big role in sparking anti-war sentiments. He explained that black soldiers serving in Vietnam were supposed to be fighting for 'freedom' for the Vietnamese, but their own government did little to eliminate the discrimination they themselves faced at home. Whites do not like it, Featherstone asserted, when 'we Negroes' criticise the Vietnam War. But African-Americans had to speak out about US foreign policy, because they recognised the inequities, and also the devotion of resources to waging war in Southeast Asia rather than effectively pursuing the War on Poverty at home. In this way, Featherstone offered a thorough and convincing explanation to the Japanese audience of why he and SNCC were active in the anti-war movement, one that went beyond mere antipathy to violence and war.

In Tokyo, Featherstone explicated the link between the struggle 'to protect human rights' (*jinken o mamoru undô*) and the anti-war movement. He pointed to the failure of the US government to protect the 'right to happiness and all the rights' of blacks, even as it claims to protect South Vietnam from the North; the US government seeks to ensure 'free elections' in Vietnam, even though blacks in America are often deprived of their rights at the ballot box.[37] He elucidated the contortions of US Cold War policy, made possibly partly by the hubris resulting from the nuclear threat that the United States wielded as it competed with the Soviets.

Searching for a common ground

Featherstone and Zinn were surrounded at the Japanese teach-ins mostly by progressive and Marxist intellectuals, workers, and engaged citizens who, as they did, understood the Vietnam war as part of the global Cold

War, with the United States not as the untarnished leader of the Free World but as a military aggressor and neo-imperialist power. Older participants in the teach-ins, such as novelist Kaikô Ken, spoke frankly of their roles during the Asia Pacific War, and were not apologists for Japanese militarism. It was Howard Zinn, who had served as a bomber pilot in the European theatre in the Second World War, who brought to light the continuities in air war and highly mechanised warfare in the twentieth century. According to Judy Wu, some American radicals regarded the atomic bombings of 1945 and the 'massive destruction wrought on Vietnam by the American military' in the same light, and indeed an entire critique of US military's predilection for air war developed.[38]

The New Left activists encouraged awareness of agency and complicity in reference to recurring narratives of Japanese victimisation. Some Hiroshima participants such as Professor Nihei cautioned that fellow Japanese must not regard the hated Security Treaty merely as a mechanism that will draw Japan unintentionally into America's war of aggression in Vietnam.[39] Japan was actively and willingly supporting America's Cold War policies and strategies, including the Vietnam War, through the bases, munitions supplies, and so on, as it had during the Korean War. Tokyo Beheiren leader Oda Makoto concurred, but also drew on the language of the Civil Rights movement as he pronounced 'that Japan and the U.S. are linked by the security treaty so Japanese have the right and responsibility *(kenri to sekimu)* to protest the Vietnam War'. He went beyond the connection by the Security Treaty, and emphasised a connection to Zinn and Featherstone, and to a global discourse about human rights and race.

Howard Zinn's view of the New Left resonated with that of Tsurumi Shunsuke's generation in Japan. Too young to have experienced the Japanese Communist Party's purges and the convulsions among the Left caused by anti-Stalinism from the mid-1950s, the organisers of the Beheiren teach-ins, like SNCC, exhibited no uniform political ideologies or allegiances. SNCC and other student movements in the States condemned the racial hierarchy, but also questioned the unequal distribution of wealth, the failure to attend to the public good, and renounced, in Zinn's words, 'without the pretense of martyrdom ... the fraud and glitter of distorted prosperity'.[40]

Defining wars

Several of the Hiroshima participants did find a way to explore the link between the nuclear weapons, hibakusha and Vietnam by invoking the framework of the Cold War. Hiroshima journalist Kanai Toshihiro (1914–74) adopted a notably historical and structural approach to the question of how the atomic bombing related to the topic at hand – opposition to the Vietnam War. This was not only because he represented an older generation than most of the participants in the Hiroshima teach-in; Kanai had been covering nuclear issues for the Hiroshima regional newspaper the *Chûgoku shinbun* for more than a decade.

The journalist himself posed the question of how the experiences of Hiroshima relate to the topic at hand – the Vietnam War. Instead of answering the question directly, he offered comparison of wars. Combat – fighting on a battlefield – is experienced only by those designated by the state as combatants. Kanai distinguished the battlefield from war experienced by non-combatants in Total War, when families experience war in the form of separation from loved ones, families breaking up, and communities fracturing due to by separation and death. War haunts each family's kitchen. In other words, many citizens in a situation of Total War have experiences of war, but not of the battlefield.

The journalist scrupulously avoided mention of the victims of immediate acute radiation exposure from the atomic bombing in Hiroshima and Nagasaki, or of napalm in Vietnam. Everyone in the room knew about them. They had seen the pictures; they had seen with their own eyes. Or they themselves were there on 6 August and 9 August.[41] The Japanese media in the mid-1960s was full of stories and photographs about Vietnamese peasants maimed and killed by napalm, and their burned villages and fields.[42] It is not that Kanai was callous about those who died. He wanted to make a point about what happens when war reaches beyond the battlefield and into towns and cities where people live, in Japan, in Vietnam, anywhere. His reserve in critiquing the ongoing American war was not merely out of politeness for the American visitors. Nor was it because he wanted to obscure Japan's militarist past – he too had been a soldier in China. Those were topics for other speakers. Others spoke with conviction about Japan's role as 'accomplice' to America's wrong-headed foreign policy in Asia, in providing bases for B-52 bombers and manufacturing napalm and 'jungle shoes' for use in Vietnam.

It was doubtless such interactions that would encourage Howard Zinn to describe his impression that

> [The past] lay in the Japanese people's piercing consciousness of their own recent history. Again and again, at virtually every meeting, there arose the accusation, directed at the Japanese past and the American present: 'You are behaving in Asia as we once did' … There is a widespread and vocal

recognition of Japan's own sins, from the Manchurian invasion of 1931 to Pearl Harbor. Japanese scholars have done much research on those years, and see in American actions in Vietnam many of the same characteristics displayed by Japan in the '30s.[43]

Mr Kanai had two points he wanted to make – one about the unrecognised war that continued in Hiroshima and Nagasaki, and a related point about human rights in the atomic age. He explained that it took five years after the atomic bombings before the Japanese government finally saw fit to count the number of survivors. That meant that no one knows, Kanai continued, exactly how many people died from the effects of the bombing between 1945 and the time of a government survey in 1950. Because they were classified as non-combatants, the government had no obligation to keep track of those who died during those five years. Its only obligation was to provide care and support towards combatants and people who directly supported their missions. Those designated as 'ordinary citizens' (*ippan shimin*) (meaning non-combatants mobilised during Total War), ended up with nothing, in wartime or in this case long after the war. For example, during the war, pregnant women were considered by the government to be incapable of holding a bamboo spear, and therefore not part of the numbers, no matter what damage or injury they sustained.

The journalist was hyperbolic in his insistence that the state washed its hands of non-combatants who were injured in wartime. However, people who worked extensively with hibakusha in Hiroshima, as Kanai did, knew that the government had not provided adequate recognition, medical care for those who suffered from the effects of radiation sickness, or social support for the hibakusha subject to discrimination and unemployment. Kanai employed military metaphors to describe the contemporary plight of the hibakusha in his city: they were non-combatants subject to indiscriminate attack, as were many others. But the atomic bomb extended their suffering to the present day, many long years after the cessation of hostilities. Despite John Hersey, despite all the fuss about how powerful the atomic bomb was, nuclear weapons had become so entrenched, so essential to security, that no one dared to ban them – or to really care for the survivors of the time when they were used on humans. It took the government more than a decade before it passed the Law Concerning Medical Care for the Atomic Bomb Exposed (1957), which provided only limited support and recognised only a limited number of survivors as qualifying. Kanai defined as needless cruelty leaving these survivors in a state of 'perpetual battle'.

The Cold War for the survivors, then, was not the state of anticipation of apocalypse, represented vividly in films and novels, but the forever-present symptoms of the first atomic moment: despised, injured from internal exposure to high dosages of radiation. Although Kanai did not invoke the language of human rights, his talk is clearly informed by the ideas of the 'Declaration': the rights of the hibakusha, who were robbed of their health and economic security by the bomb during war. He spoke of their medical and economic rights since their injuries and vulnerability lasted far in to 'peacetime'. Although the defeated Japanese state had renounced any right to compensation from its wartime enemies, the individual had the right to demand medical and social support from the state.

It is not that the atomic bomb survivors in Hiroshima and Nagasaki were ignored. This was far from the case. Lurking in the background of the journalist's advocacy for hibakusha rights in the 1960s present is the two-decades long, convoluted history of medical–scientific institutional and governmental interaction with individual hibakusha and survivor groups and advocates. By framing the continued struggle for medical and social support of the survivors of radiation exposure in terms of human rights, a dominant concept in the 1960s, Kanai is able to redefine them. They were not just victims of a past war, but citizens of a Cold War present dependent on a nuclear economy and nuclear 'security', whose economic and social rights must be ensured. He moved them out of the moment of the iconic 6 August 1945 bombing and its immediate aftermath and presented them as part of the Cold War present. The righteousness of Featherstone's emphasis on civil rights for long discriminated-against minorities in the United States in the same forum provided another confirmation that it was important to advocate for the rights of the hibakusha.

Many of the Hiroshima residents present at the teach-in such as Moritaki had taken the lead in advocating for government support for the medical and social needs of the hibakusha, which would only from the late 1960s become more comprehensive (yet still partial). The case of the hibakusha, of all people injured in wartime who seek compensation and support, was complicated considerably by the ongoing research and development in nuclear technologies during the Cold War arms race. Governments were not so much interested in the hibakusha's visible surface wounds, the peeling skin and burns, but instead the invisible effects of high and low radiation dosages delivered by the bomb and lurking in the environment. The US government formed the Atomic Bomb

Casualty Commission (ABCC) immediately after the war for the purpose of studying the biological effects of the new weapons (and by implication, those yet to be designed). What were the various causes of death after the atomic explosion? Did the radiation result in genetic mutations? What other effects did these bombs that emit high dosages of radiation have on the human body that differed from conventional weapons? And what would be the effect of the still controversial low-dose exposure over time?

The ABCC studies in Hiroshima and Nagasaki were hotly debated for two reasons. First, the ABCC had a policy of only examining and collecting data from the survivors, and not treating them. Second, the ABCC, while described as a 'joint' US–Japanese project, was in fact dominated by American military and research agendas, and did not give a say to the Japanese physicians and scientists who collaborated extensively, much less to the survivors themselves. Historian Susan Lindee describes the ABCC as an example of colonial medical research.[44] For the US government, it was a fine line between affirming that the atom bomb was indeed destructive in unique ways because of radiation and acknowledging that nuclear weapons, as many critics claimed, are inhumane weapons of mass destruction that should be banned, as poison gas had been.

Not surprisingly, many of the survivors in Hiroshima and Nagasaki who continued to live with the social stigma and the various medical problems that resulted from their exposure, resented the implication that research and development project regarded them as guinea pigs (*morumotto*), rather than as human beings with rights and dignity. In Japan, the hibakusha were viewed by some as shameful symbols of Japan's defeat in the war and of Japan's technological inferiority. It took a long time to connect the notion of human rights to the hibakusha needs and abject status, just as it took time for the UN 'Declaration' to permeate popular and political discourses.

At the Hiroshima University symposium, local presenters emphasised the broader ethical considerations and the importance of education. Even the head of the Japan Confederation of A- and H-Bomb Sufferers Organisations (Hidankyô) Professor Moritaki did not mention the experience of the bombing, but instead boldly defined nuclear weapons as 'unethical' (*hijindôteki*), again invoking the condemnation of brutality in the UN 'Declaration'.[45] With a strong partner such as journalist Kanai to advocate for hibakusha issues, Moritaki felt able to move beyond A-bomb concerns and express solidarity with the Vietnam protestors. He urged the local audience to 'channel anti-nuclear feelings and actions into opposition to the Vietnam War'. In the Featherstone and Zinn's presence, furthermore, Moritaki exhorted the other participants to demonstrate and protest but never to resort to violence.[46]

Conclusion

Unfortunately, Ralph Featherstone did not publish his viewpoints on the Japan tour or his interaction with Hiroshima residents. He died young, killed by a car bomb, and never wrote a memoir, nor was he part of the reunions of the 'large pantheon of individuals' that gathered to remember and tell the story of the organisation that was SNCC, which, by virtue of its decentralisation and democratic bent, is still regarded as 'heroic'.[47] In a memoir, Tsurumi Shunsuke wrote that Featherstone tended to give the same talk in venue after venue, without varying it for the audience as Zinn and the other presenters did.[48] However, Featherstone did alter his remarks for the audience in Okinawa. He described the Okinawans as being most like 'Negroes' in America, because they had been robbed of their past, and lived in the company of a majority that discriminated against them. 'Our history in America is short [compared with Okinawa]', yet the violence implied by the US occupation of Okinawa even in the 1960s resonated with the weight of violence tolerated against blacks in the United States.[49] He pledged solidarity with the people he met in Okinawa.

After his return to America, Howard Zinn offered an activist intellectual's viewpoint of the ways the Vietnam War – the first 'television' war – had entered global awareness, and the rationale that American leaders offered for a proxy war now widely regarded with regret. Zinn's (and perhaps Featherstone's) impressions that all Japanese opposed America's war came from the intense encounters at the teach-ins with literally thousands of like-minded people:

> The war [in Vietnam] we are waging, no matter how sharply we feel it on occasion, has the quality of fiction as it appears on television screens or in news columns. Always at hand to "explain" the bombing of villages, the death toll of civilians, the crushing of Buddhist dissidents, are earnest 'liberals' (Humphrey and Goldberg), 'realistic' experts (Rostow), genial spokesmen for the administration (Rusk and McNamara). We listen with the languor of a people who have never been bombed, who have only been the bombardiers. So even our flickers of protest somehow end up muted and polite ... The Japanese have had a more intimate association with death, both as killers and as victims ... For the Japanese, the recollection of themselves as kamikaze pilots, and then the turn-about-Hiroshima and Nagasaki, wore off all the sheen. Out of their experience, the Japanese want desperately to speak to us.[50]

Japan's Cold War

By exploring the interaction of the 'collective imaginations' of citizens in the so-called Free World – the United States and its premier client states in Asia during the Vietnam War, we can gain a better understanding of the evolving Cold War, as well as its links to transnational citizen engagement from earlier in the twentieth century. In Ralph Featherstone's journey to Japan, he was able to illuminate links between the presence of violence and 'the bomb' in Japan and in the exclusionary zones of the USA, the superpower and (post-)colonial battlefields. His own violent death, only a few short years after his return to Washington, D.C. (along with the compromised bodies of Mr Moritaki and other injured hibakusha), embody the scars of violence in the Cold War. The great act of imagination on the part of those gathered at the Hiroshima teach-in was their steadfast invocation of human rights as the global norm that motivated them to act.

Notes

1 'Hibakusha' here is used to mean survivors of the atomic bombings. The term is also used now to refer to people exposed to high radiation dosages or lower doses over time, as a result of nuclear weapon testing, or unsafe nuclear waste storage. – The author is indebted to the Hiroshima University Archives, Koike Seiichi, Ishida Masaharu, Tashiro Akira, Shelley Lee, Renee Romano, and Pam Brooks.
2 See J. Masco, *The Nuclear Borderlands: The Manhattan Project in Post-Cold War New Mexico*. (Princeton, 2006), pp. 15-6. See also L. Yoneyama, *Hiroshima Traces: Time, Space, and the Dialectics of Memory* (Berkeley, 1999); A. Sherif, *Japan's Cold War: Media, Literature, and the Law in Postwar Japan* (New York, 2009).
3 K. Tsutui and H. J. Shin, 'Global norms, social activism, and social movement outcomes: global human rights and resident Koreans in Japan', *Social Problems*, 55:3 (2008), pp. 391-418.
4 Beheiren (*Betonamu ni heiwa o! shimin rengô*), a coalition of anti-war groups, was the most prominent of such movements during the Vietnam War era. For a history of Beheiren, Th.R.H. Havens, *Fire Across the Sea: The Vietnam War and Japan 1965-1975* (Princeton, 1987); O. Makoto M. Oda, '*Beheiren' kaisôroku denai kaisô* (Tokyo, 1995). The group also published a newsletter called *Beheiren News* and was frequently featured in the *Asahi Journal*. Primary sources and recent scholarship can be found at: www.jca.apc.org/beheiren/ (accessed 19 February 2016).
5 An extensive literature exists on the Cold War and human rights. See for example J. N. Wasserstrom, L. Hunt, M. B. Young and G. Grandin (eds), *Human Rights and Revolutions* (New York, 2007), A. Iriye, P. Goedde and W. I. Hitchcock (eds), *The Human Rights Revolution: An International History* (New York, 2012).

6 T. Shunsuke, O. Makoto, and K. Takeshi S. Tsurumi, M. Oda and T. Kaiko (eds), *Nichibei Hansen kôen kiroku* (Tokyo, 1967).
7 Among sources on 'Sixty Eight', see J. Suri, *The Global Revolutions of 1968* (New York, 2007); and C. Fink, Ph. Gassert and D. Junker (eds), *1968: The World Transformed* (New York, 1998).
8 Iida Momo, 14 June 1966, in Tsurumi Shunsuke, Oda Makoto and Kaikô Takeshi. eds., *Nichibei Hansen kôen kiroku* (Tokyo: Kawade Shobo Shinsha, 1967), p. 91.
9 L.S. Wittner, *Confronting the Bomb: A Short History of the World Nuclear Disarmament Movement* (Stanford, 2009), p. 14. See also 'Kenshô Hiroshima – 1945-95, Tsutaeru hyôgensha tachi" #29, Hiroshima Peace Media Center, original in the 6 August 1995 *Chûgoku shinbun* morning edition.www.hiroshimapeacemedia.jp/mediacenter/article.php?story=20120529115548184_ja&query=%25E3%2583%2599%25E5%25B9%25B3%25E9%2580%25A3 (accessed 22 May 2015).
10 The Featherstone-Zinn tour was one in a series of major events organised by Beheiren. It hosted other American anti-war protestors such as Dave Dillinger of the SDS.
11 J. Wu, *Radicals on the Road: Internationalism, Orientalism, and Feminism during the Vietnam Era* (Ithaca, 2013), p. 5.
12 Wu notes the proactive approach of the NLF in 'foreign relations' with U.S. opponents of America's war (p. 7), a topic explored extensively in R. K. Brigham's *Guerrilla Democracy: The NLF's Foreign Relations and the Vietnam War* (Ithaca, NY, 1999). See also F. Fitzgerald, *Fire in the Lake* (New York, 1972).
13 M. Duberman, *Howard Zinn: A Life on the Left* (New York, 2012), pp. 268-9.
14 Relevant works in the extensive literature on air war include M. Sherry's *The Rise of American Air Power: The Creation of Armageddon* (New Haven, 1987).
15 L. Wittner, *The Struggle Against the Bomb*, vol. 2 (Stanford, 1997), p. 244.
16 Alperovitz' renowned 'revisionist' *The Decision to Use the Atomic Bomb* (first edition) was published in 1965, during the Vietnam controversy. He revised the book in 1995.
17 M. Dudziak, *Cold War Civil Rights: Race and the Image of American Democracy* (Princeton, 2000), p. 12.
18 Peter Ling notes that no civil rights group is 'more revered' than SNCC, in his essay 'SNCC: Not One Committee, But Several', in I. Morgan and Ph. Davies (eds), *From Sit-Ins to SNCC: The Student Civil Rights Movement in the 1960s* (Gainesville, 2012), p. 81.
19 Zinn had studied with Reischauer when he was on a Ford Foundation fellowship for East Asian Studies at Harvard in 1960-61 because he wanted to be able to contribute to a curriculum in non-Western studies at Spelman College, a traditionally black college in Atlanta (his first teaching job). Duberman, *Howard Zinn*, pp. 40-1. Oda Makoto spent two years at Harvard

on a Fulbright Fellowship in 1957–58. Zinn and Featherstone met with the US ambassador in Japan, Edwin Reischauer. Tsurumi Shunsuke graduated from Harvard during the war, and returned during the 1960s to visit.
20 Tanaka, in his introduction to Howard Zinn, 'Hiroshima: Breaking the Silence', *The Asia Pacific Journal*, www.japanfocus.org/-Howard-Zinn/3375 (accessed 22 May 2015).
21 One of SNCC's earliest public documents was an 'Appeal for human rights', which was first published in Atlanta newspapers and then reprinted in *The Nation* in 1960. Duberman, *Howard Zinn*, p. 38.
22 Dudziak, *Cold War Civil Rights*, pp. 43–4.
23 On the Declaration of Human Rights, see J. Winter and A. Proust. *René Cassin and Human Rights: From the Great War to the Universal Declaration* (New York, 2013). Also, Dudziak, *Cold War Civil Rights*, pp. 44–5.
24 Comfort women protests in S. Korea also emerge from these discourses.
25 Dudziak, *Cold War Civil Rights*, p. 13. See also R. Lieberman, 'Anticommunism and the dividing of U.S. social movements', in B. Ziemann (ed.), *Peace Movements in Western Europe, Japan and the USA during the Cold War* (Essen, 2007), pp. 91–106.
26 T. Shunsuke, O. Makoto, K. Ken S. Tsurumi, M. Oda and T. Kaiko (eds), *Hansen no ronri* (Tokyo, 1967), p. 113.
27 R. Featherstone, 'Nagoya', in Shunsuke Tsurumi *et al.* (eds), *Hansen no ronri*, p. 112.
28 *Ibid.*, p. 116.
29 *The Movement, June 1965*, vol. 1, in Clayborne (ed.), *The Movement*, p. 41.
30 M. Nzinga Orange, 'Now She Flies: Dr. Charlotte Orange-Featherstone', ed. P. Lee. Originally printed in the *Michigan Citizen*, 13–20 December 2009. Reposted by permission of Michigan Citizen. www.crmvet.org/mem/feathers.htm (accessed 22 May 2015). See also Dudziak, *Cold War Civil Rights*, p. 226. Tsurumi Shunsuke notes that Featherstone went to Havana for a conference in 1968 (T. Shunsuke, S. Tsurumi, *Hokubei taiken saikô* (Tokyo, 1971), p. 144).
31 Dudziak, *Cold War Civil Rights*, pp. 250–1.
32 Featherstone, 3 June 1966, Tohoku University, in Shunsuke Tsurumi *et al.* (eds), *Hansen no ronri*, p. 24. The author's translation of the Japanese transcript of his talk.
33 Shunsuke Tsurumi *et al.* (eds), *Hansen no ronri*, p. 25.
34 Wu, *Radicals on the Road*, p. 31. See C. Anderson, *Eyes off the Prize: The United Nations and the African American Struggle for Human Rights, 1944–1955* (Cambridge, 2003), pp. 6, 19–20, 189, 200. See also M. Newman 'Civil rights and human rights', *Reviews in American History*, 32:2 (2004), pp. 247–54.
35 R. Zwigenberg analyses the Old and New Left in 'A sacred ground for peace: violence, tourism, and sanctification in Hiroshima 1960–1970', in B.S. Turner (ed.), *War and Peace. Essays on Religion and Violence* (London, 2013), pp. 131–7.
36 Shunsuke Tsurumi *et al.* (eds), *Hansen no ronri*.

37 Featherstone, 'Osaka', in Shunsuke Tsurumi *et al.* (eds), *Hansen no ronri*, pp. 132-3.
38 Wu, *Radicals on the Road*, p. 134. Michael Sherry's work on air war is the best known critique.
39 Shunsuke Tsurumi *et al.* (eds), *Hansen no ronri*, pp. 194-5.
40 Zinn, 'Hiroshima', p. 237.
41 Shunsuke Tsurumi *et al.* (eds), *Hansen no ronri*, p. 195.
42 Both national newspapers (Asahi, Mainichi, and even the conservative Yomiuri) and regional newspapers during the 1960s included daily coverage of the war in Vietnam, including photographs and coverage of violence towards non-combatants.
43 H. Zinn, 'On Fish', in *The Zinn Reader: Writings on Disobedience and Democracy* (New York, 2011), p. 304.
44 On the ABCC, see M. S. Lindee, *Suffering Made Real: American Science and the Survivors at Hiroshima* (Chicago, 1994).
45 Yuki Miyamoto studies the ethical and religious dimensions of hibakusha witnessing and the aim of creating 'a community of memory unrestricted by national boundaries' in *Beyond the Mushroom Cloud: Commemoration, Religion, and Responsibility after Hiroshima* (New York, 2012), quote p. 29.
46 Shunsuke Tsurumi *et al.* (eds), *Hansen no ronri*, p. 200.
47 Peter Ling contrasts the 'exalted reputation' SNCC with the 'revisionist assessments' of Southern Christian Leadership Conference (SCLC) 'SNCC, Not One Committee, But Several', pp. 81-2.
48 *Hokubei*, pp. 137-8.
49 Ralph Featherstone, 13 June 1966, Ryukyu University, Okinawa, in Shunsuke Tsurumi *et al.* (eds), *Hansen no ronri*, pp. 57-9.
50 Zinn, *The Zinn Reader: Writings on Disobedience and Democracy* (New York, 2011), p. 302.

9

Catholic anti-communism, the bomb and perceptions of apocalypse in West Germany and the USA, 1945–90

Daniel Gerster

Christian religion and war have shared a common history for centuries. There is, in fact, a long and entangled Christian discourse on 'war', even though Christianity has repeatedly emphasised the founding myth of it being purely a 'peace religion'.[1] Yet, since the late third century at the latest, such self-perception has conflicted with different Christian concepts that justified war and thus made it conceivable. Most influential in this regard has been the so-called 'just war theory', which was primarily introduced to Christian doctrine by Saint Augustine. It ensured that war could be justifiable if its cause was just, its intention right and the belligerent authority legitimate.[2] Related to the Neo-Scholastic rise of natural law, the concept regained crucial influence in Roman Catholic discussions on war and peace from the nineteenth century onwards. In addition to the just war theory, further concepts of 'Holy War' or 'crusades' have informed the ways in which Catholics understood war. They drew upon a dualism between 'Good' and 'Evil' and justified war against heretics or non-believers as God-wished or God-made.[3] In addition, Christians affected by war and violence were always looking for explanations for war in order to come to terms with their fate. They found relief by imagining the violent act of war as 'God's revenge' or as the beginning of the apocalypse.[4] During the Cold War, Christians could employ these centuries-old discourses when experiencing the ongoing nuclear arms race as a mental threat – an imaginary war.

In this chapter, I examine how Roman Catholics in West Germany and the United States used these Christian concepts of war to face the permanent nuclear threat of the Cold War years from 1945 to 1990. I focus on the question of whether the Cold War confrontation simply modified traditional arguments that oscillated between justifying limited warfare and appeals for peace, or whether the ideological and military conflict after 1945 developed a distinctive dynamic, which 'turned [religion] into a vehicle of general political appeal'.[5] Interpretations of 'Cold War religion' that underscore the Christian underpinnings of US Cold War policy take seriously the structural compliance between political interests of the United States and the concerns of the Holy See during the early years of the conflict, based on a stern anti-communism. However, they tend to underestimate the intrinsic value of religion and neglect to differentiate between various religious actors. In so doing, they run the risk of simply reproducing the ideological image of 'god-fearing versus godless' and do not fully explain the transformation of religion during the Cold War period.[6] However, the 'Cold War religion' approach is certainly right in stressing that Christian anti-communism is of crucial importance in understanding how Roman Catholics perceived the inherent threats of the nuclear arms race.

An examination of Roman Catholic perceptions of nuclear deterrence should not only look at the concepts themselves but also ask who supported them. Furthermore, it is essential to take into consideration the fundamental organisational structures of the Roman Catholic Church during the twentieth century. From the nineteenth century onwards, a hierarchical power structure has been a distinctive feature of the Roman Catholic Church: local parishes are subordinate to dioceses, which themselves are subject to the Pope in Rome. Beyond the clerical hierarchy and parochial structures, laymen are allowed to establish their own associations and societies, but they have always been under the strict tutelage of the clergy.[7] While the organisational structures largely determine the legal positions of Catholics within their own community and towards other social groups, they only partly reflect and encompass the whole range of religious phenomena. Historians have therefore often discussed religious performances and practices beyond the official doctrine by employing the problematic term of 'popular belief'.[8] Both fundamental social changes and controversies about the role and structure of religious organisations challenged the Roman Catholic Church, as well as other religious groups, during the second half of the twentieth century. But instead of understanding this transformation as a linear and steady decline of religion in modern society, it should rather be seen as a general reframing of the relation between religion and society at different levels.[9] With regard to the Catholic community this includes, for example, the decline of churchgoers on the one hand and various efforts by the Roman Catholic Church's officials to open up the agenda for new topics, structures and media on the other hand.[10]

Catholic perceptions in West Germany and the USA

To what extent did the Cold War nuclear threat contribute to these developments? How did Catholics in the United States and West Germany discuss the potential reality of an all-out nuclear war? Despite differences in the constitutional status of religion, both communities in general shared similar organisational church structures as well as fundamental challenges of the post-1945 era.[11] Catholics in the United States were still met with much scepticism by the Protestant majority, at least until the presidency of the Catholic John F. Kennedy, from 1961 to 1963. As in the two world wars, the Roman Catholic Church, headed by the cardinal of New York, Francis Spellmen, fully supported the foreign policy of the US administration to prove Catholic loyalty.[12] West German Catholics, on the other hand, found themselves in a very different situation after the end of the Second World War. Owing to large-scale territorial and population shifts, they were no longer a minority in West Germany but exerted massive political and social influence by dominating the governing conservative party Christian Democratic Union (CDU).[13] In addition, the clerical hierarchy of the Roman Catholic Church and the leaders of the Catholic laity openly supported the government and its foreign policy of Western integration and rearmament.[14] Yet different starting points subsequently brought about the same result in the United States and West Germany.

I will look more closely at how Catholics in both countries developed different notions and ideas of 'war' during the Cold War period. For that purpose, I will, first of all, analyse the concepts and metaphors of war that came to light in Catholic popular belief during the immediate post-war years. I will suggest that powerful images of war were more likely to emerge during rituals such as pilgrimages or devotions than in official remarks of religious leaders and intellectuals. The highly emotional dimension of rituals enabled Catholics to express their fear of an atomic war and of a supposed communist threat. These images of war were largely influenced by collective experiences and memories in the respective nation. Second, I will examine how anti-communism, along with the traditional Roman Catholic teaching of just war, underpinned Catholic support for Western nuclear armaments during the early decades of the Cold War. This reasoning has rarely been examined in the context of a broader imagination of an atomic war. It was this rationale (which existed in different forms), that determined Catholic discourse during the Cold War, depending on changing international circumstances and different national developments. Finally, I will look at shifting Catholic conceptualisations of 'peace' in the wake of the continuous nuclear threat since the late 1950s that were largely influenced by the dialogue with other social actors. I will argue that, even though these attempts to redefine war and peace offered an excellent opportunity to incorporate vivid imaginations of nuclear warfare into Catholic discourse, Catholic thinking about the atomic conflict remained predominately abstract because it considered itself part of the official Catholic discourse. The anti-communist foundations of political discourse among Catholics forced even opponents of nuclear armaments to present their case in abstract terms in order to demonstrate the credibility of their arguments.

Images of a nuclear war in Catholic popular belief

Fear of communism and of an imminent nuclear World War was widespread among Catholics in the United States and West Germany during the immediate post-war period; these perceptions mainly found expression in religious practices that are usually labelled as Catholic popular belief. Many of these performative practices were not part of the official ecclesiastical tradition, but they were steeped with important metaphors and reflect in many ways how ordinary Catholic laypersons thought about the nuclear threat. Thus, they can be juxtaposed with official Roman Catholic Church statements and intellectual and theological articles. In this context, apparitions of the Virgin Mary, which regained influence in Catholic popular belief during the nineteenth century, were of particular significance during the early Cold War years. In 1993, historian David Blackbourn offered a captivating analysis of the Marian apparition that took place in the small mining community of Marpingen near the German-French border in the late 1870s, at the height of the 'cultural struggle' over the place of the Roman Catholic Church in the newly founded nation-state. Blackbourn emphasised that these apparitions were important examples for the continuing – and often underestimated – presence of religion in modern society, and showed how they enabled the Catholic faithful to express suppressed political and social demands.[15]

Following Blackbourn's study, a large body of historical and sociological research on Marian apparitions in the modern age has emerged. Yet Marian apparitions were not a new phenomenon of the nineteenth and twentieth century, but had a long tradition in Christian religion. They feature a vision of Mary, mother of Jesus Christ, who reveals herself to one or more seers and confides a secret message to them. Since the nineteenth century, there has been a remarkable increase of female seers, a development that has transformed Marian apparitions into rather emotive cults, which allow believers to express not only actual claims, but also their feelings and fears. Usually these events start at the local level but subsequently generate a high level of mobilisation among Catholics. They are therefore often critically observed by the church hierarchy, while local clergy and Catholics are broadly supportive of them. When apparitions were not officially recognised, conflicts between local supporters and the church hierarchy a were often inevitable.[16]

During the first decade of the Cold War, especially between 1949 and 1953, there was a significant increase in Marian apparitions in West Germany as well as in the United States. Such a development can be explained by referring to the generally increased appreciation of the cult of Mary during the pontificate of Pope Pius XII, who dogmatised 'The Assumption of Virgin Mary into Heaven' in 1950. On the other hand, the renewed interest in Mary may also be associated with the intensive fear of a nuclear war during this period. For the United States, the Catholic historians Thomas A. Kselman and Steven Avella have stressed this aspect in their research on the cult of Mary in Necedah, Wisconsin. In this little village, more than 100,000 people gathered at the farm of Fred Van Hoof on 15 August 1950 – the day of the official dogmatisation –, because his wife Mary Ann claimed that she had seen Mary the previous month and that she would reappear that very same day. Her vision attracted massive media attention throughout the United States. Yet the increasing personality cult around the farmer's wife Mary Ann also led to great scepticism amongst Catholics, and finally to a condemnation of the vision by the Roman Catholic Church.[17]

With regard to the emotions and threat perceptions of the early Cold War among Catholics, the Marian apparition of Necedah reveals that American Catholics had already internalised the fear of an atomic war. This was summarised in the warning the 'Blessed Mother' expressed according to Mary Ann on 15 August 1950:

> All religions must go together against the enemy of God, for he is very strong right now … Remember, the time has come that the destruction is right above us. More than three-thirds [sic] of the nations is now covered with the enemy of God … America must pray right now – now, not tomorrow. Beginning is not in Korea; it will now end there unless we pray … The black clouds are coming over, not to Europe, Asia, Australia, Africa, but to America.[18]

By stressing that 'the time has come', the warning voices a collective fear that the apocalyptical age was finally approaching ('black clouds'). It is characterised by a distinctive dualism between the God-fearing 'religions' and the 'evil' 'enemy of God', who has become ever stronger and affects the whole world ('more than three-thirds of the nation'), particularly the United States ('but to America'). The warning does not name this enemy; it goes without saying that it is secular communism and its supporters. And this applies not only to the Soviet Union, but to every single nation. The threat is imminent, and the only solution is to show regret and believe in God ('pray right now'). In the light of the enormous danger even differences between religions vanish, which most probably reflects the increasing inter-faith co-operation in the United States during the 1940s and 1950s. This and the religious antagonism between good and evil that corresponded with a political dualism enabled Catholics to support the US Cold War policy and helped to integrate Catholics into US society in the long run.[19]

For West Germany, historian Monique Scheer has recently argued that Marian apparitions also allowed Catholics in the Federal Republic to express their fear of a nuclear conflict during the first post-war decade.[20] By examining detailed vision reports, Scheer provides evidence that the increase of apparitions was caused not only by the Marian devotion of the time, but by severe anxieties. The apparitions offered a strategy to deal with these fears for both the seers and the pilgrims, as shown through their language. The events in the Upper Franconian town Heroldsbach, for instance, provide a good example for the apocalyptic undertones in the semantics of Marian apparitions.[21] In 1949, several young girls in Heroldsbach claimed that they had frequently seen the Mother of God. The visions quickly gained media attention and the number of visitors increased rapidly. Although the range of topics addressed by the Franconian apparitions was very broad, remarks on a future war dominated the reports. Fears were mostly associated with the call to repentance and conversion. For instance, when asked what Mary had told her, one of the seers said: 'If people do not comply with my request, much blood will flow ... Then the Russians will come and kill.'[22] Unlike the US example, this quote does not stress the fundamental dualism between 'good' and 'evil'. Instead, it explicitly names the enemy ('the Russians') and predicts a violent attack by employing graphic imagery ('much blood will flow'). It interprets the threat as 'God's revenge' from which – as in the Necedah case – believers can only escape if they turn to God immediately.

Both examples point to the fact that prior experiences crucially influence images of war. Accordingly, German vision reports predominately articulated the lingering experiences of the Second World War, in particular bombing raids, housing shortages and hunger. Thus, fear of 'the Russians' and of communism was most present in this imagery as could be seen with regard to the apparitions of Heroldsbach. Marian visions in the United States, by contrast, were permeated with notions of an impending nuclear war, most probably owing to the experience of Hiroshima and Nagasaki in 1945. Thus, many supporters of the seer Mary Ann Van Hoof understood her warning that 'black clouds' would come over America as the prediction of a nuclear war.[23] Seen in that perspective, they expressed their own fears in words and images they took from their immediate cultural environment, which Paul Boyer has characterised as 'nuclear fear'.[24]

Yet there is evidence that images of war were not only shaped by personal experiences. Some West German supporters of the Marian cult in Heroldsbach, for instance, interpreted Virgin Mary's counsel already as a warning of a nuclear war. The Marian apparition in the Portuguese village of Fatima in 1917 had an especially significant impact among Catholics around the globe. The third and final part of Maria's prophecy given to three children became famous as the 'Third Secret'; it had been written down by one of the three in 1941, kept under tight wraps by the Vatican and only revealed in 2000.[25] Since the 'Second Secret' (the second part of the prophecy, which had been made public in 1942) had allegedly already predicted the Second World War, many Catholics expected the 'Third Secret' to refer to an eschatological war fought with nuclear weapons. One of the best-known texts related to such speculations is an article by Louis Emerich published in the German weekly *Neues Europa*. The journalist claims that the negotiations on the Nuclear Non-proliferation Treaty of 1963 had only been successful because the Vatican had revealed the 'Third Secret' to the negotiating partners.[26]

The first post-war wave of Marian apparitions in West Germany and the United States as well as in other parts of the Catholic world subsided in 1953, presumably because fear of an imminent nuclear had been decreasing since the end of the Korean War in 1953. Yet, apparitions remained the acts of popular piety most likely to use apocalyptic images to channel the fear of an all-out nuclear war. Apparitions that were reported in the Croatian village of Medjugorje in the early 1980s, for instance, are a case in point.[27] Apocalyptic undertones, albeit on a lesser scale, were also present in other practices, such as pilgrimages and devotions. For example, the Archbishop of Paderborn, Lorenz Jaeger, strongly warned about both the 'violence of modern weaponry' and of 'hysterical fear' during a peace devotion at the biennial general assembly of German lay Catholics, the 'Katholikentag', in Berlin in 1958.[28]

Finally, apocalyptic semantics of nuclear war came to light in remarks of Catholic mystics such as the American priest Thomas Merton. Born in France in 1915, Merton had taken interest in socialism during his studies in France and England, before converting to Catholicism in the 1930s. In 1941, he joined the Trappist congregation Gethsemani in Kentucky, remaining a member until his death in 1968. Living the life of an ascetic, Merton wrote more than fifty books and hundreds of articles in which he reflected his own search for God and a 'good life'. From the late 1950s, he was also involved in campaigning on issues of social justice and peace. During these activities, Merton did not create a systematic theology, but 'employed a language that was creative, inclusive'.[29] And while many of Merton's writings and technical terms were not in line with the Catholic tradition of just war, he used non-Catholic argumentations of non-violence and expressed his fear in powerful metaphors In his book *Breakthrough to Peace* of 1962, for instance, he called the atomic bombing of Hiroshima 'a calculated project of terror and annihilation'.[30] Nevertheless, compared to the imagery of Marian apparitions such rhetorics are rather reasonable and sober. In fact, it seems as if there is a correlation between the emotionality of religious performances, which is predominantly expressed in practices of popular belief, and the explicit mentioning of fears about impending nuclear war.

Catholic anti-communism and support for nuclear weapons

In contrast to emotive religious rituals and other forms of popular belief, official remarks by the Roman Catholic Church on the Cold War confrontation and the nuclear arms race were rather abstract and hypothetical, and mainly driven by fundamental opposition to communism and its materialist and secular ideas. Yet Catholic condemnation of communism was not a new phenomenon, since the Roman Catholic Church had attacked socialism ever since its rise in the nineteenth century. The new geo-political constellation after the Second World War, with the Soviet Union ruling more or less half of Europe and eager to expand its sphere of influence over the other half, intensified the antagonism and reinforced Catholic anti-communism. In consequence, fundamental opposition to communism was the main driving force behind Catholics' perception of nuclear armament, especially during the first decade of the Cold War. This can be exemplified with regard to the statements of Pope Pius XII.

Even though Pius XII had strongly advised against the uncontrollable impact of an atomic explosion as early as 1943, his attitude towards nuclear armaments and the possibility of nuclear war remained ambivalent until the end of his pontificate in 1958.[31] For instance, in a speech on international criminal law in October 1953 the Pope concluded that a legitimate state authority should be allowed to use all kinds of weapons for self-defence that are 'agreeable for a man with a healthy and reasonable sense of justice'.[32] Although the pope did not explicitly mention nuclear warfare, his audience well understood that he justified the use of nuclear weapons by democratic Western states. Yet, only two years later, during his Christmas sermon of 1955, Pius XII came to a different conclusion by strongly questioning the controllability and, thus, the usability of nuclear weaponry: 'This would happen … a blackened death cloud hanging over pulverised matter that would cover countless victims with scorched, dislocated and scattered limbs, while others would be groaning in agony.'[33]

It seems as if the Pope's perception of nuclear warfare had been substantially changed: while in 1953 an atomic war still seemed to be a genuine possibility, two years later it was a general threat ('blackened death cloud') – and was reminiscent of the Necedah warning of 1950. This transformation can be explained by changing political and social conditions. First, following the death of Stalin in 1953, Western expectations towards Socialist states shifted and many people, including the pope, hoped for a *modus vivendi* between the two blocs. Second, and most important, tests on a new generation of nuclear weapons and the continuing arms race brought the unpredictable risks of nuclear armament to everybody's mind. It is fair to assume that these developments at least contributed to, if not caused the Pope's change of mind as seen in the apocalyptic imagery of his Christmas sermon in 1955.[34]

Yet not all Catholics immediately agreed with the papal change of mind that was confirmed and strengthened by Pius' successor, John XXIII. During the 1960s, conservative Catholic moral theologians in the United States and West Germany employed anti-communism, often in combination with the traditional just war theory, to argue in favour of a war, even with nuclear weaponry. In the United States, it was first and foremost the Jesuit John C. Murray who espoused such an idea. In an essay from 1960, Murray challenged the assumption that the use of nuclear weapons would inevitably lead to 'global suicide'.[35] Believing that the Soviet Union would use the atomic bomb without hesitation, Murray demanded: 'since nuclear war may be a necessity, it must be made a possibility. Its possibility must be created … To say that the possibility of a limited nuclear war cannot be created by intelligence and energy, under the direction of a moral imperative, is to succumb to some sort of determination in human affairs.'[36]

Murray's considerations stemmed from a profound anti-communism and the fear of a nuclear first strike by the Soviet Union. Yet he strictly refused to admit his fears and argued that using apocalyptic imagery in the public discourse and ignoring the actual nuclear threat posed by the Soviet Union would weaken the US position in the conflict.[37] Instead, Murray championed the deployment and potential use of nuclear weapons by bringing forward arguments which he thought most reasonable. For this purpose he did not only refer to the Catholic concept of just war, but also drew on strategic considerations suggested by US politicians and military officials. References to non-Catholic discursive arguments have a long tradition in Catholic discussions of American foreign policy. As early as 1945, a controversy among Jesuits on the atomic bombing of Hiroshima and Nagasaki referred to general political arguments.[38] Against the backdrop of the events in Japan, these early discussions were highly emotionally charged. However, John Murray repeatedly stressed the rationality of his arguments.

In West Germany, the Jesuit Gustav Gundlach set the tone amongst Catholic supporters of nuclear armaments during the late 1950s and early 1960s and advocated nuclear deterrence against the communist states. Gundlach, a professor of Roman Catholic social philosophy and ethics at the Jesuit College St Georgen in Frankfurt am Main, was renowned through his work as an advisor to Pius XII. For that reason, he considered himself the intellectual trustee of the Pope, who had died the year before. At a conference of the Catholic Academy in Bavaria in February 1959, Gundlach underlined that the Roman Catholic teaching would allow the production and use of nuclear weapons provided a proper monitoring of their use and restrictions on nuclear proliferation were guaranteed. Unlike Pius, Gustav Gundlach did not consider this restriction a scientific problem but rather a human predicament: it would only be 'immoral' if the atomic bomb were used by a 'perverse sovereign will'. Needless to say that Gundlach associated such 'perversion' of nuclear warfare exclusively with communist regimes.[39]

In this respect, Gundlach differed significantly from Pope Pius XII and John C. Murray, who both incorporated their considerations on nuclear war into scientific discourses, rational arguments, and historical context. Gundlach, on the other hand, regarded the divine order and Roman Catholic moral teaching as the only basis for political decisions on war and peace. It is therefore little surprise that Gundlach concluded elsewhere: 'Even if only a manifestation of the majesty of God and his order ... remained as a result, the right and duty to defend the highest goods is possible. Yes, even if the world perished, this does not counter our argument.'[40] This quote shows that Gundlach's considerations closely followed a dualism between 'Good' and 'Evil' and the idea of a 'Holy War' against communism without using the term itself. In Germany, he was one of the few Catholics who publicly employed such reasoning to advocate nuclear armament. Others referred to Gundlach's remarks in order to clarify their own position, as did, for instance, seven leading West German moral theologians. They had supported the nuclear armament of the West German army in a public statement in May 1958, by stressing the 'reasonability' of their own arguments as distinguished from Gundlach's moralistic and apocalyptic approach.[41]

Despite fundamental transformations in Catholic discourses on war and peace during the 1960s and 1970s (discussed further below), support for nuclear armaments did not entirely vanish in either the United States or Germany. Yet the argumentative structure of such support substantially changed and in the end almost entirely focused on threat perceptions about a potential nuclear war. This transition can be exemplified with regard to the controversy over the NATO Double Track Decision during the early 1980s, when the Western military alliance decided to deploy new nuclear weapons in Europe to force the Soviet Union into disarmament talks. The NATO decision caused an unexpected public reaction and initiated protest movements in many Western countries. Catholics in West Germany and the United States participated in various ways in these public peace protests. Consequently, the vast amount of Catholic statements on the issue demonstrated the broad variety of Catholic opinions.[42] Against this backdrop, two pastoral letters, both published in 1983, can illuminate different views of American und West German Catholics on a potential war during this period.

Bishops in the United States and in West Germany considered their pastoral letters as appropriate Catholic contributions to political and social questions. Both sought a broad agreement amongst different Catholic opinions, although choosing different ways to do so. While in the United States the episcopate early on started publishing drafts of its letter 'Challenge of Peace' to initiate a public debate, in Germany a group of theologians wrote a first draft of 'Gerechtigkeit schafft Frieden' ('Justice brings Peace') that was amended by the bishops before its release. Both pastoral letters eventually provoked lively and wide-ranging discussions amongst Catholics on nuclear armament; the declaration of the US bishops even initiated further debates with non-Catholics in the United States and Catholics in other countries. Accordingly, the US episcopal letter was also noted in Germany.[43]

There are a lot of argumentative similarities between both pastoral letters, which refer back to the genesis and the common Catholic tradition of images on war and peace. The main difference is that the US letter directly referred to current political and social events, while the German pastoral letter reflected issues of nuclear armament in a more general context. As a result, the US bishops condemned nuclear weapons with regard to their actual military deployment: 'We do not perceive any situation in which the deliberate initiation of nuclear war, on however restricted a scale, can be morally justified.'[44] The German episcopate, on the other hand, considered the temporary deployment of nuclear weapons within a system of military deterrence as justifiable, and thus nuclear war as imaginable.[45] Apart from this (obviously crucial) difference, the two pastoral letters were based on the same argument that each nation-state has the right to defend itself with appropriate military force.

The way in which the West German pastoral letter approached the issue of nuclear armament reveals a blind spot that can be found in many – not only Catholic – statements in support of the NATO Double Track Decision.[46] It focused on general considerations about the fundamental essence of nuclear weaponry and ignored the inherent risks of an all-out nuclear war. Accordingly, a nuclear war remained imaginable in principle, and it was assumed that human society would continue in its aftermath. The US letter, on the other hand, reflected on these issues in an attempt to develop a rational argument about the consequences of nuclear war, similar to Pius XII: '[T]he crisis of the moment is embodied in the threat which nuclear weapons pose for the world and much that we hold dear in the world … Nuclear weaponry has drastically changed the nature of warfare, and the arms race poses a threat to human life and human civilisation which is without precedent.'[47] Following such considerations, nuclear war was neither feasible nor imaginable.

'Dialogue with the world' as a way to nuclear disarmament

The US pastoral letter of 1983 illuminates the scepticism towards nuclear warfare that flourished both among ordinary Catholics and at the highest levels of the church hierarchy during the final phase of the Cold War. However, Catholic criticism of nuclear armament had in fact emerged much earlier. As early as September 1945, Dorothy Day, the founder of the US 'Catholic Worker Movement', wrote in an article published in the magazine *The Catholic Worker*:

> We have created. We have created destruction. We have created a new element, called Pluto: Nature has nothing to do with it. [We have] brought into being ... this new weapon, which conceivably might wipe out mankind and perhaps the planet itself ... Dropped on a town, one bomb would be equivalent to a severe earthquake and would utterly destroy the place ... But our Lord Himself has already pronounced judgment on the atomic bomb. When James and John ... wished to call down fire from heaven on their enemies, Jesus said: 'You know not of what spirit you are. The Son of man came not to destroy souls, but to save.'[48]

Day's criticism of the atomic bomb fell into line with a general pacifism that was advocated by the Catholic Workers' Movement, since the organisation supported conscientious objectors during the Second World War. Yet the apocalyptic imagery Day used in her article had little equivalent in wider Catholic discourse and remained exceptional within Catholic criticism of nuclear weapons. Day's metaphors could be accounted for by her recent conversion and the proximity of the atomic bombings of Hiroshima and Nagasaki, which had taken place only the previous month. Other Catholic responses, which criticised nuclear weaponry, did not refer to similar apocalyptic images. For instance, Father John Hugo, also a member of the Catholic Workers', contended in September 1945 that 'There is no sound moral argument to justify the use of the atomic bomb. [... But] there are some reasons why the atomic bombing ... must be condemned as a crime. And not only as a crime, but as a great crime: the greatest crime ever committed by a nation against humanity.'[49] Thus, both Catholics considered nuclear war as unimaginable, but as a result of very different reasoning.

In general, Catholics who rejected nuclear warfare provided a sober assessment instead of employing apocalyptic doomsday scenarios, as we shall see. This was partly owing to the fact that Catholic objections to nuclear armament have often coincided with general criticism of the church hierarchy. This critical attitude was not a new phenomenon of the twentieth century but it grew stronger as a result of the above-mentioned conflicts between an increasingly ossified church and the challenges of radical social movements after 1945. In this conflict within the Catholic community, nuclear armaments became an important issue due to their controversial and wide public impact. Subsequently, Catholic critics have often used the topic of nuclear weapons to express their disagreement with the strictly hierarchical church organisation. It was especially well suited for asking for the recognition of individual freedom of conscience. Yet such an instrumentalisation of the issue was fraught with problems since it hampered an independent debate on the nuclear threat. It is this connection between opposing nuclear armaments and criticising the church in general that explains why Catholic critics of nuclear weapons have often referred to 'imageless', 'reasonable' arguments. Only by arguing in a rational way they thought to be taken seriously within the broader Catholic discourse.

Most Catholic critics of deterrence considered themselves 'nuclear pacifists', as in the debate on nuclear armaments in West Germany between 1957 and 1959. They did not condemn war in general, but thought it impossible to fight a war with nuclear weaponry. The legal scholar Ernst-Wolfgang Böckenförde and the philosopher Robert Spaemann in particular argued against the plan to equip the new German army with nuclear weapons by referring to the just war theory. Following the considerations of Pius XII and contradicting Gustav Gundlach, they argued: 'the pope neither taught the right to self-defence at all costs, nor did he argue that it did not depend on the controllability of the weapon or that in defence of a greater good one had to risk the end of the world'.[50] Although Böckenförde and Spaemann resorted to mildly apocalyptic semantics in this quote, they did so only in their response to Gundlach. In general, they worded their considerations in a plain, legal language to underscore that war in general was conceivable, but nuclear war was not and therefore had to be prevented by all means.

Other German Catholic critics also referred to the just war theory to disprove the legitimacy of nuclear weapons and nuclear warfare, among them the so-called 'Left Catholics', which was a label for those who saw themselves as Roman Catholics and had a leaning towards socialist ideas.[51] These circles revolved around the journals *Frankfurter Hefte* and *Werkhefte*, which both served as a platform to criticise nuclear armaments and to express fear of an imaginable nuclear war. In addition to legal and military political arguments they shared with other Catholics, 'Left' Catholics also drew on non-Catholic discourses to oppose nuclear weapons. For instance, Eugon Kogon, one of the editors of the *Frankfurter Hefte*, challenged the distinction between strategic and tactical atomic weapons, by quoting the statement of eighteen West German scientists who had opposed the government's plan to equip the army with atomic weapons in spring 1957, based on the same reasoning.[52] Furthermore, many Left Catholics emphasised the autonomy of military staff and politicians to make decisions based on their freedom of conscience. This argument was also clearly rooted in similar discussions among Protestants at that time.[53]

However, even more important is the fact that left-wing Catholics sometimes abandoned the rational discourse in their criticism of nuclear weapons in favour of apocalyptical metaphors. For instance, Hubertus Schulte Herbrüggen concluded 1958 in an article in the *Frankfurter Hefte* that a nuclear war would most probably result in 'mass destruction' and ventilated the 'problem of (eventually approved) mass killing'.[54] Such terminology has to be understood as an attempt to reconnect the nuclear threat to specific German experiences of genocide and mass killing during the Second World War.[55] This linkage to the discourse on the German past enabled Catholic opponents of nuclear weapons to express their fears by referring to their own experiences. Yet, apocalyptic and emotive metaphors remained rare in the writings of Catholic critics: only by repeatedly underlining the objectivity and rationality of their arguments could they hope to convince both the Catholic community and the broader public.

After the late 1950s, the position of Catholics towards nuclear armament and its hazards changed fundamentally. Pius' late remarks had already indicated this development that accelerated during the pontificate of his successor. Pope John XXIII no longer considered peace as merely 'non-war': 'There is a common belief that under modern conditions peace cannot be assured except on the basis of an equal balance of armaments'.[56] Instead, he promoted an 'expanded' peace concept that included social, economic and political aspects. In his most famous encyclical *Pacem in Terris* of 1963, he deplored the tremendous waste of resources caused by the arms race and advocated intensifying development cooperation between industrial and developing countries. In a similar way to as the nuclear pacifists, John XXIII argued as follows: 'We acknowledge that this conviction owes its origin chiefly to the terrifying destructive force of modern weapons. It arises from fear of the ghastly and catastrophic consequences of their use. Thus, in this age which boasts of its atomic power, it no longer makes sense to maintain that war is a fit instrument with which to repair the violation of justice.'[57]

How can we explain this profound change in Catholic discourse? On the one hand, we have to consider the fundamental reorganisation that took place in the Vatican curia during the pontificate of John XXIII. French scholars, who based their ethical reflections on social contexts, increasingly gained influence on the Pope's policy, while German teachers of normative ethics, such as Gustav Gundlach, were losing ground.[58]

This shift not only brought about new theological approaches but also a substantially new agenda. Subsequently, topics such as the post-colonial struggles in France and its former colonies gained more influence on Catholic discourses on war and peace. On the other hand, persistent fears of a nuclear catastrophe also contributed to the change. They were exacerbated by the arms race and nuclear tests, as John XXIII explicitly expressed in *Pacem in Terris*.[59] In this regard, he was quite in line with Pius XII during the last years of his pontificate. Accordingly, the shift in the Catholic stance on nuclear armament and – by implication – new concepts of peace were by no means a revolutionary act of John XXIII, but reflected a general development in Catholic discourse.

The results of the Second Vatican Council confirm this assumption. Between 1962 and 1965, 2,500 church leaders met to discuss the future of the Roman Catholic Church. They approved the pastoral constitution *Gaudium et Spes*, the last of the Council's documents, in December 1965.[60] Addressing issues of war and peace, nuclear armament and disarmament, the document is a balancing act between traditional Catholic attitudes and new ideas. On the one hand, it develops and emphasises a broader understanding of peace that includes demands for more development aid, disarmament and human rights. On the other hand, *Gaudium et Spes* sticks to the just war theory without explicitly using the term. In this regard, the apostolic constitution refers – without mentioning nuclear arms – to the 'horror and perversity' of modern warfare, but at the same time emphasises that 'governments cannot be denied the right to legitimate defence once every means of peaceful settlement has been exhausted'.[61] Consequently, the apostolic constitution does not abandon the idea of war as a possibility in general, but questions the use of nuclear arms and speaks in favour of amicable solutions. For this purpose, it employs rational terminology instead of emotive and apocalyptic metaphors.

This ambivalent position on nuclear armament shaped Catholic discourses on war and peace and on the question of whether or not war was imaginable during the 1970s and 1980s. The two above-mentioned pastoral letters of 1983 are excellent examples to illuminate this aspect. Most influential for this development was that in the aftermath of the Second Vatican Council all national churches had to incorporate its official decisions. In doing so, they also often adopted the tension between a broader peace concept and the continuity of just war theory into national contexts. For instance, the West German Synod, which held its proceedings between 1972 and 1975 in Würzburg, concluded in its statement on peace and development: 'Peace contains … more than the absence of war, development more than economic growth. Peaceful development, evolving peace aims at a life without hunger and oppression, in comfort and joy, and with the possibility for the individual and for society to creatively express themselves.'[62] At the same time, the Würzburg Synod confirmed the right of every country to defend itself with appropriate military force. In doing so, it did not condemn nuclear weaponry and war in general, but only praised the 'decision' of the Federal Republic of Germany not to produce, deploy and use such arms.[63]

This example already indicates to some extent that the individual view on actual political situations became more and more important in shaping Catholic stances on nuclear armament and its hazards. A broad majority of Catholics were asking for nuclear disarmament, and with increasing urgency, without objecting to a potential war in principle. From the 1960s onwards, Catholic peace activists such as the members of the transnational organisation Pax Christi, founded in 1944–45 to encourage reconciliation among European Catholics, repeated this claim.[64] Statements of West German and US Pax Christi groups indicate that they demanded even more steps towards disarmament during the protests against the NATO Double Track Decision and in the context of the Freeze Now Movement in the early 1980s.[65] Their claim mainly resulted from their close cooperation with other, non-Catholic activists in the peace protests, especially with Protestant (in the American case, Jewish) groups. In addition, they based their assessment on the conclusions of peace and conflict research, which had become fashionable since the early 1970s. All in all, Catholic peace activists proved to be highly critical of nuclear armaments, yet without abandoning Catholic discourse in general, which was mainly shaped by the hierarchy.

In the end, the question of how Catholics positioned themselves towards nuclear weapons during the 1980s depended on their view of the Soviet Union and communism in general. Yet the anti-communism of those supporting nuclear armament during the 1980s was no longer the same as the anti-communism of the 1950s. Numerous disarmament efforts and peace talks in the 1970s had broadly discredited anti-communist stereotypes, even though in Germany some Catholics still held on to them. But they became an extremely marginal group in the 1980s.[66] However, for the majority of those Catholics who supported the deployment of new nuclear weapons such as the leaders of Catholic laity in Germany, the image of an aggressive Soviet Union, equipped with nuclear weapons, remained decisive for their position. At the same time, they criticised the West German opponents of nuclear armaments for their naive belief in the peaceful intentions of the Communist regimes, and accused them of fanning unfounded fear.

Conclusion

For the vast majority of Catholics in the United States and West Germany, war was still imaginable at the end of the Cold War. The important question was not if war in general, but nuclear war in particular, was conceivable. The answer was different for each individual Catholic and depended on their respective position on communism, their religious practice and the historical context. Dorothy Day, for instance, resolutely condemned a nuclear war in the immediate aftermath of the bombing of Hiroshima and Nagasaki, while Catholic bishops in West Germany still justified the use of nuclear weaponry as a deterrent during the early 1980s. Despite the broad variety of opinions, a general development in Catholic discourse can be observed. While initially a nuclear war was considered conceivable, at least for church leaders as Pope Pius XII and the Catholic establishment, 'nuclear pacifism' gained increasing support among Catholics as the Cold War developed. This transformation was caused by various factors. First of all, the continuing arms race and nuclear weapons tests made the unpredictable risks of nuclear weaponry visible for a wider public. Second, the attitude towards communism and the socialist states in Eastern Europe fundamentally changed, starting with Stalin's death in 1953 and continuing throughout the 1960s and early 1970s. Third and most importantly, the self-perception and the organisation of the Roman Catholic Church had changed, particularly in the wake of the Second Vatican Council and the reconceptualisation of the Catholic peace concept. These developments led to a shift in Catholic perception and conceivability of nuclear war and underscored the intrinsic value of religion in handling the Cold War conflict.

The attitude towards war *per se* was certainly a crucial precondition for the question of which concepts and ideas Catholics drew on to picture and imagine war. Yet it was not the only decisive factor. Catholics largely referred to traditional images of Catholic discourse on war and peace already mentioned at the beginning of this chapter. The just war theory provided a 'reasonable' basis for those Catholics who still thought war, with or without nuclear weapons, to be practicable, including Pope Pius XII and the West German episcopate. Supporting a defensive, but nevertheless violent war they shied away from picturing the actual consequences of an all-out nuclear war, or, like John C. Murray, openly condemned apocalyptic semantics. Only few supporters such as Gustav Gundlach employed such imagery to underscore a fundamental dualism between 'God'-fearing Western and 'evil' socialist states. In doing so, Gundlach pronounced the idea of a 'Holy War' or 'crusade' against communism without using the term. Even Catholic opponents of nuclear armaments, who could have applied powerful imagery to peace advocacy, did so very rarely. Their restraint was caused by the fact that Catholic criticism was mostly part of a more fundamental criticism towards the Roman Catholic Church and therefore repeatedly underlined the 'reasonability' of its arguments. As a result, Catholics were most likely to use apocalyptical images to picture war when they spoke outside the official discourse. This applies, for example, to Dorothy Day's statement of September 1945 that mirrored her emotional state immediately after the bombing of August 1945. In addition, we have established that the most powerful images of nuclear war were conjured up in practices of Catholic popular piety. Marian apparitions proved most productive in this respect during the years from 1949 to 1953. They referred to the concept of God's revenge and used apocalyptical images.

Marian apparitions of the early Cold War period also provide a good starting point for comparing perceptions of war among American and West German Catholics. Beyond the above-mentioned differences between both Catholic communities – the constitutional status of religion and social position of Catholics after 1945 – Marian apparitions reveal how collective national experiences and memories shaped Catholic images of war: it was mainly the Second World War and a widespread fear of 'the Russians' that influenced the discourse in West Germany, while American Catholics very early on referred to an impending nuclear war and a communist threat. Such national framing of the Catholic discourses on war facilitated Catholic support of their respective governments' foreign policies during the early Cold War years, and in the long term enabled the integration into the political culture of their countries. This general support could occasionally include criticism of nuclear weaponry, as seen in the American bishops' pastoral letter from 1983, which was a step that was not taken by the West German episcopate. This chapter has shown that despite their differences, the two communities shared many similar developments under the umbrella of the universal Catholic Church. Most important in this regard is the general pluralisation of Catholic discourses beyond discussions on war and peace. Catholic remarks on the NATO Double

Daniel Gerster

Track Decision showed that individual answers became increasingly important. And for that reason, apocalyptic images took on greater significance in religious discussions of a conceivable war during the 1980s.

Notes

1 H. Stadtland (ed.), *"Friede auf Erden". Religiöse Semantiken und Konzepte des Friedens im 20. Jahrhundert* (Essen, 2009).
2 C. Daryl, *Between Pacifism and Jihad: Just War and Christian Traditions* (Downers Grove, Ill., 2005) and B. Kane, *Just War and the Common Good: Jus ad Bellum Principles in Twentieth Century Papal Thought* (San Francisco, 1997).
3 A. Angenendt, *Toleranz und Gewalt. Das Christentum zwischen Bibel und Schwert* (Münster, 2007), pp. 372–484.
4 A. Holzem (ed.), *Krieg und Christentum. Religiöse Gewalttheorien in der Kriegserfahrung des Westens* (Paderborn, 2009), pp. 13–104; M. N. Ebertz and R. Zwick (eds), *Jüngste Tage. Die Gegenwart der Apokalyptik* (Freiburg, 1999).
5 D. Kirby, 'The Cold War, the hegemony of the United States and the golden age of Christian democracy', in H. McLeod (ed.), *World Christianities c.1914–c.2000* (Cambridge, 2006), pp. 285–303, p. 303.
6 D. Kirby (ed.), *Religion and the Cold War* (Houndmills and New York, 2003). This publication as well as later ones lacks a deeper reflection on the essence and role of religion. They focus more on the global political perspective, as does the following: Ph. E. Muehlenbeck (ed.), *Religion and the Cold War: A Global Perspective* (Nashville, Tenn., 2012); or stress the influence of religion on 'secular' institutions in the United States: J. Herzog, *The Spiritual-Industrial Complex: America's Religious Battle against Communism in the Early Cold War* (Oxford, 2011).
7 S. Gilley, 'The papacy', in Gilley and B. Stanley (eds), *World Christianities c. 1815–c.1914* (Cambridge, 2005), pp. 13–29.
8 For criticism of the term 'popular belief', see A. Holzem, '"Volksfrömmigkeit". Zur Verabschiedung eines Begriffs', *Theologische Quartalschrift* 182 (2002), pp. 258–70.
9 The investigation is based on the idea that different (semantic) areas such as 'religion' and 'politics' do not represent static, distinct and separated areas, but stand in a 'constructivist and relational "relationship"'. P. Eitler, 'Politik und Religion. Semantische Grenzen und Grenzverschiebungen in der Bundesrepublik Deutschland 1965–1975', in U. Frevert and H. G. Haupt (eds), *Neue Politikgeschichte. Perspektiven einer historischen Politikforschung* (Frankfurt and New York, 2005), pp. 268–303, p. 269.
10 H. McLeod, *The Religious Crisis of the 1960s* (Oxford, 2010). For the German case, see B. Ziemann, *Encounters with Modernity. The Catholic Church in West Germany 1945–1975* (New York, 2014).

11 A. Liedhegener, *Macht, Moral und Mehrheiten. Der politische Katholizismus in der Bundesrepublik Deutschland und den USA seit 1960* (Baden-Baden, 2006), pp. 39–44.
12 M. Hochgeschwender, 'Waffenbrüderschaft auf Zeit. Der Vatikan, der US-amerikanische Katholizismus und die NATO', in W. Kremp and B. Meyer (eds), *Religion und Zivilreligion im Atlantischen Bündnis* (Trier, 2001), pp. 292–306.
13 F. Bösch, *Die Adenauer-CDU. Gründung, Aufstieg und Krise einer Erfolgspartei 1945–1969* (Stuttgart, 2001).
14 Th. Gauly, *Katholiken. Machtanspruch und Machtverlust* (Bonn, 1991) and Th. Großmann, *Zwischen Kirche und Gesellschaft. Das Zentralkomitee der deutschen Katholiken 1945–1970* (Mainz, 1991).
15 D. Blackbourn, *Marpingen. Apparitions of the Virgin Mary in Bismarckian Germany* (Oxford, 1993).
16 In this paragraph, I refer to M. Scheer, '"Unter Deinen Schutz und Schirm fliehen wir". Religiöse Ausdrucksformen in der Angstkultur des Kalten Kriegs', in B. Greiner, Chr. Th. Müller and D. Walter (eds), *Angst im Kalten Krieg* (Hamburg, 2009), pp. 322–46, pp. 325–9. Scheer's results are published in more detail in Scheer, *Rosenkranz und Kriegsvisionen. Marienerscheinungskulte im 20. Jahrhundert* (Tübingen, 2006).
17 Th. A. Kselman and S. Avella, 'Marian piety and the Cold War in the United States', *The Catholic Historical Review* 72:3 (1986), pp. 403–24.
18 Quoted in *ibid.*, pp. 403/4.
19 M. Hochgeschwender, '"God's Own Nation". Der gerechte Krieg im Selbstbild der USA', in N. Buschmann and D. Langewiesche (eds), *Der Krieg in den Gründungsmythen europäischer Nationen und der USA* (Frankfurt am Main and New York, 2003), pp. 286–319, p. 303.
20 Scheer, 'Angstkultur'. See also M. Geyer, 'Der Kalte Krieg, die Deutschen und die Angst. Die westdeutsche Opposition gegen Wiederbewaffnung und Kernwaffen', in K. Naumann (ed.), *Nachkrieg in Deutschland* (Hamburg, 2001), pp. 267–318.
21 Scheer, 'Angstkultur', pp. 323 and 333/334. See also S. Zimdars-Swartz and P. F. Zimdars-Swartz, 'Apocalypticism in Modern Western Europe', in S. J. Stein (ed.) *Apocalypticism in the Modern Period and the Contemporary Age* (New York, 2003), pp. 265–92.
22 Qutoted in Scheer, 'Angstkultur', p. 334.
23 Th. A. Kselman and S. Avella, 'Marian Piety', p. 418.
24 P. Boyer, *By the Bomb's Early Light: American Thought and Culture at the Dawn of the Atomic Age* (New York, 1985), p. 275, in Scheer, 'Angstkultur', p. 336.
25 S. Zimdars-Swartz and P.F. Zimdars-Swartz, 'Apocalypticism', pp. 280–3.
26 *Ibid.*, p. 282.
27 *Ibid.*

28 'Festpredigt von Erzbischof Lorenz Jaeger', in Zentralkomitee der deutschen Katholiken (ed.), *Unsere Sorge der Mensch. Unser Heil der Herr. Der 78. Deutsche Katholikentag vom 13. August bis 17. August 1958 in Berlin* (Paderborn, 1958), p. 347.
29 P. F. McNeal, *Harder than War. Catholic Peacemaking in Twentieth-Century America* (New Brunswick, NJ, 1992) p. 107. For more details on Thomas Merton, see *ibid.*, pp. 105–30.
30 Quoted in 'Hiroshima', in W.H. Shannon, Chr. M. Bochen and P. F. O'Connell (eds), *The Thomas Merton Encyclopedia* (Maryknoll, NY, 2002), p. 205. For more details on *Breakthrough to Peace*, see *ibid.*, p. 32.
31 Pius XII quite likely owed his knowledge in nuclear science to the German physicist Max Planck, who was member of the Pontifical Academy of Sciences. See F. X. Winters, *Remembering Hiroshima: Was It Just?* (Farnham, 2009), pp. 225–7.
32 Pius XII, 'Über das internationale Strafrecht', *Herder Korrespondenz* 8:2 (1953), pp. 77–83, p. 78.
33 Quoted in E. J. Nagel and H. Oberhem, *Dem Frieden verpflichtet. Konzeptionen und Entwicklungen der katholischen Friedensethik seit dem Zweiten Weltkrieg* (Munich, 1982), p. 24.
34 H. Oberhem, 'Zur Kontroverse um die bellum-iustum-Theorie in der Gegenwart', in N. Glatzel and E. J. Nagel (eds), *Frieden in Sicherheit. Zur Weiterentwicklung der katholischen Friedensethik* (Freiburg, 1981) pp. 41–68, pp. 55–62.
35 J. C. Murray, *We Hold These Truths* (New York, 1960), p. 246. For further details on Murray, see McNeal, *Harder than War*, pp. 71–82, 110–11, 154–5.
36 J. C. Murray, 'Remarks on the moral problem of war', *Theological Studies* 20 (1959), p. 58.
37 Murray, *Truths*, pp. 244–5.
38 Winters, *Remembering Hiroshima*, pp. 224–8.
39 G. Gundlach, 'Die Lehre Pius XII. vom modernen Krieg', in K. Forster (ed.), *Kann der atomare Verteidigungskrieg ein gerechter Krieg sein?* (Munich, 1960), pp. 105–34.
40 G. Gundlach, *Die Ordnung der menschlichen Gesellschaft* (Cologne, 1964).
41 'Wort zur christlichen Friedenspolitik und zur atomaren Rüstung', KNA, 05.05.1958. With regard to the clarification process see J. Hirschmann, 'Kann atomare Verteidigung sittlich gerechtfertigt sein?', *Stimmen der Zeit* 162 (1957–58), pp. 284–96, and N. Monzel, 'Die ethische Problematik des Krieges mit Atombomben', in Forster (ed.), *Verteidigungskrieg*, pp. 41–72.
42 D. Gerster, *Friedensdialoge im Kalten Krieg. Eine Geschichte der Katholiken in der Bundesrepublik 1957–1983* (Frankfurt am Main and New York, 2012), pp. 220–314. For more details on the peace movement against the NATO Double Track Decision in general, see A. Holmes Cooper, *Paradoxes of Peace: German Peace Movement since 1945* (Ann Arbor/MI, 1996), pp. 151–201.

43 A. Liedhegener, "'The challenge of peace" – "Gerechtigkeit schafft Frieden". Der amerikanische und deutsche Katholizismus in der außen- und sicherheitspolitischen Konntroverse um NATO-Doppelbeschluss und Nachrüstung', in Kremp and Meyer (eds), *Religion und Zivilreligion*, pp. 273–91. For the US pastoral letter, see McNeal, *Harder than War*, pp. 211–58.
44 *The Challenge of Peace: God's Promise and Our Response* (Washington, D.C., 1983), II. A. 2.
45 Sekretariat der DBK (ed.), *Gerechtigkeit schafft Frieden. Wort der deutschen Bischofskonferenz zum Frieden* (Bonn, 1983) pp. 40–2.
46 F. Böckle, 'Bergpredigt und Abschreckung – Ethische Probleme der Sicherheitspolitik', in H. J. Veen (ed.), *Argumente für Frieden und Freiheit* (St. Augustin: Forschungsbericht der KAS, 1983), pp. 39–46.
47 *The Challenge of Peace*, Summary.
48 D. Day, 'We go on record', *The Catholic Worker* (September 1945), p. 1. For details on Dorothy Day and the Catholic Worker Movement, see McNeal, *Harder than War*, pp. 29–48.
49 Fr. J. J. Hugo, 'Peace without victory', *The Catholic Worker* (September 1945), p. 2.
50 E. W. Böckenförde and R. Spaemann, 'Die Zerstörung der naturrechtlichen Kriegslehre. Erwiderung an P. Gustav Gundlach SJ', in *Atomare Kampfmittel und christliche Ethik. Diskussionsbeiträge deutscher Katholiken* (München, 1960), pp. 161–96, p. 176. For detailed information on their argument, see M. Weinzierl, 'Die Christen und die Problematik des Gerechten Krieges im Atomzeitalter', in F. Engel-Janosi (ed.), *Gewalt und Gewaltlosigkeit. Probleme des 20. Jahrhunderts* (Vienna, 1977), pp. 114–42.
51 E. Gerard and G. R. Horn (eds), *Left Catholicism. Catholics and Society in Western Europe at the Point of Liberation. 1943–1955* (Leuven, 2001). See esp. A. Lienkamp, 'Socialism out of Christian responsibility: the German experiment of left Catholicism (1945–1949)', in *ibid.*, pp. 196–227.
52 E. Kogon, 'Im heraufziehenden Schatten des Atomtodes', *Frankfurter Hefte* 12:5 (1957), pp 301–6.
53 G. Hirschauer, 'Der Fall Gundlach oder Die Kapitulation der Moral', *Werkhefte* 13:4 (1959), pp 95–9. For details on Protestant discussions, see W. Kalesse, *Atomwaffen als Herausforderung der Moraltheologie. Eine Untersuchung zu den theologischen Grundlagen der Diskussion der Evangelischen Kirche in Deutschland in den fünfziger Jahren. Ein ökumenischer Beitrag* (Linz, 1985).
54 H. Schulte Herbrüggen, 'Atomkrieg und christliche Ethik (II)', *Frankfurter Hefte* 13:10 (1958), pp. 686–94.
55 H. Nehring, 'Searching for security: the British and West German protests against nuclear weapons and "respectability". 1958-1963', in B. Ziemann (ed.), *Peace Movements in Western Europe, Japan and the USA during the Cold War* (Essen, 2008), pp. 167–87, p. 179.
56 *Pacem in Terris. Encyclical of Pope John XXIII on establishing universal peace in truth, justice, charity, and liberty (11th April 1963)*, § 110. URL:

www.vatican.va/holy_father/john_xxiii/encyclicals/documents/hf_j-xxiii_enc_11041963_pacem_en.html. (accessed 15 February 2016).
57 *Ibid.*, § 127.
58 Nagel and Oberhem, *Dem Frieden verpflichtet*, pp. 35–62.
59 *Pacem in Terris*, §110–12.
60 G. Alberigo and J. A. Komonchak (eds), *The History of Vatican II* (Maryknoll, NY, Leuven, 1995–2006).
61 *Pastoral Constiution on the Church in the Modern World 'Gaudium et Spes'*, promulgated by his Holiness, Pope Paul VI on 7 December 1965, § 79–80. URL: www.vatican.va/archive/hist_councils/ii_vatican_council/documents/vat-ii_cons_19651207_gaudium-et-spes_en.html. (accessed 15 February 2016).
62 'Der Beitrag der katholischen Kirche in der Bundesrepublik Deutschland für Entwicklung und Frieden', in L. Bertsch (ed.), *Offizielle Beschlüsse der Vollversammlung* (Freiburg, 1989 (1977)), pp. 470–510, p. 473.
63 *Ibid.*, p. 504.
64 For details on the early years of the international movement of Pax Christi, see F. Mabille, *Les catholiques et la paix au temps de la guerre froide. Le mouvement catholique international pour la paix Pax Christi* (Paris, 2004).
65 McNeal, *Harder than War*, pp. 211–58; Gerster, *Friedensdialoge*, pp. 245–67.
66 Gerster, *Friedensdialoge*, pp. 285–90.

10

'The nuclear arms race is psychological at its roots':[1] physicians and their therapies for the Cold War

Claudia Kemper

'Wars begin in the mind, but the mind is also capable of preventing war.'[2]

The Cold War from a medical perspective

Physicians are members of a respected profession and at the same time an elite minority, whose special social position is particularly called upon when state and society find themselves in a crisis, above all in armed conflict.[3] Traditionally, physicians involved in conflicts carry out their role after an episode of violence, dealing with injuries and traumas.[4] The ambivalent situation in which this puts them – saving people's lives in order to return them to the machinery of war – has repeatedly drawn objections from physicians throughout the twentieth century.[5] It is hardly surprising that the tense relationship between war, medical ethics and the desire for peace has been a constant issue of discussion among members of the medical profession.[6] Physicians opposed or committed to pacifism use their expertise in injuries and disease – in death and suffering – to give credibility to their actions. Such medical knowledge and experience help to gain popular legitimacy for their attempts to warn against war and their proposals on how to avoid it.[7] But how did physicians react to the threat of a nuclear war; that is, a war unlike any that had been experienced before?

The example of *International Physicians for the Prevention of Nuclear War* (IPPNW) clearly illustrates how physicians argued against future nuclear conflict. From their medical perspective, IPPNW doctors not only saw themselves as responsible for dealing with the medical consequences of a nuclear war, but they also believed that they had a duty before a war had even started. In the event of a nuclear conflict, medical assistance would be almost impossible. Therefore, the outbreak of war had to be avoided in the first place. The physicians saw their responsibility as providing treatment to ward off the future disaster before it occurred. They thus transplanted the notion of preventative medicine to their work in peace advocacy.[8]

However, the picture that IPPNW painted of nuclear war went further. For them, a nuclear war did not begin with the firing of a missile, but with the psychological effects of the nuclear threat. This raised the question of why most people were willing to accept the prospect of total destruction. IPPNW diagnosed the logic of nuclear deterrent, which large swathes of society and politics had internalised, as a form of disease that prevented people from recognising the solutions to the conflict. In their view, these societal and political attitudes were affected by the Cold War in a pathological way and had hence to be treated as a disease. This diagnosis operated at two levels. First of all they attributed the climate of mutual suspicion and the arms race itself to repressed fears among politicians and the public. People's consciousness was prepared for conventional wars through prejudices and misperceptions. By contrast, the Cold War continually ran riot in the public's mind. Thus, it prevented people from seeing the constructive possibilities for solving the conflict, which was the starting point for the therapeutic endeavours of IPPNW.[9] Second, IPPNW diagnosed a discrepancy between knowledge and action. On the one hand, the likely consequences of atomic bombs were known in some detail. Yet governments were, on the other hand, busy preparing themselves for such an apocalyptic event, for instance through civil defence measures, instead of making preparations for preventing nuclear war.

Both observations contributed to an elaborate pathology of society: it was repressing its 'natural' fears and behaviour by redirecting its activities into a cul-de-sac. In accordance with this insight, not only psychiatrists and radiation specialists were involved in IPPNW, but also public health experts, who called attention to the nuclear war as 'the last epidemic'.[10] As a consequence, IPPNW focused on society and politics as if they were patients who had to be enlightened: 'It is the belief of the founders of IPPNW that public understanding of these medical consequences of nuclear war will have a major impact on nuclear disarmament and the prevention of nuclear war, and that prominent physicians from around the world can assist in promotion this understanding.'[11]

The idea for IPPNW can be traced back to the 1960s. Already in 1961, a group called Physicians for Social Responsibility (PSR) was established in the United States. Writing in the *New England Journal of Medicine* in 1962, this organisation used an attention-grabbing scenario to describe the medical situation in the Boston area after a nuclear attack.[12] In 1980, PSR and the Harvard cardiologist Bernard Lown helped to found IPPNW as an umbrella organisation at Harvard Medical School.[13] As an international medical federation, it campaigned against the arms race and aimed to develop a special understanding of the anticipated nuclear war for this purpose. The following chapter explores how IPPNW was able to consider and articulate the Cold War in a medical context, focusing on the military and political aspects of the nuclear bomb. Only by doing so could physicians lay claim to a political mandate as a peace organisation. I shall argue that IPPNW, and in particular the IPPNW branches in Western countries, was effective because it plausibly explained in medical and psychological terms what by the early 1980s had become a highly complex international situation. By enabling doctors and laypeople to understand the Cold War as a disease, it appeared to bring a cure within reach.

IPPNW as a peaceful alternative model to the Cold War

Disease is an elusive term: while countless images and ideas are associated with it, it has never been conclusively defined. Because the concept of disease is so difficult to pin down, the abstract realm of politics has long used it as a metaphorical tool.[14] In academia, however, metaphors of disease are not highly regarded. All too often, they do not simply illustrate a state of affairs, but also create meanings that may be exploited politically.[15] An example of this is the metaphorical connection between disease and war. Politicians often declare a state of 'war' in order to attack social problems that they describe as a 'disease'.[16] Medical metaphors serve in turn to depict self-destructive forces in society.[17] In political communication, metaphors of disease often provide the precursor to imagining a reality. They form part of a bio-political discourse of legitimacy,[18] depicting an enemy as a 'social ill' – for example the description of 'organised crime' as a cancer.[19] The term 'disease' has a dual function here. First of all, it underscores the negative consequences of the illness from which people actually suffer. Second, the use of the word 'cancer' stigmatises entire social groups. Deploying images of disease as metaphors thus not only describes social realities, but also creates them.

The concept of disease is not only a crucial part of a semantic field, but also embedded in contemporary contexts. It is incorporated in socio-political discussions and perceptions, for example, when diseases are interpreted as social crises.[20] The depiction and communication of medical challenges – whether issues of public health, common disorders or incurable infectious diseases – reflect the social context in which they are negotiated.[21] Decoding the epistemology of medical discourses thus also offers an insight into how societies understand social normality and deviation from it.[22] In this context, we may analyse how doctors seek to discover social influences that trigger diseases, for example the experience of war.[23] Conversely, social psychology enquires the causes of war, hypothesising that it arises from the psychological disposition of its participants.[24] Metaphors of disease that construct social realities and social conditions that influence diseases – this was the interrelationship between medicine and society in which the physicians of IPPNW developed their interpretation of the Cold War. They did not use the term 'disease' metaphorically. Rather, they applied a contemporary concept of disease to the political situation and situated their interpretation at the interface of medicine and public.

During its first years the organisation grew rapidly. It included several doctors in high-profile positions, who published in respected professional journals as well as in the daily press, and gave talks to medical associations, college students or senator meetings.[25] In all these settings, they defined the Cold War and the nuclear arms race as a pathological condition. Explaining the causes of the Cold War in psychological terms achieved two things. First of all, the physicians adapted the abstract concept to a social reality and made it comprehensible to a broader public. Second, as psychological experts they put themselves in charge of treating the conflict between the power blocs. Prominent social psychologists such as Jerome D. Frank, Robert Jay Lifton, John E. Mack in the United States and Horst Eberhard Richter in West Germany contributed to IPPNW's arguments with their own experiences and studies.[26] Their diagnoses emphasised the psychological mechanisms that made politicians and society at large repress their fears of nuclear destruction and thereby increased the danger of a nuclear war. The IPPNW co-president, Bernard Lown, also saw a psychological pathology at work in the arms race. He believed that it was generated by 'socially engineered public misperceptions', which in turn led to collective repression.[27] Only by recognising and accepting this pathogenesis could society reframe the nuclear logic and eliminate its effectiveness.[28] Overcoming the self-inflicted arms race, he insisted, depended on humanity's self-awareness.

IPPNW developed a programme of therapeutic intervention that combined scientifically focused expert knowledge with the objectives of education and mobilisation that were typical of a grassroots organisation.

Lown, a renowned cardiologist at Harvard Medical School, wanted to take advantage of the academic recognition and moral authority of physicians in order to legitimise IPPNW as an anti-nuclear peace movement that acted across both power blocs and on the basis of political neutrality. In order to attract attention as a credible participant in the discussion about nuclear weapons in the early 1980s, IPPNW had to ensure that people perceived it not just as medically competent, but also as politically neutral. This was all the more complicated given that the medically based IPPNW campaigns were supposed to influence specific political decisions. The IPPNW physicians would only be seen as academically legitimate and politically neutral if the political arena accepted their medical perspective as relevant to policymaking. They worked on two levels in order to achieve this.

On the first level, the doctors agreed internally on medical parameters for their peace work. Furthermore, they provided medical expert knowledge not only on demand but rather as a result of their commitment against the nuclear deterrence. Under the umbrella of IPPNW they laid claim to both the medical problem and the therapy to resolve this issue. This turned the abstract scientific community of cardiologists, internists and psychologists from the East and the West into a specific epistemic community sharing the assumption that medical assistance would be impossible after a nuclear attack and that it was therefore irrational to prepare for it.[29] This medical agreement was enabled by professional contacts that American and Soviet doctors had maintained for years.[30] Based on these shared professional experiences, Lown and his colleagues in 1979 attempted to convince the high-ranking Soviet medical functionary Evgenij Chazov of the merits of a joint conference on medical consequences of a nuclear war.[31] A preparatory meeting between the Americans and the Soviets took place in December 1980, where a first joint conference was agreed.[32] IPPNW, like other forms of co-operation between the East and the West, was initially about academic exchange,[33] a stable ground where scientific discussions and professional experience could create mutual trust. Only then could the specialist discussion extend its focus beyond medical research and hospital practice.[34] The professional basis of the cooperation between American and Soviet physicians at the top of IPPNW, symbolised by the friendship between Lown and Chazov, was necessary to convince physicians in other countries of the idea's merits.

In addition to reaching internal agreement, IPPNW sought, on a second level, to legitimise its work in public, both in terms of content and presentation. This meant making medical statements in visual form, for example, public appeals in the form of medical prescriptions or combined with medical symbols (such as the Aesculapium staff), and carrying out performative actions to enable people to understand them. The demonstrative co-operation of physicians from the United States and the Soviet Union, for example, at the international conventions that took place every year, fulfilled precisely this role. After the first meeting in 1980, the IPPNW was able to organise the first international conference in the United States with physicians from over twelve countries, including the Soviet Union and Japan. At the same time their activities encouraged peace groups of medical doctors, especially in Europe, to join the umbrella of IPPNW as national sections. Subsequently, international conferences were held every year in varying countries, ranging from Great Britain, the Netherlands, Finland, and Hungary to West Germany and, in 1987, even the Soviet Union.

Behind every joint appearance was the idea that the physicians represented a positive, civilising alternative to the devastating power of the nuclear bomb. The bomb's psychologically destructive force could only be countered by cooperation and trust across both power blocs.[35] The meetings and dialogues between Lown and Chazov were therefore designed to offer a tangible experience in which the public could take part. One impressive appearance, for example, took place at an award presentation in San Francisco and Moscow in 1984. A satellite link – then a relatively new piece of technology – enabled the two co-presidents of IPPNW to speak to each other and accept the prize from two different countries.[36] It was this presence of physicians on a stage that first made the therapies for overcoming the Cold War proposed by IPPNW tangible, both for the audience and for the members of the organisation.[37]

Out of pragmatic necessity, IPPNW also adopted a strategy of scientisation that used the academic rationality and respectability of physicians for their anti-war stance. Talking about the nuclear issue in a rational way was only the first step to increase public credibility. In order to distinguish themselves from other scientific groups that promoted arms control, IPPNW used its medical background for a 'medicalisation of nuclear disarmament claims', including misperceptions between East and West.[38] This strategy was born out of the physicians' lack of political experience but also owing to mechanisms of public and political awareness. If IPPNW wanted to remain credible and to survive as a peace organisation, it was important to influence the political sphere without becoming a 'political' organisation.[39]

Physicians and their therapies for the Cold War

A perennial question with regard to the decision-making within the organisation was the impact on IPPNW's credibility and academic independence. In order not to complicate further its sensitive position as a joint American–Soviet organisation, the physicians from the East and the West decided prior to their first meeting to limit the group's objectives strictly to preventing nuclear war. If IPPNW had opposed nuclear power in general or even conventional weapons, it would have been impossible for any Soviet physician to take part in the joint initiative. For this reason, and in the light of the important role of the media, they made the following point: 'In discussing the short- and long-term consequences of nuclear war, the group will try to avoid politics by staying close to health effects and medical capabilities in the wake of nuclear exchange. At the same time … we have no doubts that everything we say will have tremendous political implications.'[40] The external political setting thus influenced the thematic focus.

Medical considerations and external factors ultimately shaped the perspective from which IPPNW diagnosed the pathology of the arms race. In this perspective, the organisation placed the power interests of both blocs in a psychological rather than political context. Taking a cue from disaster studies and trauma research, psychologists and psychiatrists in particular developed the theory of a type of pre-traumatic repression. For decades, disaster studies had been investigating the physical and psychological consequences of surviving disasters.[41] This research had established that disaster survivors have difficulty dealing with their past experiences and tend to repress them. Similarly, the doctors now diagnosed numerous symptoms suggesting that people in the United States and West Germany were repressing their fear of a future disaster. The looming nuclear catastrophe was thus triggering individual and social traumata in the present.

Psychological expertise in IPPNW

A crucial feature of the peace movement during the 1980s was the way in which it acknowledged its own fear of the nuclear apocalypse.[42] The fear of annihilation and its understanding formed the starting point for initiatives and was placed at the centre of demonstrations and campaigns. It was a distinctive characteristic of these campaigns to connect subjective emotions with science.[43] A series of experts shared their specialist knowledge of bomb technology, military strategies and potential impact on the population, thus providing an objective and social framework for their fear.⁴⁴ IPPNW and its national sections were part of this emotional regime in the peace movement and sought to offer specifically medical explanations.⁴⁵ Psychiatrists and psychologists in IPPNW observed that the openly expressed fear of the peace movement stood in opposition to the latent fear of mainstream society.⁴⁶ Even though the peace movement was popular in the United States and Europe, most people appeared to treat their own fears of the nuclear threat as the proverbial elephant in the room. Everybody was aware of the political problem but as long as nobody mentioned the inner fear of extermination, they all were able to ignore it.⁴⁷ The psychological reading was that recognising these fears was only possible if individuals were empowered to express and realise what had so far been unimaginable. For IPPNW, this gave rise to a two-pronged strategy: first of all, the physicians would instil the 'justified' fear of annihilation in people's consciousness. Second, they would reduce the 'unjustified' fear of the 'enemy', much-invoked by stereotypical rhetorics. As in psychotherapy, both objectives were to be achieved by confronting politicians and the public with their 'justified' and 'unjustified' fears.

The explanation of the repression of fear drew on well-known interpretive models. In IPPNWs' first anthology, John E. Mack simply wrote the following: 'the ultimate responsibility for the arms race resides in the hearts and minds of human beings who are unable to comprehend the real nature of the monster we have created'.⁴⁸ Mack was clearly drawing a comparison to the well-known story of Dr Frankenstein, whose irresponsible use of all available technology creates an unforeseeable threat to human life. In order to understand the effects of repressed fears, American psychologists conducted a series of questionnaires among children and young adults. These included Mack's study of the psychosocial effects of the nuclear threat on high-school students and the research filmed by Eric Chivian in 'There's a Nuclear War Going on Inside Me'.⁴⁹ Their work assumed that the weakest members of society suffered most from the nuclear threat and the silence surrounding nuclear fear.

In West Germany, the family therapist and IPPNW co-founder Horst Eberhard Richter drew his diagnoses and reflections on psychosocial effects of the nuclear threat from his experiences with group therapy and family conflicts. He had observed that children and members of groups suffer when collective conflicts are repressed rather than being resolved. According to Richter, strong personalities could only develop if individual and collective emotions were aired.⁵⁰ Richter identified similar patterns with regard to the nuclear threat. The widespread wilful ignorance could be explained by the 'incomprehensibility of the effects of modern weapons of mass destruction, which renders the horror abstract and nebulous'.[51] For all the technical details, figures and diagrams put into circulation, the impact of such warfare remained abstract. Richter compared the way in which people had become used to living under the nuclear threat to a repressed conformity with authoritarian constraints and structures of compulsion.[52] People were unable to imagine nuclear war as a possibility and so, diagnosed Richter, deceived themselves into believing that something so unimaginable could not really happen.

Psychological explanations that treated the Cold War as a disease drew upon academic discussions and on common knowledge. The use of psychiatric terminology to interpret the political present was closely linked to the specialist discussion about the cause of psychological disorders from 1945 to the 1970s.[53] Meanwhile, in the United States and West Germany, psychological knowledge permeated many areas of societal life, promoted by social movements and alternative lifestyles.[54] Talking about psychological dispositions, private fears and individual needs was popular not only in clinical practice, but also on television and in the many self-help books that were published in this decade.[55] Against the backdrop of a 'therapeutic culture',[56] interest increasingly focused on the individual.[57] If social conditions could not be changed, their effects on people were to be considered and recognised in order to prevent psychosomatic illnesses.[58]

Emotions and politics: IPPNW's legitimacy in the political arena

Predicting medical consequences of a nuclear war was the first step in considering the nuclear arms race as a disease. However, it was only through the interplay of all the discursive and performative elements of medical science that the nuclear threat became a real, already existing illness to be treated by physicians. One of these elements was the public performance of physicians, who co-operated in an atmosphere of mutual trust with each other. The conferences, which took place in accordance with academic standards, were another element, both the international conventions and gatherings of the national sections.[59]

It would be short-sighted to see IPPNW as a cross-current to the established medical profession. On the contrary, IPPNW physicians were part of the mainstream. Key staff in the central office in Boston, the co-presidents, Lown and Chazov, and the board of directors were made up of high-profile doctors who did not jeopardise their profession's procedures and analyses in general and the state-of-the-art knowledge concerning the nuclear issue in particular. Most, if not all, credible physicians during the 1980s confirmed a nuclear detonation would have unimaginable medical consequences. Yet, in the same way as other professions, they were divided over controversial definitions of professionalism in regard to the nuclear question and how their expertise could be used in a social and political context.

While IPPNW agreed internally on medical parameters as an epistemic community of knowledge-based experts, they presented their counter-expertise in public as based on state-of-the-art medical research. Calling IPPNW an epistemic community underlines their ability to create a network of medical doctors which multiplied medical knowledge about nuclear issues and at the same time generated political authority. On the public stage, representatives of IPPNW competed for and created credibility in the manifold discussions about whether or not to deploy new nuclear weapons and to extend civil defence measures, and on humanity's chances of surviving a nuclear war. Since their authority depended on their status as scientists, the physicians claimed that nuclear issues belonged to their field of knowledge and could not be left to politicians.[60] This 'boundary work' between the political and academic spheres was 'consequential, because whether a question is classified as "scientific" or "political" shapes judgments about who should resolve it'.[61] Beyond the issue of credibility, the performance of physicians in the public nuclear debate also involved theatrical forms of stage management, dramaturgical cooperation and information control.[62] Moreover, experts such as the IPPNW physicians were part of a long-established process that continued to drive the 'scientisation of politics' in the late twentieth century.[63]

Already during the early work of PSR in the 1960s, Bernard Lown had developed an argument that physicians could use to legitimise themselves in the eyes of the public and politicians. As medical expertise included researching and labelling unknown diseases, it was the duty of the medical profession to scientifically comprehend the unknown consequences of a nuclear apocalypse; that is, 'to take the incomprehensible and give it scientific credibility'.[64] Not only the substance of their work, but also the public presentation of the co-presidents, international conventions and protest campaigns by national sections of IPPNW during the 1980s had to be structured according to medical and scientific rules. At demonstrations, physicians in national sections frequently appeared in doctors' white coats before demonstrably taking these off at the end of the protest.[65] The message of such actions was easy to grasp and underlined the content of resolutions, brochures and speeches: we will be helpless in the event of a nuclear war and are thus unwilling to accept responsibility for preparing for one. A further performative method was the organisation of conventions, which followed the standards of international events for medical professionals. This involved strictly ensuring equal representation in the event programme, time management, the provision of a supporting programme and inviting specialists from other disciplines.[66] IPPNW thus presented itself as a clearly recognisable group to physicians and the peace movement alike, both through the substance of its work and the way it pitched its message through protest work. It positioned itself using arguments against nuclear armament that could be understood by a broader public rather than only by medical professionals.

IPPNW's first international conference impressively showed how important these performative displays were in making the organisation's work more prominent. In March 1981, the first official convention that involved representatives from both power blocs, especially from the United States, the Soviet Union and Japan, took place at Airlie House near Washington, D.C. The participation of Japanese physicians was essential to underscore the medical message of the conference. Although they were not the only doctors with relevant experience in the long-term effects of radioactivity, they stood for something more in the field of applied medicine: they had experienced the disaster in Hiroshima and Nagasaki and seen its consequences. Initially, the Japanese physicians were rather pessimistic about the initiative's chances of success, especially with regard to the Soviet Union.[67] Lown was able to convince them to take part by pointing out the scientific value of their presence: 'You and your associates can bring significant testimony relating to the aftermath of the first detonation of atomic bombs against human beings.'[68]

The IPPNW organisers corresponded over weeks and months in order to ensure that internationally renowned physicians participated in the first conference. Finally, the podium was filled with academic luminaries including Herbert D. Abrams from Harvard Medical School, Takeshi Ohkita from Hiroshima University, L. A. Ilyin and M. I. Kuzin from the executive board of the Soviet Academy of Medical Sciences, and Sir Douglas Black from the British Royal College of Physicians. Observers and guests from twelve countries attended. Four working groups covered the topics 'Consequences of Nuclear War', 'What physicians can do in a post-attack period', 'Costs of the arms race', and 'What physicians can do to prevent'. All in all, the agenda was meant to represent a professional approach to the issue of nuclear war. The organisers gave equal attention to the political balance of the event. The US–Soviet initiative took place during the diplomatic ice age between the two countries and the political atmosphere was thus highly charged. In order to secure the neutral status of IPPNW, Secretary James Muller visited the Russian ambassador and the State Department shortly before the conference to prepare for potential objections.[69] When he learned that neither side wanted this international conference or its final resolution on unilateral disarmament, IPPNW made efforts to take these concerns into account. The result was that the final resolution agreed on points that both sides had declared acceptable: negotiations on a stop to nuclear weapons testing and a scientifically founded public education programme.

The mood at the meeting was relaxed and professional at the same time. A Canadian journalist reported about 'teach-ins' and 'informal wanderings' as a 'backlash' by the medical 'establishment' against the arms race:

> Indeed, the conference had none of the 'what do we do for amusement later on' levity of most professional get-togethers. Soberly clad doctors – dressed rather for a college dinner than for the chicken-farming countryside – spoke to each other in low, intense tones. Even West Coast delegates kept jeans and turtlenecks to the bottom of their valises. The Soviet delegation, flanked at first by Tass news agency members and interpreters in squeaky leather jackets, relaxed as the meeting progressed and the media were barred from closed sessions.

Despite the relaxed tone, the report stated, the participants avoided discussing controversial political views, as there were rumours that CIA and KGB agents 'were tiptoeing through the broadloomed corridors'.[70] The description of the decidedly matter-of-fact discussions and friendly atmosphere during the non-public part of the conference, which was not entirely free from political inhibitions, emphasised seriousness but also exclusivity. Restricting discussions to medical consequences of a nuclear attack had originally been a pragmatic necessity in order to enable Soviet physicians to participate. Already during the first conference, however, it became evident that this restriction was also an opportunity to inject scientific expertise into the political discussion. Avoiding any complications or political entanglement can be seen as boundary work for the authoritative stance of IPPNW. Although the physicians were discussing a highly charged political issue, their appearance and behaviour drew a clear demarcation line between the scientific and the political field.[71]

All talks at the Airlie House conference and the subsequent resolution took as their reference point a scenario of all-out war between the United States and the Soviet Union in the mid-1980s, presuming that

'200,000,000 men, women and children will be killed immediately'.[72] The scenario not only presented material destruction, but also the collapse of all civilised co-existence. This was the picture from which the physicians derived their psychological diagnoses of the present. One of the speakers was Robert Jay Lifton, famous for his work with survivors in Hiroshima and Nagasaki.[73] The social psychologist had examined the after-effects of the Hiroshima bomb and used his experiences with the hibakusha – Japanese survivors of the atomic bomb – to predict the psychological state of survivors of a future nuclear war. Lifton's starting hypothesis was that people were better able to deal with the experience of a disaster, the more specifically it had been imagined beforehand. As the residents of Hiroshima and Nagasaki had had no chance to imagine the atomic bomb, they experienced the blast and its consequences in 1945 without any concept of what was happening to them. Alongside the serious physical injuries, Lifton therefore observed equally high psychological stress on the survivors. In the long term, this burden became part of the hibakusha identity. From this perspective, the hibakusha experienced the atomic bomb as a never-ending intrusion into their lives, leading the nuclear disaster to become an indissoluble part of their psyche.[74] Because they were unable to comprehend the destruction and were cognitively unprepared for it, the survivors subsequently fell silent and lived in spiritual isolation. Lifton argued that contemporary society was equally unable to prepare itself for destruction:

> Our inability to imagine death, and the elaborate circle of denial, the profound inner need of human beings to make believe they will never die, are universal psychological barriers to thought about death. The enormity of the scale of killing in a nuclear disaster and the impersonal nature of the technology are still further impediments of comprehension.[75]

Just as people react to disasters by resisting and repressing thoughts about them, Lifton believed that contemporary society was repressing its fear of a future nuclear disaster. This psychic numbing could only be cured by continually visualising the forces of nuclear destruction in the present.

Scenarios of insanity; enlightenment as therapy

Beginning with the Airlie conference in March 1981, the international IPPNW conferences that took place annually at different locations provided a stage not just for the medical knowledge of the participants, but also for their ability to develop professional cooperation and trustful working relationships.[76] IPPNW used these tools to produce both scientific knowledge and authoritative advice.[77] In addition, IPPNW used the media and created an image of trust that was supposed to serve as an example to the political world dominated by the bloc confrontation. This image proved decisive in legitimising IPPNW's initiative across both power blocs. In 1982, Lown and Chazov, together with two further physicians from the Soviet Union and two from the United States, appeared on Soviet television and discussed the medical consequences of a nuclear bomb explosion triggered by a technical failure.[78] The studio arrangement was reminiscent of a round-table discussion and deliberately avoided creating any impression of hierarchy. In addition, the programme's tone combined the familiar atmosphere of the round table with the openness of a journalistic conversation: the subtle flower decorations underlined the friendly atmosphere in which each of the six participants spoke to illuminate a particular aspect. The round-table discussion became a media event as it was broadcasted on Soviet television to a domestic audience. As the lack of media freedom was one of the greatest reservations against 'peace policy' in the Eastern bloc,[79] the TV programme offered a powerful argument against critics of IPPNW: 'For many Soviet viewers, the programme provides the first real glimpse of the horrors of nuclear war', emphasised the London *Times*, for example.[80] In the United States, the discussion was broadcast on PBS as a documentary titled 'Nuclear War: the Incurable Disease'.[81] The central office in Boston recognised the persuasive impact of the broadcasts and made efforts to replay the TV programme to influential audiences in the United States, such as members of Congress, supporters of FREEZE and potential donors.[82]

The first congress in 1981 had stimulated the foundation of national sections around the world, especially in Europe. As early as the 1970s, West German physicians had initiated several campaigns against the civil and military use of nuclear energy. Also, transnational activists such as Helen Caldicott, chair of PSR, inspired national sections. In her speeches she provided profound technical details about nuclear bombs and at the same time used catchwords like 'Nuclear Madness'.[83] With their motivation boosted by the international initiative, German physicians organised the first national convention in 1981 under the following slogan: 'The survivors will envy the dead. Physicians warn of nuclear war.'[84] Shortly afterwards, some of the active physicians including internists, anaesthetists, general practitioners and psychologists resolved to establish a new national section of IPPNW. In line with other European sections, the basic idea of the West German section was to use the dialogue across the

Iron Curtain as a form of therapy against the arms race that was deemed to be pathological. At the same time, different national circumstances, memories, and professional traditions influenced the work of the different sections. They helped to shape the performative and discursive style in which IPPNW imagined nuclear war.[85]

All sections covered the issue of civil defence, as this was most conducive to creating scenarios of a world affected by nuclear war. Drawing on a range of technical details the physicians reviewed state-of-the-art knowledge in their profession and considered civil defence to be essentially ineffectual in the event of a nuclear war.[86] According to this combination of technical and psychological approaches, IPPNW argued the expansion of nuclear civil defence in the early 1980s was in fact an indication of psychological repression at the political level.[87] The extent to which civil defence represented a political manifestation of repressed fears could be seen, they claimed, in the excessive faith in technology it revealed, combined with its inability to acknowledge technological and medical uncertainties.[88]

IPPNW's educational work focused on exposing civil defence as a false promise of security. To achieve this, it aimed to invalidate the political definition of rationality by making predictions based on scientific criteria. Government officials admitted that millions would die in the event of a nuclear war, but assumed that a post-attack situation would be manageable in principle.[89] IPPNW countered this by questioning the conclusions of official rhetoric. A strategy paper from 1982 stated that IPPNW should offer arguments to the political opposition by deconstructing the official claims: 'The medical material has been utilised to great advantage, the matter of accidents, systems failure, human failure, can all be elaborated on. Physicians can serve an important role in demythologising the concept of nuclear weapons as a great mystery and magic known only to the military.'[90] The physicians made use of scientific and technical knowledge from other disciplines and combined their predictions with their own experiences from emergency medicine.

The discourse on civil defence was also an important target for IPPNW because it took conventional disasters as the starting point for preparing for a nuclear attack.[91] Basic research on civil defence had to make recourse to prior experiences of disasters in order to predict the technical, medical and 'psychobiological' impact on behaviour.[92] In the past, disaster experts had gained experience of emergency care for merely several hundred people. For nuclear civil defence planning, they had to expect injuries of tens and hundreds of thousands of people in a small area.

IPPNW, too, used the existing plans and forecasts of the military in order to draw their own conclusions. While those involved in civil defence tried to present a nuclear attack as an unlikely event that could be overcome by using conventional means, IPPNW took precisely the opposite approach. It considered a nuclear attack very likely and coping with it almost impossible. A scenario for London began with the words: 'The NATO "Square Leg" exercise, which took place in 1980, provides a credible pattern of missile strikes, which can be used as a model to assess the possible consequences of a nuclear attack on Great Britain.'[93] Scenarios always described the devastation of their authors' homeland: British physicians imagined the devastation of London, Japanese physicians assumed an attack on Tokyo, and American physicians looked at Chicago.[94] Supplemented with photographs of Hiroshima and Nagasaki, diagrams and maps, disaster scenarios became tangible futures for the first time. In these scenarios, familiar images were used to trigger people's imagination and traces of memory. In Europe, this meant tapping into memories – still living or recently passed on – of the continent's last conventional war.[95] Texts by American IPPNW authors mostly mentioned spectacular natural disasters in the country's history to unleash fearful memories and images.[96]

To enable the realisation of the enormous consequences of a nuclear attack, all IPPNW scenarios described not only material and environmental devastation, but also the destruction of civil society, rationality, reason and emotion. The helplessness of physicians in these scenarios underlined the importance of this message: all preparations for a nuclear war were futile, and hence insane. In this sense, the creation of images of this helplessness was also a strategy to convey scientific knowledge by transforming it into generally accepted objectivity. Physicians sought to illustrate the anticipated material future in the event of a nuclear attack. Scenarios of total destruction were based on complex medical prognosis but were provided in tangible images that demonstrated everyone's own mortality. The triggered personal concern was then embedded in further explanations about the psychological mechanism of repressed fears. In this manner, the scenarios provided by IPPNW incorporated images of both humanity's self-destruction through nuclear weapons and the psychological disease as its root.

IPPNW's definition of the Cold War as a disease that could be treated and cured represented a strict counter-position to the allegedly rational strategy of the balance of deterrence. In the attempt to frame the assumed rational substructure of Cold War conflict, politicians and experts endeavoured to talk about security measures in the run-up to an atomic bomb detonation rather than commenting on the explosion itself. IPPNW's argumentation took aim at the way in which those in power had taken linguistic and psychological ownership of the nuclear threat and had blurred its contours. As politicians and experts normalised the unimaginable event of a nuclear bomb explosion, an atomic catastrophe became increasingly likened to a natural disaster – something unexpected and almost impossible to influence. IPPNW countered this with its own imagining of nuclear war.

Conclusion

The image of nuclear confrontation as a disease was perhaps not a simplistic, but certainly a simplifying, way of grasping the conditions and implications of the Cold War. For IPPNW, this notion was a necessary and obvious way of attracting attention as a peace organisation of physicians. Three elements were at work in this notion of disease. First of all, by interpreting the state of affairs in medical terms, IPPNW was able to justify the physicians' medical objections to nuclear weapons. Just as physicians are considered to be neutral figures in medical emergencies, so too could they emphasise their neutrality with respect to the nuclear threat. It was on this basis that co-operation between physicians from the East and the West was possible. Second, imagining the Cold War as a disease offered a medical–scientific frame for physicians from different nation-states. Away from the concerns of the national sections, the physicians could communicate with each other through their specialist knowledge. Third, the image of a disease was plausible and accessible to non-medics too. On the one hand, there were the repressed fears of the 'patients': the politicians, the military and the public at large. And on the other, the 'healers' of IPPNW, who were communicative, capable of dialogue and offered trustful encounters with therapeutic effects.

IPPNW went beyond defining concepts to offer therapies that were supposed to put a stop to the 'nuclear madness'. Its own organisational structure was supposed to serve as a model here, and the vivid scenarios of nuclear war were designed to have a deterrent effect. As in psychotherapy, the realisation of the unsayable was coupled with the aim of changing behaviour. Politically, the physicians placed themselves in opposition to the mainstream of their profession, but in diagnostic and therapeutic terms they met the usual standards. This was the basis of IPPNW's credibility in the eyes of their colleagues. Remarkably, the medically agreed parameters of IPPNW's work and the message it presented to the public showed significant links to the medical zeitgeist of the 1970s and 1980s. Criticism of technology and calls for a reform in the doctor–patient relationship were just as much topics of IPPNW as psychologising individual and social circumstances. In the same way, photographs, narratives and scenarios were supposed to have an effect on politicians and the general public, comparable to the notion of 'working through' and confronting one's problems in a therapeutic setting. The patient was to face the threat in order to become capable of eliminating its causes.

Creating scenarios for an all-out nuclear war became a constant strategy. IPPNW used to highlight its concerns. These scenarios provided vivid, but not sensational illustrations of the supposed aftermath of a nuclear detonation. And they stressed the organisation's firm conviction that medical doctors would be incapable of rescuing anyone in the event of a detonation. At the same time, they criticised established scenarios that promoted civil defence concepts by arguing that these were unrealistic. In reality, IPPNW pointed out, civilians would suffer first in the aftermath of an explosion and sooner or later everybody would be affected. The scenarios had public impact because they were based on generally accepted assumptions about the environmental effects of an atomic bomb explosion. They were described in detail in hundreds of scientific journals, books and publications. In addition to these descriptions, IPPNW offered elaborate calculations to demonstrate the evident absurdity of every civil defence concept. The rows of figures were linked to concrete scenarios in familiar environments. They were supposed to trigger individual imaginations in the minds of the readers, which were then acknowledged by the final sentence: if such an event occurred, no physician, not even a military physician, would be able to help.

Yet it still seemed to be impossible to grasp fully the reality represented by these scenarios. The physicians therefore made efforts to use their medical competence and expertise to develop a way out of the seemingly inescapable vicious circle of nuclear armament. By anatomising societal collectives, the IPPNW physicians transformed common political and military categories into a new, but at the same time intelligible psychological category, revealing the core of the conflict: repressed fear. Their strategy – education through facts: details, graphs, serious calculations – was equivalent to the psychological therapy of 'paradox intervention'. This method, developed by Horst Eberhard Richter, is based on the principle of strengthening a negative impulse in order to provoke a constructive reaction.[97] Ultimately, IPPNW's psychological explanations and therapies had little influence on policy making.⁹⁸ However, they provided an opportunity for the physicians to reach agreement with each other and become legitimate participants in the nuclear debate. IPPNW had much more influence when, as a result of the self-confidence instilled in the physicians by its campaigning work, the organisation came into contact with politicians, made demands and underlined its positions with the moral authority of the medical profession: listen to us, undergo therapy and you will be healthy again.

Notes

1. J. E. Mack: 'Psychosocial effects of the nuclear arms race', *Bulletin of the Atomic Scientists* (Apr. 1981), p. 18.
2. E. Chivian, S. Chivian, R. Lifton and J. Mack (eds), *Last Aid: The Medical Dimensions of Nuclear War* (San Francisco, 1982), p. 310.
3. M. K. Wynia, 'Medical professionalism in society', *New England Journal of Medicine (NEJM)* 341 (1999), pp. 1612–16.
4. E. Crawford, *The Treatment of Combatants and Insurgents under the Law of Armed Conflict* (Oxford, 2010).
5. J. Bourke, Der Heilberuf und das Leiden. Die Erfahrungen der Militärmedizin in den beiden Weltkriegen, in M. Larner, J. Schmitz and C. M. Peto (eds), *Krieg und Medizin* (Göttingen, 2009), pp. 119–31.
6. F. Allhoff (ed.), *Physicians at War: The Dual-Loyalties Challenge* (Dordrecht, Berlin and Heidelberg, 2008).
7. C. Goschler, *Rudolf Virchow: Mediziner, Anthropologe, Politiker* (Cologne, 2002); C. Jenssen,'"Die Aufrüstung ist die Mikrobe des Krieges …". Rudolf Virchow (1821–1902), schillernder "Apostel des Friedens und der Versöhnung"', in T. Ruprecht (ed.), *Äskulap oder Mars? Ärzte gegen den Krieg* (Bremen, 1991), pp. 75–97.
8. On the idea of prevention, see M. Lengwiler and J. Madarász (eds), *Das präventive Selbst. Eine Kulturgeschichte moderner Gesundheitspolitik* (Bielefeld, 2010).
9. This definition differs from Mary Kaldor's definition of 'imaginary war'. She uses the concept to refer to the planning, conducting, and escalation of the Cold War on political and military levels. M. Kaldor, *Imaginary War: Understanding the East-West-Conflict* (Oxford, 1990).
10. 'US, Soviet doctors agree N-defence an illusion', *Boston Globe* (7 Dec. 1980).
11. IPPNW statement to the first congress, in: IPPNW Records (MC 408), Harvard Medical Library in the Francis A. Countway Library of Medicine, box 3/folder 1 Prospectus bound with corrections.
12. V. W. Sidel, J. Geiger and B. Lown, 'The physician's role in the post-attack period', *New England Journal of Medicine* 266 (1962), pp. 1126–55.
13. See on the history of the origin of IPPNW: I. Abrams, 'The origins of International Physicians for the Prevention of Nuclear War: the Dr James

E. Muller diaries', *Medicine, Conflict and Survival* 15:1 (1999), pp. 15-31; M. Evangelista, 'Transnational organisations and the Cold War', in M. P. Leffler and O. A. Westad (eds), *Cambridge History of the Cold War, vol. III: Endings* (Cambridge, 2010), pp. 400-21; B. Lown, *Prescription for Survival: A Doctor's Journey to End Nuclear Madness* (San Francisco, 2008). Following the foundation of IPPNW in Boston, national chapters developed in forty countries. Eastern bloc countries arranged their chapters top-down, while most in the West were built from the bottom up. There were some differences among the Eastern chapters. While Hungarian doctors were allowed to become members on an individual basis, the GDR chapter was composed entirely of functionaries.

14 See D. Porter, 'Introduction', in D. Porter (ed.), *Doctors, Politics and Society: Historical Essays* (Amsterdam, 1993), pp. 1-29, see pp. 2-4.
15 See on metaphorical aspects: O. Nohr, 'Vernunft als Therapie und Krankheit', *Forum Interdisziplinäre Begriffsgeschichte (FIB)* 2 (2013), pp. 8-20.
16 K. Malinowska-Sempruch and S. Gallagher, *War on Drugs, HIV/AIDS, and Human Rights* (New York, 2004).
17 P. Sarasin, *'Anthrax': Bioterror as Fact and Fantasy* (Cambridge, Mass., 2006).
18 Nohr, 'Vernunft als Therapie', pp. 8-9.
19 R. J. Kelly, Ko-lin Chin and R. Schatzberg (eds), *Handbook of Organized Crime in the United States* (Westport, Conn., 1994), p. 252.
20 D. Pick, *Faces of Degeneration: A European Disorder, c.1848-c.1918* (Cambridge, 1993).
21 D. Serlin (ed.), *Imagining Illness: Public Health and Visual Culture* (Minneapolis, 2010).
22 M. Hermes, *Krankheit: Krieg* (Essen, 2012).
23 J. T. V. M. de Jong (ed.), *Trauma, War, and Violence: Public Mental Health in Socio-cultural Context* (New York, 2002).
24 O. Kinberg, 'Mental disease as a present factor in the causation of war: a psycho-pathological study', *The Hibbert Journal* 37 (1938-/39), pp. 513-32. This connection was not only drawn in medical context but also from intellectuals and pacifists like Albert Einstein. See, e.g., *Why War: A Correspondence between Albert Einstein and Sigmund Freud*, trans. Stuart Gilbert (London, 1939).
25 Update IPPNW, May 1981, in: IPPNW Records (MC 408), Harvard Medical Library in the Francis A. Countway Library of Medicine, box 9/folder 65 Updates.
26 J. D. Frank, *Sanity and Survival in the Nuclear Age: Psychological Aspects of War and Peace* (New York, 1982); R. J. Lifton and R. A. Falk, *Indefensible Weapons. The Political and Psychological Case Against Nuclearism* (New York, 1982); H.-E. Richter, *Alle redeten vom Frieden. Versuch einer paradoxen Intervention* (Reinbek, 1981).
27 Lown, *Prescription for Survival*, p. 49.

28 B. Lown, 'Physicians and nuclear war', in Chivian et al. (eds), Last Aid, pp. 7–15, p. 15.
29 P. M. Haas (ed.): *Knowledge, Power, and International Policy Coordination* (Columbia, S.C., 1997); L. Dobusch and S. Quack, 'Epistemic communities and social movements. Transnational dynamics in the case of creative commons' MPIfG Discussion Paper 08/8 (2008), URL: http://edoc.vifapol.de/opus/volltexte/2009/1166/pdf/dp08_8.pdf (accessed 10 May 2015).
30 See Abrams, *Origins*.
31 Another important character during the start-up phase of IPPNW was James Muller, with experience in the USSR as visiting physician. See also Lown, *Prescription for Survival*, pp. 32–46.
32 The meeting was joined by the psychiatric Eric Chivian, who at the same time re-established 'Physicians for Social Responsibility' together with the pediatrician Helen Caldicott and the emergency doctor Ira Helfand. H. Caldicott, 'Die "Physicians for Social Responsibility" Ärztinnen und Ärzte in sozialer Verantwortung', in Ruprecht (ed.), *Äskulap*, pp. 501–6.
33 A. Iriye, *Global Community: The Role of International Organizations in the Making of the Contemporary World* (Berkeley, 2002), pp. 149–50.
34 See K.-H. Barth, 'Catalysts of change: scientists as transnational arms control advocates in the 1980s', in J. Krige and K.-H. Barth (eds) *Global Power Knowledge: Science and Technology in International Affairs* (Chicago, 2006), pp. 182–206.
35 See for the American protest: 'A crisis of confidence in the secular state', *Boston Sunday Globe* (20 June 1982).
36 See Statement to the Press: Beyond War. Working together we can build a World Beyond War, 5 Dec. 1984, in: IPPNW Records (MC 408), Harvard Medical Library in the Francis A. Countway Library of Medicine, box 16/folder 2 Beyond War Award 1984.
37 On the basis of Erving Goffman's sociological work on individual interaction and actor-network theory, Stephen Hilgartner examines modern scientific credibility as performance, focusing on American controversies over health and diet. S. Hilgartner, *Science on stage. Expert advice as public drama* (Stanford, Calif., 2000).
38 See Abrams, *Origins*, p. 16 with reference to M. R. Nussbaumer and J. A. Dilorio, 'The medicalization of nuclear disarmament claims', *Peace & Change* 11:1 (Apr. 1985), pp. 63–73.
39 E.g. Newsletter, Jan. 1981 from IPPNW, in IPPNW Records (MC 408), Harvard Medical Library in the Francis A. Countway Library of Medicine, box 1/folder 3 Geneva Meeting 1980. See also 'How do we influence the political process without becoming a political group? What are the bounds for a national affiliate without compromising the IPPNW charter?', in: Telex Bernard Lown to Andy Haines, 18 November 1984, in: IPPNW Records

(MC 408), Harvard Medical Library in the Francis A. Countway Library of Medicine, box 19/folder 5 Governance June–November 1984.
40 'US, Soviet doctors agree N-defense an illusion', *Boston Globe* (7 Dec. 1980).
41 As an early example: E.G. Virginia and T.G. Blocker, 'The Texas City disaster: A survey of 3000 casualties', *American Journal of Surgery* (November 1949), pp. 756–71.
42 S. R. Weart, *Nuclear Fear: A History of Images* (Cambridge, Mass., 1988); B. Ziemann, 'The code of protest: images of peace in the West German peace movements, 1945–1990', *Contemporary European History* 17 (2008), pp. 237–61.
43 W. M. Reddy, *The Navigation of Feeling: A Framework for the History of Emotions* (Cambridge, 2001), p. 129.
44 S. Schregel, 'Konjunktur der Angst. "Politik der Subjektivität" und "neue Friedensbewegung", 1979–1983', in B. Greiner, C. Th. Müller and D. Walter (eds), *Angst im Kalten Krieg* (Hamburg, 2009), pp. 495–520.
45 J. Bourke, *Fear: A Cultural History* (London, 2005).
46 Psychological Stress and Nuclear War. Report to Groups I and II on 22 March 1981, by James Titchener, M.D. [Airlie-House-Conference], in: IPPNW Records (MC 408), box 3/ folder 15: 1981.
47 E. Zerubavel, *The Elephant in the Room. Silence and Denial in Everyday Life* (New York, 2008).
48 J. E. Mack, 'Prologue', in Chivian et al. (eds) *Last Aid*, pp. 1–4, p. 1.
49 J. E. Mack: 'Psychosocial effects of the nuclear arms race', *Bulletin of the Atomic Scientists* (Apr. 1981), pp. 18–19. A video tape recording 'There's a Nuclear War going on inside me – what young people are saying about nuclear weapons' by Eric Chivian and Roberta Snow, in: Acc 94A-073 Series I, Box 8, Swarthmore Peace Collection.
50 H.-E. Richter, *Die Gruppe. Hoffnung auf einen neuen Weg sich selbst und andere zu befreien; Psychoanalyse in Kooperation mit Gruppeninitiativen* (Reinbek, 1978).
51 Report on the Cambridge Congress, UK 'Die Lebenden werden die Toten beneiden' *Süddeutsche Zeitung* (19 Apr. 1982).
52 H.-E. Richter, Engagierte Analysen – Interview mit Elena Pasca, URL, www.psychanalyse.lu/articles/RichterInterview.htm (accessed 10 May 2015).
53 A. D. Kauders, 'Drives in dispute: the West German student movement, psychoanalysis, and the search for a new emotional order, 1967–1971', *Contemporary European History* 44:4 (2011), pp. 711–31.
54 S. Maasen, J. Elberfeld, P. Eitler and M. Tändler (eds), *Das beratene Selbst. Zur Genealogie der Therapeutisierung in den 'langen' Siebzigern* (Bielefeld, 2011).
55 G. R. Bach and H. Molter (eds), *Psychoboom. Wege und Abwege moderner Therapie* (Reinbek, 1979). See M. Tändler and U. Jensen (eds), *Das Selbst zwischen Anpassung und Befreiung. Psychowissen und Politik im 20. Jahrhundert* (Göttingen, 2012).

56 L. Raphael, 'Embedding the human and social sciences in Western societies, 1880-1980: reflections on trends and methods of current research', in K. Brückweh, D. Schumann, R. F. Wetzell and B. Ziemann (eds), *Engineering Society: The Role of the Human and Social Sciences in Modern Societies, 1880-1980* (Basingstoke, 2012), pp. 41-58, p. 53.
57 E. S. Moskowitz, *In Therapy We Trust: America's Obsession with Self-Fulfillment* (Baltimore, Md., 2008); E. Illouz, *Saving the Modern Soul: Therapy, Emotions, and the Culture of Self-Help* (Berkeley, 2008).
58 Oncology also saw a psychologisation during this time identifying so-called 'cancer personalities' with a particular disposition to their illness. Susan Sontag describes the way in which the psychological description of disease primarily aims at the psychological classification of the patient. S. Sontag, *Illness as Metaphor* (London, 1988).
59 E. Kurz-Milcke and G. Gigerenzer (eds), *Experts in Science and Society* (Boston, 2004); M. Szöllösi-Janze, 'Der Wissenschaftler als Experte: Ko operationsverhältnisse von Staat, Militär, Wirtschaft und Wissenschaft 1914-1933', in D. Kaufmann (ed.), *Geschichte der Kaiser-Wilhelm-Gesellschaft im Nationalsozialismus. Bestandsaufnahme und Perspektiven der Forschung* (Göttingen, 2000), pp. 46-64.
60 Hilgartner, *Science on Stage*, p. 10.
61 *Ibid.*
62 *Ibid.*, pp. 7-19.
63 Brückweh, Schumann, Wetzell and Ziemann (eds), *Engineering Society*.
64 Lown, *Prescription for Survival*, p. 9.
65 Physicians Rally in Bonn to Protest Deployment, in: IPPNW Report, 2:1 (Winter 1984), p. 5.
66 On serious problems concerning fundraising, organisation and procedures during the congress, see Memo: Problems encountered in Cambridge, n.d., probably October 1982, in: IPPNW Records (MC 408), box 13/23.
67 Newsletter, Jan. 1981, IPPNW, in: IPPNW Records (MC 408), box 1/3.
68 Bernard Lown to Takeshi Ohkita, Research Institute for Nuclear Medicine and Biology Hiroshima University, 7 Nov. 1980, in: IPPNW Records (MC 408), box 6/8.
69 Memo Dr. Muller to IPPNW Members, Meeting with Officials from the State Department, Soviet Embassy and National Security on 5 March 1981, in: IPPNW Records (MC 408), box 4/31.
70 O. Ward, 'Physicians battle the nuclear threat', *Toronto Star* (3 Mar. 1981).
71 T. F. Gieryn, *Cultural boundaries of science: credibility on the line* (Chicago, 1999).
72 *Bulletin of Atomic Sciences* 37:6 (1981), p. 20.
73 R. J. Lifton, *Death in life. Survivors of Hiroshima* (New York, 1982). A critical approach to Lifton's theory: I. Chernus, *Nuclear madness. Religion and the psychology of the nuclear age* (Albany, 1991).

74 R. J. Lifton, 'Psychological effects of the atomic bombings', in E. Chivian et al. (eds), *Last Aid*, pp. 48–68.
75 R. J. Lifton, 'Script: Psychological effects of the atomic bomb [1981]', in IPPNW Records (MC 408), box 2/7.
76 Hilgartner, *Science on Stage*, p. 8.
77 'An expert committee, for example, not only provides advice but also explains, in direct and indirect ways, who it is and why it should be believed. Self-presentation is central to the science advisor's work.' *Ibid.* p. 9.
78 Video Cassettes of 'Moscow Telecast' in: PSR Papers, I Box 8, Acc. 94A-073 Series, Swarthmore Peace Collection.
79 'Der Frieden muss bewaffnet sein', *Die Zeit* (23 September 1983).
80 'Eye Opener', *The Times* (London) (7 July 1982).
81 Compilation 'Moscow Telecast of IPPNW', 1982, in: IPPNW Records (MC 408), box 5/9.
82 Notes of Administrative Meeting, 5 August 1982, in: IPPNW Records (MC 408), box 9/30.
83 J. Lofland, *Polite protesters: the American peace movement of the 1980s* (Syracuse, NY, 1993), pp. 237–8; H. Caldicott, *Nuclear Madness: What You Can Do!* [With a new chapter on Three Mile Island] (New York, 1980).
84 Bayerische Ärztinnen und Ärzte gegen Atomenergie; Berliner Ärzteinitiative gegen Atomenergie; Hamburger Ärzteinitiative gegen Atomenergie (eds), *Die Überlebenden werden die Toten beneiden: Ärzte warnen vor dem Atomkrieg. Materialien des Hamburger 'Medizinischen Kongresses zur Verhinderung des Atomkrieges' vom 19./20. September 1981* (Cologne, 1982).
85 C. Kemper, 'International, national, regional. Die Organisation 'Internationalen Ärzte zur Verhütung des Atomkrieges' und der Wandel im anti-atomaren Protest in der ersten Hälfte der 1980er Jahre', *Archiv für Sozialgeschichte* 52 (2012), pp. 555–76.
86 On the UK, see John W. Gleisner, 'The futility of civil defence', *Lancet* (Oct. 1980), p. 748 and L. Jones, 'Civil defence', *Lancet* (Nov., 1980), pp. 976–77.
87 In October 1981 Ronald Reagan announced efforts in civil defense to 'revitalize our strategic forces and maintain America's ability to keep the peace well into the next century'. Federal Emergency Management Agency. Civil Defense Program Overview, 1981, in: IPPNW Records (MC 408), box 5/20.
88 On national differences in the discussion see R. A. Jacobs, '"There are no civilians, we are all eat war": nuclear war shelter and survival narratives during the early Cold War', *Journal of American Culture* 30:4 (2007), pp. 401–16; G. Oakes, *The Imaginary War: Civil Defense and American Cold War Culture* (New York, 1994).
89 On West Germany until the 1960s, see F. Biess, '"Everybody has a chance": nuclear angst, civil defence, and the history of emotions in postwar West Germany', *German History* 27 (2009), pp. 215–43.

90 Summary of the IPPNW Meeting at the Harvard Faculty Club, 7 Oct. 1982, by Herbert Abrams, in: IPPNW Records (MC 408), Harvard Medical Library in the Francis A. Countway Library of Medicine, box 12/3.
91 As an example the arguments of Eric Chivian in 'Civil defence based on false assumption: MD', *Toronto Globe* (7 Dec. 1981).
92 F. Biess, 'The concept of panic in postwar Germany: military psychiatry and emotional preparation for nuclear war in the West German army', in F. Biess and D. Gross (eds), *Science and Emotions after 1945: A Transatlantic Perspective* (Chicago, 2014).
93 A. Haines, 'The possible consequences of a nuclear attack on London', in Chivian *et al.* (eds), *Last Aid*, pp. 163–72, p. 163.
94 About this widespread technique in the peace movement, see S. Schregel, *Der Atomkrieg vor der Wohnungstür. Eine Politikgeschichte der neuen Friedensbewegung in der Bundesrepublik 1970–1985* (Frankfurt am Main, 2011).
95 By contrast, the official rhetoric in West Germany avoided explicit connections. Biess, 'Everybody', p. 222.
96 Exemplary because of its psychiatric evaluation was the dam break at Buffalo Creek in 1972 with 125 deaths. See J. L. Titchener, 'Family and character change at Buffalo Creek', *American Journal of Psychiatry* 133 (1976), pp. 295–9; K. Erikson, *Everything in Its Path: Destruction of Community in the Buffalo Creek Flood* (New York, 1977).
97 Richter, *Alle redeten vom Frieden*, p. 12.
98 J. G. Blight, 'How might psychology contribute to reducing the risk of nuclear war?', *Political Psychology* 7:4 (1986), pp. 617–60.

11

Imagining the apocalypse: nuclear winter in science and the world

Paul Rubinson

Imagining Mars; imagining nuclear war

Although rigorously trained in the rules of the scientific method, the astronomer Carl Sagan frequently relied on his imagination. At times, in fact, he could only use his imagination, since his proclaimed field of exobiology consisted of the study of life in outer space – something not yet proven to exist. Sagan's imagination was especially active when it came to Mars; at one point he even pondered whether the moons of Mars were actually disguised alien vessels. In 1976, he finally had a chance to see the red planet for himself, thanks to photographs sent back to Earth from NASA's Viking missions. Although the experiments conducted there dashed Sagan's hopes by failing to find signs of life, the photographs provided him a particular thrill. At one point, he fashioned a large panoramic photo of the Mars horizon into a cylinder with the photo facing inwards, and placed it around his head. With this crude but effective virtual reality device, Sagan took himself to Mars. Coming along for the 'ride' was *Rolling Stone* journalist Timothy Ferris; the two men took turns at gazing at the Martian landscape, silent and awestruck.[1]

Sagan's imagination eventually shifted back to Earth, where, for decades, scientists, strategists and other thinkers had attempted to give a realistic portrayal of the massive death and suffering a nuclear war would cause. But in 1979, people around the world experienced a resurgence of nuclear fears as détente, a lessening of Cold War tensions, came to an end. Additionally, the increasingly hawkish rhetoric of the Reagan administration, starting in 1981, and the deployment of new nuclear missiles to both NATO and Warsaw Pact nations in 1983 made the threat of nuclear war more real than ever. Since a full-scale nuclear war had never happened, however, those hoping to prevent a nuclear disaster had to imagine what a nuclear holocaust would look like. This task eventually fell to Sagan and his scientific colleagues.

While nuclear weapons dominated the headlines in the early 1980s, Sagan and his colleagues looked at data from the Viking missions, especially ways in which particulate matter in the atmosphere cooled the surface of Mars during dust storms. They intuitively realised that something similar might happen on Earth in the aftermath of a nuclear war. When Sagan's group used this data to develop an innovative, scientific and controversial computer model of the effects of nuclear war, they were, in a sense, presenting a reliable image of an imaginary, post-apocalyptic world. After its creation in the lab, the nuclear winter theory then took on a life of its own, spanning the globe and forcing people worldwide to contemplate the destruction of the entire human species.[2] Fears that nuclear war would result in the end of humankind were not new. But never before had these fears been supported by such strong scientific evidence. Owing to this new scientific understanding, the nuclear apocalypse imagined by so many could be debated in increasingly real and accurate terms. These sobering predictions in turn increased the urgency of the global anti-nuclear movement and forced policymakers to reassess or reaffirm their established nuclear policies. Furthermore, by showing that nuclear war would result in an indiscriminate global slaughter, the nuclear winter theory encouraged the growth of a shared global ethos and a vision that nuclear war mattered not just as a part of the geopolitical chess match between the superpowers, but as a life or death issue for the entire planet.

Nuclear winter

In the late 1970s, Carl Sagan had begun to make the rare transition from scientist to media celebrity. In 1977, he had published a Pulitzer Prize-winning book called *The Dragons of Eden* on the origins and evolution of the human brain, and in 1980 he starred in *Cosmos*, the most-watched public television programme of the decade. Sagan's book that was based on the *Cosmos* TV series eventually became, according to the journal *Nature*, 'the best-selling science book ever published in the English language'. Equally at home in the lab or in Hollywood, Sagan served as a consultant for NASA missions as well as the in-house astronomer on *The Tonight Show with Johnny Carson*, a popular late-night variety show.[3]

Aside from his role as a populariser of science, Sagan was equally a committed political activist. In the early 1980s, Sagan began to speak out against nuclear weapons, and by 1983 he focused his efforts on the climatic effects of nuclear war. Writing in the journal *Science*, Sagan described how nuclear war would be worse than anyone imagined. Thinking on a scale beyond the nation-state, Sagan knew that, while tragic, a nuclear war would actually spare most of the world's population. This meant that the long-term effects might be as important as the war itself. Indeed, while the direct effects of nuclear war (i.e. thermonuclear explosions) would kill untold millions, that would be just the beginning of the carnage. The fires set by these explosions would release tonnes and tonnes of smoke, soot and particulate matter into the atmosphere, blotting out the sun and initiating a drastic cooling of the planet. 'Most striking are the extremely low temperatures occurring within 3 to 4 weeks after a major exchange', Sagan and his peers wrote. 'Even the smallest temperature decreases on land are ... enough to turn summer into winter.'[4] Elsewhere, Sagan explained that the soot in the atmosphere would block light and ruin the greenhouse effect that keeps the Earth temperate and liveable. Instead, nuclear war 'kicks the blanket off' and rapidly cools the atmosphere, unleashing an assault on global agriculture that would result in mass starvation. A nuclear war would be 'the equivalent of a hundred million Chernobyls', Sagan wrote, referencing the Soviet nuclear power disaster, 'a witch's brew of deadly assaults of life on Earth.'[5] Sagan and his co-authors evocatively called this phenomenon 'nuclear winter'.

The development of the nuclear winter hypothesis and the need to ensure its scientific credibility challenged Sagan to transform his vision from an imaginary threat into a scientific possibility. Well before the term 'nuclear winter' entered the public discourse, Sagan and his colleagues Richard P. Turco, Owen B. Toon, Thomas P. Ackerman and James B. Pollack – a group abbreviated as TTAPS – had analysed data of dust storms on Mars gathered during the Viking and Mariner missions; their analysis showed that debris in the atmosphere could drastically cool the planet. This finding seemed ominous to TTAPS when they looked at it in light of a recent hypothesis that a tremendous collision between an asteroid and the Earth drastically transformed the climate and sparked the extinction of the dinosaurs. The TTAPS team took this theory to mean that a severe climate change could cause mass extinctions on Earth. Finally, a 1982 article in an environmental science journal explained that the fires resulting from nuclear explosions released enough smoke to obscure sunlight for a substantial amount of time.[6]

During 1982 and 1983, the TTAPS scientists combined these three strains of thought and used a computer model from their volcanic studies to calculate the specific temperature drops that would follow various levels of nuclear wars on Earth. The TTAPS team set their analysis apart by paying special attention to the unique nature of fires in urban areas, which, because of the massive amounts of metal and plastic present, create particularly thick, dense smoke when burned. Obscuring the sun in this manner, TTAPS found, would cause temperatures on earth to plummet to −15 or −20 °C. Depending on the scale of the nuclear war, the particulate matter could spread to the Southern Hemisphere in as little as one or two weeks. Photosynthesis and food production would grind to a halt, meaning that anyone who survived a nuclear war would be unlikely to survive its aftermath. With about 17,000 nuclear warheads on Earth, the TTAPS scientists estimated that a nuclear winter scenario could be triggered by explosions equivalent to just 100 megatonnes.[7]

The peer review process

As a lifelong opponent of pseudoscience and self-appointed protector of the scientific method, Sagan knew that rigorous peer review of the nuclear winter hypothesis by his fellow scientists was essential. But since the urgency of an activist equally possessed Sagan, he was also anxious to present nuclear winter to the greater public. With Trident, cruise and SS-20 nuclear missiles scheduled for deployment in Europe in 1983, and increasingly belligerent rhetoric coming from the Reagan administration, Sagan decided to speed up the process. In fact, in early 1983 he had already begun to plan a conference at which he would publicly announce the theory of nuclear winter. Cognisant of the potential for controversy, the TTAPS scientists made a conscious effort to balance their desire for publicity with attempts to boost the theory's scientific credibility by subjecting it to peer review, or at least something resembling it. Rather than going public immediately, Sagan put the conference on hold and sent a long paper summarising his group's work to numerous colleagues. He also convened an unconventional meeting with scientists to review the theory in person, achieving something close to, yet in some ways still far from, conventional peer review.

Sagan arranged for between seventy and 100 physical and biological scientists to attend two meetings over five days in late April 1983 at the American Academy of Arts and Sciences in Cambridge, Massachusetts. One account of these meetings notes that 'It was understood that only if the [nuclear winter] data held up after peer review would the proposed public Conference be scheduled.' First of all, forty physicists and ten biologists heard the TTAPS presentation and commented on the paper draft. The scientists 'generally agreed with the conclusions of the report' regarding reduced sunlight and severe climate changes, though they did suggest 'minor adjustments'.[8] One observer later explained that the physicists 'had numerous questions about details but very little quarrel with the findings. Several of the scientists went home resolved to try the scenarios on *their* atmospheric models'. Next, the remaining scientists examined the 'the consensus results' of the first group and found 'general agreement' upon the 'devastating' and 'previously unforeseen' effects, including possible 'extermination' of humans and many wildlife species.[9] With this positive response, planning for the conference recommenced. At the same time, TTAPS submitted their nuclear winter research to the journal *Science*, where it would face traditional peer review and, if accepted, receive a boost in transforming nuclear winter from rough conjecture into scientific hypothesis.

While the TTAPS paper was being evaluated by *Science*, Sagan and many other scientists appeared at an elaborate scientific conference and press event titled 'The World after Nuclear War', where they dramatically announced the concept of nuclear winter to the public. On 31 October 1983, in Washington, D.C., scientists took turns at spelling out the threat, though political recommendations were strictly avoided. Soon after the conference, the TTAPS paper appeared in the 23 December 1983 issue of *Science*, having passed peer review, along with a companion piece on the biological effects of nuclear winter. This second paper was arguably the more dramatic one, as it insisted that 'the possibility of the extinction of *Homo Sapiens* cannot be excluded'.[10] Long the stuff of science fiction and American nightmares, the destruction of humankind now gained credence as a scientific possibility. And yet not everyone was convinced that, in developing the nuclear winter theory, Sagan's imagination had not got the better of him.

Much of the resistance to Sagan's claims about nuclear winter came from his ensuing campaign to use nuclear winter to argue for a drastic change in US and Soviet nuclear policies. The link between science and politics was obvious to Sagan. In the Winter 1983–84 issue of *Foreign Affairs*, he described how nuclear winter undermined the hubristic nuclear strategies devised by the superpowers over the nearly 40 years of the arms race. First, a nuclear first-strike would be 'tantamount to national suicide for the aggressor – *even if the attacked nation does not lift a finger to retaliate*'. Second, even nations far removed from a nuclear war were gravely threatened by nuclear winter. Third, nuclear winter revealed civil defence as pointless, since survivors would simply starve to death in the wake of biological and agricultural collapse.[11]

Despite Sagan's urgency, the public was not immediately convinced. The *New York Times* greeted nuclear winter with harsh scepticism in an editorial, comparing it with ABC's melodramatic anti-nuclear TV film *The Day After* and asking, 'Why this deluge of restating the obvious?' Surely everyone already knew 'that nuclear disaster is hazardous to human health'. Deterrence remained the best way to prevent nuclear war; 'Deterrence works because it is based on horror ... There's no visible alternative to deterrence, no matter how ghastly the ways nuclear war would kill.'[12] At this point in the 1980s, the public seemed to have accepted the belief that nuclear war would create something approaching apocalypse; in fact, this view was so common that the *New York Times* editors were apparently tired of hearing it. When members of the Reagan administration began referring to 'winnable' nuclear wars, however, many Americans began to wonder if US policy had shifted from deterrence to actually preparing to wage a nuclear war. If each superpower maintained huge stockpiles of nuclear weapons merely to deter an attack, the threat of nuclear war was, to some extent, imaginary. But, with a Pentagon official casually remarking that 'with enough shovels to go around, everyone's going to make it', nuclear war no longer seemed a hypothetical scenario.[13]

In trying to scientifically prove the possibility of billions of deaths, Sagan inevitably faced heavy scepticism from a number of scientists. S. Fred Singer, a professor of environmental sciences and a consultant to the White House science advisor, challenged the theory on both scientific and political grounds. In the *Wall Street Journal*, Singer, like most opponents of the nuclear winter hypothesis, attacked the theory as ultimately too uncertain to be useful. The 'range of uncertainty is so great', Singer wrote, 'that the prediction isn't particularly useful.'[14] Sagan responded by emphasising the large number of scientists who 'carefully reviewed' the TTAPS study and who drew 'roughly similar conclusions'. Singer, according to Sagan, 'offers no calculations. Our extensive computer modelling takes account of a variety of plausible values of parameters associated with coagulation of particles, rainout and other scavenging mechanisms.'[15]

Sagan's assertions of scientific reliability frequently fell on deaf ears. In the *Bulletin of the Atomic Scientists*, Joseph V. Smith reviewed the published proceedings of the World after Nuclear War conference. Smith instantly cast doubt on the theory, asking, 'If we cannot accurately forecast the weather a week in advance, what is the meaning of "nuclear winter"?'

Smith also questioned the TTAPS scientists' objectivity: 'the more uncertain a prediction', he wrote, 'the more likely an emotional discussion'.[16] By questioning the objectivity of scientists involved in the study of nuclear winter, critics robbed the theory of its value as an anti-nuclear argument.

Acceptance from the editorial staff of *Nature*, perhaps the most prestigious science journal of the time, would have given the nuclear winter theory unimpeachable scientific credentials, but this was not to be. Instead, the journal's editor, John Maddox, openly scoffed at nuclear winter in his initial editorial on the theory, asking that TTAPS's conclusions 'be plainly stamped with the label QUALITATIVE for fear that their apparent precision may prove spurious'. The TTAPS paper, he wrote, 'is less than convincing', as was demonstrated by 'the pardonable simplicity' of its authors' calculations.[17]

In contrast to the journal's editor, however, *Nature*'s pages bristled with healthy debate, as scientists from around the world weighed in on the significance of a wide array of data to the study of nuclear winter, including meteors, volcanoes, sunspots, atmospheric humidity and even 'long-term seasonal cryospheric interactions with ... sea ice/thermal inertia feedback'. The debate over nuclear winter fell within the realm of normal scientific discourse, and the participants held each other to the standards of science. When S. Fred Singer contended that a nuclear war would cause mere 'patch clouds which thin out rapidly – hardly a cataclysmic nuclear winter', other scientists criticised Singer for having 'not offered quantitative grounds' for his doubts about nuclear winter.[18]

The obvious political significance of the nuclear winter hypothesis, however, meant that debate over the theory would go well beyond the scientific discussions of complex data and events. Edward Teller, the physicist, co-developer of the thermonuclear bomb and long-time nemesis of the anti-nuclear movement, rushed to challenge Sagan's anti-nuclear science head-on. In one article, Teller scolded Sagan: 'Highly speculative theories of worldwide destruction – even the end of life on Earth – used as a call for a particular kind of political action serve neither the good reputation of science nor dispassionate political thought.'[19] Because nuclear winter had become an argument for a political demand (one with which Teller disagreed), its critics could dub the theory as more exaggerated imagination than hard science.

Sagan held fast to the scientific reliability of nuclear winter studies. In *Nature* he rebutted Teller's assertions on fallout and the ozone layer as having 'no quantitative foundation'. His claim that the climatic effects of dust would be 'by no means severe' was 'a conclusion with insufficient technical base and in the face of contrary evidence'. Teller could only explain away nuclear winter by 'invoking a "meteorological miracle" … that is, speculative "abnormal mechanisms," as opposed to careful quantitative calculations'.[20]

Although Sagan had utter confidence in the science behind nuclear winter, spending time on intricate debates over scientific details was best left to others. The National Academy of Sciences (NAS) began a study (eventually published in 1984), as did the Scientific Committee on the Problems of the Environment (SCOPE) (launched in October 1983 and completed in late 1985), studies that Sagan felt would confirm the accuracy of the theory. Arguing with partisan scientists such as Teller and Singer promised only to waste Sagan's strengths: the ability to speak to non-scientists.

After appearing at three major congressional hearings on nuclear winter between July 1984 and March 1985, Sagan had clearly grown weary of defending the scientific integrity of nuclear winter studies in the face of hostile attacks more political than scientific in nature. Science did not translate easily into political action. He attempted to address the dilemma faced by nations that confronted a threat that was at once very real but also uncertain in many respects in a 29 December 1984 letter to the *New York Times*. Obsessing over the uncertainties of nuclear winter, Sagan began, was simply an excuse for inaction. 'Nuclear winter is not amenable to experimental verification – at least not more than once', he wrote, 'and few of us wish to perform the experiment. It is possible to diminish the range of uncertainty, but not to be absolutely sure, short of nuclear war itself. This is not an unfamiliar circumstance for policymakers who must make decisions in the face of uncertainty'. No natural disaster was ever entirely predictable, and yet governments frequently took measures to protect against floods, droughts and earthquakes. So, he reasoned, a refusal to take steps against nuclear winter was simply evidence of folly.[21]

Nuclear winter and the world

Although scientists, the public, and political leaders in the United States struggled (or refused) to accept the implications of nuclear winter, the threat it posed quickly mobilised people around the world. While nuclear winter had implications for the residents of the United States and Soviet Union, the most dramatic – and arguably cruel – revelations were for those living beyond the borders of the superpowers. In Europe, where a powerful anti-nuclear movement had already begun, residents pounced on nuclear winter as evidence of nuclear madness in Moscow and Washington, since even a first strike would result in suicide for the aggressor, regardless of retaliation. Europeans thus used the opportunity to move towards more Eurocentric ways of ending the Cold War. For many nations in the developing world, the realisation that, even far removed from any nuclear conflict, they faced certain doom served to enhance efforts towards a non-aligned approach to the Cold War. As Sagan put it, 'Nuclear Winter is a way for nuclear weapons to find and kill those who live far from cities.'[22]

Demands for Sagan's time came even from some unexpected sources. In 1984, John Paul II invited Sagan to brief him on the concept of nuclear winter. Despite being an avowed and intense atheist whose popular novel *Contact* pitted science against religion, Sagan accepted the invitation. After the meeting, the Pope released a statement warning the world of the danger of nuclear winter.[23] International organisations saw nuclear winter as a sobering reminder of reality without the contentious debate over models and uncertainties. An open letter to Reagan and Soviet leader Yuri Andropov from the International Physicians for the Prevention of Nuclear War mentioned nuclear winter as one of the reasons that nuclear weapons have put 'all human life … in critical condition'.[24] In Britain, the Christian Campaign for Nuclear Disarmament, an offshoot of the larger CND organisation, relied on nuclear winter as evidence that the threat of nuclear weapons 'has grown worse', referring to the nuclear winter hypothesis as laying bare 'the probably catastrophic consequences of a nuclear war for our environment and all living things, and therefore the risks which the nuclear powers are taking with God's creation'.[25] To coincide with the third European Nuclear Disarmament (END) Convention in Perugia, Italy, the editors of the *ENDpapers* reprinted Sagan's 'Nuclear War and Climatic Catastrophe' in summer 1984.[26]

On 28 January 1985, the leaders of Argentina, Greece, India, Mexico, Sweden, and Tanzania gathered in New Delhi to issue a 'Declaration on the Arms Race'. Their statement showed that nuclear winter had indeed alerted peripheral states to their own powerlessness at the hands of the superpowers. 'Almost imperceptibly, over the last four decades', they stated,

> every nation and every human being has lost ultimate control over their own life and death. For all of us, it is a small group of men and machines in cities far away who can decide our fate … As a result of recent atmospheric and biological studies, there have been new findings which indicate that in addition to blast, heat and radiation, nuclear war, even on a limited scale,

would trigger an arctic nuclear winter which may transform the earth into a darkened, frozen planet, posing unprecedented peril to all nations, even those far removed from the nuclear explosions. We are convinced that this makes it still more pressing to take preventive action to exclude forever the use of nuclear weapons and the occurrence of a nuclear war.[27]

Since the mass destruction of the United States was all but guaranteed in a nuclear war, the ensuing destruction of the non-aligned world remained, perhaps, somewhat abstract in American minds. But to those living far from ground zero of the Third World War, nuclear winter was no abstraction.

Geography alone did not dictate the response to nuclear winter. Although Europe stood at the centre of nearly every nuclear war scenario, nuclear winter still managed to inspire anti-nuclear sentiment there. In an April 1985 address to the Council on Foreign Relations, Willy Brandt, former chancellor of West Germany and head of the Social Democratic Party at the time, declared that 'there is general agreement now that even a limited nuclear war would trigger an arctic nuclear winter which may transform the earth into a darkened frozen planet posing unprecedented peril to all nations, even those far removed from the actual nuclear weapons'. He went on to declare the possession of nuclear weapons to be 'a crime … worthy of universal contempt'.[28]

The threat of nuclear winter also resonated with religious groups. In April 1986, Bishops of the United Methodist Church released a statement on Cold War nuclear policy that drew moral outrage from nuclear winter. Their pastoral letter stated: 'We have said a clear and unconditioned "no" to nuclear war and to any use of nuclear weapons. We have concluded that nuclear deterrence is a position which cannot receive the church's blessing'. A 'foundation document' that accompanied the letter directly linked their challenge to nuclear winter: 'We write in defense of Creation. We do so because the Creation itself is under attack. Air and water, trees and fruits and flowers, birds and fish and cattle, all children and youth, women and men live under the darkening shadows of a threatening nuclear winter'. The Bishops concluded that 'The ideology of deterrence must not receive the churches' blessing'.[29]

Increasingly in Europe and elsewhere, nuclear winter brought together critiques of nuclear war, human rights violations and environmental degradation. After France paid New Zealand reparations for sinking Greenpeace's *Rainbow Warrior* vessel, the New Zealand government used the money to fund a study of nuclear winter, while the British Labour Party relied specifically on nuclear winter for their opposition to the nuclear defence of Europe in 1986.³⁰ At a European Nuclear Disarmament conference in June 1985, a workshop on British–French co-operation recommended the dubbing into French of a nuclear winter film.³¹ Although rooted in the Cold War, the nuclear winter theory allowed critics of the Cold War to envision transnational values that rose above the bipolar conflict.

Nuclear winter in the Soviet Union

On 8 December 1983, Senators Edward Kennedy (Democrat, Massachusetts) and Mark Hatfield (Republican, Oregon), co-sponsors of the 1982 House Freeze resolution, brought Sagan to their forum on the worldwide consequences of nuclear war. Sagan mentioned the broad array of scientific institutions in the United States and overseas studying nuclear winter, and claimed that three-dimensional models appeared to confirm the TTAPS study. He adamantly implored his Congressional hosts to rethink nuclear policies. If US nuclear weapons can accidentally destroy the United States, he asked, is a huge arsenal even a credible deterrent? Sagan made it clear that a minimum deterrent – with a maximum explosive power below the nuclear winter threshold – was feasible and patriotic for both superpowers. He described a nuclear first strike as 'An elaborate way of committing national suicide', adding that 'The ashes of communism and capitalism will be indistinguishable.'³²

The forum notably included Soviet scientists who had also been studying nuclear winter. Soviet scientist Vladimir V. Alexandrov discussed how his three-dimensional model showed 'significant cooling' and presented other evidence that the post-nuclear war environment would be 'hostile to human beings'. Alexander S. Pavlov stated that a nuclear war would destroy humanity, while Sergei Kapitza dubbed deterrence 'dubious' because of nuclear winter. Yevgeny P. Velikhov spoke last and described nuclear weapons as suicidal. A commentary in the *New York Times* saw the forum as having 'made short work' of the Pentagon's arguments for SDI and its claims that a nuclear war could remain limited and winnable.³³

Throughout his nuclear winter campaign, Sagan had blamed both US and Soviet officials for the dangerous predicament in which the world found itself by the mid-1980s. Sagan accordingly paid attention to the extent to which the nuclear winter theory circulated in the Soviet Union. Based on articles in *Pravda* and coverage of nuclear winter on Soviet television, Sagan estimated that 'there is continuing public discussion in the Soviet Union about nuclear winter', and that 'there has been at least some permeation of the understanding of nuclear winter to the Soviet public'.[34] A brief survey of Soviet articles on nuclear winter shows that Sagan was perhaps overly optimistic in even this modest assessment. One article from late 1983 in the Soviet newspaper *Sovetskaya Rossiya* used nuclear winter to rip into the 'inhuman aspirations of the US imperialists, who are pushing the world towards nuclear catastrophe'.[35] *Izvestia* at one point described the nuclear winter hypothesis as 'incontrovertible', explaining that 'anything that survives the nuclear massacre will freeze to death'. Another article, from February 1986, emphasised that even a war fought with conventional weapons could cause an effect 'similar to the "nuclear winter" one'.[36]

The appearance of these sporadic news stories gives some small indication that, as Sagan and Alexandrov claimed, the Soviet public had perhaps a degree of awareness of the nuclear winter threat, if not the contentious arguments over its scientific validity and political implications. But other sources indicate that small segments of the Soviet population felt that authorities under the direct control of the state were not being as forthcoming as possible about nuclear winter. The theory inspired at least one anti-nuclear protest in Moscow on 12 April 1985, where protesters shouted 'tell the truth about the Nuclear Winter phenomenon to our people'. Mass arrests followed the demonstration, and one of the participants was arrested a few months later for 'requesting greater publicity about the nuclear winter'.[37]

Not all nuclear winter activism in the Soviet Union resulted in repression, however. In October 1985, the Nobel committee awarded the 1985 Peace Prize to the International Physicians for the Prevention of Nuclear War (IPPNW), a global organisation led by one US physician (Bernard Lown) and one Soviet physician (Evgeni Chazov). The Nobel Peace Prize presentation speech hailed the group and specifically mentioned its efforts to enlighten the public about 'atomic winter' in the West and the East.[38] In their respective Nobel lectures, both Chazov and Lown mentioned nuclear winter in order to justify calls for nuclear disarmament. Lown in particular expounded at length on the scientific evidence from nuclear winter studies.

> The advent of the nuclear age posed an unprecedented question: not whether war would exact yet more lives but whether war would preclude human existence altogether ... Nuclear war, they found, could blanket the sky with smoke, dust, and soot, creating a pall of all-pervasive darkness and frigid cold. The impact on climate could last for several years, not sparing

the Southern Hemisphere. But there is more. Since cities are enormous storehouses of combustible synthetics, raging fire storms would release into the air a Pandora's box of deadly toxins. When dust, poisons, and soot finally cleared, another plague would be visited on the unfortunate survivors; high levels of ultraviolet light caused by depletion of atmospheric ozone would take an additional toll.

For his part, Chazov had appeared on Soviet television expressing how nuclear war meant 'death to all human beings', and in his Nobel lecture, Chazov described nuclear winter as 'bound to cap the catastrophe' of nuclear war.[39] While Chazov's Nobel prize was not without controversy among Soviet peace activists, the prestige of the award went a long way to legitimise both nuclear winter and the Soviet anti-nuclear movement.

Over time, Soviet officials appeared to endorse the theory as a call for a change in the arms race. Soviet Foreign Minister Eduard Shevardnadze bemoaned nuclear winter in a speech at the United Nations, and hoped that, in the future, 'the word "winter" … [would] retain in all languages of the world the one and only meaning, its original one, and be identified solely with the season of the year which is beautiful and joyful in its own way'. Mikhail Gorbachev had clearly absorbed the implications of nuclear winter when in an August 1986 speech he mentioned that using even a 'small' number of nuclear weapons 'would be a catastrophe, an irreversible catastrophe, and if someone still dares to make a first nuclear strike, he will doom himself to agonising death, not even from a retaliatory strike, but from the consequences of the explosion of his own warheads'.[40] Gorbachev by that point had begun to advocate for nuclear disarmament and pursue negotiations with the West.

Nuclear winter as metaphor

The TTAPS team chose the phrase 'nuclear winter' to serve as a metaphor, albeit only barely. The climatic effects of a nuclear war would indeed resemble a severe winter, according to their predictions. And yet the evocative phrase served to awaken in the mind a vision of what the planet would look like after a nuclear conflict – a vision that its creators hoped would remain imaginary. Nuclear winter stands out among metaphors of the nuclear age in that it derives from the nuclear age itself. Previous words used to describe a nuclear war came from earlier, even ancient, times. Apocalypse, Armageddon, holocaust – all these were used at times to alert humanity to the unthinkable destruction of a nuclear war, but these metaphors also derive from events with their own meaning. In fact, many of these end-of-the-world scenarios have been part of human culture for millennia, with nuclear war playing a resonant, but not necessarily new role.[41] Nuclear winter, by contrast, reminded the public of the present and the future, one very much threatened by nuclear weapons.

The scientists thinking about nuclear war and the end of life on Earth hoped to bring scientific credibility to the concept, but also needed to communicate with the greater public. Nuclear war remained all but invisible to the people of the 1980s; aside from Hiroshima and Nagasaki, the idea inevitably remained elusive and imaginary. Adding a level of obscurity was the fact that, aside from the direct effects of a nuclear explosion, nuclear war killed in nearly invisible ways, including fallout, radiation, and climate change. Even deterrence, which had allegedly kept the nuclear peace since 1949, was premised on a bluff, the imagined assurance that retaliation would come swift and deadly. But the false confidence produced by deterrence had lulled people around the world into seeing nuclear war as unlikely, frustrating generations of anti-nuclear activists in the process. So new metaphors and similes appeared frequently in the 1980s, aimed at rousing the public from its apathy towards nuclear weapons.

At first, Sagan had discussed the Third World War in terms of the Second World War: just a single nuclear weapon contained 'the destructive force of the entire Second World War', he wrote, while nuclear missiles were 'genies of death patiently awaiting the rubbing of the lamps'. The speed and destructive power of a nuclear war was the equivalent of 'a World War II every second for the length of a lazy afternoon'.[42] But nuclear war would be very different from any previous conflict, and so the descriptors became more unique. One of the earlier studies of the environmental impacts of nuclear war in 1982 had the subtitle 'Twilight at Noon', while Paul Ehrlich, the author of *The Population Bomb*, a warning about overpopulation, predicted that nuclear winter would kill 'virtually all land plants' in the Northern Hemisphere, and most animals would die, leaving 'rats, roaches, and flies the most prominent animals shortly after World War III'.[43] Jonathan Schell's masterwork *The Fate of the Earth*, about the destruction of the planet following a nuclear war, contained a section entitled: 'A Republic of Insects and Grass'. For many observers in the 1980s, the combination of science and metaphor proved convincing. At a congressional hearing, the aptly named Sidney G. Winter of the Yale economics department exclaimed that the TTAPS study 'is quite unprecedented in the credibility and explicitness of its apocalyptic speculations' and 'must be considered to inaugurate a new era in the discussion of nuclear armaments'.[44]

Not everyone in the debate found these metaphors convincing. Although science ostensibly reflects the reality of nature, it is not immune to counter-claims. Ronald Reagan frequently dismissed the anti-nuclear movement's arguments as out of touch with reality. In a speech to evangelicals, Reagan blasted advocates of a nuclear Freeze as pursuing 'merely the illusion of peace. The reality is that we must find peace through strength.'[45]

By 1986, nuclear winter had been roundly criticised by many scientists and politicians. The theory nevertheless retained some credibility, and so some scientists rushed to come up with a less apocalyptic version of the theory, complete with a new metaphor. In the summer of 1986, Thompson and Schneider of the NCAR published 'Nuclear Winter Reappraised' in *Foreign Affairs*, the same venue in which Sagan announced the dire policy implications of nuclear winter three years earlier. Its authors intended this article to sound the death knell for the nuclear winter theory. Their survey of recent studies had convinced Thompson and Schneider that nuclear winter had been reduced 'to a vanishingly low level of probability'. The original 'global freeze scenarios' and 'apocalyptic conclusions' predicted by TTAPS were not likely 'on scientific grounds', nor was there evidence of any threshold. Thus the two aspects of nuclear winter 'with the most important implications for policy have been removed'. The three-dimensional models showed, according to Thompson and Schneider, that average temperature changes 'are considerably smaller' than the TTAPS one-dimensional model, changes that 'more closely describe a nuclear "fall" than a nuclear winter'. Specifically, ocean warmth, smoke rainout and a smoke-enhanced greenhouse effect would prevent severe cooling. They somewhat incongruously added that the remaining problems of nuclear 'fall' could 'produce unprecedented worldwide human misery', such as 'mass starvation' in India. In all, Thompson and Schneider concluded, the global effects could still outweigh the direct effects of nuclear war.[46] Although heralding the defeat of the nuclear winter theory, Thompson and Schneider's article merely gave the effects of nuclear winter a different and less-catchy name.

The *New York Times* picked up the metaphor in a 1986 article about 'nuclear autumn', in which Thompson regretted how scientists had gone public with nuclear winter: 'People really have in their minds the image of frozen lakes and frozen cornfields and having to dig through frozen ground to bury the dead, and those images are too extreme. It was an excellent attention grabber, but those deep-freeze images are an exaggeration.' One member of the TTAPS team disputed the notion that a milder scenario overturned the original concern, asking 'Does the world have to freeze to an ice cube before people become concerned about what's going to happen?' Schneider admitted receiving 'a lot of unhappy reaction from our former friends', but consoled himself by pledging his allegiance to scientific objectivity: 'One has to clear the air sooner or later ... We're trying to substitute credibility for drama.'[47]

The metaphor mattered little, however, since in either scientific scenario, billions of people would perish. The studies that largely confirmed the accuracy of the nuclear winter theory explicitly described the effects of a nuclear war without relying on metaphor. A February 1987 workshop on the environmental effects of nuclear war that took place in Bangkok reaffirmed that agricultural systems 'are the most vulnerable to the physical and societal disruptions that could follow a large-scale nuclear war'. Agriculture in the Northern Hemisphere would be limited or even shut down for the first (and maybe other) growing seasons after nuclear war. 'For most countries, and thus for most of the people on earth', the scientists agreed, 'the food would run out in a matter of a few months if there were no agricultural production for just one season ... *Consequently, the majority of the earth's human populations is vulnerable to starvation following a large-scale nuclear war.*' As had Sagan, SCOPE pointed out that

> people living far from the scenes of direct destruction and playing no central role in a nuclear war would be at a risk of losing their lives through the *indirect* effects of nuclear war. The number of people who might starve or die from diseases associated with insufficient food could vastly exceed the number of people who would die from direct effects of such a war.[48]

By the end of the 1980s, the nuclear winter metaphor may have disappeared, but its predictions remained.

Conclusion

Nuclear war was never an abstract threat – at numerous points in the Cold War, the superpowers came dangerously close to the real thing. Yet the threat the weapons posed was in some ways imaginary, since outside of Hiroshima and Nagasaki, the world had no chance of witnessing such an event. Films, songs and other works of art frequently portrayed nuclear war, but by existing only in people's imagination, nuclear weapons in some ways became easier to live with. Carl Sagan's nuclear winter theory dealt with this imagination gap in three ways. First of all, it recognised a threat that many had feared in general terms but no one had reliably foreseen – a death toll in the billions and perhaps approaching human extinction. Second, nuclear winter made the leap from imagination to scientific probability. An event predicted by science makes a much stronger case for policy change, which perhaps explains why US policymakers felt compelled alternately to endorse, co-opt, or deny the theory. Finally, the threat of nuclear winter underpinned the idea of nuclear war as catastrophic event that risked billions of lives at a time when government figures in the United States claimed nuclear war was survivable, if not winnable.

The theory endured beyond the Cold War, being used to warn against the burning of oil fields during the Gulf War and receiving further verification in studies from the 1990s and 2000s.[49] Nuclear winter earned the ultimate sign of maturation in the early 1990s when one science textbook devoted an entire chapter to the concept.[50] After the Cold War, Sagan transformed nuclear winter into an environmental argument incorporating the greenhouse effect and global warming. In 2006 and 2007, further analyses by Robock using the most recent computer models indicated that in some scenarios, just '100 Hiroshima-sized' nuclear weapons could trigger a nuclear winter, a number startlingly lower than the original TTAPS estimate.[51] During his lifetime, Sagan had received mostly scorn for his foray into nuclear winter studies and anti-nuclear activism. But the theory spread nevertheless, influencing activists and governments. The SCOPE study of the climatic effects of nuclear war, conducted under the auspices of the International Council of Scientific Unions, affirmed the global threat of climate change caused by nuclear war, and downplayed the uncertainties associated with nuclear winter studies. Mark Harwell, a participant in the SCOPE study, argued that biological systems were so fragile 'that many of the uncertainties … are unimportant'. In a nuclear war, he estimated that more people would die in India than in the United States and Soviet Union combined; more would die in Africa than in Europe.[52]

Meteorologist Alan Robock summarised new experiments in 1989, stating that 'The basic theory of nuclear winter has remained unchanged since it was first described.' The cold and the dark would ruin at least one growing season, 'resulting in a global famine … In a nuclear war between the United States and the Soviet Union, more people would die in India or China than in the target countries combined.' Continued research since 1983 had only 'strengthened the scientific basis of the theory'. The concept of nuclear fall, he wrote, allowed people to believe that the effects would be mild, while they would actually be quite awful. 'The consensus on nuclear winter is broad', he asserted, citing studies by the NAS, the Soviet Academy of Sciences, Los Alamos, Livermore and many others. Noting with regret the decreased interest in Congress, Robock maintained that the 'implications of nuclear winter are clear: the use of nuclear weapons would be suicide for all the peoples of the planet'. Still other experiments and analyses added to the consensus.[53] Thus the nuclear winter theory offered to show the destruction of nuclear war without the world having to witness one. Certainly, not everyone believed the theory's predictions, and no one can know how many concrete changes occurred because of the theory. But in revealing the truly global threat that nuclear winter presented to the world, people around the world could see their shared peril in scientific terms.

Notes

1 K. Davidson, *Carl Sagan: A Life* (New York, 1999), pp. 126–30, 185, 281; W. Poundstone, *Carl Sagan: A Life in the Cosmos* (New York, 1999), pp. 55–58, pp. 144–6, 205.
2 On nuclear winter, see L. Badash, *A Nuclear Winter's Tale: Science and Politics in the 1980s* (Cambridge, 2010), and P. Rubinson, 'The global effects of nuclear winter: science and antinuclear protest in the United States and the Soviet Union during the 1980s', *Cold War History* 14:1 (2014), pp. 47–69.
3 C. Chyba, 'An exobiologist's life search', *Nature* 401 (28 Oct. 1991), p. 857; Davidson, *Carl Sagan*, p. 281; Poundstone, *Carl Sagan*.
4 R. P. Turco, O. B. Toon, T. P. Ackerman, J. B. Pollack and C. Sagan, 'Nuclear winter: global consequences of multiple nuclear explosions', *Science*, New Series, 222:4630 (23 Dec. 1983), pp. 1283–92.
5 C. Sagan and R. P. Turco, *A Path Where No Man Thought: Nuclear Winter and the End of the Arms Race* (New York, 1990), pp. 23–4, 53–9.
6 Sagan and Turco, *Path*, pp. 95–101; L. W. Alvarez, W. Alvarez, F. Asaro and H. V. Michel, 'Extraterrestrial cause for the Cretaceous-Tertiary extinction', *Science*, New Series, 208:4448 (6 June 1980), pp. 1095–108; P. Crutzen and J. Birks, 'The atmosphere after a nuclear war: twilight at noon', *Ambio* (1982), pp. 114–25.
7 Turco *et al.*, 'Nuclear winter', pp. 1283–92.
8 P. Ehrlich, C. Sagan, D. Kennedy and W. Orr Roberts, *The Cold and the Dark: The World After Nuclear War* (New York, 1984), pp. xv–xvi, 31; A. Ehrlich, 'About the conference', in 'Nuclear winter: a forecast of the climatic and biological effects of nuclear war', *Bulletin of the Atomic Scientists*, 40:4 (Apr. 1984), pp. 12S–13S.
9 Ehrlich, 'About the conference', pp. 12S–13S; Ehrlich *et al.*, *Cold and the Dark*, p. xvi. (Emphasis in the original.)

10 Ehrlich *et al.*, *The Cold and the Dark*, p. xviii, 35; Turco *et al.*, 'Nuclear winter', and P. Ehrlich *et al.*, 'Long-term biological consequences of nuclear war', *Science*, New Series, 222:4630 (23 Dec. 1983), p. 1299.
11 C. Sagan, 'Nuclear war and climatic catastrophe: some policy implications', *Foreign Affairs* (Winter 1983/ 1984), p. 276, p. 292. (Emphasis in the original.)
12 'The Winter After the Bomb', *New York Times*, 6 Nov. 1983, E20.
13 R. Scheer, *With Enough Shovels: Reagan, Bush, and Nuclear War* (New York, 1982).
14 S. F. Singer, 'The big chill? challenging a nuclear scenario', *Wall Street Journal*, 3 Feb. 1984, p. 22. See also S. F. Singer, 'Nuclear winter and nuclear freeze', *Disarmament: A Periodic Review by the United Nations* VII:3 (Autumn 1984), pp. 63–71.
15 'The chilling aftermath of a nuclear war', reprinted in *Congressional Record*, Senate, 98th Congress, 2nd Session, 23 Feb. 1984, p. 3083.
16 Review of *The Cold and the Dark: The World after Nuclear War*, by J. V. Smith, *Bulletin of the Atomic Scientists* 41:1 (Jan. 1985), pp. 49–51.
17 J. Maddox, 'From Santorini to Armageddon', *Nature*, 307 (12 Jan. 1984), p. 107; J. Maddox, 'Nuclear winter not yet established', *Nature*, 308 (1 Mar. 1984), p. 11. (Emphasis in the original.)
18 T. Reuter, 'Telling all', *Nature* 311 (25 Oct. 1984), p. 700; A. D. Brown, 'Teller's cold comfort', *Nature* 312 (13 Dec. 1984), p. 587; V. C. LaMarche Jr. and K. K. Hirschboeck, 'Nuclear war models', *Nature* 309 (17 May 1984), p. 203; W. H. Bown and J. Peczkis, 'Nuclear war – counting the cost', *Nature* 310 (9 Aug. 1984), p. 455; A. Robock, 'Snow and ice feedbacks prolong effects of nuclear winter', *Nature* 310 (23 Aug. 1984), pp. 667, 670; J. Katz, 'Atmospheric humidity in the nuclear winter', *Nature* 311 (4 Oct. 1984), p. 417; S. F. Singer, S. L. Thompson, S. H. Schneider and C. Covey, 'Is the "nuclear winter" real?' *Nature* 310 (23 Aug. 1984), p. 625.
19 E. Teller, 'Widespread after-effects of nuclear war', *Nature* 310 (23 Aug. 1984), pp. 621–4.
20 Sagan, 'Confidential draft: on minimizing the consequences of nuclear war', late 1984, Folder 22.25: Sagan, Box 22, HB Papers, 1–2. See also C. Sagan, 'On minimizing the consequences of nuclear war', *Nature* 317 (10 Oct. 1985), pp. 485–8.
21 C. Sagan, 'A nuclear theory that can't be tested', *New York Times*, 29 Dec. 1984, p. 20; J. Katz, 'Nuclear winter effects not settled', *New York Times*, 5 Jan. 1985, p. 20.
22 Sagan and Turco, *Path*, p. 73.
23 Davidson, *Carl Sagan*, pp. 57, 80, 349, 37–78.
24 P. Kerr, 'Physicians urge end to arms race', *New York Times*, 10 Jan. 1984, p. 17.
25 'Open letter to the General Synod of the Church of England', 15 Nov. 1984, doc. 73, 6/1 Christian CND (33/127), CND Additions (I), CND Archive, London School of Economics and Political Science.

Nuclear winter in science and the world

26 'Introduction', *ENDpapers Eight*, Spokesman 46, Summer 1984, p. 1.
27 'New Delhi declaration on the nuclear arms race, 1985', in E. J. Ozmanczyk, *Encyclopedia of the United Nations and International Agreements*, 3rd edn, ed. A. Mango (New York, 2003), pp. 1548–50. See also Sagan and Turco, *Path*, p. 179.
28 W. Brandt, 'Remarks on East-West relations', Willy Brandt Archive, A3, 992, Rede Brandt vor Council on Foreign Relations. Also published in Willy Brandt, Berliner Ausgabe, 10 (Bonn, 2009). Accessed through the Wilson Center Digital Archive, http://digitalarchive.wilsoncenter.org/document/111078 (accessed 17 February 2016).
29 'Excerpts from pastoral plan', *New York Times*, 27 Apr. 1986, p. 34. (Emphasis in the original.)
30 Sagan and Turco, *Path*, p. 181.
31 END French Group Newsletter, No. 2 (Sept. 1985), p. 3, END Papers.
32 'A partial transcript of the DC forum on the world-wide consequences of nuclear war, sponsored by Senators Kennedy and Hatfield, Dec. 8, 1983', in *Disarmament: A Periodic Review by the United Nations* VII: 3 (Autumn 1984), pp. 34–5, 37–8; P. Shabecoff, 'U.S.-Soviet panel sees no hope in an atomic war', *New York Times*, 9 Dec. 1983, A13.
33 'A partial transcript', pp. 40–2, 47, 54, 56–7, 62; T. Wicker, 'A grim agreement', *New York Times*, 12 Dec. 1983, A27.
34 Ehrlich *et al.*, *The Cold and the Dark*, p. xviii; *The Climatic, Biological, and Strategic Effects of Nuclear War: Hearing before the Subcommittee on Natural Resources, Agriculture Research and Environment, House of Representatives, ninety-eighth Congress, Second Session*, 12 Sept. 1984 (Washington, D.C., 1985), p. 45; *Nuclear Winter: Joint Hearing before the Subcommittee on Natural Resources, Agriculture Research and Environment and the Subcommittee on Energy and the Environment, U.S. House of Representatives, Ninety-ninth Congress, First Session*, 14 Mar. 1985 (Washington, D.C., 1985), p. 34.
35 N. Zheleznov, 'Symposium: Scientists Warn', from *Sovetskaya Rossiya*, 23 Dec. 1983, First Edition, 5, III, 30. Dec. 1983, USSR International Affairs, United States & Canada, A9. Box 34, Folder: Files of Cathy Fitzpatrick: USSR: Nuclear Winter/War, 1983–87, Human Rights Watch Records, Columbia University.
36 'Staging a "nuclear winter"', by A. Palladin, in *Izvestiya*, 28 July 1985, morning edition, 5, III, 31 July 1985, USSR International Affairs, United States and Canada, A6. Box 34, Folder: Files of Cathy Fitzpatrick: USSR: Nuclear Winter/ War, 1983–87; '"Nuclear winter" possible from conventional war', 28 Feb. 1986, AA3, III, 5 Mar. 1986, USSR International Affairs, Arms Control and Disarmament, Box 34, Folder: Files of Cathy Fitzpatrick: USSR: Nuclear Winter/ War, 1983–87.
37 'Visit to Yuri and Olga Medvedkov 7.11.85', 7 Nov. 1985, S1-85-11-7-1, END Papers; 'Yori to Oleg Popov', 4 Aug. 1985, S1A-85-8-4-1, END Papers; Letter from Peter Murphy, 12 Sept. 1985, S1B-85-9-12-1, END Papers.

38 From *Les Prix Nobel: The Nobel Prizes 1985*, ed. W. Odelberg, [Nobel Foundation] (Stockholm, 1986), http://nobelprize.org/nobel_prizes/peace/laureates/1985/presentation-speech.html (accessed 17 February 2016).
39 L. Wittner, *Toward Nuclear Abolition: A History of the World Nuclear Disarmament Movement, 1971 to the Present* (Stanford, 2003), pp. 228, 269–70, 360–1; 'International Physicians for the Prevention of Nuclear War – Nobel Lecture: Tragedy and Triumph of Reason'. *Nobelprize.org.* Nobel Media AB 2013. Web. 19 July 2013. www.nobelprize.org/nobel_prizes/peace/laureates/1985/physicians-lecture.html. (accessed 17 February 2016).
40 'Excerpts From U.N. Speeches by Shultz and Shevardnadze', *New York Times*, 25 Sept. 1985, p. A8; quoted in Sagan and Turco, *Path*, p. 183.
41 S. Weart, *Nuclear Fear: A History of Images* (Cambridge, Mass., 1989).
42 'To preserve a world graced by life', 1982, Folder 22.27: Nuclear Winter continued, Box 22, Hans Bethe Papers, Cornell University (hereafter HB Papers). Also appeared in shortened form in *Bulletin of the Atomic Scientists* 39:1 (Jan. 1983), pp. 2–3.
43 Ehrlich *et al.*, *Cold and the Dark*, pp. 43–59, 128, 155.
44 *The Consequences of Nuclear War, Hearings before the International Trade, Finance, and Security Economics Subcommittee of the Joint Economic Committee, ninety-eight Congress, Second Session,* 11/12 July 1984 (Washington, D.C., 1986), p. 147; 'Pentagon aides agree on a "nuclear winter"', *New York Times*, 13 July 1984, A13.
45 'Remarks at the Annual Convention of the National Association of Evangelicals in Orlando, Florida, March 8, 1983', www.reaganfoundation.org/pdf/Remarks_Annual_Convention_National_Association_Evangelicals_030883.pdf
46 S. L. Thompson and S. H. Schneider, 'Nuclear winter reappraised', *Foreign Affairs* 64:5 (Summer 1986), pp. 981–3, 989, 993–4, 998, 1005.
47 J. Gleick, 'Less drastic theory emerges on freezing after a nuclear war', *New York Times*, 22 June 1986, p. 1.
48 M. A. Harwell and C. C. Harwell, 'Updating the "Nuclear Winter" Debate', *Bulletin of the Atomic Scientists* 43:8 (October 1987), pp. 42–4. Emphasis in the original; 'Statement – SCOPE Press Conference', 28 May 1987, Folder 7: Nuclear Winter – Correspondence, Box 195, TEW Papers.
49 'The technology of Wednesday's war', *Nature* 349 (10 Jan. 1991), p. 91; P. Aldhous, 'Oil-well climate catastrophe', *Nature* 349 (10 Jan. 1991), p. 96; K. A. Browning, R.J. Allam, S. P. Ballard, R. T. H. Barnes, D. Bennetts, R. H. Maryon, P. J. Mason, D. McKenna, J. F. B. Mitchell, C. A. Senior, A. Slingo and F. B. Smith, 'Environmental effects from burning oil wells in Kuwait', *Nature* 351 (30 May 1991), p. 363.
50 J. W. Birks, 'The end of innocence', *Nature* 349 (7 Feb. 1991), p. 472.
51 The yield of the bomb used against Hiroshima was approximately 12.5 kilotonnes, R. Rhodes, *The Making of the Atomic Bomb* (New York, 1986), p. 711.

Sagan, *Billions*, pp. 99–107; R. Dalton, 'What happens when two nations battle with nukes?' *Nature* online, 12 Dec. 2006; H. Leifert, 'Extreme events: climate catastrophe', *Nature Reports: Climate Change* 4 (Sept. 2007), p. 50. In 2010, members of IPPNW and PSR mentioned nuclear winter and the 'billions of people' who would starve in an editorial arguing for ratification of the recent START treaty. I. Helfand, L. Ringenberg, and D. Mellman, 'A New START for the World', *Tampa Tribune*, 8 (Apr. 2010).

52 *Nuclear Winter and Its Implications: Hearings before the Committee on Armed Services, United States Senate, 99th Congress, 1st Session*, 2/3 Oct. 1985 (Washington, D.C., 1986), pp. 2, 5–9, 15–18.

53 A. Robock, 'New models confirm nuclear winter', *Bulletin of the Atomic Scientists* 45:7 (1989), pp. 32–5; J. Nelson, 'Fractality of sooty smoke: implications for the severity of nuclear winter', *Nature* 339 (22 June 1989), p. 611.

12

Images of nuclear war in US government films from the early Cold War

Lars Nowak

If one essential element of the Cold War was the terrifying imagination of a possible future war that would be fought with nuclear weapons, a particularly powerful means of articulating this emotionally charged fantasy was the medium of cinema, whose moving images and sounds are capable of lending preconceptions of the vividness of reality and thus evoking the spectator's feelings in a very direct way. For this reason, a deeper look into cinematic representations of nuclear war promises to be a fruitful venture. The following essay will undergo this task on the basis of American motion pictures from the period between 1945 and 1962, a time span that was framed by the atomic bombardments of Hiroshima and Nagasaki on the one hand and the Cuban Missile Crisis on the other – two events in American history that fuelled collective imaginings about nuclear war by making it clear that such a war was not an abstract possibility, but a concrete danger.

In the United States, the cinema's contribution to the nuclear imagination was not limited to fictional feature films such as Gordon Douglas' *Them!* (1954) or Stanley Kramer's *On the Beach* (1959), but also included instruction and propaganda films that were produced on the authority of the federal government. Among these state-sponsored films – whose viewing figures were in no way inferior to those of the commercial films – those concerning questions of civil defence still possess a certain public notoriety and have also attracted a considerable amount of scholarly attention. However, another group of official films on nuclear war has been almost completely forgotten by the general public and largely neglected by academic research: during the era in question, the US government also commissioned thousands of films about its atmospheric nuclear weapons tests.[1] Although these films shared some characteristics with the civil defence films, they also differed from them in several significant aspects.

Most importantly, by means of their reference to actual test explosions and material stagings of nuclear attacks, they could heighten their medium's inherent reality effect and thus grant their speculations about nuclear war an even greater credibility. This article will examine both classes of governmental films and compare them not only in terms of their explicit content, to which some of the earlier research was confined, but also with regard to their peculiarities of form, which were equally influential on the pictures of a possible nuclear war that were drawn by these films.

Civil defence films – limited destruction and effective protection

A new branch of bureaucracy for protecting the American population in the event of a nuclear disaster was created in 1950 by the establishment of the Federal Civil Defense Administration (FCDA), which was later followed by the Office of Civil and Defense Mobilisation and the Office of Civil Defense. All three agencies spent a great share of their funds on producing propaganda that aimed at instructing the American population on how to prepare for a possible nuclear war and how to act in the event of its actual occurrence. Right from the outset, the media used for this purpose included not only dioramas and booklets, but also films.[2] Essentially the same ideas were promoted in all three media, sometimes in combination, where, for instance, a corresponding pamphlet would also be provided in relation to a film. Nevertheless, civil defence officials considered motion pictures their most important propaganda instrument,[3] which was probably based on the notion that this medium's great popularity made it particularly suitable for popularising the ideology of civil defence as well.[4] In order to produce the necessary films, the civil defence administration sought the co-operation of commercial studios, such as Archer Productions, Norwood Studios or RKO, which took care of their complete fabrication or at least contributed to their manufacture by providing technology and personnel.[5] The resulting films were generally not shown in commercial cinemas, but rather at neighbourhood meetings or in schools, churches and other public institutions.

As to their formal principles of composition, the nuclear civil defence films combined rhetorical, categorical and narrative elements.[6] Reflecting the civil defence administration's general intention of reinforcing the willingness of the American people to fight a nuclear war if necessary,[7] the films sought to achieve this end, not only by specifying the different targets and destructive effects of nuclear attacks and protective measures against them, but also by connecting these attacks to stories that involved individual characters.

In both the civil defence propaganda in general and the civil defence films in particular, the creation of the desired attitude was based on the attempt to mould the population's emotional response to nuclear weapons in a way that would avert them from two extremes. On the one hand, overwhelming terror and a fatalistic attitude that could result from it had to be overcome. For instance, the film *Medical Aspects of Nuclear Radiation* (1950) argued against what it understood as the panic-mongering of the mass media by pointing out that the real danger was not the bomb itself, but excessive, paralysing fears about it that kept people from effective acting. On the other hand, the civil defence rhetoric could not completely ignore the population's anxieties about nuclear weapons but had to acknowledge them in some way. The civil defence officials even tried to remind those citizens who, for one reason or another, tried to suppress all thoughts about nuclear war, of such a war's very possibility, because they felt that people would only follow their advice if they were convinced of the necessity to do so. Therefore, the civil defence films also 'exposed the horrors of atomic warfare to citizens and attempted to impress upon them the need for self-protection'.[8] In sum, the civil defence films attempted to generate an understanding of nuclear war as a problem that was serious but at the same time manageable.[9]

The first strategy of creating this attitude was representing a nuclear attack in certain ways. In order to rouse those who preferred to ignore the dangers of nuclear war, as well as to gain the acceptance of those who were fully aware of them, the civil defence films generally acknowledged these dangers. While the first of these dangers was that of the outbreak of a nuclear war itself,[10] the films also pointed out the various destructive effects of a nuclear explosion, which not only included the blast and heat waves, but also the nuclear flash and the radioactivity. Towards the end of the 1950s, the films even started to take into account the growing fears of many Americans about radioactivity by putting special emphasis on this phenomenon and its harmful effects on the human body.[11] For instance, *Radiological Defense* (1961) admitted that a nuclear war would not only involve an immediate destruction of cities, but also a long-term radioactive contamination of the countryside. The film also presented a map which indicated that no less than 'two thirds of the nation'[12] would be covered with fallout and also transferred the huge area that had been contaminated by the *Castle Bravo* explosion, a Pacific H-bomb test conducted in February 1954, to a map of the American east coast, where it stretched from Washington, D.C. to New York City. In addition to the utilisation of the synoptic view offered by maps, the civil defence films also represented the destructive processes and results caused by nuclear detonations in moving photographic images in order to take advantage of these pictures' realistic impression as well.

At the same time, the civil defence films tried to play down the destructive effects. One way of doing so was to point out the limited character of those effects whose existence had been acknowledged, as exemplified by *Survival Under Atomic Attack* (1951), which, in its first part, graphically depicted the atomic annihilation of Hiroshima and Nagasaki, but in the second part, which dealt with a hypothetical A-bomb attack on an American city, only presented minor damage.[13] Since, among all the effects of nuclear detonations, radioactivity provoked the greatest anxieties, many films were particularly eager to deny the dangers of the radiation, such as the causation of long-term contamination and genetic defects. To this effect, *Medical Aspects of Nuclear Radiation* even resorted to using animated drawings of gamma rays that resembled sperm cells, thus connecting the lethal technology of the atom bomb to its opposite, the reproduction of life (Figure 1). While *You Can Beat the A-Bomb*

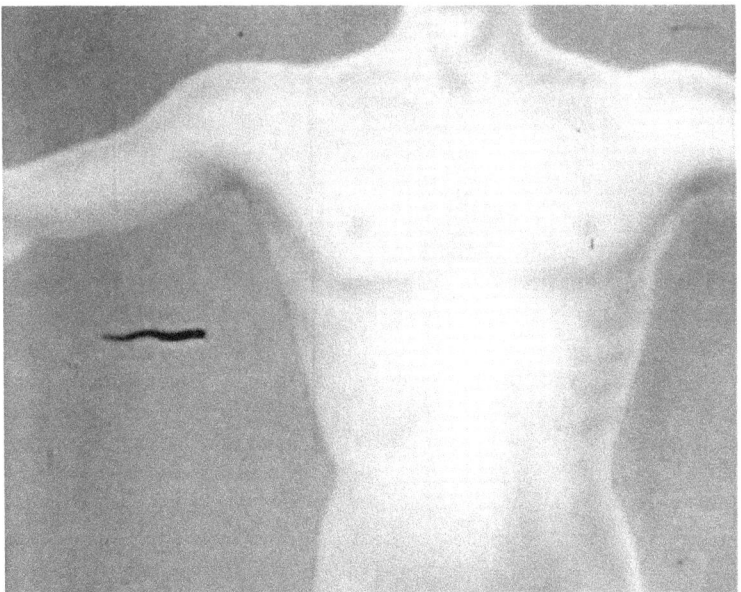

Figure 1 Being visualised by an animated drawing, gamma rays bear a surprising resemblance to sperm in *Medical Aspects of Nuclear Radiation* (1950)

(1950) maintained that the blindness induced by the nuclear flash would only last for a short time, *Duck and Cover* (1952) transformed the flash into an early sign of an atomic explosion, which could warn the victims of an unannounced attack about the other effects that would follow. Sometimes, the civil defence films also completely left out certain destructive effects; for example, *Operation Alert* (1956) did not address the serious problems that would be faced by those Americans who had escaped the immediate bombings.[14]

Several formal features of the civil defence films also contributed to their belittlement of a nuclear bomb's destructive power. Although *Survival Under Atomic Attack* and other films included shots of the real devastation that had been brought about by the A-bomb attacks on Japan, in many other cases the realism of the films' photographic images was undermined by the fact that these images only showed staged damages, injuries and deaths. Furthermore, numerous civil defence films represented the dangers of nuclear explosions in drawings, which, although often animated, were even more removed from reality. Finally, films such as *Our Cities Must Fight* (1951) and *A New Look at the H-Bomb* (1954) did not offer any visual depictions of these dangers at all, but only referred to them verbally. Switching from photographic pictures to other means of representation could have a reassuring effect for other reasons as well. The radioactivity's imperceptibility did not only challenge the films' capability of depicting it photographically, but, as was remarked by the commentator of *Medical Aspects of Nuclear Radiation*, also contributed to the fears this phenomenon provoked among Americans. Therefore, the population's concern about the radioactivity could also be contained by the fact that the films devised other ways of visualising it. The use of drawn pictures and diagrams was one of these alternative visualisations; another one, that was deployed in *Radiological Defense*, was the application of a red filter, which alluded to the fogging of photosensitive surfaces by gamma radiation. This semiotic mastery over the radioactivity suggested that the latter could be controlled in reality as well. In a similar manner, films such as *Duck and Cover* and *Atomic Alert (Elementary Version)* (1951) signified the nuclear flash by means of overexposures that turned the whole image field white, thereby negating all representation. However, the image always completely returned just a moment later, which confirmed the claim that the blinding effect of the flash was only temporary. Finally, the dangers of nuclear explosions were played down by comparing the latter to less harmful phenomena, which included other sources of radioactivity, such as radium watches, dynamite and other conventional weapons and also natural events such as fires or sunburns.[15] Just as the conventionalisation of nuclear weapons negated their fundamental alterity and historical singularity, their naturalisation denied man's responsibility for their existence and use.

The civil defence propaganda also tried to ease the population's fears by claiming that the dangers of a nuclear attack could be fended off with the help of several protective measures, which were sometimes even quite simple and inexpensive and, therefore, available to everyone. The first group of countermeasures consisted in steps taken *before* a possible nuclear attack. One preparing measure, which was recommended in *Target: You!* (1953) was keeping the household tidy in order to prevent rubbish from being set on fire by a nuclear explosion's heat wave.[16] Another, more labour-intensive preparation was the building and furnishing of shelters, which the civil defence films started to promote in the late 1950s. Although it was generally acknowledged at that time that shelters would not protect against a thermonuclear explosion's shock and heat waves,[17] staying in them for two weeks was presented as a protection against fallout. As demonstrated by the film *Bombproof* (1956), shelters were also intended for the storage of documents,[18] whose alleged importance even after a nuclear war suggested that the latter would not seriously disrupt social life.

The second group of protective measures that were pointed out by the civil defence films concerned the citizens' behaviour *during* a nuclear attack. As a protection against the latter's mechanical, thermal and optical dangers, many films advised American citizens to take particular body positions such as lying down, getting shielded by a building and covering their eyes.[19] Suggesting that fallout could simply be wiped or washed off, the films also recommended ordinary household routines as decontamination procedures. Although civil defence in general referred to the suburbs, some civil defence films were concerned with the city centres. Early films such as *Survival Under Atomic Attack*, *You Can Beat the A-Bomb* and *Our Cities Must Fight* insisted that urban populations should remain rather than evacuating, since the danger of radioactivity was overrated and a mass escape would not only invite enemy occupation, but would also cause a breakdown of economic and social life. However, since the civil defence agencies considered the evacuation of cities a reasonable protective measure if it was carefully planned,[20] later films such as *Target: You!* and *Radiological Defense* did not require a renunciation but a better organisation of it.

During the 1950s, private basement and backyard shelters were given preference over public sheltering on the grounds that the latter were 'communist', while the former were in accord with the high esteem in which the American society held private initiative.[21] In reality, it was hoped that the privatisation of civil defence would make it seem less militaristic and save large sums of public money, which would be spent better on the development and production of nuclear weapons.[22] Therefore, the Eisenhower administration only funded the building of shelters for the political, military and industrial elites, not for ordinary citizens.[23] However, the latter were supposedly cared for when in the early 1960s President Kennedy launched the National Fallout Shelter Survey in which numerous basements and corridors of public and commercial buildings were declared community shelters and even partially stocked with supplies.[24]

In a similar manner, the civil defence films further reassured the American citizens by pointing out that many steps against the consequences of a nuclear war were taken by the civil defence agencies and other governmental authorities themselves, which would tend to them. Films such as *Radiological Defense* and *Fallout: When and How to Protect Yourself Against It* (1959) tried to make clear that the state bureaucracy employed a lot of experts and volunteers who would provide the population with data about radioactive fallout and other important information via CONELRAD (Control of Electromagnetic Radiation) radio messages and carry out life-saving rescue operations. However, since most of the various measures of protection against a nuclear attack were expected from the citizens, the civil defence films also stressed that the population could not exclusively rely on the government's activities, but was called upon to make its own contribution to the nation's civil defence effort. This appeal to everybody's active participation also included children, who were not only addressed by civil defence drills at schools and specially designed booklets,[25] but also by films such as *Atomic Alert (Elementary Version)* and *Duck and Cover* which presented children as protagonists.[26]

The privatisation of civil defence was particularly focused on the family, which was not only regarded as the ultimate object of protection, owing to its role as the foundation of America's value system, but also as one of its essential means, because of its supposed social cohesion and capability to fend off other dangers, such as communist subversion.[27] However, since the family's interests did not always harmonise with those of the society at large, it also had to be adapted to the needs of civil defence by being subjected to a paramilitary reorganisation that was not only propagated by written manuals, but also by several civil defence films.²⁸ At the same time, the family's militarisation had to be made to look like ordinary familial activities, because it also served an inverse end: a normalisation of nuclear weapons, which in addition to the latter's conventionalisation and naturalisation also comprised their domestication.²⁹

Since women were regarded as the core of the family, civil defence's particular attention to the family implied a focus on them as well. Special emphasis was put on mothers, who were traditionally associated with values such as the reproduction and protection of life, which were also closely connected to the purposes of civil defence.³⁰ Women's central role was also foregrounded by the civil defence films, which showed them 'quieting their happy children in home bomb shelters' they had earlier stocked with 'food, water, and children's games'.³¹ The great importance of women could even include the acquisition of professions conventionally reserved for men, since in films from the second half of the 1950s, women were shown 'working as emergency ambulance drivers, police officers, firefighters and medical doctors'.³² Nevertheless, because the political situation was tense, but not as urgent as in the Second World War, the patriarchal hierarchy between the sexes remained basically intact,³³ as is exemplified by the film *Atomic Alert (Elementary Version)*, in which a small girl, whose knowledge about civil defence was quite limited, depended on the help of her older and more knowledgeable brother. This preservation of traditional gender roles was particularly evident in connection with the families' militarisation, which constructed the husband as 'sergeant' and his wife as 'second in command'.³⁴ For instance, in *You Can Beat the A-Bomb*, two fathers who were quite unimpressed by an atomic attack gave explanations, demonstrations and orders to the other members of their respective families, which owing to their visible fear only hesitantly followed and supported them (Figure 2).

In spite of their emphasis on the responsibility of individuals and families, the civil defence films stressed the importance of co-operation among the citizens themselves as well as between the citizens and the civil defence officials. Just as in *Atomic Alert (Elementary Version)* the sister was assisted by her brother, both children were later helped by two civil defence workers. *Alert Today – Alive Tomorrow* (1956) presented the 8,000 civil defence volunteers of a small town in Pennsylvania as a harmonious community, exemplifying the principle of mutual assistance.³⁵ And the voice-over of *Survival Under Atomic Attack* tried to evoke a sense of unity among the recipients by frequently using the pronoun 'we' and its derivatives.³⁶

Although civil defence officials also sought the co-operation of non-whites and, therefore, presented their films in African-American communities,[37] the films' appeal to everyone's team spirit did not include ethnic minorities. Instead, films like *Alert Today – Alive Tomorrow* were completely dominated by whites and devoid of all other ethnic groups.[38] This exclusion of non-whites helped the civil defence films to avoid mentioning several problems that resulted from racial inequalities and prejudices. Most important in that respect was the fact that blacks were often unable to afford a private shelter, but were among the primary targets of nuclear attacks because, after the Second World War, they constituted the principal population of the inner cities.[39] Another issue was that their close contacts with whites, who would have to share public shelters with them or even accept them into their suburban homes as evacuees, would probably cause tensions.[40]

In order to persuade the American population to adopt the correct attitudes and actions concerning nuclear war, the civil defence films employed different rhetorical-narrative strategies. Sometimes, as in the case of *Atomic Alert (Elementary Version)*, they presented characters

Figure 2 A militarised father instructs his family in protective measures against an atomic explosion in *You Can Beat the A-Bomb* (1950)

who behaved in wrong ways, which gave other characters the opportunity to advise them – and the spectators as well. At other times, the films offered role models whose perfect knowledge, emotional self-control and efficient acting could directly be imitated by the viewers. One extreme example of this strategy was *Operation Alert*, a film about the nationwide air-raid drills of the same name that were held every summer between 1954 and 1961 and typically simulated nuclear attacks on 50–100 American cities. All the participants in this exercise, although enacting a catastrophic event, expressed neither fear nor any other affects and fulfilled their respective functions faultlessly.[41] In spite of the fact that the role models' perfect behaviour was only a staged ideal, the medium's reality effect created the impression that it had already been realised. Finally, a third group of civil defence films presented the replacement of a wrong behaviour by a right one in order to offer this learning process for imitation by the uninitiated spectator. One example can be found in the film *Warning Red* (1956), whose protagonist, in an implausibly short time, turned from a completely ignorant citizen into a competent, exemplary helper of civil defence.

As a result, the civil defence films reassured the citizens that, thanks to the limited destructiveness of nuclear explosions and the availability of effective countermeasures, they could survive a nuclear war.[42] Sometimes, such as in the case of *Atomic Survival* (1951) and *Survival City* (1955), this message was already conveyed by the films' titles. When *Operation Alert* concluded with everybody's return to normal life after the exercise had ended, the film even implied a similar restoration of normalcy after an actual nuclear attack. Since the film suggested that the institutions and values of American society had been left unchanged, nuclear war was completely normalised.[43]

In reality, of course, all means of protection that the civil defence films recommended were ineffective. For example, evacuation was not only confronted with the problem that the location chosen for the reception of the evacuees could be targeted as well. In the mid-1950s, H-bomb tests also made it clear that the fallout of the new generation of nuclear weapons would contaminate areas of such large dimensions that it could also include the receiving sites. Finally, in 1957 the successful launching of the Sputnik satellite demonstrated the Soviets' capability of transporting their nuclear bombs by missiles instead of airplanes, which reduced the warning times to such a high degree that evacuations became completely obsolete.[44] The real objective of the civil defence programme, therefore, was not to create safety for the citizens, but to give them simply a feeling of safety in order to prevent conflicts with the elites, who would be protected in better ways, and to generate a willingness to fight a nuclear war that could be used as a means of deterrence.[45]

In their attempt to mobilise the American population for the purpose of public protection in the event of a nuclear attack, however, the civil defence films ultimately failed. On the one hand, many children were traumatised by the civil defence activities, which communicated to them that their previous safety had been destroyed by the prospect of an inevitable and imminent nuclear war.[46] This message did not only emanate from the civil defence drills, but also from films such as *Duck and Cover*, in which the minors could not expect any protection from the grown-ups (who, after all, were responsible for the new situation), but had to help themselves.[47] One the other hand, adults tended to ignore the civil defence agencies' propaganda during the whole period in question because they were neither deceived by the government's claims about the possibilities of protecting civilians against a nuclear attack, nor were they willing to prepare for the next military conflict so soon after all the hardships endured during the Second World War.[48]

Nuclear test films – real explosions and deeper ambiguities

The time span between the end of the Second World War and the beginning of the 1960s was not only marked by the nuclear bombings of Japan and the Cuban Missile Crisis, but also by the first test of an atomic bomb, called 'Trinity', in 1945, and the signing of the Limited Test Ban Treaty in 1963, which bound the USA, the USSR and the UK to relocate their nuclear weapons tests below ground. Between these two events the three countries conducted hundreds of those tests in the atmosphere. This fact calls into question Paul Virilio's claim that nuclear war has been infinitely postponed by being constantly prepared for in the form of a 'pure war' of deterrence characterised by an 'ecologistical' 'zero growth' that corresponds to an ecological one.[49] In reality, the Cold War, at least during its first two decades, was very dirty, for the atmospheric nuclear tests, which are often justified as an important contribution to the deferral of a nuclear war, also anticipated such a war by releasing amounts of radioactivity on a par with those that would probably be produced by a global nuclear conflict. As the harmfulness of the radioactive fallout already became evident during the 1950s, the collective imaginings of a future nuclear war at that time were also stimulated by the constant testing of nuclear bombs, which anchored the possibility of such a war in reality once more.

Images of nuclear war in US government films

In the United States, which not only carried out the first of the nuclear tests, but also the largest number of them, the cinematic record of these tests began even before the production of the civil defence films, namely, at the *Trinty* test. Most of the American nuclear test films were produced by the US Air Force 1352nd Photographic Group, which was entrusted with documenting all tests from 1947 to 1969 in still and motion pictures.[50] Just as commercial film studios participated in the production of the civil defence films, the 1352nd Photographic Group, which was stationed at the Lookout Mountain Air Force station in Hollywood, employed personnel including technicians, cameramen, directors and actors who also worked for studios such as Warner Brothers, RKO and MGM.[51]

As opposed to the civil defence films, which always addressed the entire American population, most nuclear test films were only screened for selected audiences who were directly involved with the weapons tests. These audiences were composed of servicemen, employees of administrative bodies such as the Atomic Energy Commission (AEC) or the Department of Defense and members of political institutions such as the Congress. This restricted circulation could be one explanation for the obscurity of the nuclear test films that were mentioned at the beginning of this chapter; however, the internal audiences were of quite considerable sizes, and selected test films were additionally presented to the general public via TV broadcasts or screenings at schools, churches and similar institutions, where they reached even more people.[52]

Like the civil defence films, the nuclear test films, which were sometimes quite lavishly produced,[53] combined categorical, rhetorical and narrative elements. Most of them classified the various experimental programmes carried out during the tests and the contributions of the different military services that participated in them. They also tried to justify the testing programme by declaring almost every test a scientific success and an indispensable contribution to the national security. Finally, the test films usually constructed a temporal chain of events, which started with a test's preparation, proceeded to its performance, observation and recording and ended with its analysis and evaluation. However, the nuclear test films differed from the civil defence films in that they also integrated a fourth aesthetic principle, since they always included, as their dramatic climaxes, spectacular images of the test explosions, whose extensive presentation as 'attractions' interrupted the narrative flow.[54]

Far from merely depicting the nuclear weapons tests of the recent past, the test films also aimed at preparing their viewers for a possible nuclear war in the future and in this way contributed to the era's imagination of such a war. Just as, for example, *Military Participation on Tumbler/ Snapper* (1952) began with remarks on 'atomic warfare', *The United States Air Force Presents Its Part in 'Operation Sandstone'* (1948) ended with the claim that the preceding pictures had offered 'a grim warning of what the next war ... can be like'. One reason for these references to atomic war was that the nuclear weapons tests themselves already referred to it, because they were not only scientific experiments with new types of nuclear bombs, but also theatrical stagings of the latter's use in a military conflict. This was particularly true in the case of the 'effects tests', which did not only enable an observation of the explosions' various physical effects (which were in the focus of the 'diagnostic tests'), but also an examination of the damage, destruction and contamination these effects caused in laboratory animals and on test objects that comprised samples of different materials and objects, basic architectural shapes, scale models and mannequins. As physical stagings in which the animals and puppets embodied human beings and the other test objects functioned as props, the military effects tests went beyond pure fantasies of a nuclear war and gave them some material reality. For these war games, two different scenarios can be distinguished, both of which also involved human actors.

On the one hand, civil defence was also an issue at those military effects tests whose test objects included civilian vehicles, infrastructure and buildings. Questions of civil defence played a particularly important role at the Nevada tests *Doorstep* and *Cue*, which were documented in *Operation Doorstep* (1953), *Operation Cue* (1955) and *Let's Face It* (1955). Both tests were carried out with the participation of the FCDA, which derived some of its claims about the possibilities of civil defence from them. The *Cue* test deployed several test houses, which were even equipped with appliances, furniture and food and simulated a whole settlement, thus transforming the landscape of the Nevada desert into an imaginary cityscape. Being called 'a creation right out of science fiction' in *Let's Face It*, the test town was placed at such a distance from ground zero that it represented the suburb of a city whose centre was hit by a nuclear bomb. While FCDA personnel performed field exercises that simulated some of its typical services during both civil defence tests,[55] the *Cue* test also included a psychological experiment with civilian test persons who experienced the explosion from trenches.[56]

On the other hand, the nuclear test films went beyond the civil defence films in that they also represented tests that made use of military test objects or even integrated military manoeuvres. After the first tests of

Images of nuclear war in US government films

this kind, the test series *Crossroads*, which was represented in *Operation Crossroads* (1946), had exposed nearly 100 ships and submarines to an air burst and an underwater explosion, later military effects tests also employed military vehicles and equipment, foxholes, trenches and weapons, including the casings of nuclear bombs,[57] as shown in films such as *Military Participation on Buster Jangle* (1951), *Operation Teapot: Military Effects Studies* (1955) or *Operation Redwing* (1956). Additionally, at several Nevada tests, members of all four US military services watched the test explosions and later entered the test areas in order to inspect the detonations' effects on the test objects and participate in tactical exercises. Most of these exercises belonged to the *Desert Rock* manoeuvres of 1951–57, which were depicted in *Exercise Desert Rock* (1951) and *Military Participation on Tumbler/Snapper*.[58] While the real atomic explosions were located at staged places during the civil defence tests, the military exercises embedded them in a chain of staged events. The soldiers' involvement in the nuclear tests did not only serve to instruct them in and make them accustomed to nuclear warfare, but also to study their reactions to the explosions with the help of questionnaires, interviews, direct observations and cardiological measurements.[59] As opposed to the first *Desert Rock* manoeuvre in which the soldiers had watched the explosions from a distance of seven miles and entered the test zones only several hours after a detonation, later exercises tried to make the simulation of a nuclear war more realistic by drastically reducing the distances from ground zero and the waiting times before moving towards it.[60]

In their fantasies about a nuclear war, the nuclear test films, like the civil defence films, transformed the United States from an attacker who had actually dropped two atom bombs on Japan into the hypothetical victim of a nuclear attack by another country, which was mostly identified as the Soviet Union. This reversal characterised both the films on the civil defence tests and those on the military manoeuvre tests, albeit in slightly different forms. While the test buildings and towns that were attacked with atom bombs in the former tests imitated typical American houses and communities, the latter tests persistently staged an invasion of enemy armed forces into American territory which had to be repulsed by the US military's own employment of tactical A-bombs.[61]

Again, like the films on civil defence, those about the nuclear tests aimed at producing an evaluation of nuclear war that would neither overestimate nor underestimate its dangers and thus produce neither terror nor carelessness. Likewise, claiming that 'panic, not nuclear destruction, was ... the real danger in nuclear warfare',[62] the nuclear test films also tried to dispel such fear by emphasising that the destructive potential of nuclear detonations was limited. Again, particular efforts were made to belittle the dangers of radioactivity. Some films, including *Operation Crossroads* and *Military Participation on Operation Buster Jangle*, plainly denied these risks in their commentaries.[63] Others, however, such as the manoeuvre test films *Exercise Desert Rock* and *Military Participation on Tumbler/Snapper*, cited alleged experts who confirmed that in the case of an air explosion the radioactivity was carried up into the stratosphere and, therefore, responsible for no more than 10 per cent of the detonation's victims. Additionally, the nuclear test films sometimes also completely left out particular dangers, such as long-term contamination and firestorms. At other times, they avoided to mention the massive destructiveness of hydrogen bombs and instead focused on smaller atom bombs.[64] For example, *Operation Doorstep*, although produced two years after the first successful test of an H-bomb, addressed the 'atomic age' and documented the explosion of a 15-kiloton A-bomb, which was even less powerful than the bombs that had been dropped on Japan eight years earlier.[65]

The nuclear test films also resembled the civil defence films in that they, too, pointed out several measures that would offer protection against those dangers of nuclear detonations which they had admitted. Again, some of these measures were expected from the average citizens, who were called upon to make their homes bomb-proof. While *Operation Doorstep* and *Operation Cue* recommended the building of outdoor and basement shelters as well as reinforced concrete buildings, *The House in the Middle* (1954) admonished the viewers to keep their homes in order and paint them white so that they would not be ignited by a nuclear explosion's thermal radiation. In addition to this contribution to the militarisation of the civilian population, films about manoeuvre tests, such as *Exercise Desert Rock*, advised soldiers to take refuge in foxholes and trenches and to decontaminate themselves by wiping radioactive dust from their uniforms.[66] All these protective steps were supplemented by aid measures provided by the civil defence agencies, which, according to *Operation Cue* and *Let's Face It*, were well prepared for this task, as it was basically identical to the relief measures they had accomplished during other disasters.[67]

Since these disasters included natural events such as hurricanes, earthquakes and storm tides, the reference to the civil defence administration's other activities implied a naturalisation of nuclear war. This implication was reinforced when in *Let's Face It* a tornado was shown that bore a striking resemblance to a mushroom cloud and one of the depicted test explosions was called a 'hurricane of fire and blast'. Other films compared nuclear bombs to gunpowder or even to a cement mixer.[68] Thus, like the civil defence films, the nuclear test films aimed at denying the nuclear weapons' radical otherness by comparing them to conventional weapons, civilian technology and natural phenomena.

Another correlation between the films on civil defence and those about the nuclear tests was that the latter also presented characters whose initially negative attitudes about nuclear war shifted towards becoming more positive. Just as in the former, where ordinary citizens acquired the knowledge and optimism necessary for withstanding a nuclear attack, *Exercise Desert Rock* and *Military Participation on Tumbler/Snapper* showed that the attitudes of servicemen who participated in atomic test manoeuvres were changed by witnessing a test detonation and receiving explanatory instructions. Both films suggested that, owing to this experience, the soldiers' initial fears, which were based on the 'misconception[s]' that the explosion would make them deaf, blind and sterile, were replaced by the confidence that a nuclear war could be fought, survived and won.[69]

As representations of actual nuclear explosions, the nuclear test films had an important rhetorical advantage over the civil defence films: they were apparently able to substantiate their assertions by giving empirical evidence. Just as, for example, *The House in the Middle* could show different houses and fences after their exposure to the test explosion to prove that their thermal damages depended on their state of preservation, *Operation Doorstep* only had to present the detonation's effects on sheltered and unsheltered mannequins to demonstrate that sheltering offered substantial protection against a nuclear explosion's shock wave. In a similar manner, *Exercise Desert Rock* supported its contentions about an atomic test's positive effects on soldiers' attitudes towards nuclear warfare by including an interview with two servicemen who confirmed that they had undergone the transformation described above (the only problem being that this interview was actually and obviously staged).

As a result of all the different strategies deployed to play down the dangers of nuclear explosions, nuclear war was declared feasible, as it happened at the conclusion of *Exercise Desert Rock* and *Military Participation on Tumbler/Snapper* (Figure 3). Some nuclear test films, though, did not content themselves with dispelling common anxieties about nuclear weapons, but even aimed at transforming them into the fear that the testing of a new type of nuclear bomb could *fail*. A good example of this tendency was the film *Operation Ivy* (1952), which focused on the Ivy Mike

Figure 3 The determined expression on the face of a soldier who has just participated in an atomic test manoeuvre testifies to the feasibility of nuclear warfare in *Military Participation on Tumbler/Snapper* (1952)

test, the world's first full-scale test of a hydrogen bomb. The film tried to create narrative suspense by pretending to document the last hour before the test explosion and by suggesting that the latter's outcome was unknown. However, since the very existence of the film, which of course had been finished after the test, excluded the possibility of a catastrophic surpassing of all expectations about the bomb's explosive force, the only remaining uncertainty that could be the object of concern was that the bomb had fallen short of the expectations.

Just as by way of this emotional reversal the nuclear test films went far beyond the civil defence films in their attempt to play down the dangers of nuclear weapons, the other side of the latter's ambiguous representation, the exposure of their extreme destructiveness, was more developed in the nuclear test films as well. For one thing, the test films indicated the enormous spatial extensions of the explosions' mechanical and thermal activity, radioactive fallout and electro-magnetic pulse, which in the case of the two last-mentioned effects could even exceed the boundaries of the test zones. Often, the ranges of these effects were illustrated with the help of maps showing not only the Pacific test sites, but also American cities and conurbations (Figure 4).[70] Although this representational strategy, as mentioned above, was also applied by some civil defence films, none of these went as far as the nuclear test film *Operation Argus – Report of Chief, AFSWP to ARPA* (1958), which by means of several world maps demonstrated that the three explosions of the *Argus* series, which had taken place at a height of 300 miles, had affected the entire magnetic field of the earth.[71] Furthermore, the nuclear test films added a number of other devices to emphasise the large dimensions of nuclear detonations. One of these devices was a comparison to familiar objects that did not equate both entities but pointed out their differences and, therefore, did not trivialise nuclear weapons, but stressed their uniqueness. Just as *Let's Face It* demonstrated the typical size of a mushroom cloud by placing tiny human figures in front of it, *Operation Ivy* made use of popular American buildings as measuring units for the *Ivy Mike* explosion. In addition to inserting the complete skyline of Manhattan into the fireball, the film also put thirty-two images of the Empire State Building on top of each other to measure the height of the mushroom cloud and filled the bomb crater with fourteen versions of the Pentagon.[72] Furthermore, the commentator stated that the force of the explosion was four times bigger than that of all conventional bombs dropped by the United States and Britain during the Second World War. Finally, the nuclear tests films illustrated the detonations' spatial sizes by relating them to the dimensions of the image fields in which they appeared. While in *Operation Ivy*, the *Mike* fireball was cut through by the picture's edges so that it seemed to burst the frame itself, other films, such as *Operation Castle: Commander's Report* (1954), indicated the explosions' huge dimensions by giving the height and width of their images in miles.

Besides, the nuclear test films conveyed the types of destruction that could be caused by a nuclear explosion's physical effects more clearly than the civil defence films. Like these, the test films represented these destructive aspects not only verbally, but also in graphic and photographic moving pictures. They also concurred with the civil defence films in that they, too, showed not only the results, but also the processes of demolition. While in *Exercise Desert Rock*, for instance, the camera accompanied the soldiers who after a test explosion inspected the test objects, which in some cases were heavily damaged or even completely destroyed, civil defence test films such as *Operation Doorstep* and *Operation Cue* contained slow-motion shots that revealed that the test buildings were set alight and swept away by the detonations' heat and shock waves in a few seconds (Figure 5). However, the nuclear test films were more powerful than the civil defence films in regard to their formal means of expressing a nuclear explosion's destructive force. Whereas the civil defence films' red filters and white image fields only simulated the fogging and overexposure of their photographic stock by a nuclear explosion's emissions of radioactivity and light (which suggested a semiotic mastering of these dangers), the nuclear test films expressed the test explosions' destructive forces in indexical ways, since here the photographic materials and cameras had really been affected by these forces, whose uncontrollable nature was thus made clear. Again, pictures that were suddenly turned white signified a nuclear flash; but now, the shapes of objects did not return immediately but only after a while, which indicated that the film had actually been overexposed. In addition, nuclear test films such as *Let's Face It*, *Operation Ivy* and *Operation Hardtack: Military Effects Studies. Part Three: Underwater Tests* (1958) made the explosions' shock waves palpable by way of their mechanical impact on the camera, as they contained shots of test explosions whose blast waves raced across the Pacific towards the camera and at the moment of their arrival gave it a heavy blow.

Finally, not all nuclear test films tried to dissimulate that thermonuclear weapons had a much greater destructive force than atomic ones. For example, *Operation Cue* and *Let's Face It* explained that the destructiveness of the A-bomb used in the *Cue* test was spatially exceeded by a typical H-bomb by several hundred times. Although both films maintained that a hydrogen bomb's mechanical and thermal range was still finite, *Operation Cue* added that because of its longer blast duration even at the fringe these destructive effects were more severe. This statement was supported by *Military Effects on Operation Redwing* (1956), in which, precisely for this reason, a thermonuclear detonation completely destroyed all test buildings. Similarly, *Special Weapons Orientation: The Thermonuclear Weapon. Part VI* (1956) clarified that the destructive power of hydrogen bombs could be increased indefinitely (while that of A-bombs had physical limits) and that it allowed for the elimination of entire countries and civilisations.[73]

Thus, the nuclear test films exceeded the civil defence films both in their dissimulation and in their revelation of the destructive potential of nuclear weapons. This peculiarity can be explained in three different manners, which are related to each other in rather complicated ways. The first explanation refers to the fact that the test films were made for three different target groups, which, according to Joseph Masco, were approached with the use of different emotional strategies that were

Figure 4 The area of thermal-mechanical activity of the hydrogen bomb explosion *Ivy Mike* is superimposed on a map of Washington, D.C. in *Operation Ivy* (1952)

Figure 5 A test house is violently destroyed by the atomic explosion of the civil defence test *Cue* in *Operation Cue* (1955)

based on divergent assessments of the nuclear threat.[74] The dangers of nuclear war were more openly acknowledged in the films for the servicemen, which paid particular attention to the tests involving military exercises, than in those for the general public, which generally focused on the civil defence tests. These dangers were even more frankly depicted in the films for the bureaucrats and politicians, which dealt with technical details as well as the long-term patterns of nuclear weapons development. This discrimination between different audiences is also illustrated by the film *Operation Ivy*, which had initially been made for internal usage but was later modified for public release. In order to soothe fears about the potential harm of atmospheric testing that had been prompted by the massive fallout of the *Castle Bravo* test, the AEC and the FCDA produced a public version of this film, which was broadcast on TV in April 1954. As compared to the original version, the modified one had been cut from 60 to 28 minutes and sanitised, since it did not mention the fallout produced by the *Ivy* test series, which had been conducted 14 months earlier.[75]

Second, the nuclear test movies did not only attempt to prepare viewers for a possible nuclear war in the future, but were also designed to justify the nuclear bomb tests themselves, which were both harmful to the environment and quite expensive. To attain this aim, two contradictory strategies were employed. On the one hand, the films played down the dangers of nuclear bombs in order to present these weapons' experimental testing as 'safe'.[76] Thus, they sought primarily 'to reassure American G.I.s about the protection of their safety while participating in nuclear test maneuvers'.[77] On the other hand, the films tried to generate public support for the nuclear tests by stirring up anxieties about a nuclear attack by the USSR, which could be averted, they argued, by building up the United States' own nuclear weapons arsenal.

Third, although the nuclear test films, from both the civilian and the military points of view, always imagined a nuclear war in which the United States played the role of the attacked party, the nuclear tests' real purpose was not only to improve the protective measures against nuclear weapons, but also to develop and refine these weapons themselves. After all, the areas of destructive activity that were applied to American cities in several films did not really belong to Soviet bombs, but rather to American ones. Therefore, if some of the test films openly depicted the massive destruction that could be brought about by these bombs, this openness did not only increase existing fears about the Soviet Union's nuclear weapons, but also served to convince the spectators of the enormous military power connected to the United States' own possession of such weapons. Against the backdrop of the availability of A- and H-bombs to the United States themselves, the films glorified their enormous destructive force to evoke in the spectators, not fear, but a feeling of omnipotence.[78] Since this offensive perspective was only implied and dissimulated by the explicitly assumed defensive one, the tests films did not even need to express moral reservations about using nuclear weapons to kill millions of human beings living behind the Iron Curtain.

The nuclear test films were apparently more successful in achieving their propagandistic objectives than the civil defence films. For although the *Castle Bravo* accident of 1954 induced many ordinary citizens to revise their former approval of their country's nuclear weapons tests, which were now criticised for their radioactive pollution of the environment, the members of the Congress constantly approved big budgets for hundreds of those tests and continued to do so even after the public protests had forced them below ground.

Lars Nowak

Conclusion

This examination of the US government's civil defence and nuclear test films from the first two decades of the Cold War has demonstrated that they shared several features. Films of both types, in effect, transformed the United States from being a nuclear aggressor into being the potential victim of a nuclear attack, while trying to instil in their viewers a moderate emotional stance on such an event that would enable them to protect themselves effectively. If people followed the films' advice regarding this protection, it was suggested, a nuclear war would neither extinguish the American people nor seriously endanger the social order of the United States, thereby giving the impression that the country could, in fact, emerge victorious from it.

At the same time, the civil defence and the nuclear test films differed from each other in two important respects. First of all, although in both cases the manipulation of the spectators' emotions was based on an ambivalent image of nuclear weapons, the indecision of the civil defence films between disguising and revealing the destructive power of these weapons was pushed to extremes in the test films. There were several complex and interconnected reasons for this difference, one of which was that the latter, as opposed to the former, did not limit their focus on the consequences of nuclear war for civilian life, but also took military and political perspectives into consideration.

Secondly, both groups of films made use of the reality effect of moving photographic images to intensify their speculations about a nuclear war. But in the case of the civil defence films, this apparent realism was more frequently diminished by the replacement of these scenes with other kinds of images, such as drawings, diagrams and maps, in contrast to the nuclear test films. Inversely, in the case of the test films, it was more often amplified through the images' contents than in that of the civil defence films; for the test films based their imaginings of nuclear war on real nuclear detonations affecting real test objects and real laboratory animals, and the violence of these detonations was not only conveyed by pictures showing how the test objects were destroyed by their blast and heat waves, but also inscribed onto the cinematic images themselves, which were physically shaken and overexposed. By comparison, the civil defence films' stagings of nuclear war were basically the products of pure imagination, but occasionally complemented their thematic references to the bomb tests with the inclusion of footage that had actually been shot at them. While most of these real-life scenes of the explosions depicted fireballs and mushroom clouds, films such as *Bombproof* and *Radiological Defense* also contained shots showing the destruction of the test objects. Using this strategy, the civil defence films obviously attempted to participate in the enhanced realism that gave the nuclear test films' imaginings of a future nuclear war a quasi-corporeal existence.

Acknowledgement

The research for this chapter was conducted as part of the research project 'Die Wissensräume der ballistischen Photo- und Kinematographie', funded by the Deutsche Forschungsgemeinschaft (project NO 916/2-1).

Notes

1 B. Mielke, 'Rhetoric and ideology in the nuclear test documentary', *Film Quarterly*, 58:3 (2005), pp. 28–37, p. 29.
2 A. Winkler, *Life Under a Cloud: American Anxiety About the Atom* (New York and Oxford, 1993), p. 114.
3 A. C. Titus, 'Back to ground zero: old footage through new lenses', *Journal of Popular Film and Television* 11:1 (Spring 1983), pp. 2–11, p. 6; G. Signori, 'Loving the bomb: Cold War audiovisual propaganda in the United States', in K. Starck (ed.), *Between Fear and Freedom: Cultural Representations of the Cold War* (Newcastle, 2010), pp. 69–81, pp. 71–2.
4 In addition to the established medium of cinematic film, the civil defence authorities also utilised the newer medium of television. Co-operating with the networks, they produced single TV films as well as complete film series, whose messages were also similar to those of the other materials. G. Oakes, *The Imaginary War: Civil Defense and American Cold War Culture* (New York and Oxford, 1994), pp. 100–4, 120–9, 184; M. Matthews, *Duck and Cover: Civil Defense Images in Film and Television from the Cold War to 9/11* (Jefferson, 2010), pp. 73–84.
5 Titus, 'Back to ground zero', pp. 3, 7–8.
6 This terminology is from D. Bordwell and K. Thompson, *Film Art: An Introduction* (New York, 2008), pp. 343–55.
7 D. Garrison, *Bracing for Armageddon: Why Civil Defense Never Worked* (Oxford, 2006), pp. 36, 47.
8 Titus, 'Back to ground zero', p. 6.
9 L. McEnaney, *Civil Defense Begins at Home: Militarization Meets Everyday Life in the Fifties* (Princeton and Oxford, 2000), p. 5; Signori, 'Loving the bomb', p. 71.
10 Titus, 'Back to ground zero', p. 8.
11 *Ibid.*, pp. 6–7.

12 If no source for a quotation is given, as in this case, it was taken from the film that is currently being discussed.
13 T. Lefebvre, 'Filmer la bombe A: premières images, premiers usages', *1895* 39 (Feb. 2003), pp. 127–46, pp. 145–6.
14 Oakes, *Imaginary War*, p. 100.
15 Matthews, *Duck and Cover*, pp. 11–12, 31; Signori, 'Loving the bomb', p. 72.
16 In many civil defence films, tidiness and cleanliness were also characteristics of the diegetic world after a nuclear attack. One extreme example of this textual strategy, which served to emphasise that the attack had not brought about any real change, was *Operation Alert*. Oakes, *Imaginary War*, pp. 96, 98–9.
17 Garrison, *Bracing for Armageddon*, pp. 40, 109.
18 E. Zuckerman, *The Day after World War III: The U.S. Government's Plans for Surviving a Nuclear War* (New York, 1984), pp. 275–6; P. Boyer, *By the Bomb's Early Light: American Thought and Culture at the Dawn of the Atomic Age* (Chapel Hill, 1994), pp. 319, 326.
19 Titus, 'Back to ground zero', p. 6.
20 Zuckerman, *The Day after World War III*, p. 133.
21 McEnaney, *Civil Defense Begins at Home*, p. 7.
22 Ibid., pp. 7–8, 69; Garrison, *Bracing for Armageddon*, pp. 35–7, 40–2.
23 Winkler, *Life Under a Cloud*, p. 120; Garrison, *Bracing for Armageddon*, p. 49.
24 Zuckerman, *The Day after World War III*, p. 139; Winkler, *Life Under a Cloud*, p. 127; Garrison, *Bracing for Armageddon*, p. 123.
25 Garrison, *Bracing for Armageddon*, pp. 44–6.
26 Titus, 'Back to ground zero', p. 6; B. Jacobs, 'Atomic kids: *Duck and Cover* and *Atomic Alert* teach american children how to survive atomic attack', *Film & History* 40:1 (Spring 2010), pp. 25–44, pp. 28–34.
27 McEnaney, *Civil Defense Begins at Home*, pp. 70–1, 78–80.
28 Ibid., pp. 72, 76–7, 80–2.
29 Ibid., pp. 5, 73.
30 Ibid., p. 77; Garrison, *Bracing for Armageddon*, pp. 36–7.
31 Ibid., p. 37.
32 Ibid., p. 38.
33 McEnaney, *Civil Defense Begins at Home*, p. 78.
34 Ibid., p. 77.
35 Oakes, *Imaginary War*, pp. 3–5.
36 Signori, 'Loving the bomb', p. 75.
37 McEnaney, *Civil Defense Begins at Home*, pp. 136–7.
38 Garrison, *Bracing for Armageddon*, p. 37; Oakes, *Imaginary War*, p. 3.
39 D. MacCannell, 'Baltimore in the morning ... after: on the forms of post-nuclear leadership', *Diacritics* 14:2 (Summer 1984), pp. 33–46, pp. 39, 42–4.
40 McEnaney, *Civil Defense Begins at Home*, pp. 146, 149–50; Garrison, *Bracing for Armageddon*, pp. 39–40. The racist bias of the civil defence bureaucracy was

noticed by the National Association for the Advancement of Colored People, which criticised that it would only protect whites against nuclear attacks, while coloured people would be sacrificed. McEnaney, *Civil Defense Begins at Home*, p. 8. Connecting civil defence to civil rights, African-American groups were only willing to participate in it on the condition that this racism was overcome. *Ibid.*, pp. 9, 136, 145.

41 Oakes, *Imaginary War*, pp. 96–100.
42 Titus, 'Back to ground zero', p. 6.
43 Oakes, *Imaginary War*, pp. 100, 104.
44 Zuckerman, *The Day after World War III*, p. 134; Garrison, *Bracing for Armageddon*, p. 39.
45 Garrison, *Bracing for Armageddon*, pp. 36, 47, 50.
46 Matthews, *Duck and Cover*, pp. 24–6; Jacobs, 'Atomic kids', pp. 26–7.
47 Jacobs, 'Atomic kids', pp. 31–2.
48 Winkler, *Life Under a Cloud*, pp. 116, 123, 129–31; McEnaney, *Civil Defense Begins at Home*, p. 84; Garrison, *Bracing for Armageddon*, pp. 36, 126.
49 P. Virilio and S. Lotringer, *Pure War: Twenty-Five Years Later* (Los Angeles, 2007), pp. 68, 103–4, 131–2, 148–9.
50 Mielke, 'Rhetoric and ideology', p. 29.
51 Titus, 'Back to ground zero', p. 7; P. Kuran, *How to Photograph an Atomic Bomb* (Santa Clarita, 2006), p. 39.
52 For instance, the public version of the nuclear test movie *Operation Ivy* (1952) had more viewers than any other film produced by a government institution after the Second World War. Kuran, *How to Photograph an Atomic Bomb*, p. 39. Additionally, some nuclear tests, among them the civil defence tests *Doorstep* and *Cue*, were filmed by TV reporters from the Nevada Proving Ground's News Nob and partly broadcast in real time. McEnaney, *Civil Defense Begins at Home*, p. 170; Kuran, *How to Photograph an Atomic Bomb*, p. 112; Joseph Masco, 'Target audience', *Bulletin of the Atomic Scientists* 64:3 (July–Aug. 2008), pp. 22–31, 45, p. 28; Matthews, *Duck and Cover*, pp. 84–9. During the 1990s, a selection of about fifty nuclear test films was declassified by the US Department of Energy and thus made available for scholarly examination. These movies were transferred to videotapes, which can be purchased at the Nuclear Testing Archive (www.nv.energy.gov/library/films/testfilms.aspx), and are now also available as digital files on several websites, such as the Internet Archive (www.archive.org). (accessed 16 February 2016).
53 Kuran, *How to Photograph an Atomic Bomb*, pp. 38–9, 48.
54 Mielke, 'Rhetoric and ideology', pp. 30, 33–4.
55 A. C. Titus, *Bombs in the Backyard: Atomic Testing and American Politics* (Reno and Las Vegas, 1986), pp. 63–4.
56 Masco, 'Target audience', pp. 28–9.
57 Titus, *Bombs in the Backyard*, p. 63; Masco, 'Target audience', p. 26.

58 Masco, 'Target audience', p. 26; Titus, *Bombs in the Backyard*, p. 61.
59 Titus, *Bombs in the Backyard*, pp. 59–61; Masco, 'Target audience', p. 26.
60 Titus, *Bombs in the Backyard*, pp. 62–3. Volunteers underwent even more extreme experiments. For example, in an experiment performed during operation *Buster-Jangle* and depicted in the film *Military Participation on Buster Jangle* (1951), some of them deliberately exposed their eyes to the nuclear flash so that their temporary loss of sight could be studied.
61 Titus, *Bombs in the Backyard*, pp. 60, 74; Masco, 'Target audience', p. 26.
62 Masco, 'Target audience', p. 27.
63 Mielke, 'Rhetoric and ideology', p. 31.
64 Masco, 'Target audience', p. 27.
65 T. Vanderbilt, *Survival City: Adventures Among the Ruins of Atomic America* (New York, 2002), pp. 89–92.
66 Masco, 'Target audience', p. 27.
67 *Ibid.*, p. 29.
68 Mielke, 'Rhetoric and ideology', p. 31.
69 *Ibid.*, p. 31; Masco, 'Target audience', pp. 26–7.
70 Masco, 'Target audience', p. 31; L. Nowak, 'Karte – Kino – Krieg: Zum Gebrauch von Karten in zwei "Subgenres" des amerikanischen Kriegsfilms', in S. Günzel and L. Nowak (eds), *KartenWissen: Territoriale Räume zwischen Bild und Diagramm* (Wiesbaden, 2012), pp. 421–49, pp. 436, 443–6.
71 *Ibid.*, p. 439.
72 *Ibid.*, pp. 436, 443.
73 Masco, 'Target audience', pp. 30–1.
74 *Ibid.*, p. 24.
75 S. Weart, *Nuclear Fear: A History of Images* (Cambridge, Mass. and London, 1988), p. 183; Oakes, *Imaginary War*, pp. 59, 149.
76 Titus, 'Back to ground zero', p. 8.
77 *Ibid.*, p. 7.
78 Masco, 'Target audience', p. 24.

Index

Literary works can be found under author's name.

1968 93, 106, 131, 133, 168

A New Look at the H-Bomb 264
A Short Vision 102
ABC 83, 243
Abel Archer-83 3
Abrams, Herbert D. 223
Acheson-Lilienthal plan 77
Ackerman, Thomas P. 240
activism 76, 78, 81–2, 129, 141, 167, 169–70, 175, 249, 254
Adenauer, Konrad 60, 119–26, 133
Adorno, Theodor W. 141, 159n.11, 164n.123
Aesculapium staff 218
AFCENT 134
Afghanistan 25, 81
Africa 193, 254
Airlie House 223–5
Alabama 81
Alamogordo 80
Alaska 86
Aldermaston marches 126
Alert Today – Alive Tomorrow 267
Alexandrov, Vladimir V. 248–9
American Academy of Arts and Sciences 242
American Revolution 177
Anders, Günther 9, 18–19, 33–5, 40, 46–7, 125, 140–57
  Burning Conscience 145
  On the Bomb and the Roots of our Blindness to Apocalypse 143
  The Dead 151
  Faust is Dead 143
  The Man on the Bridge 145–6, 148
  The Obsolescence of Human Beings 141, 143, 146–50, 152
  Theses on the Atomic Age 34
Andropov, Yuri 246
anthropology 34, 142–3, 152
anti-communism 126, 175, 190–1, 196–8, 205
anti-nuclear activism 129, 254
anti-nuclear movements 140–1, 146, 165, 167–71, 173, 239, 244, 246, 250, 252
anti-nuclear protests 5, 111, 134, 166, 249
anti-Stalinism 179
anti-war
  activists/groups 170, 175–6, 185n.4
  discourse 65
  movements 167, 170, 172, 178
  tour 168

Index

antiquity 25
apocalypse 15–16, 30–1, 34–5, 38, 45–7, 52, 102, 117, 143, 149–52, 155–6, 165, 169, 182, 189, 219, 222, 239, 243, 250
Archer Productions 261
Arendt, Hannah 142
Argentina 246
Armageddon 51, 62, 87, 95, 154, 250
Armageddon 86
arms race 14, 20, 52, 57, 78, 81, 131, 145, 156, 168, 170–1, 182, 189–90, 196–7, 200, 203–4, 206, 214–16, 219–21, 223–4, 227, 242, 250
Asahi journal 188n.42
Asia Pacific War 170, 179
Atomic Alert (Elementary Version) 264, 266–8
Atomic Bomb Casualty Commission (ABCC) 183
Atomic Café 89n.14
Atomic Energy Commission (AEC) 72n.67, 78, 271
Atomic Fireball 81
Atomic Survival 269
Atomic Underwear Company 77
atomic
  age 10, 13, 75, 77, 84, 110, 119, 141, 147–8, 156–7, 181, 274
  anxiety 53, 111
  attack 18, 61, 97–100, 267
  blast 7–8, 80, 122, 128
  cars 96
  death 125–6, 146
  explosion 60, 183, 196, 264, 268, 273, 280
  future 94, 101
  missiles 57, 116
  tests 75, 77, 101, 119, 275–6
  weapons 47, 51, 56–8, 62, 70n.35, 70n.38, 111, 119, 122–3, 202
Attack of the Crab Monsters 80

Attlee, Clement 96, 99–100
Auschwitz 74n.104, 145, 148, 157, 161n.43, 162n.62
Australia 79, 193

B-29 19, 145
balance of terror 39, 41, 44
Bali 86
Barbusse, Henri 130
Batman 87
Baudissin, Wolf Count von 134–5
Bavaria 198
BBC 6–8, 68n.4, 97–8, 108, 112n.18
Beauvoir, Simone de 168
Beheiren 166–9, 175–6, 179, 185n.4, 186n.10
Belgium 116
Benjamin, Walter 142
Bennett, Alan 108
Benson, Arizona 61
Berlin, 31, 41–2, 78, 83, 132–3, 142, 195
Bert the Turtle 79
Beyond the Fringe 108
Bible 77, 91n.38
Bikini Atoll 58, 75, 79, 119, 171
bishops 8, 199–200, 206–7, 247
black activism 167
Black, Sir Douglas 223
Blank, Theodor 120–1
Blitz 18, 68n.8, 93–4, 99–100, 104, 111
Blumenberg, Hans 47
Böckenförde, Ernst-Wolfgang 202
Bogensberger, Wolfgang 163n.85
Bombproof 265, 283
Bonn 59, 127
Boston 168, 215, 221, 226, 232n.13
Boulting Brothers 100
Brandt, Willy 247
Brazil 86
Brecht, Bertolt 142
Brezhnev, Leonid 61–2, 65, 72n.73

288

Index

Britain 7–8, 18, 70n.43, 72n.84, 81, 92, 94, 96–106, 108–11, 143, 218, 228, 246, 277
    see also United Kingdom
British Museum 103
British Royal College of Physicians 223
Brodie, Bernard 33, 39
Broken Arrow 85
Bronowski, Jacob 94
Brown, H. Rap 176
Buchanan Brothers 77
Bulletin of the Atomic Scientists 31, 40, 42, 243
Bultmann, Rudolf 151
Bundeswehr 17, 119–23, 125, 133–4
Burdick, Eugene 50n.50, 79
Bush, George W. 75, 86

Caldicott, Helen 226, 233n.32
California 82, 142
Cambridge, Massachusetts 242
Cameron, James 102
Campaign for Nuclear Disarmament (CND) 7–8, 92, 104–11, 126, 246
capitalism 55, 177, 248
Carmichael, Stokely 175–6
'carpet bombing' 124
Carte Blanche 121
Carter, Jimmy 81
cartoons 54, 56, 59–60, 63, 72n.74, 87
Castle Bravo 262, 280–1
Catholic Academy 198
Catholic Workers' Movement 201, 211n.48
Catholicism 196
CBS 78, 82, 128–9
Central Committee 54, 66
Central Europe 121, 126, 129, 146
Central Park 78, 82
'Challenge of Peace' 199
Chazov, Evgenij 217–18, 221, 226, 249–50

Chernobyl 65–6, 73n.97, 240
Chicago 81, 88, 228
China 13, 81–2, 180, 254
China Syndrome 82
Chivian, Eric 220
Chrichton, Michael 31
Christian Campaign for Nuclear Disarmament 246
Christian Democratic Union (CDU) 119–21, 123, 125–7, 191
Christian
    culture 66
    doctrine 189
    eschatology 149, 151
    religion 189, 192
    tradition 117
Christianity 51, 151, 189
Chûgoku Shinbun 169, 180
Churchill, Winston 105
CIA 85, 224
cinematography 9–10
Cities of Peace 165
Civil Defence Corps 93, 97
civil defence 7–9, 12, 15, 21, 35–6, 43, 68n.4, 93–5, 97–102, 104–6, 108, 110–11, 214, 222, 227–8, 230, 243, 260–78, 280–3, 284n.40
    administration 261, 274
    films 7, 260–78, 281–3
    propaganda 68n.4, 93, 104, 262, 265
civil nuclear energy 13–14
civil rights movements 166–70, 172, 174, 176–9
civilians 120, 184, 230, 270, 274
civilization 18, 21, 51, 53, 58, 93–6, 101–2, 150–5, 157, 200, 278
Clancy, Tom 82, 85
    The Hunt for Red October 82
    The Sum of all Fears 85
class 56, 61, 103, 156, 175–7
climate change 240, 242, 251, 254
Clooney, George 85

Index

collective imagination 24, 53, 69n.16, 185
colonialism 19, 145
Columbia Pictures 75
commercial films 260, 271
Commoner, Barry 79
communication 33, 41–3, 45–6, 123, 145, 215
communism 52, 55, 67, 105, 134, 172, 178, 192, 194–6, 199, 205–7, 248
Communist Party of Great Britain 109
Communist Party of Japan 179
concentration camps 124, 153
CONELRAD (Control of Electromagnetic Radiation) 266
Confessing Church 120, 124
Connery, Sean 82
conscription 125
consequences of nuclear war 3, 8, 12, 20, 36, 97, 99, 119, 128, 200, 219, 223, 246, 248, 266, 282
   medical 213–14, 217, 221–2, 224, 226
   of nuclear weapons 11, 14, 16, 21, 133
consumerism 169, 175
contamination 36, 262–3, 272, 274
Cook, Peter 108
Cosmos 239
Council of the Affairs of the Russian Orthodox Church 66
Coventry 104
Crimson Tide 84
Critical Theory 142
Crozier, William 23
cruise missiles 116–17, 127, 131, 241
'crusades' 53, 62–3, 146, 189, 207
Cuba 107, 110, 176
Cuban Missile Crisis 6, 43, 61, 64, 78, 84, 107, 126, 168, 260, 270

Dagwood Splits the Atom 78
Daily Mail 97
Daily Mirror 95, 97, 101, 109

Day, Dorothy 200–1, 206–7
Dayton, Ohio 76
decontamination 265
defence planners 7, 15, 101, 103
Defence White Paper 105
DeLillo, Don 84
   Underworld 84
democratisation 1
Denver 76, 85
Department of Defense 271
Derrida, Jacques 38, 52
destruction
   mass 32, 57, 87, 124, 147, 154, 183, 203, 221, 247
   total 4, 96, 107, 214, 228
destructiveness 2, 93, 98, 269, 274, 276, 278
détente 16, 24, 238
deterrence 33, 35, 37–40, 92–3, 104–8, 111, 200, 202, 228, 243, 248, 251, 270
   nuclear 3–5, 7–8, 22, 25, 45–7, 94–5, 117, 131, 133–4, 198, 217, 247
Deutscher Gewerkschaftsbund (DGB) 124
Dillinger, Dave 168, 186n.10
dinosaurs 83, 240
diplomacy 11
disarmament 12, 40, 95, 105, 107–8, 145, 150, 171, 199, 204–5, 214, 218, 224, 249–50
discourse
   on the bomb 18, 31, 47, 118, 171
   Catholic 19, 191–2, 199, 201–7
   Christian 189
   Cold War 24, 165, 167, 173
   on human rights 165, 169, 173–5, 179
   political 94, 183, 192, 215
   public 98, 132, 198, 240
   on radioactivity 32
   scientific 198, 216, 244

Index

on security 5
victimization 119, 122
on war 65
discrimination 171, 174, 176, 178, 181, 280
diseases 20–1, 213–16, 221, 226, 228–9, 235n.58, 253
'doomsday clock' 30
Doomsday Device 40, 43–4, 46–7
Douglas, Gordon 260
Dresden 118–19
DuBois, W.E.B. 174
Duck and Cover 264, 266, 270

earthquake 82, 201, 245, 274
East Asia 19, 178
Easter March movement 123, 126, 132
Eastern Europe 206
Eatherly, Claude 19, 145, 152
economic growth 168–9, 175, 205
Economist 97
Edwards, Ralph 80
Eggebrecht, Axel 119
Ehrlich, Paul 252
  The Population Bomb 251
Eighteen Nation Committee on Disarmament 60
Einstein, Albert 58, 119, 150, 232n.24
Eisenhower, Dwight D. 70n.40, 266
electricity 78, 96
Eley, Geoff 98
Empire State Building 277
end of the world 30, 33, 35, 45, 47, 53, 60–2, 65–7, 94, 101, 117, 151, 202, 251
Enola Gay 19, 24, 80, 86, 145
episcopate 199–200, 206–7
equality 47, 172, 175–6
Erenburg, Il'ia 60, 62
escalation 6, 11, 25, 35, 37, 42, 52, 66, 146, 231n.9
eschatology 149, 151
Essex 23

Eugen, Heinrich 124
Eurocommunism 11
European Nuclear Disarmament (END) 246, 248
evacuation 99–100, 265, 269
Exercise Desert Rock 273–5, 277
exobiology 238
extermination 30, 33–4, 154, 220, 242
extinction 30, 52, 75, 102, 153, 157, 240, 242, 254

FALLEX '63 108
Fallout: When and How to Protect Yourself Against It 266
Falwell, Jerry 62
Fantastic Four 87
Far East 57
fascism 52, 55, 63
Fatima, Portugal 195
Faulkner, William 86
FBI 172
Featherstone, Ralph 19, 167–70, 172–3, 175–9, 182–5, 186n.10, 187n.19, 187n.30
Federal Civil Defense Administration (FCDA) 261, 272, 280
Federal Constitutional Court 123
Federal Republic of Germany *see* West Germany
Federation of American Scientists 77
Ferrara, Nello 81
Ferrara Pan Candy Company 81
Ferris, Timothy 238
Feuerbach, Ludwig 156
'Fight against Atomic Death' 123–4, 126
Finckh-Krämer, Ute 137n.46
Finding Nemo 87
firestorms 6, 118, 274
first strike 3, 39, 44, 198, 242, 246, 248
First World War 9, 23, 31–2, 37, 124, 151
Flanders 10
Florida 85

Fonda, Henry 79
Fonda, Jane 82
Fontainebleau 122, 134
Foreign Affairs 242, 252
Fort Leavenworth, Kansas 129
France 13, 15, 72n.84, 81, 143, 158n.1, 196, 204, 247
Frank, Jerome D. 216
Frankfurt 130, 142, 159n.11, 198
Frankfurter Hefte 202–3
FREEZE 226
Freeze Now Movement 205
Freundlich, Elisabeth 142, 159n.16
Fulda 17, 128–9
fundamentalism 102
'futurology' 35, 43, 48n.14

game theory 39–41, 43
Gaudium et Spes 204
GDR 128–9, 232n.13
General Electric 78
genetic defects 38, 263
Geneva summit 58
genocide 125, 146–7, 157, 159n.14, 203
George, Peter 38
   Red Alert 38
Germany 48n.1, 101, 118, 120–3, 125–6, 128–9, 132–4, 142–3, 161n.57, 199–200, 205
   see also Federal Republic of Germany; West Germany
Gerstenmaier, Eugen 120
Gethsemani, Kentucky 196
Geyer, Michael 3–4, 69n.16, 125, 157
global warming 254
Godzilla 80
Goldwater, Barry 83–4
Göll, Franz 133–4
Gorbachev, Mikhail 25, 51, 65, 67, 83, 146, 250
Göttingen 123
Great Plains 5
Greece 246

greenhouse effect 240, 252, 254
Greenpeace 247
Greens 127
Grosz, George 142
'ground zero' 24, 128, 247, 272–3
Grushin, Boris 63–5
Guha, Anton Andreas 130
   Diary from the Third World War 130
Gundlach, Gustav 198–9, 202–3, 207

H-bomb 18, 36, 41–2, 51, 58, 60–1, 68n.4, 70n.43, 78–9, 81, 93, 101, 120, 123, 125, 142–3, 166, 171, 183, 262, 269, 274, 276, 278–9, 281
H-Bomb War: What It Would Be Like 108
Hackett, Sir John 129
Hackman, Gene 84
Haig, Alexander 82
Haley, Bill 51
Hamburg 118–19, 161n.57
Hanford 88
Harris, Brian 130
Harry Potter 87
Harwell, Mark 254
Hatfield, Mark 248
Hattenbach 128–9, 134
Healey, Denis 107–8
Heidegger, Martin 142
Heroldsbach 194–5
Hersey, John 77, 87, 181
   Hiroshima 77, 85
Hesse-Nassau 123–4
hibakusha 19, 119, 165–7, 169, 171, 173, 179, 181–3, 188n.45, 225
   see also survivors
Hidankyô 166, 183
Hiroshima
   activists 166–7, 169, 173, 179
   after Hiroshima 57, 70n.35, 75, 94–5, 103, 141, 146–7, 157
   anniversary of 57, 75

Index

Auschwitz and 145, 148, 157, 161n.43, 162n.62
  bombing of 9, 16, 18–19, 23–4, 51, 70, 76, 93–6, 101–3, 110, 118–19, 122, 131, 142, 171, 196, 198, 201, 206, 258n.51, 260
  destruction of 4, 77, 263
  'Hiroshima Maidens' 80
  Nagasaki and 4, 9, 16, 23, 75, 77, 95, 99, 118–19, 141, 145, 147–9, 165, 168, 170–1, 173, 180–4, 195, 198, 201, 206, 223, 225, 228, 251, 253, 260, 263
  nuclear cloud over 56
  peace conference in 58
  photographs of 228
  residents 171, 182, 184, 225
  ruins of 99, 149
  solidarity with 156
  survivors 166, 182–3, 225
  symposium 175
  teach-in 176–7, 180, 182, 185
  university of 166, 169, 183, 223
Hitler, Adolf 142, 151
Hoban, Russell 108
  Riddley Walker 108
Hoegh, Leo 90n.18
Hofer, Karl 23
Hokkaido 166
Holland 31
Hollywood 76–7, 102, 239, 271
Holocaust 142, 144, 148–8, 152
'Holy War' 189, 199, 207
Home Office 6, 106, 113n.32
'Honest John' rocket 120
Houses of Parliament 103
Hudson Institute 35, 38
Hughes, Ted 107
Hugo, Fr. John 201
human race 75, 83, 93, 102, 107, 144, 149, 155
human rights 11, 19, 165, 167, 169, 173–9, 181–3, 185, 204, 247

Hurley, Frank 10
Husserl, Edmund 142
  hypothetical historiography 37

If It Fell on Hampstead 98
Iida, Momo 167–8
Illustrated London News 98
Ilyin, L.A. 223
imagery 38, 45, 65, 87, 98, 194–8, 201, 207
imperialism 19, 166
Incredibles 87
Independence Day 85
independence movements 168
India 81, 246, 252, 254
industrialism 153
inequalities 268
Institute of Public Opinion 63
intercontinental ballistic missiles (ICBMs) 78
international control 77–8, 96–8, 171
International Council of Scientific Unions 254
International Institute of Strategic Studies 127
International Physicians for the Prevention of Nuclear War (IPPNW) 20–1, 130, 213–31, 232n.13, 233n.31, 249, 259n.51
internationalism 140, 156
Invasion of the Body Snatchers 88
Iran 25, 85–6
Iraq 87
Iron Curtain 15, 21, 25, 51, 130, 227, 281
irrationality 20, 44, 46, 108
Israel 81
Italy 116, 246
Izvestiia 57–8, 249

Jaeger, Lorenz 195
Jansson, Tove 10
  Comet in Moominland 10

Index

Japan 16, 19, 36, 76, 145, 152, 166–73, 175–6, 179–81, 183–5, 187n.19, 198, 218, 223, 264, 270, 273–4
Japan Confederation of A- and H-Bomb Sufferers Organisations 166, 183
Jaspers, Karl 30–1, 35
Jesuits 197–8
John Paul II 246
John XXIII 197, 203–4
Judeocide 146
Jungk, Robert 35
'just war theory' 189, 197, 202, 204, 206
'Justice brings Peace' 199

Kahn, Albert 61
Kahn, Herman 7, 33, 35–8, 40–1, 43–5, 47, 50n.44, 80, 133
   On Thermonuclear War 7, 35–7, 41, 80
   Thinking about the Unthinkable 37
Kaikô, Ken 179
Kanai, Toshihiro 169, 180–3
Kansas 75, 83, 129
Kapitza, Sergei 248
Karpov, 66
Katholikentag 195
Kennedy, Edward 248
Kennedy, John F. 42–3, 61, 191, 266
Kent 6
Kentucky 196
Kerry, John 87
Key to Hell 124
KGB 82, 224
Khrushchev, Nikita 42–3, 58–9, 61, 70n.40, 71n.47, 72n.84, 84
Kidman, Nicole 85
Kiseleva, Evgeniia Grigor'evna 64–5, 67
Koestler, Arthur 75
   Darkness at Noon 75
Kogon, Eugen 202
Kohl, Helmut 146
Kola peninsula 63

Komsomol'skaia pravda 63
Korean War 66, 78, 98, 179, 195
Kosmodem'ianskaia, Zoia 55
Kramer, Stanley 21, 79
   On the Beach 51, 59, 79, 85, 90n.18, 260
Kremlin 43, 54
Krokodil 52, 54, 56, 60, 63
Kubrick, Stanley 33, 40, 44–7, 80, 84, 87
   Dr. Strangelove or: How I Learned to Stop Worrying and Love the Bomb 37–8, 40, 44–7, 75, 80, 83–5, 108
Kurasawa, Akira 86
Kuzin, M.I. 223
Kyushu 166

Labour Party 106–8, 177, 247
Law Concerning Medical Care or the Atomic Bomb Exposed 181
Left Behind 87, 91n.38
Lehrer, Tom 80
Lem, Stanislaw 31
Lessing, Doris 109
   The Golden Notebook 109
   The Truth about Billy Newton 109
Let's Face It 272, 274, 277–8
Levy, Benn W. 106
Liberal Democratic Party (LDP) 169, 171–2
Libya 81, 86
Life magazine 77
Lifton, Robert Jay 78, 157, 216, 225
Lilienthal, David 78
Limited Test Ban Treaty 270
Lion Noir 121
Listener 97
Livermore 255
Loader, Jane 89n.14
London 32, 86, 95, 98, 100, 119, 127, 228
Lopushanskii, Konstantin 51
   The Letters of a Dead Man 51

Index

Lord of the Rings 87
Los Alamos 88, 255
Los Angeles 82
Lou Grant 82
Lovejoy, Sam 81
Lown, Bernard 20, 215–18, 221–3, 226, 249
Lucas, George 87
Lucky Dragon 58, 171
Lumet, Sidney 33, 45–6, 50n.50
  Fail-Safe 37, 44, 46–7, 79, 83, 85

Mack, John E. 216, 220
Mad magazine 80
Maddox, John 244
Madrid 86
Mainichi 188n.42
Majdanek 74n.104
Malenkov, Georgii 58, 71n.48
Malraux, André 151
'Man and the Atom' exhibit 78
Manhattan 24, 277
Manhattan Project 31–2, 76, 88
Marcuse, Herbert 145
Maresʹev, Aleksei 55
Marian apparitions 20, 192–6, 207
Marian cult 195
Mariner missions 240
Markusen, Eric 157
Marpingen 192
Mars 238–40
Marx, Karl 143, 156
Marxism 56, 150, 156, 158n.2, 164n.127, 175, 178
Masereel, Franz 124
mass media 17, 97, 129, 162n.58, 262
mass protests 92, 127
Massachusetts 82, 241, 248
Matthau, Walter 45
McNamara, Robert 6, 184
MDK 84
mechanization 145–6, 153–4

Medical Aspects of Nuclear Radiation 262–4
Medjugorje, Croatia 195
Merton, Thomas 196
  Breakthrough to Peace 196
metaphors 1–2, 4, 10, 20–1, 24–5, 33, 36, 55, 98, 122, 124, 148, 181, 191–2, 196, 201, 203–4, 215–16, 250–3
Mexico 246
MGM 271
Military Effects on Operation Redwing 278
Military Participation on Buster Jangle 273, 285n.60
Military Participation on Tumbler/Snapper 272–6
military 2, 5, 22, 66, 119–20, 122, 125, 131, 133, 179, 183, 227–9
  action 24
  base 76, 130, 172
  circles 12, 119
  commanders/officials 54, 62, 198, 266
  conflict 25, 41, 189, 270, 272
  exercises/manoeuvres 272–3, 280
  history 153
  personnel 9, 38, 44, 128, 178, 203
  planners 3, 7, 10, 12, 133–4
  policy 16
  science 32, 37, 169
  strategy 33, 92, 134, 219
Miller, Walter 79
  A Canticle for Leibowitz 79
minorities 94, 104, 151, 177, 182, 191, 213, 268
Minuteman missiles 5
Mississippi 174, 177
mobilisation 125, 130, 141, 175, 193, 216, 261
modernity 34, 148, 162n.58
Molotov, Viacheslav 51
Moritaki Ichirô 166, 169, 173

Index

Moscow 3, 42–6, 54, 59, 64, 71n.53, 72n.67, 81, 83, 218, 246, 249
Moscow peace conference 55
Muller, James 224, 233n.31
Murray, John C. 197–8, 207
mushroom cloud 2, 8, 30, 59–60, 62, 71n.53, 71n.61, 82, 86–7, 119, 124, 126, 275, 277, 283
mutants 51, 80
mutations 59, 102, 183
Mutual Assured Destruction (MAD) 39–41, 43–6

NAACP 174, 177
Nagasaki 59
Nagasaki
  anniversary of 75
  bombing of 9, 16, 23, 76, 95, 118–19, 145, 162n.67, 165, 172, 180, 198, 201, 206, 260
  destruction of 4, 77, 149, 263
  Hiroshima and 4, 9, 16, 23, 75, 77, 95, 99, 118–19, 141, 145, 147–9, 165, 168, 170–1, 173, 180–4, 195, 198, 201, 206, 223, 225, 228, 251, 253, 260, 263
  photographs of 228
  residents of 86, 171, 225
  ruins of 99
  survivors of 182–183, 225
  victims of 148
Nagoya University 175
Naha 169
napalm 180
Napoleon 143
NASA 238–9
National Academy of Sciences (NAS) 245
National Association for the Advancement of Colored People 284n.40
National Education Association 78
National Fallout Shelter Survey 266

national liberation movements 167
National Socialism 146, 150
NATO 3, 8, 17, 116, 119, 121–2, 126–7, 133–4, 228, 238
NATO Double Track Decision 116, 127, 146, 199–200, 205, 207, 210n.42
Nature 239, 244
Nazis 60, 118, 124, 142, 146–7, 161n.57
Nazi Germany 174
NCAR 252
Necedah, Wisconsin 193, 197
neo-imperialism 166
Neo-Scholastic 189
Netherlands 116, 218
Neu-Ulm 127
neutral countries 15–16
neutrality 15, 217, 229
Nevada 87, 272–3, 285n.52
New Delhi 246
New England 82
New England Journal of Medicine 214
New Haven 76
New Jersey 61
New York 46–7, 60, 77–8, 82, 120, 142, 191, 262
New York Times 243, 245, 248, 252
New Yorker 77, 83, 157
New Zealand 247
News Chronicle 95
Newsweek 145
Niemöller, Martin 124–6, 132
Nieuwenhuys, Constant 23
Nike-Hercules missiles 78, 120, 128
'Nikel' 63
Nine Power Conference 119
Nixon, Richard 79
Nobel Peace Prize 249–50
non-combatants 180–1, 188n.42
North Korea 86
Norwood Studios 261

Index

novels 6, 31–2, 38, 40, 50n.50, 51, 79, 82–5, 87, 91n.38, 98, 102, 108–9, 182, 246
Nuclear Non-proliferation Treaty 81, 195
Nuclear Test Ban Treaty 126, 171
nuclear
  allergy 169, 171
  annihilation 2, 25, 63, 126, 130, 144, 147, 165
  anxiety 17, 64, 116, 132
  autumn 252, 254
  catastrophe 4, 8, 81, 129, 131, 204, 219, 249
  chain reaction 32
  cloud 56, 60
  confrontation 6, 11–12, 14, 17, 92, 229
  consciousness 51
  crisis management 11, 44
  culture 13, 18, 52–3, 60
  destruction 3–4, 6, 14, 16–17, 85, 92–3, 95, 103, 119, 127, 131–3, 156, 165, 216, 225, 273
  deterrence 3–5, 7–8, 22, 25, 45–7, 94–5, 117, 131, 133–4, 190, 198, 217, 247
  detonation 222, 230, 263, 274, 277, 282
  devastation 3–4, 128–9, 134, 157
  'era' 93–4
  explosion 8, 21–3, 30, 240, 247, 251, 262, 264–5, 269, 274–5, 277–8
  fears 16, 52, 79–80, 83, 86, 195, 220, 238
  fission 31–2
  holocaust 51, 56, 93, 239, 250
  knowledge 12–14
  madness 226, 229, 246
  militarization 128
  missiles 7, 85, 116, 123, 125, 128, 238, 241, 251
  pacifism 19, 124

  physics 24, 31
  politics 11–12, 145
  question 141, 143, 222
  reality 76–6, 103, 111
  stand-off 3, 21
  strategists 3, 7
  technology 13, 24, 119, 169, 182
  test films 22, 271–8, 281–3, 285n.52
  threat 2, 5–6, 35, 51, 58, 67, 76, 82, 85, 109, 128, 142, 145, 157, 178, 189, 191–2, 198, 202–3, 214, 220–1, 229, 280
  warheads 17, 75, 84–6, 120–2, 126, 133–4, 241
  waste 6, 76, 87, 124, 185n.1
  'winter' 21, 239–55, 259n.51
nuclearisation 143
Nuremberg Trials 174

Oak Ridge 88
occupation 19, 56, 87, 94, 118, 168, 171, 184, 265
Oda, Makoto 167–70, 177, 179, 186n.19
Ôe, Kenzaburô 166
  Hiroshima Notes 166
Office of Civil and Defense Mobilisation 261
Office of Civil Defense Management 90n.18
Ogonek 54–5, 59–61
Ohkita, Takeshi 223
Okinawa 166, 184
Oklahoma City 85
Operation Alert 264, 269, 284n.16
Operation Argus – Report of Chief, AFSWP to ARPA 277
Operation Atomic Vision 78
Operation Castle: Commander's Report 277
Operation Crossroads 273–4
Operation Cue 272, 274, 277–8, 280
Operation Doorstep 272, 274–5, 277

Index

Operation Hardtack: Military Effects Studies. Part Three: Underwater Tests 278
Operation IVY 70n.43, 275, 277–80, 285n.52
Operation Redwing 273, 278
Operation Teapot: Military Effects Studies 273
opinion polls 20, 63–4, 102, 107, 125, 132
Oppenheimer, Robert 83
Oregon 248
Orwell, George 1, 4, 24–5, 100
 Nineteen Eighty-Four 100
Our Cities Must Fight 264–5

Pacem in Terris 203–4
pacifism 19, 56, 124, 126, 130, 201, 206, 213
pacifists 3, 52, 98, 124, 168, 202–3, 232n.24
Paderborn 195
Pakistan 81, 86
Paris 31, 41, 54, 142, 151
Paris summit 63, 72n.84
pathology 20, 214, 216, 219
patriotism 56, 64
Pavlov, Alexander S. 248
Pax Christi 205, 212n.64
peace
 activists/campaigners 3, 17, 22, 60, 102, 131, 133, 205, 250
 campaigns 53–4, 57–8, 66, 69n.21
 conferences 55, 58
 movements 12, 52, 60, 63, 107, 127–9, 131, 134, 145–6, 156, 159n.8, 210n.42, 217, 219–20, 223, 237n.94
 protests 59, 127, 199, 205
 researchers 3, 35
peaceful coexistence 61
Peace Park 166
Pearl Harbor 181

Pennsylvania 82, 267
Pentagon 44, 62, 82–3, 243, 248, 277
People 62
Perle, Richard 116
Pershing II 116
Perugia 246
Physicians for Social Responsibility (PSR) 214–15, 222, 226, 233n.32, 259n.51
Picasso, Pablo 98
Pius XII 19, 193, 196–8, 200, 202–4, 206, 210n.31
Plessner, Helmuth 142
Polaris missiles 166
Pollack, James B. 240
popular belief 20, 190–2, 196, 208n.8
popular culture 5, 10, 12–14, 17, 24, 82, 84–8, 93, 95, 98, 100–1, 103–4, 106
post-nuclear
 future 102, 117
 society/world 9, 104, 148
 war 79–80, 83, 248
Prague 54
Pravda 54, 57–63, 72n.75, 248
Preservation 75
prisoners of war 119
Pritt, D.N. 107
Promethean gap 34, 144, 146–7, 151
propaganda 5, 8, 54, 60, 68n.4, 78, 93, 97, 100, 104, 106, 111, 118, 260–2, 265, 270
protests 95, 123, 132, 171, 174, 176, 184, 222–3, 249
 events 127
 movements 5, 59, 123, 167, 170, 199
 international 157
 mass 92, 127
 public 172, 281
 social 166
 student 177
Protestant Church 124
psychotherapy 220, 229

Index

public health 214, 216
Pugwash initiative 58

race 172, 175, 177–9
radiation 10, 48n.2, 53, 58–9, 67,
 79–80, 102, 104, 118, 120, 124,
 180–3, 185, 214, 246, 251, 262–4,
 266, 274
Radio Moscow 59
radioactive
 cloud 79–80
 contamination 36, 262
 fallout 36, 58–9, 79, 101, 171, 266,
 270, 276
 waste 76
radioactivity 31–2, 79, 102–3, 223,
 262–5, 270, 274, 278
Radiological Defense 262, 264–6, 283
radium 32, 265
Rafferty, Kevin 89n.14
RAND 7, 33, 35–6, 38–9, 80
Rapacki, Adam 125
rational choice theory 39, 45
rationality 45, 98, 107–8, 111, 131–2,
 198, 203, 218, 227–8
Reagan, Ronald 53, 62, 65, 67, 82–3,
 86, 146, 236n.87, 238, 241, 243,
 246, 252
rearmament 17, 59, 116, 119, 125, 191
Red Army 121
'red telephone' 43, 50n.46
Reichstag 142
religion 19, 189–94, 206–7,
 208n.6, 246
repression 168, 176, 216, 219–20,
 227, 249
Resnais, Alain 79
 Hiroshima Mon Amour 79
retaliation 17, 41, 120, 130, 246, 251
retaliatory strike 39–40, 250
Revenge of the Sith 87
Reykjavik 146
Rhapsody in August 86

rhetorics 16, 33, 53–6, 58, 61, 65–6,
 97, 106, 110, 116, 167, 172, 196,
 220, 227, 237n.95, 238, 241, 262
Rhine river 121, 130
Rhineland 123, 151
Rice, Condoleezza 87
Richter, Horst Eberhard 130–1, 216,
 220–1, 230
 Everyone talked about Peace 130
RKO 261, 171
Robards, Jason 83
Robock, Alan 254–5
Rochester 6, 8
Rogers, Buck 83
romanticism 116, 133
Rome 190
Russell, Bertrand 58, 93, 103, 108
 Has Man a Future? 93
Russian Revolution 52, 55

Sagan, Carl 21, 238–46, 248–9, 251–4
 Contact 246
 The Dragons of Eden 239
Saint Augustine 189
Sakharov, Andrei 59
San Francisco 218
SANE 79, 170
Sapporo 169
Sartre, Jean-Paul 145, 163
satellites 83, 153
Sato, Eisaku 172
Saturday Evening Post 79
Scheler, Max 142
Schell, Jonathan 83, 157, 251
 The Fate of the Earth 83, 157, 251
Schlesinger, John 109
 Darling 109–10
Schmidt, Helmut 127
Schnez, Albert 122
Schnittke, Alfred 59
Schrödinger, Erwin 153
Schulte Herbrüggen, Hubertus 203
Schwarzenegger, Arnold 85

Index

Science 240, 242
science fiction 23–4, 32, 42, 79, 82, 102, 242, 272
Scientific Committee on the Problems of the Environment (SCOPE) 245
scientisation 20–1, 218, 222
Scott, George C. 80
Second Vatican Council 204, 206
Second World Peace Congress 54
Second World War 18, 37, 47, 56, 63, 70, 92–6, 98–100, 103, 110, 116, 118, 124–5, 147, 155, 170–1, 177, 179, 191, 194–6, 201, 203, 207, 251, 267–8, 270, 277, 285n.52
security 2, 4–5, 33, 39–41, 45–7, 64, 87, 116, 130, 171–2, 174, 179, 181–2, 227, 229, 271
self-destruction 33–4, 46, 51, 228
self-determination 143, 167
Sellers, Peter 44, 80
Serling, Rod 80, 87
Seven Days to Noon 100
SHAPE 122
Shaw, Tony 7
Sheffield 54
shelter 61, 67, 78, 103, 265–8, 274–5
Shevardnadze, Eduard 250
Shoah 145
Shute, Nevil 21, 51, 79, 102
  On the Beach 21, 51, 102
Singer, Fred S. 243–5
Skupy, Hans-Horst 163n.88
Slessor, John 93
Smith, Joseph V. 243–4
Smithsonian Institute 24, 86
Social Democratic Party (SPD) 119, 123, 127, 137n.46, 247
social psychology 216
socialism 14, 51, 196
Soddy, Frederick 32
Somerville, John 159n.9
Sontag, Susan 52, 235n.58

South Africa 81
South Korea 81
South Pacific 17, 134
South Vietnam 170, 178
Southeast Asia 178
Southern, Terry 80
sovereignty 96, 119–20
Sovetskaya Rossiya 249
Soviet Academy of Medical Sciences 223
Soviet Committee for the Defence of Peace 57
Soviet government 54, 57, 61
Soviet Union 11, 14–17, 21, 40–1, 44–5, 54, 56, 65, 72n.84, 82, 84, 96–9, 105, 126, 131, 143, 170, 172, 194, 196–9, 205, 218, 223–4, 226, 245, 248–9, 254, 273, 281
  see also USSR
Spaemann, Robert 202
Special Weapons Orientation: The Thermonuclear Weapon. Part VI 278
Spellmen, Francis 191
Spider Man 87
Spiegel magazine 121, 130
Spielberg, Steven 87
Sputnik satellite 269
SS-20 missiles 127, 241
St. Louis 79
St. Paul's Cathedral 103
Stalin, Joseph 51, 53–4, 56, 58–9, 62–3, 67, 69n.27, 70n.35, 72n.73, 142, 149, 197, 206
Stasi 134
State Department 172–3, 224
Statue of Liberty 60, 71n.58
Stern, William 142, 161n.57
Sting (Gordon Sumner) 83, 85
Stockholm 54, 57, 70n.36
Stockholm Peace Appeal 57, 70n.36
Strategic Arms Limitation Treaty (SALT I/II) 81

Index

strategic defence initiative (SDI) 23–4, 83, 248
stratosphere 274
Strauß, Josef 122
Strontium-90 79
Student Nonviolent Coordinating Committee (SNCC) 19, 167–8, 172, 175–9, 184, 186n.18, 187n.21, 188n.47
Students for Democratic Society (SDS) 168, 186n.10
Stuttgart 127
submarine 124
Suez Crisis 143
surveys 20, 63–4, 79, 97, 155, 181, 249, 252, 266
survival 9, 18, 33, 42, 85, 94, 103–4, 106, 108, 111, 117, 121, 131–2
Survival City 269
Survival Under Atomic Attack 263–5, 267
survivors 7, 21, 32, 36, 77, 79, 84, 102, 110, 119, 130, 132–3, 145, 154, 165–6, 173, 181–3, 185n.1, 219, 225–6, 243, 250
  see also hibakusha
swastika 55
Sweden 15, 246
Switzerland 15
symbolism 20, 98
symbols 1–2, 4, 17, 35, 47, 71n.53, 86, 95, 110, 118–19, 148, 183, 218
Synod 204–5
Szilard, Leo 32–3, 40–3, 46
  The Mined Cities 41–3, 49n.38
  The Voice of the Dolphins 41–3

Tanzania 246
Target: You! 265
Tass news agency 224
television 6–8, 65, 102, 106, 108–9, 128–9, 144, 184, 221, 226, 239, 248, 250, 283n.4

Teller, Edward 30, 244–5
terrorism 16, 84, 87
Thatcher, Margaret 146
The Beginning or the End 76
The Catholic Worker 201
The Creature from the Black Lagoon 80
The Day After 83, 85, 243
The Day the Earth Stood Still 77
The House in the Middle 174–5
The Incredible Shrinking Man 80
The News of the World 101
The Peacemaker 85
The Simpsons 84
The Tonight Show with Johnny Carson 239
The Twilight Zone 80
The United States Air Force Presents Its Part in 'Operation Sandstone' 272
The War Game 6–9, 68n.4, 82, 108, 115n.83
Them! 80, 260
theology 19, 34, 157, 196
There's a Nuclear War Going on Inside Me 220, 234n.49
thermonuclear
  bomb 86, 244
  era 94, 101, 104
  explosion 240, 265, 278
  tests 58
  war 38, 75, 79, 83, 86, 94, 133
  weapons 53–4, 86, 102, 105, 171, 244, 278
Third Reich 120, 134, 153
Third World War 37, 130, 133, 141, 151, 154–6, 247, 251
This is Your Life 80
Threads 108
Three Mile Island 82
Tikhonov, N.S. 57
Time magazine 82
Times (London) 72n.73, 97, 226
Tohoku University 176

Index

Tokyo 80, 145, 149, 169, 178–9, 228
Tolkunov, A. 62
Toon, Owen B. 240
Topchiev, A.V. 58–9
total war 25, 92, 180–1
town meetings 82
Toynbee, Philip 103, 107
Travolta, John 85
Trident missiles 241
Trinity 270–1
tropes 7, 23, 73n.97, 129
True Lies 95
Truman, Harry S. 57, 76, 78, 149
Tsurumi Shunsuke 167–9, 179, 184, 187n.19, 187n.30
TTAPS 240–4, 248, 250–2, 254
Tugendhat, Ernst 132
Turco, Richard P. 240

Under Siege 85
United Kingdom 6–8, 11, 15, 68n.4, 101, 116, 270
   see also Great Britain
United Methodist Church 247
United Nations (UN) 60, 125, 174, 177, 183
   UN Commission on Human Rights 174
   UN General Assembly 174
United States 11, 13–15, 18–21, 24, 41, 46, 56, 75–6, 80–2, 84–6, 99, 101, 103, 134, 142, 166, 169–70, 178–9, 182, 184–5, 189–95, 197, 199–200, 206, 214, 216, 218–21, 223–4, 226, 245, 247–8, 254–5, 260, 271–3, 277, 281–2
   see also USA
United States–Japan Security Treaty 172, 179
Universal Declaration of Human Rights 174, 182–3
Updike, John 83
   Rabbit at Rest 83

US government 6, 172, 174, 178, 182–3, 260, 282
USA 52–4, 56–8, 60–5, 68n.4, 70n.43, 72n.74, 72n.84, 74n.104, 170, 185, 270
   see also United States
USSR 25, 51–2, 54, 56–8, 60, 62–3, 65, 70n.38, 71n.53, 173, 233n.31, 270
   see also Soviet Union

V-2 missiles 120–1
Van Dijk, Paul 140
Van Hoof, Fred 193
Van Hoof, Mary Ann 193, 195
Vatican 195, 203
Velikhov, Yevgeny P. 248
Verne, Jules 31
victimisation 119, 122, 179
Vienna 142, 159n.16
Viet Cong (National Liberation Front of South Vietnam) 170
Vietnam 19, 81, 166–71, 173–81, 183–5, 186n.16, 188n.42
Viking missions 238–9
Virgin Mary 192–3, 195
Virilio, Paul 9, 270
visualisation 56, 264
Vladivostok 84
Voronezh region 66
Voting Rights Bill 176

Waco, Texas 145
Wall Street Journal 243
War Games 82
War of the Worlds 87
war
   games 3, 7, 22, 121, 128, 272
   scenarios 79, 129, 247
   'on terror' 24, 86–7
warfare 4, 9, 12, 19, 37, 45, 58, 135, 221
   atomic/nuclear 7, 36, 53, 56–7, 94–6, 110–11, 117, 121, 152–3,

192, 197–8, 200–2, 262, 272–3, 275–6
industrial 9
limited 10, 30, 36, 45, 61, 120, 133, 153, 189, 197, 247–8
mechanisation of 154, 179
modern 204
traditional 70n.35
virtualisation of 23
Warner Brothers 217
Warning Red 269
Warsaw 54
Warsaw Pact 238
Washington 43, 61, 78, 81–2, 86, 185, 223, 242, 246, 262, 279
Washington University 79
Washington, Denzel 85
Watergate crisis 81
Watkins, Peter 6–9, 108
weapons technology 1–2, 4, 31, 33, 37
Wehrmacht 119–20, 123
Weimar 142
Weinstein, Adelbert 121
Wells, H.G. 31–2, 37, 40–2, 87
    The World Set Free 31–2, 37, 41
Werkhefte 202
Wesker, Arnold 109
    Menace 109
West Germany 14–15, 17–20, 116, 117, 123, 126–9, 133, 143, 189, 191–5, 197–9, 202, 205–7, 216, 218–21, 236n.89, 237n.95, 247
    see also Germany
Western Europe 22, 60, 82, 151

Westinghouse 78
Wheeler, Harvey 50n.50, 79
White House 43, 53, 172, 243
Whitehall 7
Willis, Bruce 86
Winter, Sidney G. 251
Wisconsin 82, 193
Wohlstetter, Albert 39
Woolf, Leonard 96
World Congress of Intellectuals for Peace 54
World Congress of the Partisans of Peace 54
World Council of Churches 124
world peace 41, 96, 105
worst-case scenarios 44, 128
Wrocław 54
Würzburg 204–5
Wyndham, John 102
    The Chrysalids 102

X the Unknown 102

Yomiuri 188n.42
Yorkshire Post 95
You Can Beat the A-Bomb 263, 265, 267–8
youth culture 177

Zadra, Robert 163n.85
Zelka, Charlotte 145, 160n.38
Zinn, Howard 167–70, 172–5, 178–80, 183–4, 186n.10, 186n.19, 187n.19

EU authorised representative for GPSR:
Easy Access System Europe, Mustamäe tee 50,
10621 Tallinn, Estonia
gpsr.requests@easproject.com

www.ingramcontent.com/pod-product-compliance
Ingram Content Group UK Ltd.
Pitfield, Milton Keynes, MK11 3LW, UK
UKHW021839140426
5217IPUK00022B/1519